The Origins of Buddhist Monastic Codes in China

CLASSICS IN EAST ASIAN BUDDHISM

The Origins of Buddhist Monastic Codes in China

An Annotated Translation and Study of the *Chanyuan qinggui*

YIFA

A KURODA INSTITUTE BOOK
University of Hawai'i Press
Honolulu

14 13 12 11 10 09   6 5 4 3 2 1
Paperback edition 2009

Library of Congress Cataloging-in-Publication Data
Yifa.
The origins of Buddhist monastic codes in China :
an annotated translation and study of the Chanyuan qinggui / Yifa.
p. cm.
Includes bibliographical references and index.
ISBN 978-0-8248-2494-5 (hardcover : alk. paper)
ISBN 978-0-8248-3425-8 (pbk : alk. paper)
1. Zongze, d. 1092. Chan yuan qing gui.   2. Monasticism and reli-
gious orders, Zen—Rules.   I. Title: Annotated translation and study of the
Chanyuan qinggui.   II. Zongze, d. 1092. Chan yuan qing gui. English.   III. Title.
BQ9295.Z653 Y54   2002
294.3'657'0951—dc21   2002000245

Figure Credits
P. xxv: Walking stick. *Butsuzo hyoshikigi zusetsu*, by Gikai, 1694. *NBZ* 73.
    Guazi. *Butsuzo hyoshikigi zusetsu*, by Gikai, 1694. NBZ 73.
    Shoes. *Butsuzo hyoshikigi zusetsu*, by Gikai, 1694. NBZ 73.
P. xxvi: Compartment. Zengaku daijiten.
    Pianshen. Butsuzo hyoshikigi zusetsu, by Gikai, 1694. NBZ 73.
P. xxvii: Bowl set. *Zusetsu Zen no subete: ikite iru Zen*, by Shinohara Hisao and Sato Tatsugen.
    Tokyo: Mokujisha, 1989.
    Sangha hall. *Zusetsu Zen no subete: ikite iru Zen*, by Shinohara Hisao and Sato Tatsugen.
    Tokyo: Mokujisha, 1989.
P. xxviii: Assembly quarters. *Zusetsu Zen no subete: ikite iru Zen*, by Shinohara Hisao and Sato
    Tatsugen. Tokyo: Mokujisha, 1989.
    Dining room bell. *Zusetsu Zen no subete: ikite iru Zen*, by Shinohara Hisao and Sato Tatsu-
    gen. Tokyo: Mokujisha, 1989.
P. xxix: Wandering monk. *Zusetsu Zen no subete: ikite iru Zen*, by Shinohara Hisao and Sato
    Tatsugen. Tokyo: Mokujisha, 1989.
    Arrival at the monastery gate. *Zusetsu Zen no subete: ikite iru Zen*, by Shinohara Hisao and
    Sato Tatsugen. Tokyo: Mokujisha, 1989.
P. xxx: Bowing. *Zusetsu Zen no subete: ikite iru Zen*, by Shinohara Hisao and Sato Tatsugen.
    Tokyo: Mokujisha, 1989.
    Answering questions. *Zusetsu Zen no subete: ikite iru Zen*, by Shinohara Hisao and Sato
    Tatsugen. Tokyo: Mokujisha, 1989.
    Drum. *Zusetsu Zen no subete: ikite iru Zen*, by Shinohara Hisao and Sato Tatsugen. Tokyo:
    Mokujisha, 1989.

The Kuroda Institute for the Study of Buddhism and Human Values is a nonprofit,
educational corporation founded in 1976. One of its primary objectives is to
promote scholarship on the historical, philosophical, and cultural ramifications
of Buddhism. In association with the University of Hawai'i Press, the Institute also
publishes Studies in East Asian Buddhism, a series of scholarly investigations of
significant themes and topics in the East Asian Buddhist tradition.

University of Hawai'i Press books are printed on acid-free
paper and meet the guidelines for permanence and durability
of the Council on Library Resources.

Designed by Cindy Chun
Printed by The Maple-Vail Book Manufacturing Group

**Kuroda Institute
Classics in East Asian Buddhism**

**Kuroda Institute
Studies in East Asian Buddhism**

For my spiritual teacher and my parents

Contents

Acknowledgments

In making my acknowledgments, I must first express my indebtedness to the monks throughout the ages who have, through their diligence, bequeathed to us so many treasures. Chinese monks made careful translations of Indian Vinayas, wrote detailed treatises and commentaries on Vinayas, and painstakingly composed monastic codes. Japanese monks deserve recognition for preserving the text and continuing the tradition of Vinaya scholarship. The commentaries of Mujaku Dōchū (1653–1744) were especially valuable to the present translation for the great light they shed on the sometimes abstruse text of *Chanyuan qinggui*.

I extend my most devoted gratitude to my advisor, Professor Stanley Weinstein of the Department of Religious Studies, Yale University, who impressed on me his meticulous standards of scholarship and gave me the solid training necessary to complete my dissertation. He should not, however, bear the slightest blame for any insufficiencies found in my work. Special thanks should also go to Lucie Weinstein for her compassion and encouragement.

While in Japan I received the generous assistance of Professor Kosaka Kiyū at Komazawa University, who took the time to meet with me regularly, answer my questions, and arrange visits to the Eiheiji monastic headquarters and the Eiheiji branch temple in Tokyo, whose members I would like to thank. I would like to express my gratitude to Professor Ishii Shūdō (also of Komazawa University) and his wife, Emi, for their kind efforts and for providing useful material. I must acknowledge Ms. Suzuki Eiko, the librarian at Komazawa University, for her extreme kindness and untiring aid.

I do not know how to thank my friend and fellow graduate student Lee D. Johnson, without whose editorial assistance and enormous time commitment this work would not have been possible. Also invaluable were the generous editorial contributions of Anne Lazrove and John N. Jones, my colleagues in the Department of Religious Studies. I must also thank Yamabe Nobuyoshi, who supplied me with bibliographical suggestions and who, while simultaneously working on his own dissertation, took the time to argue with me over details and provide encouragement. I am also grateful for the advice and support of Richard Jaffe of Duke University and Morten Schlütter. For their help in readying this work for publication, I thank Paul Kjellberg of Whittier College, Mizuko Ichinose of Yale University Library's East Asian Collection, and Margaret Weatherford, who spent many hours reorganizing and editing the final draft. Thanks go, also, to the Kuroda Series publications committee and reviewers for their encouragement and helpful suggestions.

Finally, I would like to express my deep appreciation to the members of Fo Guang Shan Monastery for their sponsorship and encouragement. I thank especially my spiritual teacher, Hsing Yun (Xingyun), who inspired me to enter the Buddhist order and provided a nun with the opportunity to pursue a formal education. I also acknowledge my great indebtedness to my family and to all the devotees of Fo Guang Shan who went to great lengths to make my studies at Yale possible.

Abbreviations

AOS	Journal of the American Oriental Society
BKN	Bukkyōgaku kenkyūkai nenpō 佛教學研究會年報
BS	Bukkyō shigaku 佛教史學
BYQG	Chanlin beiyong qinggui 禪林備用清規
CBQG	Chixiu Baizhang qinggui 敕修百丈清規
CHSS	Chokushū Hyakujō shingi sakei 敕修百丈清規左觽
CSJ	Chu sanzang jiji 出三藏記集
CYQG	Chanyuan qinggui 禪苑清規
DSL	Da Song sengshi lüe 大宋僧史略
DSW	Da biqiu sanqian weiyi 大比丘三千威儀
DXQZ	Da Tang xiyu qiufa gaoseng zhuan 大唐西域求法高僧傳
DZDL	Da zhidu lun 大智度論
DZZ	Dōgen Zenji zenshū 道元禪師全集
FYZL	Fayuan zhulin 法苑珠林
FZTJ	Fozu tongji 佛祖統記
GJZ	Gozan jissatsu zu 五山十剎圖
GSP	Genben Shuoyiqieyou bu pinaiye 根本説一切有部毘奈耶
GSP(A)	Genben Shuoyiqieyou bu pinaiye anjushi 安居事
GSP(B)	Genben Shuoyiqieyou bu baiyi jiemo 百一羯磨
GSP(C)	Genben Shuoyiqieyou bu pinaiye chujiashi 出家事
GSP(J)	Genben Shuoyiqieyou bu pinaiye jiechinayishi 羯恥那衣事
GSP(N)	Genben Shuoyiqieyou bu nituona mudejia 尼陀那目得迦
GSP(O)	Genben Shuoyiqieyou bu pinaiye posengshi 破僧事
GSP(P)	Genben Shuoyiqieyou bu pinaiye pige shi 皮革事
GSP(S)	Genben Shuoyiqieyou bu pinaiye song 頌

GSP(Y)	Genben Shuoyiqieyou bu pinaiye yaoshi 藥事
GSP(Z)	Genben Shuoyiqieyou bu pinaiye zashi 雜事
GSZ	Gaoseng zhuan 高僧傳
HKDK	Hokkaidō Komazawa Daigaku kenkyū kiyō 北海道駒澤大學研究紀要
IBK	Indogaku Bukkyōgaku kenkyū 印度學佛教學研究
JA	Journal asiatique
JDQG	Conglin jiaoding qinggui zongyong 叢林校定清規總要 (Jiaoding qinggui 校定清規)
JIABS	Journal of the International Association of Buddhist Studies
JXXL	Jiaojie xinxue biqiu xinghu lüyi 教誡新學比丘行護律儀
JYQG	Jiaoyuan qinggui 教苑清規
KBK	Komazawa Daigaku Bukkyō gakubu kenkyū kiyō 駒澤大學佛教學部研究紀要
KBR	Komazawa Daigaku Bukkyō gakubu ronshū 論集
KDBKN	Komazawa Daigaku daigakuin Bukkyōgaku kenkyūkai nenpō
KZKN	Komazawa Daigaku Zen kenkyūjo nenpō 禪研究所年報
LBWL	Lebang wenlei 樂邦文類
LYSG	Lüyuan shigui 律苑事規
MN	Monumenta Nipponica
Mochitsuki	Mochitsuki daijiten 望月大辭典
Morohashi	Dai kanwa jiten 大漢和辭典 (*Morohashi Tetsuji* 諸橋徹次, *ed.*)
MSL	Mohe sengqi lü 摩訶僧祇律
NBZ	Dai Nihon Bukkyō zensho 大日本佛教全書
NJNZ	Nanhai jigui neifa zhuan 南海寄歸內法傳
PNMJ	Pini mu jing 毘尼母經
QTS	Qingyuan tiaofa shilei 慶元條法事類
RRQG	Ruzhong riyong qinggui 入眾日用清規
SBS	Shina Bukkyō shigaku 支那佛教史學
SFL	Sifen lü 四分律
SGJY	Shimen guijing yi 釋門歸敬儀
SGK	Shūgaku kenkyū 宗學研究
SGSZ	Song gaoseng zhuan 宋高僧傳
SJLP	Shanjian lü piposha 善見律毘婆沙
SJZ	Shisan jing zhushu 十三經注疏
SK	Shūkyō kenkyū 宗教研究
SKKK	Sōtōshū kenkyūin kenkyūsei kenkyū kiyō 曹洞宗研究院研究生研究紀要

SOAS	Bulletin of the School of Oriental and African Studies
SSL	Shisong lü 十誦律
SSYL	Shishi yaolan 釋氏要覽
STGK	San Tendai Godaisan ki 參天台五台山記
SXC	Sifen lü shanfan buque xingshi chao 四分律刪繁補缺行事鈔
SXCZ	Sifen lü xingshi chao zichi ji 四分律行事鈔資持記
T	Taishō shinshū daizōkyō 大正新修大藏經
WFL	Wufen lü 五分律
XGSZ	Xu gaoseng zhuan 續高僧傳
YZS	Yakuchū Zennen shingi 訳註禅苑清規
ZBKK	Zen bunka kenkyūjo kiyō 禪文化研究所紀要
ZD	Zengaku daijiten 禪學大辭典
ZSS	Zenrin shōkisen 禪林象器箋
ZTSY	Zuting shiyuan 祖庭事苑
ZZK	Dai Nihon zokuzōkyō 大日本續藏經
ZZKX	Zokuzōkyō 續藏經 (*Xinwenfeng* 新文豐 *edition*)

Conventions

I have based my translation of *Chanyuan qinggui* on the critically edited text found in *Yakuchū Zennen shingi (YZS)* by Kagamishima Genryū, Satō Tatsugen, and Kosaka Kiyū. I have followed the punctuation and paragraph divisions given in *YZS* but have made corrections when necessary. Because *YZS* often identifies several textual variants, I have alerted the reader to the relevant manuscript whenever a significant choice was made on my part. I cite the corresponding pages in *YZS* throughout my translation, providing the page numbers in boldface and brackets (e.g., **[18]**). Readers who wish to refer to the text of *Chanyuan qinggui* published in *Dai Nihon zokuzōkyō (ZZK)* may make use of the Finding List included at the end of this book. The original work contains a great deal of interlinear commentary, which appears here in smaller type to distinguish it from the rest of the text. To facilitate reading comprehension, I refer to well-known sutra and Vinaya works (such as the *Four Part Vinaya* and the *Ten Section Vinaya*) by their English titles throughout my analysis and translation. However, in the notes they are identified by the abbreviations of their Chinese titles (*SFL* and *SSL*, respectively).

Many of the terms used in the Chinese text can be understood only in their historical context and are unfathomable even to the modern-day native speaker of Chinese. Although my translation of *Chanyuan qinggui* is intended to be as true to the letter of the original as possible, rendering the work in contemporary English called for great caution, as well as creativity. I hope that the scholarly-minded reader will approve of my attempts to convey everything recorded in the Chinese manuscripts and forgive any irregularities in the English text produced for the sake of deeper comprehension and out of loyalty to the original.

After consulting the vocabulary list in Roger Jackson's "Terms of

Sanskrit and Pāli Origin Acceptable as English Words," which itself makes use of *Webster's Third New International Dictionary,* I have decided not to italicize a number of Sanskrit and Pāli terms commonly accepted in English. I have omitted the Chinese characters for the names of provinces and dynasties, since they will be apparent to readers who know Chinese. For modern East Asian place-names such as Tokyo, Kyoto, or Taipei, I have used the common "postal spellings."

For transliterations of Japanese Zen names and terms, I have relied on *Zengaku daijiten.* For transliterations of Sanskrit names and terms, I have followed Franklin Edgerton's *Buddhist Hybrid Sanskrit Grammar and Dictionary,* M. Monier-Williams's *Sanskrit-English Dictionary,* and Nakamura Hajime's *Bukkyōgo daijiten.*

The illustrations have been taken for the most part from Japanese resources. Through the process of my research, I discovered that materials shown in these resources have been preserved to closely depict those found in *Chanyuan qinggui.*

Introduction

Compiled in 1103 by the Chan Buddhist monk Changlu Zongze (?–1107?), *Chanyuan qinggui* (Rules of Purity for the Chan Monastery) is regarded as the earliest Chan monastic code in existence. This text is a comprehensive set of rules, written to regulate virtually every aspect of life in the large public monasteries of the era. Before *Chanyuan qinggui*, monastic codes were limited and scattered; they did not attempt to establish a definitive code for Chan Buddhism. Any extensive codes that may have existed prior to *Chanyuan qinggui*, including one allegedly compiled by Baizhang (749–814), have been lost.

In laying out the regulations for monastic life, *Chanyuan qinggui* covers a remarkably wide range. The text defines very specific guidelines for itinerant monks,[1] emphasizes the importance of studying under masters at various monasteries, prescribes the proper protocol for attending a retreat, and details the procedure for requesting an abbot's instruction. A significant portion of the text addresses the administrative hierarchy within the monastery, including the duties and powers of the various monastic officers. An important thread running through the text is the proper social deportment of the monks vis-à-vis each other, especially at tea ceremonies, chanting rituals, and monastic auctions. In addition, *Chanyuan qinggui* details the proper procedures for such mundane activities as packing one's belongings for travel, bathing, and using the toilet.

Chanyuan qinggui is of course valuable to modern scholars for its wealth of information about monastic life in twelfth-century Song China. It was also extremely influential at the time of and directly following its compilation, both in China and abroad. The Japanese monk Eisai (1141–1215), who traveled to China to study Chinese Buddhism, reported its preeminence among existing codes. *Chanyuan qinggui* continued to be the dominant influence on compilers of regulatory texts well into the Song and Yüan eras. In Japan it served as the model for generations of monastic codes. Dōgen (1200–1253), for example, was strongly influenced by *Chanyuan qinggui* and adapted it for use in Japan, paraphrasing many of its passages in his own works.

Structure of the Work

This book consists of two parts: the first delineates the Chinese historical and cultural contexts in which *Chanyuan qinggui* arose and traces the code's heritage to the Indian Vinayas; the second is an annotated translation of *Chanyuan qinggui,* its first complete rendering into English.

In Part 1, I argue that a work as comprehensive as *Chanyuan qinggui* could not have risen up like a monolith during the Song era. It was preceded in China by a long history of translations, adaptations, and formulations of monastic codes. This evolutionary history can roughly be divided into three stages: the introduction to China of the Indian Vinayas *(jielü);* the compilation of Sangha regulations *(senggui)*[2] by Chinese monks; and the composition of Rules of Purity *(qinggui),*[3] or comprehensive monastic codes such as *Chanyuan qinggui.* In my examination of the first of these stages in Chapter 1, I discuss the introduction into China of five complete Indian Vinaya texts *(guanglü),* four of which were translated into Chinese as early as the fifth century. These texts from five schools provided the basic framework within which Chinese Buddhism formed its initial understanding of traditional monastic discipline.

But even before these complete Vinayas had been introduced, partial and abbreviated versions of Vinaya texts had already been translated and brought to China. Monks arriving from the West—from India and Central Asia—served as living instructors, carrying with them the knowledge and habits of the Indian Buddhist orders. However, the Indian Vinayas and the Indian and Central Asian monks were often from diverse schools of disciplinary philosophy. The monks came to China haphazardly, arriving at different times and settling in different regions. As a result, the Chinese lacked a unified monastic code. But it was not long before Chinese monks recognized the need to collect and systematize whatever Vinaya texts were available and, supplementing them with their observations of foreign monks' practices, to compile them into unified monastic codes.

In my discussion of the second historical stage, I consider the important role played by the Chinese monks who first attempted to create rules specifically suited to monastic life in China. The first such set of Sangha regulations on record is the work of Daoan (312–385), who compiled a set of rules for his own monastery. Significantly, many of the regulations established by Daoan were to become standard practices in later monastic codes such as *Chanyuan qinggui*. As I will illustrate, Daoan inherited a profound respect for monastic discipline from his master and subsequently engendered this quality into his disciples. These pupils, among them Huiyuan (334–416), were renowned for their own meticulous adherence to the Indian Vinaya precepts, which they combined with their indigenous Sangha regulations to form rules tailored to the needs of individual monasteries in China.

The influence of Daoan and his respect for monastic discipline is evident in other regulatory codes, such as the work of Lü master Daoxuan (596–667), which, in turn, influenced later monastic codes. This interest in monastic discipline animated the Tiantai school, whose founder, Zhiyi (538–597), and his successor three centuries later, Zunshi (964–1032), each developed Sangha regulations of his own. Along with these works, I examine the importance of the alleged first Chan Rules of Purity, the so-called *Baizhang qinggui*, which predates many of the Sangha regulations discussed here. This nonextant code, traditionally ascribed to Chan master Baizhang, has been a source of great controversy. Because of his supposed role as author of the first comprehensive Chan monastic code, Baizhang was long considered responsible for initiating Chan independence from other Buddhist schools. However, many modern scholars have come to doubt the existence of *Baizhang qinggui*. Although my own approach has been to trace elements of Chan monastic codes to influences that far precede Baizhang's time, I dispute the methodology of those who claim that Baizhang's regulations were never formally codified.

This brings us to the third stage of monastic regulations: Rules of Purity, comprehensive monastic codes of which *Chanyuan qinggui* is the earliest surviving example. I hope to demonstrate a clear line of continuity between Chinese monastic regulations, beginning with the original Indian Vinayas, moving through the Sangha regulations, and finally culminating in *Chanyuan qinggui* and the many Rules of Purity that followed in its wake.

In Chapter 2, to give the reader a more complete understanding of *Chanyuan qinggui*, I discuss a number of external factors that influenced its composition. Foremost among these influences are the

Indian Vinayas, from which can be traced a tremendous amount of the material in *Chanyuan qinggui*. In this connection, I refer frequently to the works of the Lü masters Daoxuan and Yijing (635–713) for the light they shed on the earliest Vinaya translations produced in China.

The Chinese government left its mark on *Chanyuan qinggui* as well. This is evident in the text's conformity to state decrees concerning travel permits, the sale of tonsure and titular certificates, the election of abbots, the conversion of public monasteries into private ones, and the creation of monastic offices charged with governmental supervision of the order. I discuss the cultural context within which the text was produced and its effects: In *Chanyuan qinggui* we find echoes of court protocol in monastic ceremonies, the tea ceremony borrowed from popular custom, and the introduction of rituals, such as circumambulation and expressions of humility, from the three Confucian books of rites.

In Part 2, as an introduction to the translation itself, I offer a biography of the author of *Chanyuan qinggui* and a discussion of the various extant editions of the text. I argue that Changlu Zongze was influenced not only by his own Chan tradition, the Yunmen school, but by the thought and practices of the Pure Land school as well. This influence is borne out clearly in *Chanyuan qinggui*, wherein the author incorporates Pure Land concepts and rituals into the funeral liturgy.

In addition to the seven fascicles translated here, the original text includes a three-fascicle appendix. Because the content of the appendix is so different in nature from the first seven fascicles, I have left their translation and annotation for a future project.

I hope that my translation of *Chanyuan qinggui* will prove valuable to Buddhist scholarship, given that until now there has been no more comprehensive English translation of the text. I have endeavored to be as literal as possible in translating the text, attempting to preserve the letter, and perhaps the spirit, of the original literary Chinese wherever feasible. My annotations introduce a great deal of historical material that will elucidate the text and show the evolution of regulations within *Chanyuan qinggui*. They include, for example, documentation of many borrowings and influences from the Indian Vinayas that were too numerous and disparate to discuss completely in Chapter 2.

I believe that a deeper understanding of *Chanyuan qinggui*'s place in the continuous evolutionary progression of monastic regulations, in conjunction with a reading of the text itself informed by the numerous borrowings and points of influence from Indian Vinayas and other early works, will lead the reader to conclude that Rules of Purity, long thought to have begun with the innovative work of Baizhang, were not a Chan invention. It is my intention to show that with the exception of its attempts to accommodate Chinese social and cultural norms, *Chanyuan qinggui* largely represents the continuation of a monastic tradition that is traceable to the very roots of Indian Buddhism.

Walking stick

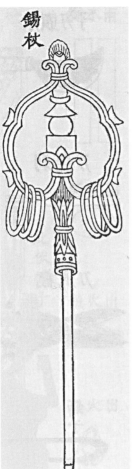

Guazi "hanging robe"

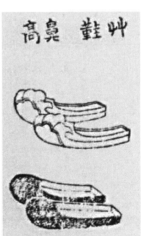

Shoes

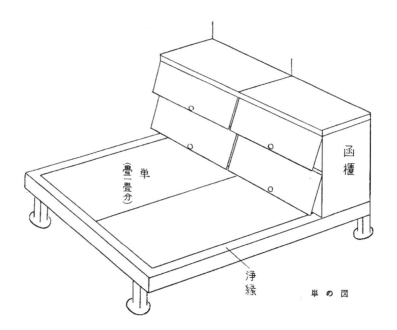

Compartment

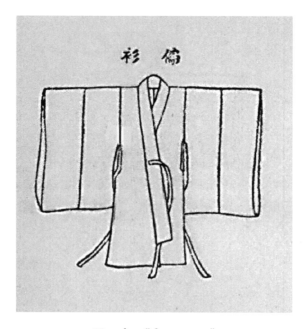

Pianshen "short gown"

Bowl set, including bowls,
chopsticks, spoon, and dining mat

Sangha hall, where monks meditate and dine

Assembly quarters, where monks study

Bell in dining room

Wandering monk

Arrival at the
monastery gate

Bowing to check in at the monastery

Drum

Answering questions from a guest master

PART ONE

Context

1.
Evolution of Monastic Regulations in China

Introduction of the Buddhist Vinayas into China

With the introduction of Buddhism into China around the first century C.E., men and women began leaving their familial households (*chujia*) and taking the tonsure. According to the earliest recorded reference to a monastic, the feudal prince Liu Jun and a woman named Apan, both took the tonsure during the reign of Emperor Ming of the Han dynasty (58–75 C.E.).[1] However, it is believed that the Vinayas[2]—the Indian Buddhist scriptures containing the formal precepts necessary for ordination—were not available in China at the time. Thus Chinese monks and nuns of this era could not have been formally ordained in the Indian Buddhist tradition.[3] Instead, they would have taken "the three refuges" (the Buddha, the Dharma, and the Sangha), looking to the religion's founder, his teachings, and the community for guidance on their spiritual path.

But taking the three refuges is also a practice of the Buddhist laity. Monks and nuns of this time were distinguished from the laity only by their shaven heads; in practice they performed their observances in accordance with traditional Chinese sacrifice and worship.[4] It was not until the middle of the third century (Jiaping era, 249–253), when Dharmakāla arrived in China from central India, that monks and nuns were first properly ordained. Dharmakāla translated part of the *Mahāsāṅghika Vinaya* from an Indic language into Chinese and titled it *Sengqi jiexin* (Essence of Mahāsāṅghika Precepts),[5] thereby supplying the clergy with at least the specific goals of a formal ordination. Deeming Chinese Buddhism to be at an early stage and not yet ready for the great complexity of a full Vinaya, Dharmakāla decided to translate only the basic rules for daily living.

Complete Vinayas generally include three parts: the *Sūtravibhaṅga*, an explanation of rules and punishments for monks and nuns based on the articles of *prāktimokṣa;* the *Skandhaka* (sometimes referred to as the *Vastu*), a discussion of the rituals and interactions of daily monastic life based on the prescriptions of the *karmavācanā*s; and appendices, which usually summarize the points made in the two preceding sections and sometimes introduce general historical information. Dharmakāla's translation enumerated the precepts themselves *(jieben; prātimokṣa)*, but omitted any instruction regarding the actual procedures for many communal activities *(jiemo fa; karmavācanā)* such as admission into the order, the ceremony for the reception of the precepts, the fortnightly confession *(upavasatha)*,[6] the protocol for large assemblies, and the execution of punishments. Dharmakāla entrusted the translations of matters of procedure to his fellow Indian monks, who subsequently took up the task in separate, supplementary translations.[7] Although no such supplementary translations have been preserved, these instructions for ceremonial procedure, used in conjunction with Dharmakāla's precepts, enabled the first Chinese clergy to be ordained in the proper fashion. This fact is attested to by the sixth-century collection of monks' biographies *Gaoseng zhuan*.[8] A later tradition based on the tenth-century history of Buddhist practices *Da Song sengshi lüe* (Abridged History of Sangha Compiled under the Song; henceforth *Sengshi lüe*) held that the source for Chinese procedural practices was *Tanwu jiemo (Dharmaguptaka Karmavācanā)*, translated in 255 by the Parthian monk Tandi. According to *Sengshi lüe*, it was the combination of Dharmakāla's *Sengqi jiexin* and Tandi's *Tanwu jiemo* that enabled Chinese clergy to receive their precepts for the first time.[9]

Another *karmavācanā* translation from the same Dharmaguptaka school is *Tanwude lübu za jiemo*, which was translated by Saṅghavarman, who arrived in China just a few years before Tandi. Both Dharmaguptaka *karmavācanā* texts are extant; however, Hirakawa Akira argues that these two were produced after the translation of the *Four Part Vinaya (Sifen lü)*—that is, after 410. If this is the case, neither text was translated by Tandi or Saṅghavarman. Ōchō Enichi makes this point as well.[10]

Before the introduction of any complete Vinayas *(guanglü)*,[11] several partial translations appeared sporadically over the next century and a half. Three texts were completed around the year 379 by the monk Tanmoshi[12] in collaboration with Zhu Fonian. These were *Shisong biqiu jieben* (Sarvāstivāda Bhikṣu Precepts), *Biqiuni dajie* (Bhikṣuni Great Precepts), and *Jiaoshou biqiuni ersui tanwen* (Essay on Instructing Bhikṣuni for Two Years), all three of which belong to the Sarvāstivāda school. Manuscripts of the latter two texts were obtained and brought to Tanmoshi by Sengchun from Kuchā. Monks translated nuns' precepts as well. Mili translated the five hundred precepts for nuns, as did Huichang, while Fatai (319–387) commissioned foreign monks to work on a translation of nuns' precepts that was never completed. All of these texts were eventually lost, and the only surviving partial Vinaya translation from this era is the *Binaiye* (Vinaya), which was translated by Zhu Fonian in 383.[13] Scholars believe that this text belongs to the Sarvāstivāda school.[14] We do know of another Vinaya text *(jiejing)* of this school, from Dunhuang, which was introduced into China before the complete Vinayas and is thought to belong to the Sarvāstivāda school as well. This text from Dunhuang may be the oldest translation of the *Sarvāstivāda Vinaya*.[15]

The first complete Vinayas appeared at the beginning of the fifth century, when the texts of four separate schools were brought to China. The *Sarvāstivāda Vinaya* was introduced by Puṇyatāra, who came to China from Kaśmīra (Jibin)[16] and was patronized by the ruler Yao Xing. In 404 Puṇyatāra began to recite the *Sarvāstivāda Vinaya* to Kumārajīva (344–413), who translated Puṇyatāra's words into Chinese, calling the work *Shisong lü* (Ten Section Vinaya). Puṇyatāra died after reciting only two-thirds of the work. The task was completed by Dharmaruci, who arrived from Kaśmīra with the *Sarvāstivāda Vinaya* in hand to help Kumārajīva finish the translation. The final text totaled fifty-eight fascicles. In 406 Vimalākṣa (?–413), who taught Kumārajīva the Vinaya at Kuchā, came to Chang'an to assist his former pupil with the final proofreading and reediting of the *Ten Section Vinaya*. The result is the sixty-one-fascicle version known to us today. Thus the first full Vinaya became available to the Chinese through the recitations of Puṇyatāra and Dharmaruci, the translations of Kumārajīva, and the editing of Vimalākṣa.

The second full Vinaya translation, the *Four Part Vinaya*, belongs to the Dharamaguptaka school and was also translated at Chang'an in northern China. At Kumārajīva's urging, Yao Xing summoned Buddhayaśas, a monk from Kaśmīra, to Chang'an, where he was sponsored by Yao and treated like a teacher by Kumārajīva. Here, in 410, with the help of Zhu Fonian, Buddhayaśas translated the forty-fascicle *Four Part Vinaya*.

As mentioned above, a number of Chinese pilgrims were traveling to India at this time in search of a complete Vinaya. One such traveler was Faxian (339?–420?), who left for India in 399, before any full Vinaya had been translated in China. By the time Faxian returned in 414, the *Ten Section Vinaya* and the *Four Part Vinaya* had already been translated; nevertheless, the Vinayas that Faxian brought with him were from different schools, and their translation offered a wealth of new material. Faxian returned with two texts: the Vinaya of the Mahāsāṅghika, found in the Aśoka Stūpa of Pāṭaliputra, the Magadha region of central India; and the Vinaya of the Mahīśāsaka, obtained in Sri Lanka. Upon his return, Faxian settled in the south at Jiankang (present-day Nanjing). After some time, he asked the Indian monk Buddhabhadra (359–429), who had come to Chang'an to work with Kumārajīva but later fled south to avoid conflict with Kumārajīva's disciples,[17] to translate the Mahāsāṅghika text into Chinese. This task was completed in 418, resulting in *Mohe sengqi lü*; however, Faxian died before the second text could be translated. It was only after several years had passed that the monk Buddhajīva, a student of the Mahīśāsaka school who had come to China from Kaśmīra in 423, took on the task of translating the *Mahīśāsaka Vinaya*, or *Wufeng lü* (Five Part Vinaya), completing the work in 424. In contrast to the first and second Vinayas, both of these translations were carried out in southern China, at Jiankang.

Within a short period of twenty-six years, the Vinayas of four different schools became available to Chinese Buddhists. While there continued to appear periodically a number of partial Vinaya texts in China, it was not until the eighth century that the full Vinaya of a fifth school would join the other four. This occurred when the Chinese pilgrim Yijing (635–713) went to India and brought back the *Mūlasarvāstivāda Vinaya (Genben Shuoyiqieyou bu lü)*, translating it himself around 700–703.[18] From this point on, one can speak of China as home to the complete Vinayas of five schools *(wuda guanglü)*, the *Mūlasarvāstivāda Vinaya* being the most extensive. However, by the time the *Mūlasarvāstivāda Vinaya* was introduced in the eighth century, the *Four Part Vinaya* had already established its dominance throughout the Chinese Lü traditions. After the Song, the Chan school, which eventually prevailed over all other forms of Chinese Buddhism, also used the *Four Part Vinaya* as its basis. Thus Yijing's translation of the *Mūlasarvāstivāda Vinaya* has never received the attention it deserves.

The *Ten Section Vinaya*—the first complete Vinaya introduced into China and the one most carefully studied by Kumārajīva's disciples— became the foremost Vinaya text during the Southern-Northern dynasties of the fifth century. Vimalākṣa was the first to advocate the use of this *Sarvāstivāda Vinaya* in southern China, prompting Huijiao (497–544), an early historiographer, to proclaim, "Due to the efforts of Vimalākṣa, the great propagation of the Vinaya was accomplished."[19] After Vimalākṣa, the disciples of Kumārajīva dedicated themselves to the teaching of the *Ten Section Vinaya*, as did the disciples of Huiyuan, the monk who had originally invited Dharmaruci to China to supply the portion of the *Ten Section Vinaya* left unrecited by Puṇyatāra. Although the *Ten Section Vinaya* was first translated at Chang'an, it went on to flourish in the south in Jiankang.

The Dharamaguptaka *Four Part Vinaya* was translated at Chang'an and circulated in the north near the Chang'an and Luoyang areas; in time this Vinaya would largely supercede the Sarvāstivāda *Ten Section Vinaya*. Scholars seeking to explain the text's popularity have pointed to the preexisting tradition of *karmavācanā (jiemo)*, the procedure for ordination used by Chinese monks before the introduction of complete Vinayas. The earliest translations of *karmavācanā* were from the Dharmaguptaka school; it is likely that when a full Vinaya was selected, it was chosen to correspond closely with these already established instructions and customs.[20] Establishing a custom requires effort, and one can find a succession of monks who advocated the use of the *Four Part Vinaya*. The monk Facong (468–559), who initially studied the Vinaya of the Mahāsāṅghika, reasoned that since the *karmavācanā* of the Dharmaguptaka was used mostly for procedural purposes, the full Vinaya text should correspond to this *karmavācanā;* accordingly, he switched to the study of the *Dharmaguptaka Vinaya*. Facong's disciple Daofu continued the work of his master by writing a commentary to the *Four Part Vinaya*. In turn, Daofu's disciple Huiguang (468–537) carried on the tradition as a staunch advocate of these monastic rules. But perhaps the most emphatic and active advocates of the *Four Part Vinaya* were Huiguang's disciples. More than a century and a half after Huiguang, Emperor Zhong of the Tang (r. 684) enacted a decree prohibiting the use of the *Ten Section Vinaya*, which was still in circulation in southern China. By the seventh century, the *Four Part Vinaya* had become the dominant text.[21]

Of the original four Vinaya texts, the two remaining, the *Five Part Vinaya* and the *Mahāsāṅghika Vinaya*, were never widely circulated. The former had almost no adherents; the latter, though first translated in the south, was studied by monks in the Guanzhong region (present-day Shanxi province) in the north. It too, however, was eventually replaced by the increasingly popular *Four Part Vinaya*.[22] Table 1 outlines the introduction of the various Vinaya texts into China.

Table 1. Introduction of Vinaya Texts into China

Date	Text	Adherents	School
249	Sengqi jiexin	Dharmakāla	Mahāsāṅghika
253 (?)	Tanwude lübu za jiemo*	Saṅghavarman (?)	Dharmaguptaka
254–255 (?)	Jiemo*	Tandi (?)	Dharmaguptaka
265–360	Vinaya text found in Dunhuang		Sarvāstivāda
371–372	Shisong biqiu jieben	Tanmoshi	Sarvāstivāda
	Biqiuni dajie	Zhu Fonian	
	Jiaoshou biqiuni ersui tanwen		
no dates	Texts on nuns' precepts	Mili	
		Fatai	
		Huichang	
383	Binaiye	Zhu Fonian	Sarvāstivāda
404–406	Shisong lü	Puṇyatāra	Sarvāstivāda
		Kumārajīva	
		Dharmaruci	
		Vimalākṣa	
410	Sifen lü	Buddhayaśas	Dharmaguptaka
	Tanwude lübu za jiemo*		Dharmaguptaka
	Jiemo*		Dharmaguptaka
418	Sengqi lü	Buddhabhadra	Mahāsāṅghika
424	Wufen lü	Buddhajīva	Mahīśāsaka
700–703	Genben Shuoyiqieyou bu lü	Yijing	Mūlasarvāstivāda

* The dates and the authors of these works are disputed. See note 10 of this chapter.

Sangha Regulations before *Chanyuan qinggui*

In contrast to doctrine, which traditionally has been the main focus of Buddhist scholarship, Sangha regulations and monastic practices have rarely been investigated. From its inception, however, Chinese Buddhism grew out of a concern with not only spiritual doctrine, but also practical matters of everyday behavior. In their zealous search for an adequate set of daily regulations, monks sought out preexisting Indian models and developed their own, thus instituting standards more suitable to their communities.

Daoan's Regulations

During the Southern-Northern dynasties, the eminent monk Daoan occupied one of the most important historical positions in the earliest stages of Chinese Buddhism. Scholars have long focused on his achievements in developing the doctrines of dhyana (meditation) and prajna (wisdom); however, his contribution to the development of

Sangha regulations deserves greater attention. Daoan created a set of guidelines for Buddhist communal living well before the appearance of the first four complete Vinayas, leading Zanning (920–1001) to praise him as "the pioneer of Sangha regulations" in China. The monastic practices codified by Daoan have been in constant use up to the present time, yet his legacy has long been underestimated and neglected by Buddhist scholars. In the work of Lü master Daoxuan we can see the full extent of Daoan's influence in many matters of monastic practice.

Because Daoan developed his Sangha regulations before the appearance of any of the complete Vinayas, it must be assumed that he and others like him learned much of what they codified from monks who had traveled to China from Western Buddhist communities and later adapted these foreign rules to the specifics of Chinese life. In his formulation of monastic codes, Daoan was undoubtedly influenced by his teacher, Fotudeng (232–348). Although he is most often remembered as the possessor of supernatural powers, another image of Fotudeng exists, one that unfortunately seems to have faded with time: that of a devout observer of the precepts, of a man who never indulged in drink or took a meal after noon in his one hundred and nine years of monkhood.[23]

Daoan, who studied under Fotudeng at Yedu (present-day Henan province), wrote that while there were numerous monks undertaking translations of Vinaya texts, very few were able to make comparative studies of the texts of different schools; only with the appearance of Fotudeng were monk-scholars able to carry out much-needed revisions and research.[24] This statement attests to the fact that not only was Fotudeng a strict adherent of the precepts in practice, but he was regarded as an authority on the various Vinayas.

Daoan must have gained much of his devotion to the practice and study of the Vinaya from his teacher. When Fotudeng died in 348 and his patron ruler Shi Hu (295–349) followed him a year later, the army of Ran Min (?–352)[25] invaded the Heluo area (Henan province), forcing Daoan to escape to Xiangyang (Hubei province). In the south, Daoan—much to his regret—was unable to continue his studies of the Vinayas.[26] For years he lamented the apparent lack of new Vinaya texts, particularly noting the absence of Vinaya for nuns.[27]

Eventually Daoan was invited (or captured) by his admirer, Fu Jian (338–385),[28] and brought to Chang'an. Here Daoan came into contact with foreign monks who had brought Vinaya texts to China and others who were assisting in their translation. Following their work closely, he wrote *Biqiu dajie xu*, a preface to Tanmoshi's translation of the *Sarvāstivāda Vinaya* text regarding bhikṣu precepts.[29] In the preface, we can see Daoan's abiding concern with the Vinaya and with the ethics of communal living. While Daoan did not live to see the introduction of a complete Vinaya into China, a random collection of various partial Vinaya translations was available at this time—albeit scattered across China. A streamlined set of guidelines was necessary to compare all the materials available and fill in apparent lacunae. Taking his lead from practices described by foreign monks, Daoan undertook just such a set of guidelines, calling it *Standards for the Clergy and a Charter for Buddhism (Sengni guifan fofa xianzhang),*[30] a work considered to be the earliest Sangha regulations intended as a supplement to the existing Vinaya. The work itself is no longer extant, and the oldest text to mention it, *Gaoseng zhuan*, tells us only that Daoan's regulations could be roughly grouped into three categories.[31] Fortunately, however, in his *Sifen lü shanfan buque xingshi chao* (henceforth *Xingshi chao*), Lü master Daoxuan of the Tang dynasty reports that Daoan was the major source of material for his own monastic code. Thus we can glean from Daoxuan's regulations much of Daoan's original work. Using the brief descriptions of Daoan's work given in *Gaoseng zhuan* as our reference point, we can discuss some aspects of Daoan's clerical regulations.

The procedure for offering incense while circumambulating the hall (xingxiang), *taking one's seat, preaching the sutra, or giving a lecture*[32]

This description of the first group of topics codified by Daoan shows us that he concerned himself with rituals that were the subject of discussion long before and long after the time of his writings. The ritual of *xingxiang* is mentioned in the earliest Indian sutras and Vinayas. There is the story given in *Zengyi ehan jing* of a rich householder's daughter, who, having married into a non-Buddhist family, has her religious beliefs challenged and calls for help by offering incense in the direction of the Buddha. When Ānanda asked what this incense meant, the Buddha replied that the incense should be perceived as a messenger summoning the Buddha.[33]

Sengshi lüe indicates that in China the custom of *xingxiang* began with Master Daoan.[34] Daoxuan's *Xingshi chao* gives a detailed description of the ceremony of *xingxiang*: "After the flowers are spread, the donors bow down three times, lift their incense, and stand holding their incense burners. Facing the seated senior monks, they all kneel down and place the incense into the incense burners. The rector then announces, 'Offer the incense and preach the verse!' This ritual was adopted from Master [Dao]an."[35] Much later, during the Tang, the travel diary of Japanese pilgrim Ennin (794–864) describes how laypeople distributed incense to the monks while circumambulating the hall.[36] During the Song, according to Zongze's *Chanyuan qinggui*, the ritual of offering incense was held on many occasions (for example, when laypeople came to the temple to sponsor a feast). Clearly, the incense rituals performed in Daoan's day continued into the Tang and Song dynasties.

Regarding the description of Daoan's regulations in *Gaoseng zhuan*, the absence of punctuation renders the meaning of each sentence ambiguous (as is so often the case with classical Chinese writing). Ōchō Enichi believes that the second and third phrases in the above quotation indicate that during a meal monks were to "arrange Piṇḍola's seat" and after it they were to "chant and preach."[37] Ui Hakuju and Tang Yongtong, however, hold that the same characters signify the "ascension to the high seat to preach the sutra."[38] Ōchō focuses on the seat itself as the direct object of a transitive verb, whereas Ui and Tang assume an implicit subject who would himself ascend to the seat. It seems to me that the fifth character of this quotation, *shang*, meaning "up," implies an action taking place in or toward an elevated position, making the latter interpretation the more plausible one. Indeed we see from other texts that a monk usually does ascend to a high position to preach. In the earliest translated text regarding the manners of clergy, *Da biqiu sanqian weiyi*, monks are described as ascending to a high seat to preach the sutra.[39] Daoxuan writes that the Lü master always sits in a high seat while transmitting the precepts.[40] Later in the Chan tradition (as evidenced in *Chanyuan qinggui*) the abbot ascends to the highest seat in the Dharma hall *(shangtang)* before preaching.[41] All of these references indicate a long tradition of ascension to elevated positions to conduct ceremonies.

Two texts attributed to Daoan that pertain to the ritual of chanting, *Daoshi yuanji* and *An Fashi faji jiuzhi sanke*,[42] indicate that in Daoan's day the rituals of reciting the sutra, giving lectures, and performing the precept observance were conducted as chants. According to *Da biqiu sanqian weiyi*,[43] once the signal was struck and the monks had taken their seats, they would chant the praise verse *(zan jibai)*, and reciting the sutra would follow: Although we do not know with certainty what Daoan's practices were for such rituals, *Gaoseng zhuan* describes how Daoan's disciple, Huiyuan, would first ascend the high seat, lead the chanting, and then preach the sutra.[44] This practice, presumably adopted from his master, remained unchanged for many generations. Most of the chanting ceremonies discussed in *Chanyuan qinggui* can be found in Daoxuan's earlier discussion on the ritual regarding the fortnightly confession in *Xingshi chao*, which, Daoxuan tells us, is directly indebted to Daoan's *upavasatha* text.[45] While we should not assume that these chanting rituals were Daoan's personal innovation, it seems clear that the ceremonies were being performed at his monastery.

The procedure for the daily practices to be performed throughout the six periods of the day, such as circumambulating the Buddha statue, taking meals, and chanting at mealtimes[46]

Circumambulation of the Buddha statue *(xiangdao)* as a means of worshiping has its provenance in Indian practice. The proper direction for circumambulation was clockwise, with the worshipper's right shoulder toward the Buddha. Although the sutras often specified three circumambulations as the standard number indicating respect for the Buddha, the actual number performed by Indian monks may have varied widely as they usually walked continuously for a set period of time.[47]

Regarding mealtime rituals, *Chanyuan qinggui* indicates that before taking their meals, monks would chant the ten epithets of the Buddhas and bodhisattvas, a custom preserved in Chinese monasteries to the present day. The content of the chant is as follows: "The Pure Dharma Body Vairocana Buddha, the Perfect Reward Body Vairocana, the Śākyamuni Buddha with His Myriad Transformation Bodies, the Venerable Buddha Maitreya Who Will Descend and Be Reborn in This World in the Future, All the Buddhas in Ten Directions and Three Ages, the Great Holy Mañjuśrī Bodhisattva, the Great Practice Samantabhadra Bodhisattva, the Great Compassion Avalokiteśvara Bodhisattva, and All the Great Bodhisattvas. Great Prajñā-pāramitā!"[48] Ui Hakuju asserts that this chant originated with Daoan and his regulations.[49]

According to the *Four Part Vinaya*, Indian monks chanted verses after their meals.[50] As Daoxuan tells us this tradition was altered in China by Daoan, who began the practice of circumambulating with burning incense and chanting prior to the meal. Daoxuan himself considered this change to be appropriate and adopted the routine for the

Chinese Lü school.[51] This represents yet another monastic practice that to the present day is thought to have originated with Daoan.

The procedure for the fortnightly confession, including the process whereby nuns send a representative to invite a monk to preside over their observance, the ritual of repentance, and so on[52]

In the section of *Xingshi chao*[53] concerning the confession ceremony, Daoxuan makes reference to two earlier texts devoted to this subject *(chujia busa fa)*, one by Puzhao[54] and one by Daoan. Again, Daoxuan relies heavily on Daoan for his interpretations, and we can glean much information about Daoan's original views from this work. The confession is a fortnightly ritual held separately by monks and nuns, usually on each new and full moon, in which the precepts are recited in their entirety. In his description of the ceremony, the author of *Xingshi chao* specifically cites Daoan as his source. First, the monks or nuns are summoned together by a signal. The rector *(weinuo)* begins with a ritual washing of the bamboo stick *(chou)*, which is traditionally used to count the number of participants at the ceremony. The precept master is then invited to ascend to the high seat, and the monks offer water, flowers, and incense. Novices who have not yet received full ordination are requested to leave. Once this is done, representatives of monks or nuns unable to attend the ceremony express the wishes of the absent parties *(shuoyu)*. All of the precepts are then recited one at a time, after which members of the clergy who have violated the rules must confess their transgressions before the assembly, while those who have not remain silent. After this recitation and confession period, the novices are asked to return for the chanting of the verses of praise to close the ceremony.

In addition to regulations directly ascribed to Daoan, a number of other monastic rituals are said to have their origin in incidents from Daoan's life. For example, *Chanyuan qinggui* states that before the assembly of monks may enter the bathhouse, the Holy Ones must first be invited to bathe, a ritual that can be traced to an episode in the biography of Daoan in *Gaoseng zhuan*.[55] The story begins with Daoan and his disciples standing before the statue of the Bodhisattva Maitreya. They are taking vows to be reborn in Tuṣita Heaven, where Maitreya dwells until his return to this world as a future Buddha. On the twenty-seventh day of the first month in the twenty-first year of the Jianyuan era (385), a strange-looking monk arrives to take up residence in Daoan's temple. Since the dormitory is full, he is accommodated in the lecture hall. That night the rector on duty spots the guest passing in and out of the hall through cracks in a window and rushes to tell Daoan of this strange phenomenon. Daoan rises immediately and goes to the guest monk to ask him the purpose of his visit. "To accompany you," he replies, referring to Daoan's vow to journey to Tuṣita Heaven. Daoan then remarks, "I have come to realize and contemplate the great weight of my bad karma; is it possible that I may yet be liberated?" "Without a doubt," the guest assures him. "To fulfill your wish, however, you must invite the holy monks to bathe." The guest goes on to demonstrate the ritual of inviting the Holy Ones to bathe. After witnessing this, Daoan asks where he will be reborn. With a gesture of his hand, the guest points to the northwest corner of the sky. The clouds immediately part, revealing to Daoan and the others the full splendor of Tuṣita Heaven. Later, when Daoan prepares the bath according to the monk's instructions, he suddenly sees an unusual child, accompanied by dozens of other children, coming to the temple, playing, and entering the bath. Feeling as though he were seeing a vision of his own future in heaven, Daoan realizes that he and his followers will receive what they seek.

Another long-standing monastic custom connected with the life of Daoan is the placing of a statue of Piṇḍola in the monastery's dining hall. Daoan is said to have dreamt of a foreign monk with white hair and long eyebrows. The monk tells Daoan two things. First, he reassures him that his annotations to the sutras are correct. Second, he tells Daoan that he is appearing in his dream because he was forbidden by the Buddha to enter nirvana and was condemned to dwell in the west. This mysterious monk then promises to help Daoan propagate the Dharma and suggests that food be offered to him at shrines within the temple. Daoan, of course, complies with this request, and the tradition of the offering was born. Not until Daoan's death and the appearance of the *Ten Section Vinaya* did his disciple Huiyuan realize that the monk in his master's vision was Piṇḍola. (According to the Vinaya, Piṇḍola was forbidden by the Buddha to enter nirvana after he showed off his supernatural powers in front of laypeople.)[56] From Daoxuan's *Xingshi chao*, which identifies the Holy Monk as Piṇḍola, it is evident that the Chinese Lü school's custom of honoring Piṇḍola with an offering of food began with Daoan.[57]

Daoan had a direct influence on yet another aspect of monastic life: the use of the surname Shi. Before Daoan, it was common practice for each monk to take the last name of his teacher. However,

Daoan thought that all monks had but one teacher, the Buddha himself, and that out of respect for their spiritual origins, monks should take the Buddha's name as their own. Śākyamuni Buddha, or "*Śākya*," was known in Chinese as "*Shijia*;" Daoan adopted the initial syllable, *shi*, to serve as the proper surname for all monks. This practice is supported in a passage in *Zengyi ehan jing:* The Buddha proclaimed that just as four different rivers empty into the same ocean and lose their individual names, so should the monks of the four different castes, upon entering the monastic order, call themselves without exception the disciples of the Śākya Buddha.[58] The use of the surname Shi among Chinese Buddhist monastics has continued for well over a millenium.[59]

Assuredly more texts on Sangha regulations were written by Daoan, but unfortunately these are no longer extant. In the early canonical catalogues, several texts are mentioned by title and attributed to Daoan, including an annotation to the Vinayas *(Lüjie)* and instructions for the striking of signal instruments *(Da jianzhi[60] fa)*.[61] Several texts were attributed to Daoan in the later Song-era canonical catalogues: *Sishi liwen* (Instruction for the Four Daily Prayers),[62] *Sengni guifan* (Clerical Standards), and *Famen qingshi ershisi tiao* (Twenty-four Pure Rules of the Dharma Gate).[63] These texts were listed in the catalogue by title only, so their actual content remains obscure. Because the earlier *Gaoseng zhuan* and *Chu sanzang jiji* make no mention of them, they may simply be excerpts from Daoan's larger compilation of clerical regulations, referred to by Sengyou as a still extant work entitled *Sengni guifan fofa xianzhang*. It may be that Sengyou himself applied an umbrella title to a grouping of varied but related writings. Certainly there are no definitive answers at this point, but it is clear from the description in *Gaoseng zhuan* that Daoan and his order were already using a well-developed set of rules and maintaining a highly disciplined monastery.

By advocating the Vinayas and his own clerical regulations, Daoan established a lasting model that "would be adopted by monasteries throughout the entire country."[64] Traces of this model can easily be discerned in Daoxuan's *Xingshi chao* and the earliest surviving Chan monastic code, *Chanyuan qinggui*. Just as Daoan learned respect for the precepts from his teacher, Fotudeng, so too did he transmit this same spirit to his own disciples. Daoan's strict implementation of discipline is illustrated in an incident involving his disciple Fayu. One of Fayu's students drank wine and forgot to offer incense. Fayu punished him (it is unclear exactly what the punishment was) but did

not expel him. When Daoan heard of this leniency, he had a cane delivered over a great distance to Fayu, who immediately understood
his master's meaning. Fayu promptly asked the rector of his temple
to flog him with the cane, all the while blaming himself for being remiss in his duties as a teacher.[65]

Huiyuan's Rules

Huiyuan, like his teacher Daoan, rigidly adhered to the precepts. On
his deathbed he refused to drink alcohol, even though elder monks
advised him to take some fermented bean wine as medicine. The
monks then offered him some rice juice, which he also rejected. Finally, they exhorted Huiyuan to drink some honey water. But before
Huiyuan would drink, he insisted that the Vinayas be consulted by
experts. The senior monks managed to get only halfway through the
Vinayas when Huiyuan passed away.

This episode reveals not only Huiyuan's appreciation of the Vinayas,
but his knowledge of them as well. The Vinayas give detailed instructions on when and how wine may be taken as medicine; when
the juice of grains and vegetables is considered legitimate; when
honey may be taken. At the time Huiyuan invited Dharmaruci to complete the translation of the *Ten Section Vinaya*, he had the opportunity to observe the translation process directly and to deepen his understanding of the precepts. The *Ten Section Vinaya* records an
incident in which Upāli asks the Buddha whether monks are allowed
to drink bitter wine after noon. The Buddha replies that wine is permissible if it is pure, without dregs or the smell of alcohol. Upāli then
asks about juice made from roots, twigs, stems, leaves, flowers, or
fruit—all of which the Buddha approved as long as the juice was not
intoxicating.[66] Elsewhere in the text, honey is included among the four
kinds of medicine conducive to digestion and therefore allowable in
treating the sick.[67] Such medicines were permissible for a period of
seven days.[68] The intake of these foods was restricted because they
were considered a great luxury: According to the *Ten Section Vinaya*,
virtuous elder monks were usually the recipients of such offerings.[69]
Honey was regarded as the "liquid not allowed after noon" *(feishi
jiang)*; it could only be taken before noon and only by those who were
sick and had received the offering.[70] Although *Gaoseng zhuan* does
not specify when the senior monks advised Huiyuan to take a drink,
one must assume that even the extremely cautious Huiyuan would
have hesitated only if it were past noon. Either Huiyuan had a broad
familiarity with the precepts without perfect retention (after all,

everything offered him was permissible) or, more likely, he knew his own death was imminent and inevitable and so sought to educate his fellow monks by setting a clear example of vigilance and profound respect for the Vinayas.

Huiyuan's teaching of the Vinaya precepts was influenced by not only his teacher Daoan but also another external factor—political pressure. Toward the end of the fourth century, during the East Jin, Huan Xuan (369–404), the son of Commander Huan Wen (312–373), seized power. At a time when numerous members of the clergy had ingratiated themselves to the imperial court to win favor and patronage, Huan Xuan took it upon himself to purge the Buddhist clergy. He wrote a letter to Huiyuan, whom he had always respected, to inform him of his decision. Huiyuan replied with a defense of the clergy, strongly advising against any government intervention. At the same time, Huan Xuan's decision forced Huiyuan into thinking that perhaps some form of renewed discipline was necessary, and that it would be better for it to come from within than without. To that end, Huiyuan took on the roles of editor and compiler, gathering an impressive number of regulations for the clergy.[71] While there is no existing information specifying the content and extent of his work, *Chu sanzang jiji* lists Huiyuan as the editor of *Fashe jiedu* (Regulations for the Dharma Association), *Waisiseng jiedu* (Regulations for Monks from Outside), *Jiedu* (General Regulations) and *Biqiuni jiedu* (Regulations for Bhikṣuni).[72] Collectively known as *Huiyuan's Regulations (yuangui)*, they soon became the basis for all later regulations. The sheer volume of Huiyuan's work demonstrates the extent of his concern for the Vinaya and his respect for monastic discipline, both of which passed from teacher to disciple through the generations—from Fotudeng to Daoan to Daoan's disciples, all of whom helped lay the foundations for Chinese monastic life.

Regulations Compiled by Daoan's Contemporaries

We have seen how Daoan and his disciples established a system of discipline in the earliest stages of Chinese Buddhism; however, many of Daoan's contemporaries throughout China were also interested in creating enduring regulations. At a time of governmental transition in the south—during the Song, Qi, Liang, and Chen dynasties—as well as in the north, there was no shortage of individuals seeking to use these windows of opportunity to buttress the existing Vinayas with supplementary rules. Making use of available records, I will briefly touch upon the lives and contributions of those who created regulatory texts other than Vinaya translations during the Northern-Southern dynasties.

One of Daoan's contemporaries, Zhi Dun (314–366), also known as Zhi Daolin, was a monastic leader in the south, with a constant following of hundreds of students.[73] His primary goal was the integration of the Daoist philosophy of "profound learning" *(xuanxue)* with Buddhist prajna thought. While some scholars of profound learning, or "pure talk" *(qingtan)* tended to lead lives unfettered by regulations of any sort, Zhi Dun insisted on the observance of the precepts. After witnessing a chick emerge from an egg, he became a lifelong vegetarian, a decision indicative of his rigor and devotion.[74] He supervised his students at the Dong'an Temple with extreme dedication, codifying his rules for their behavior in his *Boretai zhongseng jiyi jiedu* (Rules of Conduct for the Sangha Assembly on the Prajna Platform)[75] during his tenure as preacher of *Prajna Sutra*. Another monk, Sengqu (fl. 453–464), appointed Sangha rectifier *(sengzheng)* by the southern Song court, worked on the *Ten Section Vinaya* and compiled supplementary regulations for the fortnightly confession ceremony. This text, *Sengni yaoshi* (Major Activities of the Clergy), had a wide circulation at the time.[76] In 489, during the Qi dynasty (479–501), which succeeded the Song court in the south, the monk Chaodu compiled *Lüli* (Rules from the Vinaya),[77] basing this work on the Vinayas themselves. During the Liang dynasty, Fayun (467–529) was commissioned by the imperial court to compile a set of clerical regulations *(sengzhi)*, which became a popular model for later works.[78] In 504, the monk Sengsheng edited the *Jiaojie biqiuni fa (Admonitions for the Bhikṣuni)*, closely following the Dharmaguptaka Vinaya.[79] As none of these texts are extant, we can only guess at their content.

In the courts of the north, there were a number of monks living after Daoan who, in the capacity of clerical officials, codified many of the regulations added to the Vinayas. The monk Sengxian was appointed controller of clergy *(shamen tong)* and compiled *Sengzhi sishiqi tiao* (Forty-seven Articles of the Clerical Regulations) by imperial decree in the year 493.[80] As mentioned above, Huiguang encouraged the teaching of the *Four Part Vinaya*, for which he wrote a widely read commentary. Because of this text he later came to be regarded as the founder of the *Four Part Vinaya* tradition. He was recruited by the imperial court of the East Wei (534–543) as a clerical official and granted the title of Controller of the Nation's Clergy *(guotong)*. Despite these honors, Huiguang never ceased to uphold the precepts. He compiled *Sengzhi shiba tiao* (Sangha Regulations in Eighteen Articles) in hopes of streamlining and clarifying the rules for the Buddhist clergy, and his contribution to the "reformation of the [corrupt] spirit of the clergy and the spread of the teaching"[81] was considered second only to Daoan's.

Clerical regulations came from not only monks themselves but also devout rulers and members of the nobility. Prince Wenxuan (459–494) of the Qi dynasty was interested in regulation and practice for laypeople as well as the clergy. According to *Chu sanzang jiji*, his works include: *Sengzhi* (*Sangha Regulations;* most likely edited by monks), *Qingxin shinü fazhi* (Regulations for Sincere and Devoted Laywomen),[82] and *Zaijia busa yi* (The Model of Confession for Laypeople).[83] Emperor Jianwen (r. 549–551) of the Liang dynasty edited *Baguanzhai zhi* (Regulations for the Overnight Retreat for Laypeople), which contains the following regulations to be observed during a day of fasting and abstention.[84]

1. Those who sleep past the time of roll call must do a penance of twenty prostrations and must hold the incense burner while listening to three preachings of the sutra.

2. Those who are absent without permission must do a penance of ten prostrations.

3. Those who are absent and do not come back before the sutra is preached three times must do a penance of ten more prostrations.

4. Those who do not report to the rector a neighbor falling asleep during a ceremony must do a penance of ten prostrations.

5. Those who make mutual agreements with a neighbor not to report each other to the rector when they fall asleep must do a penance of ten prostrations.

6. If the rector is negligent in checking for any violators of these rules and does not assign penance, the rector himself must do a penance of twenty prostrations and must hold the incense burner while listening to three preachings of the sutra.

7. On the day of every new and full moon *(baihei)*,[85] the rectors should conduct reviews of each other. If there is any mutual agreement between rectors not to report each other, both parties must do a penance of twenty prostrations.

8. Those who are unwilling to chant the praise at the end of the sutra preaching must do a penance of ten prostrations.

9. Those who request to register for the retreat and do not attend at their allotted time must do a penance of ten prostrations.

10. Those who register incorrectly for the retreat on a new or full moon day must do a penance of ten prostrations.

Zhiyi's Rules for the Guoqing Monastery

While power in China inevitably changed hands throughout the centuries, the transmission of monastic discipline remained unbroken. During the twenty-nine-year period between the Southern-Northern dynasties and the Tang, the short-lived Sui dynasty reunified the nation. A set of regulations from this period provides us with an early example of the monastic code—one that was in use two centuries before Baizhang, the reputed formulator of the Chan monastic code. Master Zhiyi, founder of the Tiantaishan Monastery, was highly respected by rulers of the Chen (557–589) and Sui dynasties. Aside from his lifelong devotion to the teaching of the *Lotus Sutra*, Zhiyi studied Vinaya with Lü master Huikuang upon entering the order and wrote a commentary on the *Brahma Net Sutra*, the Mahayana sutra conferring the bodhisattva precepts. The crown princes of both the Chen and Sui dynasties received the bodhisattva precepts from him, and when Emperor Houzhu of the Chen dynasty (r. 583–587) attempted to purge the clergy, it was Zhiyi's opposition that prevented him.

Zhiyi laid out *Lizhi fa shitiao* (Rules in Ten Clauses), which was aimed at restraining the restlessness of novices. These rules were included at the beginning of *Guoqing bailu* (One Hundred Records of the Guoqin Monastery), a work compiled by Zhiyi's disciple Guanding (561–632). In the preface, Zhiyi expresses his concern over the deterioration of character in the members of his order. He states that when he first established his monastery on Mount Tiantai in 575, the monks possessed self-discipline and did not need any words of encouragement. But upon his return to the mountain in 595, he likened the minds of the newer members to those of "monkeys and horses" and immediately saw the need for a system of rules. These ten rules have been preserved and can be summarized as follows:[86]

1. All members of the Sangha community are categorized into one of three groups: those who concentrate on sitting meditation in the common hall *(yitang zuochan)*, those who practice repentance in separate sanctuaries *(biechang chanhui)*, and those who carry out Sangha matters *(zhi sengshi)*. Members of all three groups are equally deserving of the same supplies and personal effects. Those who do not wish to belong to any of the preceding groups should not be allowed to enter the Sangha community.

2. Those concentrating on meditation must devote four periods of time to meditation and six periods of time to worshiping the Bud-

dha. If they fail to fulfill these requirements, they must prostrate themselves and confess before the assembly.

3. During the period of worshiping the Buddha, the monks are required to put on "robes with scale-like strips" *(kāṣāya)*. They must chant in unison, maintaining their focus. Failure to do so will result in the same punishment as above.

4. The purpose of "individual practice" is to separate oneself from the rest of the assembly so that one may engage in the four types of intensive samadhi [continuous sitting, continuous walking, walking half the time and sitting half the time, and neither walking nor sitting]. However, if a monk separates himself from the assembly and does not engage in one of the four types of vigorous meditation, he should be punished by having to serve as the rector on duty.

5. Those who carry out Sangha affairs must not misuse monastic property. If, after a proper investigation, it is proven that a member of the assembly has misappropriated communal property, he must be expelled from the monastery.

6. If not suffering from illness, each monk is required to attend the two daily meals in the dining hall. Eating vessels may be made of iron or clay. Materials such as bone, bamboo, painted gourd, or shell are not allowed. Striking one's bowl, sipping noisily, talking while eating, asking for extra food, and eating alone are not permissible. Transgressors should be made to prostrate themselves and repent before the assembly.

7. Every Sangha member, whether senior or junior, whether inside the monastery or outside, whether near or far, is prohibited from surreptitiously eating meat or fish or drinking wine. Eating at the wrong time is also prohibited. If anyone violates these rules, he must be expelled. The only exceptions are cases of medical necessity.

8. To emphasize the harmony of the Sangha, members are prohibited from quarreling or fighting. Those who have quarreled must be made to prostrate themselves before each other. Those who have engaged in physical fighting must be expelled.

9. Those who commit the gravest offenses should be punished in accordance with the Vinaya. In the case of a false accusation, the one who is accused should not be punished, while the one who has made the false accusation should be expelled.

10. Those who have violated one of the above nine rules but have since repented should be allowed to remain in or return to the community; those who frequently violate the above rules or show no remorse should be expelled and should not be allowed to reenter the monastery.

Another text ascribed to Zhiyi, *Guanxin shifa* (Method of Contemplation during the Meal), addresses proper decorum at mealtime.[87] In this work, customs observed before the taking of a meal are described in detail: "After unfolding one's cushion, taking a seat, and listening for the rector to strike the signal bell, one collects one's hands and performs the Buddhist service by offering a prayer for the unity of the Three Treasures, which prevails in the realms of all ten directions. Next, food is offered to all sentient beings. Offering food to the beings in the six realms symbolizes the six paramitas [the six perfections].[88] Only then can one partake of the food oneself."[89] This description of the rituals before dining is strikingly similar to that given in the earliest Chan monastic code, *Chanyuan qinggui*. *Guanxin shifa* thus provides concrete evidence that such rituals were established long before the time of Baizhang, and that customs of the Tiantai school did not differ much from the customs of the later Chan school.

Zhiyi also wrote *Xun zhishi ren,* an admonition to the administrators of his monastery.[90] In it he warns the members against the misappropriation of public property. He then encourages them to "develop the mind" dedicated to service and personal cultivation. Zhiyi tells the story of a purity-keeper *(jingren)* who, after covertly listening to the master preach, keeps in his mind at all times the pure thoughts he has heard, even while he performs such menial tasks as grinding grain or washing rice. Eventually he attains samadhi while stoking the wood stove. Here we see spiritual cultivation linked to a regimen of physical labor within the monastery[91]—a concept that clearly existed well before Baizhang's time.

In addition to general rules for the monastic order, Zhiyi compiled several articles specifically devoted to the practice of repentance: *Jingli fa, Puli fa, Qing Guanshiyin chanfa* (Procedure for Invoking Avalokiteśvara for Repentance),[92] *Jinguangming chanfa* (Procedure for Repentance described in Golden Light Sutra), *Fangdeng sanmei xingfa* (Procedure for the Vaipulya Samadhi Repentance), and *Fahua sanmei chanyi* (Procedure for the Lotus Samadhi Repentance). This collection of rules was obviously intended for those who had chosen to practice repentance in separate sanctuaries and as a complement to Zhiyi's rules for those who had chosen meditation, such as *Mohe zhiguan* (Great Tranquility and Contemplation), *Liu miao famen* (Six Wondrous Dharma Gates), and *Xiuxi zhiguan zuochan fayao* (Essentials for Practicing the Meditation of Tranquility and Contemplation). Worship and repentance are the major rituals of Buddhism, and the texts compiled for these two practices provide guidelines on how they should be conducted. However, Zhiyi's compilation of instructions in no way implies that Tiantai was the first tradition to perform these practices. Rituals of worship and repentance were carried out by other traditions at the time of Zhiyi.[93] As mentioned above, one text regarding the worship of Buddhas was attributed to Daoan himself.

Daoxuan's Regulations for the Clergy

As we have shown, many of Daoan's monastic practices have come down to us through the works of Daoxuan, especially through *Xingshi chao*. But while clearly relying on the guidance of Daoan, Daoxuan was an innovator in his own right. He created new models for later monastic practices and rituals, and his influence on Chinese monasticism is far greater than many have realized.

Daoxuan was a prolific writer whose works covered a wide array of subjects. His non-Vinaya works include biographies of monks, catalogues of the Buddhist canon, genealogies, and apologia. However, he is best remembered as the most prominent monk in the Chinese Lü tradition. The lineage he founded, Nanshan (named after the mountain where he first sequestered himself), has survived as the main branch of the Lü school. At the beginning of the Tang, when the *Four Part Vinaya* rose to prominence over other Vinaya texts, its study was carried out by three main Lü traditions: the Xiangbu lineage, represented by Fali; the Dongta lineage, represented by Huaisu; and the Nanshan lineage, represented by Daoxuan—the name of each lineage being taken from the location of the home temple of its major advocate. Gradually, Daoxuan's Nanshan lineage dominated the other two and became the main branch of the Lü school. (It is the only Lü tradition still in existence.) In his time Daoxuan was so dedicated to the *Four Part Vinaya* that he produced five commentaries on it.[94] These enormously rich commentaries on the Dharmaguptaka Vinaya established him as the authority on the *Four Part Vinaya*. His sect's rise can also be attributed to Daoxuan's claim that the doctrine of the *Four Part Vinaya* anticipated the spirit of Mahayana teachings *(fentong dasheng)*. Other sects insisted the *Four Part Vinaya* belonged to the Hinayana tradition.

To lend credence to this claim, Daoxuan drew from not only the Vinaya texts but the Mahayana precept sutras: the *Bodhisattva Stages Sutra*, the *Bodhisattva Precepts Sutra*, and the *Brahma Net Sutra*.[95] He justifies not eating meat by citing Mahayana precepts and arguing that although meat eating is allowed in the Vinayas, the true Buddhist should abstain from the practice out of compassion for all sentient beings. He explains the apparent discrepancy between the Hinayana and Mahayana texts by claiming that heavenly beings reported to him the Buddha's intended teaching on the subject. The words of the Buddha were, "At the very beginning, when I attained enlightenment, I did allow the Vinayas to permit the consumption of three kinds of pure meat. But these three meats are not of creatures from the four statuses of living beings; they are the meats of dhyana, the food beyond comprehension which you cannot understand. Why are you slandering my teaching? In those sutras such as *Nirvana Sutra* and *Laṅkāvatāra Sutra*, I teach that one should abstain from all kinds of meat, and I forbid anyone who seeks to uphold the precepts to consume the flesh of any sentient being. If any evil bhikṣu claims that the Vinayas teach that it is permissible to eat fish or meat or to wear silk clothing, let his words be anathema."[96]

Daoxuan also expounded the now traditional view that the differences between the Mahayana and Hinayana schools are only apparent. He claimed that "there is no distinction in the intended spirit of the two vehicles of Mahayana and Hinayana. They are designed as medicine. Each is prescribed in accordance with the disposition of a sentient being, but both ultimately are intended to eliminate the disease."[97] Accordingly, Daoxuan integrates the ideas of the Mahayana precepts with the Hinayana Vinayas, thereby paving the way for the Mahayana Lü school.

Among Daoxuan's great works on the *Four Part Vinaya*, *Xingshi chao* was the most influential in the development of this Dharmaguptaka Vinaya in China. In addition to providing doctrinal interpretations of the *Four Part Vinaya*, it shows that many of the practices described had been carried out some time before. As we have shown above, *Xingshi chao* preserves a great deal of Daoan's practices. Numerous customs mentioned in Daoxuan's works are, in turn, still practiced in the Chan school of the present day. The five contemplations *(wuguan)* recited before meals can be found in *Chanyuan qinggui*, but they were first enumerated by Daoxuan in *Xingshi chao*. These contemplations—given by Daoxuan and preserved (with only slight modification) by Chan monks in the Song and even by monks in modern-day China and Japan—are as follows:

- One, to ponder the effort necessary to supply this food and
  to appreciate its origins;
- Two, to reflect upon one's own virtue being insufficient
  to receive the offering;

  – Three, to protect the mind's integrity, to depart from error,
    and, as a general principle, to avoid being greedy;
  – Four, at the same time, to consider the food as medicine and
    as nourishment for the body, which prevents emaciation;
  – Five, to receive this food as necessary to attain enlightenment.[98]

The conspicuous "hammer and stand" signal instrument placed in the center of the Sangha hall in Chan monasteries does not have its origins in the Chan school at all. As indicated in *Xingshi chao*, the "hammer and stand" was used by Daoxuan's order and most likely dates back to the time of Daoan. Daoxuan writes that in order to strike the hammer, the rector "first stands outside the gate, prepares himself, and presses his palms together. He then enters through the side door and approaches the striking position. First, standing with his palms closed, he lifts the hammer with his right hand and touches it to the stand silently. He then strikes the stand with the hammer once, being careful not to do so too loudly. After this he silently rests the hammer on the stand, holding the handle. Then he presses his palms together and makes the appropriate announcements. If there is a meal offering, a chanting benediction, or a prayer to be made, all must wait until the rector has announced the proper procedure. The hammer cannot be used for any other purposes, except to pacify the assembly."[99]

Another practice cited in *Xingshi chao* that would become a standard monastic procedure is the reception of the ten novice precepts. Comparing the ritual of the novice receiving the precepts *(shami shoujie wen)* described in this text with that in the appendix to *Chanyuan qinggui* (used for tonsuring the postulants in Chan monasteries), we find that, aside from a few minor additions, the latter work is practically identical to the former.[100] Additional proof of Daoxuan's influence on later monastic practice can be found in the admission by the Tiantai monk Zunshi that Daoxuan's *Xingshi chao* served as the primary model for his own procedure for conferring the five precepts.[101]

Besides *Xingshi chao*, Daoxuan wrote several other texts to supplement the Vinayas. He wrote *Jingxin jieguan fa* (The Method of Abstention and Contemplating the Purity of Mind) during a summer retreat and sent it to one of his disciples to encourage the members of his monastery to cultivate their minds. *Shimen guijing yi* (The Practice of Refuge and Veneration in Buddhism) fully discusses the complicated etiquette for bowing and prostration in its eighth chapter. *Shimen zhangfu yi* (Practices regarding the Robes in Buddhism) explains the making of the monk's robes. *Liangchu qingzhong yi* (Method for the Allocation of "Light and Heavy" Objects) reorganizes the rules given in the Vinaya regarding the distribution of a deceased monk's possessions. *Guanzhong chuangli jietan tu jing* (Discussion and Diagram of the Ordination Platform in Guanzhong) provides a wealth of information on the ordination ceremony, including a section on the procedure for ascending the platform to receive the precepts.[102]

Most of these works are extensive in their detail; some are perhaps too complex to be carried out in practice. Daoxuan gave simple and straighforward rules regarding etiquette and courtesies in *Jiaojie xinxue biqiu xinghu lüyi* (Exhortation on Manners and Etiquette for Novices in Training, henceforth *Xinghu lüyi*).[103] To remind newcomers that proper deportment was a necessity of spiritual life, Daoxuan composed this code as a manual for trainees. It comprises twenty-three lessons of etiquette with such titles as "Entering the Monastery," "Lodging in the Dormitory," "Washing One's Eating Bowls," and "Abstaining from Laughter on Six Occasions." The text discusses each rule briefly.

The influence of *Xinghu lüyi* is far greater than scholars have hitherto been aware. The close parallels between Daoxuan's text and *Chanyuan qinggui* are striking.[104] Daoxuan's legacy is apparent not only in the earliest regulations, but also in the later monastic code of Dōgen. The first twenty-two rules of Dōgen's *Tai taiko goge jari hō* (Etiquette of Interacting with Seniors Who Were Ordained Five or More Years Earlier, from Dōgen's *Eihei dai shingi*), are taken one by one from Daoxuan's *Xinghu lüyi*, beginning with the seventh lesson. Dōgen's remaining rules are analogous to those given in Daoxuan's twentieth lesson, "Venerating the Seniors," and other passages scattered throughout *Xinghu lüyi*. Even if one assumes that Dōgen did not borrow his regulations from Daoxuan directly, whatever source he used was undoubtedly dependent on *Xinghu lüyi*.

Another text entitled *Shimen jiseng guidu tu jing* (An Illustration and Model for the Gathering of the Assembly in Buddhism), although little studied, has been attributed to Daoxuan.[105] In this short piece, the author demonstrates the proper method of striking the big bell: three short sequences to gather the assembly; a number of long sequences to relieve the pain of those suffering in the evil realms. The latter alludes to the story of Candana Kaniṣka of the Kuṣāṇa dynasty, who accumulated a great deal of evil karma in a previous life. He was reborn as a thousand-headed fish whose heads were continually severed one at a time by a great wheel of swords. Since the wheel of swords ceased only when a monastery bell was

Table 2. Correspondences between
Two Works by Daoxuan and *Chanyuan qinggui*

Sifen lü shanfan buque xingshi chao		*Chanyuan qinggui*	
"Precept Preaching" (shuojie)	T 40:35b9–37b13	"Liturgy for Novice Ordination" *(shami shoujie wen)*	YZS **[297– 318]**
"Jiexiang"	T 40:36c9–11	"Jiexiang"	YZS **[298]**
"Chu shijie"	T 40:37a9	"Chu shijie"	YZS **[315]**
Hammer and stand	T 40:35c	Hammer and stand	YZS **[45]**
Striking hammer	T 40:146b15–18	Striking hammer	YZS **[221]**
Story of King Kaniṣka	T 40:6c19–24	Story of King Kaniṣka	YZS **[154]**
Five Contemplations	T 40:84a9–12, 128b3–c10	Five Contemplations	YZS **[52]**
"The Six Awarenesses" *(liunian)*	T 40:30b8–12	"The Six Awarenesses"	YZS **[39]**
Jiaojie xinxue biqiu xinghu lüyi			
Entering the Monastery	T 45:869b26–27	Attendance at Meals	YZS **[42]**
Serving Teachers	T 45:869c26		
Partaking of the Two Meals	T 45:871c8		
Serving Teachers	T 45:869c27–29	Small Sermon	YZS **[83]**
Staying in the Monastery	T 45:870a18–19	Small Sermon	YZS **[81]**
Partaking of the Two Meals	T 45:871b26	Attendance at Meals	YZS **[54]**
	T 45:871c16–17		YZS **[43]**
	T 45:872a1–3		YZS **[52]**
	T 45:872b2–4		YZS **[48]**
Going to the Toilet	T 45:872c29	Using the Toilet	YZS **[233]**
Entering the Bathroom	T 45:873a24–25	Using the Toilet	YZS **[233]**

struck, Kaniṣka requested that monks continually strike the bell to alleviate his pain. Thus the temple bell is struck for long sequences in the morning and at night to stop the pain of all sentient beings who have fallen into the evil realms.[106] According to *Chanyuan qinggui*, the "bell master" in the Chan monastery strikes the bell every morning and evening. The explanation given for this comes from the story of Kaniṣka.[107] In *Chanyuan qinggui*, the bell is also used to gather the assembly.[108]

Most of the regulations and practices of the Chan tradition, as collected in *Chanyuan qinggui*, can be found in the Lü master Daoxuan's work. This is a clear indication of the extent to which the Chan school shares its sources with the Lü tradition. Their common heritage is the voluminous extant material originally written by Daoxuan. Table 2 shows the degree to which Daoxuan's works affected the composition of *Chanyuan qinggui*. The left column lists sections from two prominent works by Daoxuan; the right parts of *Chanyuan qinggui* that closely correspond to these sections.

Authenticity of Baizhang's Monastic Code

Traditionally, Baizhang has been considered a revolutionary figure who fought for Chan independence from other schools, most especially the Lü school. According to several accounts,[109] Chan monks lived within Lü school monasteries from the time of the first patriarch, Bodhidharma, until the sixth patriarch, Huineng (683–713). The monks viewed this arrangement as an impingement on their freedom. Baizhang was said to have been troubled by the situation and was determined to establish a Chan monastery that would be separate from the Lü monastic establishment. It has been claimed that Baizhang established a novel code of regulations as a way of declaring this independence. This alleged Baizhang code no longer exists; all that we know of it is derived from statements written by historiographers of the later Song, who describe the regulations and practices observed by Baizhang's order as follows:[110]

> 1. Those who have a spiritual mentality and respectable virtues are called Elders *(zhanglao)*, a term used to refer to those from the West [India] who have great virtue and ordination seniority, such as Śāriputra.
> 2. If a monk reaches the rank of *huazhu*[111] [abbot], then he resides in the room of "ten square feet" *(fangzhang)*,[112] which is not unlike the room of Vimalakīrti and which [the abbot] should not consider his personal quarters. No Buddha hall need be built, but instead a Dharma hall shall be erected. This is because every current abbot should be considered a successor of the Buddha and the patriarchs and should be honored as such.
> 3. All those who assemble to learn, regardless of number, regardless of rank, enter the Sangha hall and take their places in order of ordination seniority. Inside the hall are platforms and racks for personal effects.
> 4. Monks should lie on their right side during sleep, this being the most auspicious posture. Sleeping is only to be a brief rest between the long periods of sitting meditation. Proper deportment is required at all times.
> 5. Entering the abbot's room for instruction is at the discretion

of the trainees. On such occasions, the juniors and seniors do not observe the ordinary customs associated with rank.

6. All the members of the monastery gather for morning sermons and evening meetings. The Elder [that is, the abbot] enters the hall and ascends the seat, while the administrative staff and the disciples stand in a straight line, listening with complete attention. The guests and the master engage in debate and propagate their school's traditional teachings. All of these procedures should be carried out in the proper fashion.

7. Meals are served twice a day and must be available to everyone. But they are also to be frugal. The frugality demonstrates, through the taking of meals, the accomplishments of the Dharma.

8. All members, whether junior or senior, must participate in communal labor *(puqing)*.

9. There are ten administrative offices, each one with a chief and several subordinates.

10. Those who pretend to be monks and create disturbances by mingling among the pure assembly should be singled out by the rector, have their bedding removed, and be expelled. The main purpose of this rule is to insure the purity of the assembly. Those who have committed grave offenses are to be caned by the rector, they are to have their robes, bowls, et cetera, burned in front of the assembly, and they are to be expelled from the monastery by the side door. This is to show the shame and disgrace of their behavior to the assembly.

After Baizhang established his monastic code, other Chan monasteries are said to have followed suit. As one historiographer claims, "It was Baizhang who initiated the independence of the Chan school."[113]

The famous maxim "One day without work, one day without food"[114] is attributed to Baizhang and identifies him as an early advocate of the Chan work ethic. The emphasis on labor was a defense against the accusation that monks were nothing more than parasites on society; it also represented an open protest against the prohibition on agriculture laid out in the Vinayas and therefore stood as a challenge to the stricter interpretations of the Lü school. This partial deviation from the Vinayas undertaken by the Chan school was a result of both external social factors as well as internal doctrinal disputes.

As a result of Baizhang's alleged role in the schism between the Chan and Lü schools, he was commemorated as one of the great patriarchs of the Chan tradition, along with Bodhidharma and Huineng. This hagiographic portrait of Baizhang has been challenged by modern scholars, who claim that Baizhang's reputation as the author of the Chan monastic code and creator of the independent Chan school was a fiction created during the Song. While historical documents prior to the Song are obscure on this subject, scholars argue that the establishment of the Chan community was well under way at the time of Baizhang, arguing that Chan masters before him, including the fifth patriarch Hongren (d. 674) and the sixth patriarch Huineng, had already established Chan monasteries independent of the Lü school in which meditation was central and Sangha regulations were developed.[115]

Furthermore, it has been asserted that there is no solid evidence that Baizhang ever invented a monastic code. The text that contained the rules purportedly established by him no longer exists; whether or not such a text ever existed is a matter of debate. Scholars disagree about whether the regulations were Baizhang's invention or merely a collection of longstanding customs[116] and, if the former, about the time of this work's disappearance. Piecing together references in extant materials, they have tried to reconstruct the original text. The following is a list of the five major sources of information on Baizhang's code in chronological order.

> A. The biography of Baizhang in *Song gaoseng zhuan* (Biographies of Eminent Monks Compiled in the Song), written by Zangning in 988.[117]
>
> B. The section "Bieli Chanju" in *Sengshi lüe*, compiled by Zangning in 999.[118]
>
> C. *Chanmen guishi*, appended to the biography of Baizhang in *Jingde chuandeng lu* (Transmission of the Flame Compiled in the Jingde Era), written in 1004.[119]
>
> D. *Baizhang guisheng song*, appended to *Chanyuan qinggui*, written in 1103.[120]
>
> E. The alleged preface to Baizhang's code, written by Yang Yi (968–1024), appended to *Chixiu Baizhang qinggui*, written in 1335.[121]

Ui Hakuju argues that *Jingde chuandeng lu* [C] did not borrow from *Song gaoseng zhuan* [A][122] and that their similarity can only be the result of a direct, common source—namely, Baizhang's code. The philological need for an urtext, Ui argues, provides the best proof for the existence of Baizhang's original work during the Song. Narikawa Hōyū holds a similar view,[123] seconding Ui's belief that the Baizhang code was a unique prototype that was subsequently lost. Lending credence to this idea is the fact that the regulations given in the earlier text, the biography of Baizhang [A], are rather abbreviated in nature, whereas the later *Chanmen guishi* [C] is much richer in detailed information—indicating perhaps the existence of a common source. At the same time, there can be little doubt that both the passages in *Baizhang guisheng song* [D] and in *Chixiu Baizhang qinggui* [E] are copied from *Chanmen guishi* in *Jingde chuandeng lu* [C].

Ui and Narikawa's argument for the existence of Baizhang's code[124] is also based on the content of "A Letter from Chan Master Yishan" *(Yishan Chanshi shu)*.[125] In this letter sent to his friend Yunwu Zixian, Yishan (also known as Liaowan [d. 1312]) mentions that Huiji Yuanxi (1238–1319), who lived at Baizhang Mountain, had sent him an old monastic code of Huiji's monastery two years earlier, one Yishan later identified as Baizhang's. After reading the code, Yishan discovered many errors and intended to ask Huiji to collaborate on a revision of Baizhang's text, a task that was never undertaken.[126] If one assumes that the content of this letter is accurate, then the Baizhang code must still have been extant during the second half of the thirteenth century, that is, even after the compilation of *Chanyuan qinggui*. However, in the afterword to *Chixiu Baizhang qinggui* (the Yuan version), we are informed that Baizhang's code had been lost by the time of the compilation (1335).[127] As Yishan, Huiji, and Yunwu corresponded during the era of Xianchun (1265–1274) and were regarded as "the three senior venerables of Xianchun" *(Xianchun san zunsu)*, we can deduce that the original code must have been lost at some point during the sixty years between 1274 and 1335, or some time after the Xianchun era but before the time of the compilation of *Chixiu Baizhang qinggui*.[128]

Kondō Ryōichi holds an entirely different view, however, arguing that Baizhang's monastic code was not a written codification at all, but merely a body of customs transmitted by communal example and oral instruction. In support of his thesis, Kondō uses the earliest materials available: an inscription about Baizhang, written by Chen Xu in 818, four years after Baizhang's death; and *Zutang ji*, the earliest Chan record on "the transmission of the flame," compiled in 952. Kondō points out that neither of these works mentions a written code. Even the writings of Weishan Lingyou (771–853), one of Baizhang's direct disciples, contain no references to any such code. Finally, the four-character title *Baizhang qinggui* (Baizhang's Regulations of Purity), the standard reference to this regulation, never appears in early monastic codes such as *Chanyuan qinggui* (1103) and *Jiaoding qinggui* (1274)—a surprising omission if a well-known titled document was available. Kondō also points out that *"qinggui"* was used by non-Buddhists during the Tang to designate "pure rules," or "rules for keeping oneself pure," and was not a specific genre designating Buddhist monastic codified regulations.[129] Griffith Foulk takes a similar approach in his study of historical documents written during the Tang and Five Dynasty periods and finds no mention of a Baizhang monastic code. After examining the works of Baizhang's disciples and contemporaries, he sees no evidence of a pivotal historical role for Baizhang.[130]

Kondō and Foulk's arguments are worth considering; however, an *argumentum ex silencio* is hardly conclusive. The fact that the compilation of a *qinggui* is not mentioned by contemporaries or even by disciples does not mean it never existed. The case of Zongze may serve to illustrate this point. Not long after Zongze's death, his contemporary, Yuanzhao (1048–1116), wrote a preface to a collection of Zongze's writings entitled *Changlu Ze Chanshi wenji xu*.[131] In this preface, which serves more or less as an obituary, Yuanzhao lists works by Zongze but neglects to mention *Chanyuan qinggui*.[132] In fact, none of the biographies of Zongze that appear in the various records of "the transmission of the lamp"[133] and none of the texts in the Pure Land collections (Zongze is exalted as one of the patriarchs of the Pure Land tradition) make any mention of Zongze's compilation of a monastic code. However, because *Chanyuan qinggui* is still extant, and because the author clearly identifies himself in the preface to this work, we can assume with a fair amount of certainty that Zongze did in fact compile this monastic code. Analogously, the absence of any mention of Baizhang's monastic code cannot be taken as proof of its nonexistence.

While Kondō does not deny the existence of *Baizhang's regulations*, he believes they were never compiled into a written document, or, if they were codified, the resulting document was not given the title *Baizhang qinggui* at the time. (The term *"qinggui"* does not appear until the second half of the twelfth century.)[134] Despite the absence of a clear mention of Baizhang's code, the "Letter from Yishan" suggests that it is more probable than not that Baizhang's code existed in written form, but that the original text was not called *Baizhang qinggui*. As I hope I have made clear, many monks before Baizhang compiled supplementary regulations for their own orders, but it was not until long after Baizhang that a comprehensive set of rules and regulations was compiled and given the name *qinggui;* thus it would seem that *Chanyuan qinggui* is the earliest surviving text of this sort.

Why, then, was Baizhang's work seemingly lost? The answer may lie in the fact that written works regarding the rules and regulations of monastic practice have traditionally been given less weight by historians and scholars than philosophical and doctrinal texts. Regulations, which deal with daily activities, are apt to be taken for granted, or at least regarded as a less compelling subject. We see this phenomenon clearly demonstrated by the fact that there are far more commentaries dedicated to the sutras than to the Vinayas. From Daoan to Huiyuan to Daoxuan, philosophical works have always been the main focus of scholarly research. Daoxuan, for instance, has been studied primarily for his *Xingshi chao,* with its complex annotations; his *Xinghu lüyi,* with its straightforward rules for daily living, has rarely been explored despite its great influence on later monastic practice.

Another salient feature of Kondō's argument is his belief that Baizhang's reputation as monastic code pioneer is due primarily to later political developments:[135]

> The Chan school successfully invented a history of transmission of the flame to establish a distinct genealogy. The nature of the school required that its adherents distinguish their tradition from others to imbue themselves with a special authority. One method of claiming such authority and marking the independence of their school was to emphasize the uniqueness of their regulations. Accordingly, Baizhang's monastic code was devised to fit this requirement.

Political necessity undoubtedly contributed to the exaggeration of Baizhang's historical significance; however, the question remains: Why was Baizhang singled out and who would have had an interest in advocating his position?

While Baizhang may not have been the sole originator of the Chan work ethic or monastic code, or primarily responsible for initiating the movement toward an independent Chan school, the regulations and practices depicted in *Chanmen guishi* [C] and the biography of Baizhang [A] strongly suggest that Baizhang's order was a discipline-oriented community with a clear sense of codified rules. The respect for monastic rules that Baizhang instilled in the members of his monastery and the lasting legacy of this spirit have deservedly earned him an important place in Chan tradition. That Baizhang's successors carried on this tradition of respect is evident in his disciples' codifying the following five rules immediately after their master's death, as recorded in the Chen Xu inscription:[136]

1. A fully-ordained monk should be placed in charge of master Baizhang's pagoda and a novice should be appointed to sweep the floor.

2. Nuns' quarters, nuns' tombs, or nuns' pagodas may not be placed within the boundaries of the monastery. Lay people are not allowed to inhabit the monastery.

3. Monks who come from outside seeking spiritual guidance and those postulants who join the monastery must look to the chief of the monastery [*yuanzhu*, that is, the abbot] for all things. No other monk is allowed to receive disciples of his own.

4. Beyond the "platform" [*tai*, that is, the temple grounds] the monastery should not possess any estates or lands.

5. The resident members of the assembly are not allowed to accumulate personal money or grain inside or outside the monastery.

Even if we assume that Baizhang did compile a written monastic code for his order and that the rules depicted in *Chanmen guishi* [C] reflect those practices performed in his order, there is still no assurance that Baizhang was the formulator of a monastic code. Scholars have proven that independent Chan monasteries were established long before Baizhang's time and that his practices do not represent any innovation. Yet, given the fact that historiographers have spoken of the Chan independence movement as a break with the Lü school, I have undertaken a comparison of monastic regulations followed by the Chan and Lü schools. Careful study of Baizhang's regulations and practices surprisingly reveals that each article can be traced to a Vinaya text or to a source in common with the Chinese Lü school.[137]

In summary, the reputation of Baizhang as a pioneer of Chan monastic independence and advocate of the labor ethic has been seriously challenged by modern scholarship. There remains a great deal of disagreement and speculation regarding Baizhang's alleged monastic code: some believe it did exist but was later lost; some argue it was never codified as a written document; and still others assert that the codification of Baizhang's regulations never occurred in any form. I maintain that Baizhang could have had a monastic text written for his order, as did many monks before him; however, this text could not have been given the title *Baizhang qinggui*. Nevertheless, whether his regulations were codified or not, none of the rules or practices ascribed to Baizhang are unique or represent a departure from other schools. The factors that led historiographers to designate Baizhang as a revolutionary require further investigation, but one of these may well have been Baizhang's ability to convey his profound respect for monastic discipline.

Zunshi's Regulations

As we have seen, once a tradition distinguished itself from the school out of which it developed, members sought to establish a separate school with its own unique lineage. Like Baizhang, the Tiantai monk Zunshi, one of the primary leaders of the Shanjia faction during the Song,[138] came to feel that the lack of coherence and self-reliance in his lineage made the Shanjia faction dependent on other Buddhist schools, and he resolved to create a new model:[139]

> I had observed before that among the hundreds of monasteries in the area of Qiantang [present-day Zhejiang province], not one of them represented the teaching of the Shanjia school, and that all the Dharma teachers [*fashi*, that is, monks of this school][140] dwelt as dependents in the monasteries of other lineages. Thus host and guest were mutual hindrances; having this awkward, subservient situation as the background for relations between master and disciple of the Shanjia lineage naturally breeds discord. How could Shanjia followers not be compelled to keep moving from place to place? And so it was then that I attempted to create an independent order.

Having visited all the famous monasteries of the region, Zunshi selected the abandoned temple Tianzhusi as his base. He rebuilt the facilities and founded his own school in 1015. More than a decade after he had instituted his revival (in 1030), Zunshi felt the need for a code of binding regulations that would help maintain order in his monastery.

In his *Tianzhusi shifang zhuchi yi* (Rules of the Abbacy in the Tianzhu Public Monastery), Zunshi lists ten major principles as guidelines for his successors, summarized as follows:[141]

> 1. The abbot should be knowledgeable enough to be relied on by the assembly and virtuous enough to avoid fame and privilege.
> 2. There are five rules by which monks are to be protected from the difficulties of "external conditions": monks should be given equal access to material provisions and spiritual guidance; monks

are not allowed to wander into the administrative staff's quarters; the fundraiser should be selected prudently; monks should not enter the city without permission; and monks should not slander each other.

3. The abbot is the only one with the authority to tonsure postulants; no other member is allowed.

4. The disciples of the abbot are divided into groups and assigned variously to listen to lectures in the hall, to serve the assembly to earn merit, or to practice chanting and self-cultivation. Those who fail to practice that which is assigned to them will be expelled from the monastery.

5. The abbot should provide quarters for whomever contributes their labor to the monastery, and he should provide care for retired administrators.

6. In order to safeguard the welfare of postulants, one-tenth of the income of the assembly should be collected and used for their sake.

7. No domestic animals, such as horses, cows, mules, roosters, cats, or dogs, are allowed in the monastery. There can be no possession of outside estates, no farming, no businesses for profit.

8. Monks should not misappropriate public property. Any damaged or broken public property must be replaced. An inventory record should be kept in every hall.

9. All visitors should be treated equally and with consideration. A guest master should always be on duty; any monk other than the guest master may be required to help entertain guests.

10. If a candidate for abbot is not qualified, he should voluntarily yield to one who is qualified.

These regulations are evidence of Zushi's farsighted approach to life in Tianzhusi Monastery and his efforts to prevent potential disruptions. The third rule is similar to one established by Baizhang, which prohibits individual monks from accepting private disciples and creating factions within the monastery. Retired administrators are cared for, but so are low-ranking postulants. *Chanyuan qinggui*, compiled some seventy years later, describes Zongze's followers as being engaged in farming and business for profit, clearly a violation of one of Zunshi's regulations.

In addition to the above principles, which were intended for top-ranking members of the monastic staff, Zunshi wrote a set of guidelines for the assembly of monks, *Bieli zhongzhi* (Additional Rules for the Assembly).[142] This work enumerates eighteen rules and gives the corresponding punishments for their violation, ranging from prostrations (the most common) to monetary penalties to expulsion from the monastery. Protocols for all the minutiae of everyday living, such as how to take a bath or use the latrine properly, are described in Zunshi's *Fan ru yushi lüezhi shishi* (Ten Things to *Know When Entering the Bathhouse*)[143] and *Zuanshi shangce fangfa* (Compilation to Show the Correct Method of Using the Latrine),[144] both of which have close counterparts in *Chanyuan qinggui*.

Zunshi also devoted attention to the procedures for rituals and ceremonies. He wrote two texts on the conferring of precepts: *Shou pusa jie yishi* (Procedure for Conferring the Bodhisattva Precepts) and *Shou wujie fa* (Procedure for Conferring the Five Precepts).[145] *Shou pusa jie yishi* became a model for the bodhisattva ordination and is referred to in the monastic code of the Tiantai school, *Jiaoyuan qinggui*, issued in 1347. *Shou wujie fa*, as the author himself explains, was based on Daoxuan's *Xingshi chao*.[146] Zunshi compiled several texts on the rituals for worshiping and repentance,[147] which were based on works by Zhiyi and became the standard guides for these essential practices of religious life. In addition, he wrote about the rituals of releasing animals for merit *(fangsheng ciji)* and the significance of offering food to all sentient beings *(shishi)*.[148] Zunshi composed several important essays, including *Jie jiurou cihui famen* (Admonition against Eating Meat and Wine) and *Jie wuxin pian* (Admonition against the Consumption of Five Alliaceous Vegetables), to emphasize the importance of traditional Buddhist abstentions. Another of his essay's concerns the three robes of the clergy. In his article *Sanyi bianhuo pian* (Clarification of the Rules concerning the Three Robes), Zunshi insists that clergy robes should never be worn by laypeople, even by those who have received the bodhisattva precepts. He also disagrees with the use of the robe worn by monks during communal labor *(luozi)*, asserting that there is no such garment allowed in the Vinayas.[149] In this essay, Zunshi repeatedly refers to Daoxuan's *Xingshi chao* as the source for his arguments, thus illustrating the fact that despite the existence of different schools, early models of monastic practice were nearly universal.

Legacy of *Chanyuan qinggui*

Since the monastic code ascribed to Baizhang has not come down to us and no other complete texts of monastic regulations currently exist, *Chanyuan qinggui* is considered the oldest surviving Chinese monastic code. Because of its comprehensive scope and the dominance of the Yunmen tradition from which it sprang, *Chanyuan qing-gui* quickly became the authoritative text of its time, adopted and closely followed throughout the Buddhist community.[150] It was also the prototype emulated by most of the subsequent compilers of monastic codes in both China and Japan.

The Influence of Chanyuan qinggui *in Japan*

During his two pilgrimages to China, Eisai, the founder of the Japanese Rinzai school, bore witness to the prevalence of *Chanyuan qing-gui*. Returning to Japan after his second trip, he wrote *Kōzen gokoku ron* (Essay on the Promotion of Zen and the Protection of the State), in which he praises Buddhism in Song China and suggests that *Chanyuan qinggui* be adopted as the standard in Japan. He describes for his Japanese readers not only the regulations laid out in *Chanyuan qinggui* but also the extent to which Chinese monks followed the spirit of this code. Thus Eisai's work provides invaluable testimony on the importance of *Chanyuan qinggui* in Song China and a rare glimpse of actual contemporary practices. Table 3 outlines the monks' daily regimen as observed by Eisai.

In *Kōzen gokoku ron,* Eisai makes the following observations, subdived into ten categories:

1. The monastery compound: The physical layout of monasteries throughout China is homogeneous in pattern, regardless of size. Each monastery is circumscribed by corridors with only one main gate leading into the compound. This gate, which is always guarded, is closed in the evening and reopened in the morning to prohibit nuns, other women, or any uninvited malefactors from staying overnight.

2. Ordination: Both Hinayanist and Mahayanist precepts are retained in the Chan school.

3. Upholding the precepts: The fortnightly confession ceremony is held to maintain the purity of the Sangha.

4. Acquisition of knowledge: Every monk is expected to have a fair degree of familiarity with the sutra teachings and to behave in an externally dignified manner.

5. Deportment: Monks must uphold the precepts, including a vegetarian diet.

6. Demeanor: Dressed in robes, monks greet each other by pressing their hands together and lowering their heads, regardless of their respective ranks. The monks remain together as a group while eating, walking, meditating, studying, reading, and sleeping. Hun-

Table 3. Daily Regimen for Chinese Monks in the Song

Period of the Day	Approximate Time	Activity
diandeng ("lamp lighting")	6–8 P.M.	worshiping
rending ("people's rest")	8–11 P.M.	meditation
third geng	11 P.M.–1 A.M.	sleeping
fourth geng	1–3 A.M.	sleeping
fifth geng	3–5 A.M.	meditation
mao shi	5–6 A.M.	worshiping
dawn	6–7 A.M.	breakfast
chen shi	7–9 A.M.	studying
yu shi	9–11 A.M.	meditation
wu shi	11 A.M.–12 P.M.	lunch
wei shi	1–3 P.M.	bathing
bu shi	3–5 P.M.	meditation
you shi	5–6 P.M.	break

dreds or even thousands may live in a single large hall, helping each other to maintain general decorum and discipline. But when one monk commits even the slightest infraction, the rector corrects him personally.

7. Clothing: The robes of all monks are in the uniform style of the "Great Country," that is, China.

8. Disciples: Only those who accept the wisdom of the monastic rules of discipline and are willing to diligently maintain a spiritual life are allowed to enter the order.

9. Worldly gain: Monks are to focus on meditation without the distractions of farming or the accumulation of personal wealth.

10. Summer and winter retreats: The summer retreat lasts from the full moon of the fourth month to the full moon of the seventh month. The winter retreat lasts from the full moon of the tenth month to the full moon of the first month.

Eisai also enumerates the annual monastic ceremonies and rituals held in the Song:

1. The imperial birthday: The monastery is required to chant the *Mahāprajñā pāramitā Sutra*, the *Benevolent King Sutra*, the *Lotus Sutra*, and the *Golden Light Sutra,* et cetera, for thirty days before the emperor's birthday.

2. Chanting rituals: These are held on six days of each month— the third, eighth, thirteenth, eighteenth, twenty-third, and twenty-eighth.

3. Worship of earth deities: These rites are performed on the second and sixteenth days of every month.

4. Repayment of gratitude: On the first day of every month the *Prajna Sutra* is recited to signify indebtedness to the present emperor; on the fifteenth day of every month the *Nirvana Sutra* is recited in gratitude to the previous emperor.

5. Various festivals are held each month.

6. During retreats the Lengyan ritual is held daily.

7. Each of the monks is expected to read one fascicle of a sutra per day. Thus, assuming there are one hundred monks in a temple, in the course of a year all the sutras would be read through. [In such a case, as many as 36,500 different fascicles would be read]. Sutra reading is usually sponsored by lay patrons.

8. In the True-word cloister *(zhenyan yuan)*, the Water-land service is held frequently, sponsored by lay patrons for the merit of the deceased.

9. The ritual in the Tranquility-contemplation cloister *(zhiguan yuan)* is held to practice the Lotus samadhi, the Amitābha samadhi, and the Avalokiteśvara samadhi.

10. A ceremony is held when the monks enter the abbot's quarters for instructions.

11. The ritual of confession is held every fortnight.

12. The abbot visits the assembly quarters every five days.

13. The members of the Sangha bathe every five days in winter and every day in summer.

14. Feasts are held on the anniversary of the death of late emperor, the late abbot, and the current abbot's deceased parents.

15. Feasts and various rituals, such as the incense-offering ceremony, are sponsored by government officials.

16. A ritual is held in which the Sangha members assemble to play music and turn the eight-spoked sutra-store wheel *(bafu lunzang)*.

Table 4 presents Eisai's descriptions of the twelve major monthly festivals. In addition to relying on his observations of Chinese rituals and ceremonies, Eisai undoubtedly depended on Zongze's *Zuochan yi* (Manual of Meditation) for much of the information regarding meditation in his *Kōzen gokoku ron*.

Kōzen gokoku ron strongly endorsed strict adherence to the Buddhist precepts, but it was not in itself a monastic code. The earliest Japanese monastic code was compiled by Eihei Dōgen (1200–1253), the founder of another mainstream Japanese Zen tradition, the Sōtō school. Dōgen also traveled to China, and during his five years there

Table 4. Festivals

Month	Service	Month	Service
1	Arahat Service *(luohan hui)*	7	*Prajna Sutra* Chanting Service *(bore hui)*
2	Relic Service *(sheli hui)*	8	*Prajna Sutra* Chanting Service
3	Grand Service *(dahui)*	9	*Prajna Sutra* Chanting Service
4	Buddha's Birthday Service *(fosheng hui)* and Summer Retreat	10	Ordination Ceremony
5	*Golden Light Sutra* Chanting Service *(zuisheng hui)*	11	Winter Service *(dongjie)*
6	*Golden Light Sutra* Chanting Service	12	Grand Service of Buddha's Names *(Foming dahui)*

(1223–1227) he visited Tiantongsi, where his enlightenment was certified by Rujing (1163–1228). In 1227, Dōgen returned to Japan to establish the Sōtō school, for which he developed a monastic code that came to be known as *Eihei shingi*.[151] This code is a collection of six separate works, all of which survive: *Tenzo kyōkun* (Instructions for the Monastic Cook, 1237); *Tai taiki goge jari hō* (Regulations for Interaction with Instructors Who Are Five Years Senior, 1244); *Bendō hō* (Model for Practicing the Way, 1246); *Chiji shingi* (Regulations for Administrative Officers, 1246); *Fu shukuhan pō* (Regulations for Attending Meals, 1246); and *Shuryō shingi* (Regulations for the Assembly Quarters, 1249).[152] These texts were first delivered as lectures at several different Japanese temples between the years 1237 and 1249.[153] *Chanyuan qinggui*, still the dominant text when Dōgen was traveling in China, became a major influence on his subsequent thinking, and as we will see, he freely adopted large sections of it in his own monastic codes as well as in his largest work, *Shōbōgenzō*.[154]

Of Dōgen's six works on monastic regulations, *Fu shukuhan pō* contains the rituals connected with the two daily meals. When we compare this text with the section called "Attending Meals" in *Chanyuan qinggui*, it becomes immediately apparent that the former is taken largely from the latter. With the addition of an introductory paragraph of theoretical explanations, Dōgen's text copies entire sections word for word from *Chanyuan qinggui*. It occasionally expands on the original with material gained from Dōgen's own observations in Chinese monasteries, such as his detailed account of the Chinese custom of taking down the bowls from their place on the wall before eating, a ritual that *Chanyuan qinggui* finds unnecessary to describe. Generally speaking, roughly 85 percent of *Fu shukuhan pō* is taken verbatim from *Chanyuan qinggui.*

Chiji shingi provides guidelines for the administrative offices, and here again prodigious use is made of *Chanyuan qinggui.* Most of the descriptions of the various officers' duties are drawn directly from the four sections of *Chanyuan qinggui* entitled "The Prior," "The Rector," "The Cook," and "The Superintendent." *Tenzo kyōkun,* based to some extent on Dōgen's experiences with the cooks he encountered in Chinese monasteries, is concerned with the preparation of the two daily meals and the relationship between food and Zen. Once again, Dōgen quotes frequently from the instructions to the cook given in *Chanyuan qinggui;* he even goes so far as to say that any monastic cook worth his salt, so to speak, should thoroughly study the guidelines given in *Chanyuan qinggui.*

Thus Dōgen's great dependence on *Chanyuan qinggui* for his own monastic code, especially *Tenzo kyōkun, Chiji shingi,* and *Fu shukuhan pō,* is evident. In addition, he uses excerpts from *Chanyuan qinggui* in *Shōbōgenzō.* He adopts the entire section called "Receiving the Precepts" at the beginning of *Chanyuan qinggui* for *Shōbōgenzō,* dividing it into the sections *"Shukke," "Jukai,"* and *"Shukke kudoku."* Elsewhere in the text there are more than ten explicit instances of borrowing from *Chanyuan qinggui.*

Another link between Zongze and Dōgen that has been explored by scholars is the textual borrowing from Zongze's *Zuochan yi* by Dōgen in his *Fukan zazen gi* (Manual of Zen Meditation). While over a third of Dōgen's text is taken from Zongze's work, it is clear that Dōgen does not agree with Zongze's philosophy of meditation. Instead, Dōgen sees his own approach as a return to Baizhang, whom he considered to be representative of the pure spirit of Chan. Just what Dōgen considered Baizhang's methods to be, and whether or not he had access to an existing text written by Baizhang from which he could have formed his opinion, is uncertain.[155] At any rate, Dōgen's well-known methods of meditation, such as "mere sitting" *(shikan taza)* and "silent illumination" *(mokushō),* are clearly at odds with Zongze's Pure Land-influenced forms of meditation, which emphasize first and foremost the recitation of Amitābha's name. It comes as little surprise then that the rituals for funerals prescribed in *Chanyuan qing-*

gui, centering around the recitation of Amitābha, were not adopted by Dōgen.

The monastic tea ceremony *(jiandian)*, which constituted a major part of life in the Song-era monastery, is given much attention in *Chanyuan qinggui*, but is not included in Dōgen's regulations. Unlike the recitation of Amitābha's name, however, this practice is less likely to have been deliberately neglected by Dōgen. When we examine the section *"Ango"* in *Shōbōgenzō*, we see that Dōgen borrows from *Chanyuan qinggui*'s description of the tea ceremony held at the beginning and end of the summer retreat, changing only the dates written on the tea poster to match the Japanese calendar and the time of writing, the third year of Kangen (1245). In fact, there is evidence that the Chinese tea ceremony was first introduced to Japan at Dōgen's monastery. Perhaps the reason for Dōgen's omission was a lack not of interest but of time. Dōgen passed away at the early age of fifty-three, leaving *Shōbōgenzō* unfinished. Undoubtedly at the time of his death he intended to discuss several other subjects in this work.[156]

Chanyuan qinggui and Dōgen's writings complement each other. The comprehensive nature of the rules given in *Chanyuan qinggui* helps us understand much of the Song-era monastic culture that came to permeate Japan, although such an influence would not have been recorded by Dōgen himself. Conversely, Dōgen's detailed descriptions of everyday life in a Chinese monastery shed light on aspects of Buddhism during the Song that the author of *Chanyuan qinggui* thought unnecessary to include.[157] Table 5 illustrates the influence of *Chanyuan qinggui* on Dōgen's writings. The two left columns list the various sections of Dōgen's texts that show clear signs of borrowing. The right columns indicate the corresponding sections of Zongze's *Chanyuan qinggui* and the exact pages cited or paraphrased.

The Influence of Chanyuan qinggui in Song-Yuan China

As we have seen, when Japanese pilgrims traveled to China during the Song, they reported that *Chanyuan qinggui* was the authoritative monastic code within the Buddhist community. Dōgen's testimony as to the text's dominance during the years 1223–1227 shows that the code was still in wide circulation after more than a century. Given its prominence, it is not surprising that *Chanyuan qinggui* also served as inspiration for many of the monastic codes generated during the Song-Yuan period (specifically from the twelfth century to the fourteenth centuries), the era during which most of the codes extant today were produced.

Table 5. Influence of *Chanyuan quinggui* on Dōgen's writings

Eihei shingi	*Dōgen Zenji zenshū II*	*Chanyuan qinggui*	*Yakuchū Zennen shingi*
Fu shukuhan pō	348–349	Attending Meals	42–43
	350		50
	351–352		46–48
	352–353		52–53
	353–354		54–55
	355–356		55–56
	356–357		58
Chiji shingi	331–333	Prior	105–109
	339–340	Rector	110–115
	340–341	Cook	116
	345	Superintendent	119
	341	Essay on Setting a Good Example *(guijing wen)*	269
	341		270
	342	Cook	116
	342	Essay on Setting a Good Example	273
	343		116
	345	Cook	119
	345	Superintendent	269
	345	Essay on Setting a Good Example	270
	345		275
Tenzo kyōkun	295	Essay on Setting a Good Example	269
	295		116
	296	Cook	273
	300	Essay on Setting a Good Example	276
Bendō hō	318	Manual of Meditation	279

Shōbōgenzō	*Dōgen Zenji zenshū I*	*Chanyuan qinggui*	*Yakuchū Zennen shingi*
Shukke (Renunciation of the World)	597	Receiving the Precepts	13
Jukai (Receiving the Precepts)	619	Receiving the Precepts	13
Shukke kudoku (The Virtue of Renouncing the World)	617	Receiving the Precepts	13

Continued on next page

Table 5, *continued*

Shōbōgenzō	*Dōgen Zenji zenshū I*	*Chanyuan qinggui*	*Yakuchū Zennen shingi*
Senmen (Washing the Face)	431	Upholding the Precepts	16
Ango (The Training Period)	571	Commencement of the Summer Retreat	85
	574–576		86–88
	580–581	Closing of the Summer Retreat	91
Senjō (Rules for the Lavatory)	470	Using the Toilet	233
	472	Latrine Attendant	153
	473	Using the Toilet	235
Hotsu bodai shin (Awakening the Buddha-seeking Mind)	649	120 Questions	285
Kie Bupposo bo (Taking Refuge in the Three Treasures)	667	120 Questions	285

Fukan zazen gi	*Dōgen Zenji zenshū II*	*Manual of Meditation*	*Yakuchū Zennen shingi*
	3–4		279–283

If *Chanyuan qinggui* was accorded such authority, one may wonder why there was a need to produce further monastic codes. One explanation for the appearance of alternative codes takes into account the nature of *Chanyuan qinggui* itself. Zongze's text was designed primarily for large-scale public monasteries and may have been considered less suitable for smaller, private temples. Thus, smaller-scale codes were constructed to meet the specific needs of a given monastery. Furthermore, rules were often altered to fit the changing social role of the monastery. The composition of the Buddhist community was also in flux, and new sets of regulations were needed for many of the emerging sects, such as the Lü and Tiantai schools. While all of the codes created during the Song and Yuan eras were tailored to suit changing environments, they nevertheless relied on *Chanyuan qinggui* as their model and starting point, often excerpting large sections of the earlier code verbatim.

For those who dedicated themselves solely to the practice of meditation, a set of rules entitled *Ruzhong riyong* (Daily Life in the Assembly)[158] was created in 1209 by Wuliang Zongshou n.d.,[159] a fourth-generation monk in the Yangqi lineage of Linji master Dahui Zonggao (1089–1163). Written while Zongshou occupied the the chief seat in the Sangha hall, this code was designed to regulate meditators' activities in the Sangha hall and the assembly quarters by providing strict guidelines prescribing the correct procedure for performing the most ordinary of daily tasks: getting up, washing, putting on robes, unwrapping the eating bowls, eating meals, reading sutras, using the toilet, taking a bath, and lying down to sleep. Although this second oldest surviving monastic code does not cover all aspects of monastic life, it betrays the clear influence of *Chanyuan qinggui.* *Ruzhong riyong* itself influenced future generations of monastic codes and was adopted verbatim by many subsequent compilers.

Ruzhong riyong is excerpted in abridged form in the later *Ruzhong xuzhi* monastic code (author unknown) which, judging by information given in the section entitled "Chanting" *(niansong),* can be dated around 1263.[160] Despite its dependence on *Ruzhong riyong, Ruzhong xuzhi* contains far more entries, including sections describing the protocol for sitting meditation, entering the abbot's quarters, tea ceremonies, the inauguration of a new abbot, funerals, the auctioning of robes belonging to deceased monks, and the ordination of novices *(śrāmaṇera).* These entries are summaries of sections in the earlier *Chanyuan qinggui.*

Many of the Song-Yuan monastic codes, such as *Cunsi qinggui* and *Huanzhu an qinggui* were written for use in private monasteries. *Cunsi qinggui,* written in 1281 by Danliao Jihong, seems to have been preserved well into the eighteenth century but has since been lost.[161] Fortunately, *Huanzhu an qinggui* is still extant and provides us with an excellent example of a private monastic code. It was written in 1317 by Zhongfeng Mingben (1263–1323), who, like Wuliang Zongshou, belonged to the Yangqi sect of the Linji school, the dominant school of the time.[162] As it was designed solely for Mingben's private "Mirage Hermitage" *(Huanzhu an),* this set of regulations does not include any of the rituals performed in large public monasteries, such as the ceremonies for a new abbot's inauguration. Although it makes occasional use of the material codified in *Chanyuan qinggui, Huanzhu an qinggui* is unlike the codes intended for public monasteries. *Huanzhu an* did not have the logistical needs of a large monastery, and accordingly its compiler did not borrow extensively from *Chanyuan qinggui.* Instead *Huanzhu an qinggui* contains an unusual amount of original material, devised specifically for its institution. The text is divided into ten entries: daily routines, monthly schedules, annual festivals, examples of prayers offered on various occasions, food storage and building repair, lineage customs *(jiafeng)*, titles and duties of administrative officers, personal cultivation, attending to the sick, and funerals. It is apparent throughout that the code was intended for use in the smaller private monasteries. For example, the section on the major administrative offices describes the duties of only five members: the abbot, the chief seat, the assistant abbot, the chief of storage, and the cook—a list dwarfed by the public monastery's extensive hierarchy of offices. Like Zongze, however, Mingben advocated a synthesis of Chan and Pure Land teachings, and, not surprisingly, his discussions of the rituals for the sick and the deceased, with their emphasis on the recitation of Amitābha's name, are largely adopted from Zongze's *Chanyuan qinggui.*

The Song-Yuan codes compiled for public monasteries in the tradition of *Chanyuan qinggui* include *Jiaoding qinggui* (or *Conglin jiaoding qinggui zongyao),*[163] *Beiyong qinggui* (or *Chanlin beiyong qinggui),*[164] and *Chixiu Baizhang qinggui.* The first of these was compiled in 1274 by the monk Jinhua Weimian, about whom very little is known. The most distinctive aspect of this text is its use of diagrams to illustrate the monks' positions during various monastic rituals, as well as its inclusion of examples of the public letters and documents used to announce activities such as tea ceremonies and feasts. This text does not comment on the duties of the administrative staff and focuses instead on rituals and ceremonies. For its discussion of matters of daily etiquette, it simply cites the entire text of *Wuliangshou riyong xiao qinggui.*

In 1311, thirty-eight years after the compilation of *Jiaoding qinggui,* another monk of the Yangqi sect of the Linji school, Zeshan Yixian, produced a far more comprehensive monastic code. In his preface, Yixian reveals the painstaking methods used in his text's composition. Inspired by the monastic codes he encountered at the Jingcisi and Lingyinshan monasteries while studying under Shilin Xinggong n.d., Yixian began his own compilation in 1278. Although he finished his work by 1286, he did not rush to circulate it. Instead he sought the advice of his master, Chengtian Juean, and his Dharma relatives, Xixi Guangze, Yunfeng Xiu, and Qianfeng Wan. Yixian implemented his code on an experimental basis at the three monasteries where he served as abbot from 1295 to 1311. After some thirty-three years of trial and improvement, he wrote the preface for the code's publication, in which he concludes that his work is unworthy as a primary text and recommends it be used as a secondary reference only. Yixian gave his life's work the humble title *Beiyong qinggui* (Alternate Pure Regulations).[165]

Similar to *Chanyuan qinggui* but even more comprehensive in its scope, *Beiyong qinggui* covers all aspects of monastic life. Although it adopts a great deal from *Chanyuan qinggui*, it expands on topics not mentioned in the earlier code, such as the liturgical procedures for the rituals held on the imperial birthday and for the anniversaries of the deaths of Bodhidharma, Baizhang, and the Chan patriarchs. (This expansion seems to indicate an increased role for chanting ceremonies in monastic life.) The text also prescribes in great detail the proper procedures for taking up residence in the monastery and meeting with the abbot, rules that were undoubtedly necessitated by an increased mobility among tonsured members of the Buddhist community and by a marked gain in the stature ascribed to the abbot—two changes that in turn reveal the growing size and importance of the Buddhist monastery in general. The impressive scale and meticulous organization of *Baiyong qinggui* lays the foundation for the later Yuan monastic code *Chixiu Baizhang qinggui*.

Chixiu Baizhang qinggui is the best-known monastic code in China,[166] not only because it was compiled in accordance with a decree issued by the Yuan Emperor Shun (r. 1333–1368), but largely because it has been mistakenly ascribed to Baizhang himself. Although the original title did include Baizhang's name, it was never meant to imply Baizhang's authorship. Rather the title reflects the fact that its compiler, Dongyang Dehui, was the abbot of the temple at Baizhang Mountain and is meant as a tribute to the patriarch who founded the monastery there. Under imperial sponsorship, Dehui collaborated with the abbot of the Jiqingsi Monastery, Xiaoyin Daxin, the Dharma heir of Huiji Yuanxi who, generations before, also lived at Baizhang Mountain.[167] As the preface explains, *Chixiu Baizhang qinggui* was commissioned by the emperor during the Yuan (when the Mongols ruled China) because it was assumed that the increasingly heterogeneous nature of Chinese monastic codes was a problem—one that could be remedied by the introduction of a single authoritative text for the entire Buddhist community. This ostensible need for uniformity, however, may have sprung less from a call for unity from within the Buddhist community than from the desire of a foreign government to maintain control over the local population. After all, the great diversity of codes throughout China had evolved for a reason—codes were written to suit the particular needs of each monastery.

The compilation of *Chixiu Baizhang qinggui* began in 1335 and was completed in 1338. As Dehui points out in his colophon, the code putatively written by Baizhang had been lost by this time. But Dehui cites three other codes—*Chanyuan qinggui, Jiaoding qinggui,* and *Beiyong qinggui*—as existing sources on which he had relied. (He mentions a special indebtedness to *Beiyong qinggui*.) When completed, *Chixiu Baizhang qinggui* was considered the most comprehensive monastic code of regulations ever assembled. The first chapters contain liturgies relating to prayers for the longevity of the emperor and prayers for the avoidance of natural disasters. Their placement and inclusion mark an increased consideration for the state and the imperial family. We see a similar pattern in *Beiyong qinggui*, whose author, Yixian, had initially intended to place either the section "Receiving the Precepts" or "The Entrance of a New Abbot to the Monastery" at the beginning of his text, but altered his plans when his master suggested that the liturgical ceremony for the emperors be placed first. The subsequent sections of *Chixiu Baizhang qinggui* present a schedule of various ceremonies involving the abbot. The positioning of this section highlights the increasing importance of the abbot in monastic life. The text then discusses the titles and duties of the administrative officers. Here again the abbot is assigned greater significance: his retinue of attendants is expanded into five groups, each of which assists him in his duties,—namely, the performance of liturgical ceremonies, conducting correspondence, the entertainment of guests, the management of personal property, and providing medical care. The duties of the priory are also expanded and divided between two positions, a clear indication that the overall importance of the monastery was increasing as its hierarchy became more and more complex. Only after the description of administrative duties do we find a section pertaining to individual cultivation. In this section there are several entries, such as the receiving of precepts, the upholding of precepts, a manual for meditation, and "Essay on Setting a Good Example" *(Guijing wen)*, which, along with numerous other sections and selected quotations, are adopted verbatim from *Chanyuan qinggui*.

It is worth noting that with the exceptions of Zongze, author of the earliest extant monastic code and a member of the Yunmen school, and Weimian, author of *Jiaoding qinggui* and whose affiliation is uncertain, all of the early compilers of monastic codes were connected with the Yangqi sect of the Linji school. Not surprisingly, at the time of *Chanyuan qinggui's* compilation during the Northern Song period, the Yunmen school was the dominant tradition in China. When subsequent codes were compiled during the Southern Song period, the Linji school, and more specifically the Yangqi sect, was the most prevalent Buddhist school. One might hypothesize that in each era the school considered most important would draw the most practitioners and would therefore have the greatest need to develop a body of regulations. Nevertheless, it is important to keep in mind that these texts, belonging as they did to traditions with important legacies, were themselves more likely to survive. In fact there were undoubtedly several different monastic codes circulating at the time, a fact attested to in the preface of *Chixiu Baizhang qinggui.*

The compilation of monastic codes is by no means unique to the Chan school; the Lü and Tiantai schools also compiled sets of regulations for their monasteries. The Vinaya monk Xingwu Xinzong wrote *Lüyuan shigui* in 1325, ten years before the publication of *Chixiu Baizhang qinggui.* In this work the author laments the fact that Chan monks have created monastic codes for their community while the Vinaya tradition lacked standardized regulations. Xinzong's task began twenty years earlier, when he not only consulted with senior monks of the Lü tradition, but also closely examined the monastic codes of the Chan school. As he indicates in his preface, he also completed a separate text containing a Vinaya glossary entitled *Beiyong yaoyu* (Key Auxiliary Terms), intending it as a supplement to the regulations. Unfortunately, the latter text has not survived.[168]

Xingzong concedes in the preface that his text relies on the authority of the Chan monastic code. But it also clearly emphasizes that which Xinzong considered unique to his own school's tradition. The first chapter outlines those elements that the Lü school revered as the trademarks of its teaching: the ordination ceremony, the tonsure ceremony, the invitation of the precept-granting master, the reception of the five beginning and ten advanced precepts, the ascension of the platform for full ordination, the fortnightly confession ceremony, the retreat, and the *pravāraṇa* ceremony (the confession on the last day of the retreat). All of these ceremonies concern the receiving of the precepts, which, it may be said, is the most integral element of the Lü tradition. Although the ceremony of tonsure and ordination for the novice is detailed in the appendix to the *Chanyuan qinggui,* the procedure for the full ordination ceremony is notably absent. This omission may be explained by the fact that a Chan monk, having been tonsured and having received the novice precepts at his own home temple, was then obliged to travel to a Lü monastery to receive full ordination—a practice that continued into the nineteenth century. The absence of a full ordination rite in the Chan monastic code (as well as in the Tiantai code) undoubtedly reveals a reliance on the Lü precept masters.

After its initial discussion of ceremonies derived from the Indian Vinaya, *Lüyuan shigui* lists the regulations for the liturgical prayers for the emperor and the patriarchs,[169] the tea ceremony, the administrative hierarchy, and the recitation of Amitābha's name at funerals, all of which can be found in *Chanyuan qinggui*. One particularly surprising feature of the Lü monastic code is its discussion of the positions of director of the farming village, gardern chief, and tree master—duties obviously associated with agriculture and horticulture[170] and expressly forbidden in the Indian Vinayas. But for many Chinese Monasteries landholding and farming had become major sources of income. The Lü school was no exception.

The Tiantai monastic code entitled *Jiaoyuan qinggui* was thought to have been compiled by the Tiantai monk Yunwai Ziqing in 1347, ten years after the compilation of *Chixiu Baizhang qinggui*. In fact, this text stems from a much earlier code, perhaps one even earlier than *Chixiu Baizhang qinggui*. Although the work's preface tells us nothing about the author or the date of composition, it does explain that the code's original manuscript had been kept in the Baiyun hall at Shang Tianzhu Mountain but was later destroyed in a fire. Concerned that the absence of a monastic code would contribute to a decline in ethical rigor, Ziqing took it upon himself to annotate and recompile the text based on his own personal copy, and it is this recompilation of 1347 that has come down to us today.

The Tiantai tradition described in *Jiaoyuan qinggui* is distinguished by its unusual method of instruction during the summer retreat. In sharp contrast to the Chan monastery, where the abbot bears sole responsibility for the sermons as well as for private instruction, the abbot of the Tiantai school invites the chief lecturer *(dujiang)*, who must be generally well-versed in the Tiantai doctrine, to give the sermons.[171] The rector *(weinuo)* was invited to preach from the Tiantai school's authoritative texts *(diandu)*.[172] Thus teaching in the Tiantai monastery was more of a communal obligation, as was reception of the teaching. After a lecture was given by either the *dujiang* or the rector, the audience was divided into three categories: senior monks, "capable ones" (*neng kandu zhe;* advanced junior monks), and beginners. Several monks were chosen from each group by lottery to engage in a public discussion of the sermon.[173] In addition, private written examinations (*suoshi;* "locked examinations") were given, much like those for government service.[174]

Like many of the Chan monastic codes, *Jiaoyuan qinggui* places the rituals of praying for the emperor and the patriarchs in its first chapter, followed by sections pertaining to the abbot's schedule, the administrative hierarchy, individual cultivation, and funerals. Just as the ceremonies of tonsure, observance, and *pravāraṇa* are considered unique to the Lü tradition, so is the bodhisattva precept ordination found only in the Tiantai monastic code.[175]

2.

Genesis of Chanyuan qinggui: *Continuity and Adaptation*

Heritage from the Vinaya Tradition

Chinese Chan historiographers view the establishment of *qinggui* (monastic codes) as a decisive moment in the history of the Chan tradition and the codes themselves as declarations of independence from other Buddhist schools, especially the Lü school. Traditionally, Baizhang Huaihai (749–814) was thought to have initiated this watershed movement by drawing up a set of innovative monastic rules for his own community. Baizhang's creation of a new monastic code resulted in his being celebrated as a revolutionary and as one of the great patriarchs of Chan, along with Bodhidharma and Huineng. However, modern scholars have recently challenged this portrait, claiming that Baizhang's position as the pioneer of the monastic code and the independent Chan monastery was a fiction created during the Song dynasty. They argue that the Chan community was already well under way by the time of Baizhang, and that Chan masters prior to Baizhang had established Chan monasteries that were independent from the Lü school. After comparing the Chan codes with the precepts of the Tiantai school, they claim that the rules and regulations carried out in Baizhang's monastic order had already been in practice in the Tiantai school, making them neither unique nor revolutionary.

My approach to this discussion has been to examine the earliest extant Chan monastic code—*Chanyuan qinggui,* compiled in 1103—in light of Chinese Vinaya translations and commentaries. Scrutiny reveals that a great deal of *Chanyuan qinggui*'s content is based directly on the Vinaya and the works of the great Vinaya advocate Daoan (312–385) and the Lü master Daoxuan (596–667). Such a discovery in this previously untranslated text thus challenges the widely held belief that Chan monasteries were unique and distinct from the Vinaya schools. In *Chanyuan qinggui* we find not a distinctive rhetoric but rather many similarities to the Vinaya rules and, oftentimes, a direct word-for-word transmission of the Vinaya.

The Precepts

With its opening words, *Chanyuan qinggui* establishes itself in the Vinaya lineage. The work's preface acknowledges that novices may find the complexity and detail of the regulations overwhelming and makes reference to the bodhisattva threefold pure precepts and the sravaka precepts. The threefold pure precepts are the Mahayana precepts observed by both clergy and the laity: avoiding all evil actions, doing all good deeds, and benefiting all sentient beings. The śrāvaka precepts are the Hinayana prohibitions establishing the rules of monastic discipline. According to the *Four Part Vinaya*,[1] these fall into seven categories based on the gravity of the offense: *pārājika* (offenses that result in permanent expulsion from the order—unchastity, stealing, taking life, and falsely claiming to have attained enlightenment); *saṃghāvaśeṣa* (serious offenses that do not require expulsion and may be atoned for by immediate confession before the assembly); *sthūlātyaya; pātayantika* (thirty offenses that require forfeiture of property and ninety offenses requiring simple expiation); *pratideśanīya* (mostly food-related offenses that require confession); *duṣkṛta* (misdeeds or offenses of wrong action); and *durbhāṣita* (offenses of bad speech).

"Upholding the Precepts" in Fascicle 1 begins with the admonition "A monk would rather die with the law than live without the law," and then lists the precepts that every monk must study so that he can chant them fluently. The Hinayana precepts from the *Four Part Vinaya* come first. *Chanyuan qinggui* lists these by category rather than defining them explicitly: "four 'defeats,' thirteen 'formal meetings,' two 'undetermined offenses,'" et cetera. These are the same seven categories referred to in the *Four Part Vinaya*. Next come ten major offenses and forty-eight minor offenses from the Mahayana precepts in the *Brahma Net Sutra*.[2] Though not described here, the ten major offenses are killing, stealing, engaging in sexual conduct, lying, buying and selling intoxicants, finding fault with the four groups within Buddhism (lay people who have taken the boddhisattva precepts as well as fully ordained monks and nuns), praising oneself while calumniating others, being avaricious while being uncharitable, being angry and refusing an apology from another, and slandering the Three Treasures. Minor transgressions include consuming intoxicants, eating meat, eating any of the five malodorous/alliaceous vegetables, and refusing to attend the sick.

Food and Mealtime

A great deal of *Chanyuan qinggui,* including much of Fascicle 1, concerns food and proper behavior at mealtime. These regulations and procedures offer many avenues of comparison with Vinaya texts. The vegetables prohibited explicitly in *Chanyuan qinggui* are onions, leeks, scallions, garlic, and chives.[3] Among these five forbidden vegetables, garlic is the only one prohibited in the Indian Vinayas. In fact, the Pāli Vinaya specifically states that the eating of an onion is not an offense.[4]

Two separate accounts describe the events that prompted the Buddha to prohibit nuns and monks from eating garlic. In the *Four Part Vinaya,*[5] Bhikṣuni Thullanandā led a group of nuns and female novices to a garlic patch to harvest some garlic. Although they were permitted by the owner to take five heads of garlic every day, they succumbed to temptation and pulled up all the garlic in a single day. This resulted in complaints by the layman, which in turn led the Buddha to prohibit nuns from eating garlic from that day on. The original prohibition of monks' consuming garlic is also found in the *Four Part Vinaya.*[6] A monk who has eaten garlic must avoid sitting close to the Buddha when the latter is preaching. In the first account, the prohibition stems from a concern for the economic welfare of laymen; in the second the offensive odor caused by the ingestion of garlic is the cause. The *Four Part Vinaya* does, however, reserve a place for the medicinal use of garlic. After purifying themselves of the garlic odor, recovered monks or nuns were allowed to resume communal living.[7]

Chinese Buddhists are prohibited from eating the five alliaceous vegetables largely on the basis of the Mahayana sutras, such as the *Brahma Net Sutra* and the *Śūraṅgama Sutra.* The *Brahma Net Sutra*[8] prohibits anyone who has taken the bodhisattva vows from eating these vegetables, drinking wine, and eating meat. The *Śūraṅgama Sutra*[9] prohibits the consumption of the vegetables on the grounds that "eating these five alliaceous vegetables cooked will stimulate sexual desire and eating them raw will generate anger. Those who eat these vegetables, even though they may be able to recite all the sutras, will be disgusting to all heavenly beings and immortals of all directions because of their offensive smell and will be shunned by them. The hungry ghosts will lick their lips and therefore they will always remain with those ghosts."

While *Chanyuan qinggui* expressly prohibits monks and nuns from eating meat,[10] the Indian Vinayas allow it—except under certain circumstances and with the exception of certain kinds of animals. The livelihood of the Buddhist clergy in India was based on begging; as a result, the diets of monks and nuns were determined by the foods they received. The *Four Part Vinaya* indicates that "when the monks received fish, the Buddha gave them permission to eat various kinds of fish; when they received meat, the Buddha allowed them to eat various kinds of meat."[11] However, as the same text indicates elsewhere,[12] the clerics were forbidden to partake of meat under three circumstances thought to make meat impure:[13] when the cleric saw the animal being killed, when he heard the cry of the animal being killed, and when he was aware that the animal was being killed specifically to feed him. The principle behind this rule is the nurturing of compassion. When one sees an animal killed or hears the sound it makes when it is killed, the image or sound causes one to associate oneself with the violence of the act, thus hindering the generation of compassionate thought in the eater. In the third case, the clergy must not be a motivating factor in the killing of an animal.[14]

The Vinayas also stipulate that the meat of certain kinds of animals should not be consumed. The *Four Part Vinaya* notes that the clergy are forbidden to eat the flesh of elephants, horses, dragons, dogs, and human beings.[15] The rationale behind this stipulation: elephants and horses are used by the king's military and are accorded special status; dragons possess a supernatural power that can destroy a nation; dogs can smell those who eat dog meat and will chase them; finally, the clergy should not eat the meat of their own kind. A slightly different list appears elsewhere in the *Four Part Vinaya*, which forbids the eating of elephants, horses, human beings, dogs, and beasts.[16] The text states that the clergy should also refrain from eating lion, tiger, leopard, and two species of bear.[17] The *Mahāsāṅghika Vinaya*[18] lists ten kinds of prohibited meat: human being, dragon, elephant, horse, dog, bird, eagle, pig, monkey, and lion. According to the text, dogs, birds and eagles were known to chase monks who had eaten their kin. We can assume the same reason applies to the prohibition against pig, monkey, and lion.[19]

However, the Mahayana *Brahma Net Sutra*[20] prohibits all meat. This prohibition was supported by other sutras. *Nirvana Sutra* notes, "One should not eat meat, drink wine, or eat the five alliaceous vegetables."[21] The same notion appears in *Laṅkāvatāra Sutra*.[22] The prohibition against meat eating was thought to promote great compassion, since a bodhisattva considered himself related to all sentient beings. *Aṅgulimālika Sutra*,[23] classified as one of the Mahayanist prajna texts, forbids meat eating. *Chanyuan qinggui* also prohibits all eating after noon.

Chanyuan qinggui describes mealtime protocol in great detail, providing instructions on which door to use to enter the dining hall; when, where, and how to sit; how bowls and utensils must be arranged; what verses to recite; how to eat; how to clean up afterwards; and so on. For example, "Attendance at Meals" in Fascicle 1 [42] describes the proper procedure for ringing the bell to signal the beginning of a meal. According to the Vinaya texts, the striking of a bell to indicate mealtime was already established as a practice during the time of the Buddha. Initially, monks were not in the habit of arriving in unison to receive their meals. This lack of order tended to frustrate the laypeople offering food. Thus the Buddha pronounced that a regular mealtime should be arranged.[24] When Rahula, the son of the Buddha, complained that the senior monk Śāriputra consistently received the best food offered by laypeople, the Buddha established the rule that food should be distributed equally to all. He further decreed that a special instrument should be used to summon all monks to the meals.[25]

In the *Five Part Vinaya*[26] a story is told in which several monks had started to eat their food without waiting until everyone had been served. When laypeople criticized this behavior, the Buddha instructed the monks to wait until all had received their food. On another occasion, a number of monks had been given their food and sat waiting, not knowing when to begin. The Buddha then ordered that one person should announce loudly, "*Samprāgata!*"[27] This was translated by Daoxuan as "[food will be] served equally."[28] However, Yijing's interpretation differs.[29] He insisted that the term should be thought of as a secret word or a mantra. He referred to the story in which the Buddha, along with other monks, received poisonous food. The Buddha ordered the monks to chant "*Samprāgata*"[30] before eating. After the chanting, the poisonous food was immediately transformed into healthy fare.[31]

Among the other instructions in "Attendance at Meals" is a detailed description of how to mount and descend the platforms for eating.[32] Daoxuan mentioned that the platform had previously been used in China but was reserved for scholar officials.[33] Not until the Eastern

Jin (317–419) did the use of the platform prevail in Buddhist monasteries. By Daoxuan's time (the seventh century) most temples were equipped with platforms. In China before the Eastern Jin, "rope mats,"[34] used to accommodate the assembly, were placed like straw mats on the floor. This originally gave rise to the sitting mat, which was needed as a cover for the rope mat.[35] Platforms that accommodated more than one person were not a Chinese invention. As indicated in the *Ten Section Vinaya*,[36] Upāli once asked the Buddha how many people could be accommodated on a single platform.[37] The latter replied that a platform should hold at least four people. The *Four Part Vinaya* includes a related incident: Once, when it was realized that the monastic hall could accommodate no more people if each was to have his own bed, the Buddha suggested that three senior monks share one "bed seat." If the hall was still thought to be filled beyond its capacity, the Buddha continued, platforms should be constructed.[38]

From "Attendance at Meals" we learn that in Chan monasteries monks took their two meals seated on the platforms in the Sangha hall. Yijing criticized this practice, asserting that while the custom in China is for monks to sit in rows and consume their food in a cross-legged position, such practices are unheard of in India, where monks sit on small chairs (seven inches high and one foot square on top) with their legs dropping to the floor. Yijing argued that when Buddhism was first introduced to China, monks followed the Indian practice, but beginning in the Jin dynasty the error of sitting on platforms with legs crossed was introduced. Even monks who came to China from India, Yijing contended, whether Indian or Chinese, were never able to correct this practice. According to the sacred tradition established by the Buddha, the platform should be one and a half feet in height. In China the platforms are higher than two feet. Thus it is inappropriate to sit on such a platform, Yijing concluded, for to do so violates the precepts.[39]

The origins of eating porridge, which *Chanyuan qinggui* mentions explicitly,[40] are given in the Vinaya texts. The *Four Part Vinaya*[41] states that once, when a *brāhmaṇa* had prepared porridge made with sesame oil, sesame, milk, water, ginger, pepper, and *pippalī* (a kind of pepper) and wanted to offer this to the Buddha and his monk disciples, the monks refused, insisting that the Buddha would not allow them to consume porridge made with such luxurious ingredients. When news of this reached the Buddha, he proclaimed that monks should be allowed to partake of porridge made with sesame oil and various herbs. The Buddha further explained the five benefits of taking porridge.

A similar story appears in the *Ten Section Vinaya*,[42] in which the layperson Ajita prepares eight kinds of porridge for the monks. In the *Mahāsāṅghika Vinaya*,[43] it was Nanda's mother who, after consuming some of the porridge herself, offers this salutary food to the monks, prompting the Buddha to proclaim ten great benefits accrued to the eater of porridge. The *Mūlasarvāstivāda Vinaya* depicts the Buddha as taking porridge shortly before his attainment of nirvana, clearly an indication of the power of this food.[44]

The ten benefits of porridge are given in the *Mahāsāṅghika Vinaya*.[45] It is considered conducive to appearance, strength, mental happiness, longevity, clear pronunciation, eloquence, overnight digestion, reduced flatulence, the quenching of thirst, and the suppression of hunger. *Shishi huo wu fubao jing*[46] lists the first five benefits as the Five Merits *(wufu)* and includes a detailed description of them. Daoxuan listed these same five as the Five Endurances *(wuchang)*.[47] The *Four Part Vinaya*[48] holds that porridge has five benefits *(wushi,* literally, "five matters"): overnight digestion, reduced flatulence, the quenching of thirst, the suppression of hunger, and reduced constipation. *"Wushi"* is also used in the *Ten Section Vinaya*,[49] which adds to the last four benefits in the *Mahāsāṅghika Vinaya* the alleviation of "coldness below the navel."

Monks received the porridge or other food in their own bowls, a nesting set that had to be displayed in a particular manner.[50] This ritual comes directly from the Vinaya texts. According to the *Four Part Vinaya*,[51] the Buddha instructed that the bowls be stacked in the following manner: "The *jianci* stacked into the small bowl, the small bowl into the second bowl, and this second bowl into the big bowl." The origin of the use of four bowls can be found in the *Five Part Vinaya*.[52] After attaining enlightenment, the Buddha continued to enjoy the bliss of meditation. When five hundred merchants offered him honey, the Buddha suddenly perceived that all the Buddhas in the past had received such offerings in bowls, as will all future Buddhas. And now, he, too, was receiving food in a bowl. When the four guardian deities divined his thought, each one offered him a stone bowl that contained natural and pure fragrances. The Buddha accepted all four bowls with equal gratitude. He stacked them on his left palm and with his right hand pressed them into one.

The eating utensils referred to in *Chanyuan qinggui*[53] are a definite departure from the Vinaya tradition. Monks in the Chinese Lü school were already using chopsticks and spoons.[54] Since the lay Indian custom was to eat directly with the hands, it was also the practice among Indian Buddhist monks. However, when Buddhism was introduced to China, eating with the hands seemed unsuited to Chinese custom, so monks and nuns immediately adopted the use of chopsticks and spoons. This practice was maintained by Japanese and Korean Buddhists. Dōgen provided the following defense of the use of chopsticks:

> When we look to the Buddhist customs in ancient India, we see that the Tathāgata and his disciples took their food by using their right hands to fashion rice into round balls. They used neither spoons nor chopsticks. The sons of the Buddha must remember that all the emperors, *cakravartin*, and kings took their food by rolling it in their hands. We should realize that this method is respectable. In India, all monks, aside from those ailing monks who were allowed to use spoons, would use their hands to eat. They had neither heard of chopsticks nor had they seen them. Chopsticks were used only in the countries to the east of China. Today, people use chopsticks because of regional [national, cultural] custom. As we are the descendants of the Buddha and the patriarchs, we must comply with Buddhist custom. Nevertheless, the custom of taking food by the hand has become obsolete and as we do not have teachers to consult, we use spoons and chopsticks, as well as bowls, for the sake of expediency.[55]

The ritual of offering food to all sentient beings *(chusheng)* figures prominently in *Chanyuan qinggui*.[56] Daoxuan noted that this offering could be made before taking the meal (after the chanting) or after taking the meal.[57] Since neither the sutras nor the commentaries specify a time, Daoxuan concluded that the offering could be made at either time. However, *Sifen lü xingshi chao zichi ji*, the commentary on *Xingshi chao*, indicates that in accordance with *Baoyun jing*, it is more reasonable to offer food before the meal. This sutra states that after receiving alms but *before* eating, a monk divides his food into four shares: one share for those accompanying him, one for those less fortunate, one for the spirits, and one for himself.[58]

Xinghu lüyi includes a detailed description of *chusheng* in its discussion of mealtime in Rules 45 through 48.[59] (45) If the food for the offering to all sentient beings is cake, it should be the size of half a coin. If it is cooked rice, it should not contain more than seven grains. Other foods should not be offered in excessive quantities. (46) The food for the offering to all sentient beings must be prepared properly. (47) One should not return leftover food into the food container for the offering to all sentient beings. (48) To properly offer food to all sentient beings, one should place one's food close to the edge of one's platform and allow the purity-keeper to collect the proper amount. One should not physically lift up one's own food to offer it. The purpose of this rule is to prevent the monk's hand from being soiled by the food offering.

The amount of food offered to sentient beings need not be copious, for the spirits or demons can expand what is given, thereby preventing monks from wasting laypeople's donations.[60] *Da zhidu lun* states, "When spirits or ghosts receive a mouthful of food, the food will multiply a thousand-fold."[61]

As Daoxuan indicated,[62] the provenance of the food-offering ritual can be found in the *Nirvana Sutra*. The spirit Kuangye, who lived solely on a diet of human flesh, demanded that the people of a neighboring village offer him human sacrifices. But when he was defeated and converted by the Buddha, Kuangye swore never to kill again. However, as he had always survived on flesh and blood, he asked the Buddha to reassure him that wherever he found the Buddha's disciples he would be fed. The Buddha consented and decreed that those who refuse Kuangye food, who do not make food offerings to the spirits, will no longer be counted among his disciples.[63]

The donation following the meal, *xingchen*,[64] is another ritual of Indian origin. In the *Five Part Vinaya*[65] the offering of robes and goods after the meal is called *dachen* (Skt. *dakṣiṇā*). *Dachen* refers not only to the offering of material goods by the donors, but also to the giving of Dharma by the monks. The *Four Part Vinaya*[66] describes how the Buddha instructed that monks should not leave silently after receiving meals; rather, they should perform *dachen* or chant a single verse for the donors' sake. In the *Ten Section Vinaya*,[67] *dachen* appears as the preaching of Dharma; however, *dachen* was later used to refer to the offering of material goods or money by the donor. Yijing also recorded the custom of distributing gifts after the meal.[68]

Hierarchy within the Monastery

The number of years since ordination determines the order of precedence for every occasion in the *Chanyuan qinggui*, such as taking up residence in the Sangha hall, gathering in the assembly quarters and at tea ceremonies, chanting in the Buddha shrine, and so on.[69] This custom, still carried out in modern monasteries, can be traced back to the Vinaya texts. In the Vinaya, it is related that when monks did not know how to decide the order of members of the Sangha, some suggested that the decision be based on the caste system, others suggested appearance, still others personal achievement. The Buddha then told a well-known story. A bird, a monkey, and an elephant, who all lived by a certain tree, were arguing one day about who should be considered the senior of the group. The elephant recalled that when he was young the tip of the tree touched his stomach when he passed over. The monkey contended that when was young he could bite the tip of the tree. Finally, the bird announced that long ago he remembered eating some fruit and spitting out the seed from which this tree eventually grew. Thus the bird was regarded as the most senior. The Buddha then proclaimed that, analogously, those who had received full ordination first, who had been in the monastery the longest, were to occupy the senior seats.[70]

"Server" was the title given to those who entered the monastery seeking the status of monk but could not be tonsured until they had carried out a number of menial tasks within the monastery.[71] *Samantapāsaādīkā*[72] offers the following explanation: "Why are these people referred to as *paṇḍupalāsa?*[73] Because they are noble men who are attempting to 'leave home.' Before they obtain their robes and bowls, they willingly rely on the inhabitants of the temple."[74]

Servers in China, as Dōchū informed us,[75] did not shave their heads but had their hair parted in two and draped down their backs. They were obliged to observe the five precepts. (In keeping with the third precept, the server, unlike the layperson, was not permitted to engage in any sexual activity.) Servers were assigned various tasks in departments of the monastery and were given specific titles indicating their assigned duties. In *Chanyuan qinggui*, we find titles for the food server, the servers who perform various tasks in the kitchen, the server who tends all the shrines and halls, the server in charge of striking the bell, the server in charge of the main gate, the server in charge of the fire, the tea server, the server to the chief gardener, the server in the farming village, and the vehicle server.[76] Collectively, all servers were referred to as *tongxing*,[77] and the building in which they lived was known as "postulant hall" or "hall for choosing monks."[78]

Chanyuan qinggui specifies that the serving of meals should be done by a specific class of untonsured servers called purity-keepers *(jingren)*,[79] a term adopted from the Vinayas. In the Vinaya texts, the role of the purity-keeper (Pāli *kappiya-kāraka*) is to serve as mediator, keeping monks away from activities that are improper for them to undertake yet need to be fulfilled. Thus the *jingren*, by performing these tasks, help maintain the purity of the clergy.[80] The *Mūlasarvās-*

tivāda Vinaya offers another definition of the term *jingren:* "At that time, the monks would explain to these people [i.e., to the purity-keepers] that they are only allowed to undertake pure tasks; impure deeds are forbidden them. Thus, as they carry out only those tasks deemed pure, they are known as the 'people of purity.'"[81]

The recruitment of purity-keepers into the order, according to the *Ten Section Vinaya,*[82] is said to have originated when King Bimbisara encountered Elder Mahākāśyapa laboring alone in the mountains, covered in mud. Out of compassion, the king vowed to send a few servants to help him. After five hundred days had passed, the king encountered Mahākāśyapa for the second time and suddenly remembered his promise. As if to make up for lost time, the king sent five hundred captured bandits to serve as purity-keepers. To prevent these bandits from stealing or robbing the monks' belongings, the king established a village for these five hundred people, providing them with everything they might need. After learning of this, the Buddha instructed monks to appoint a leader among the purity-keepers and to teach them the following duties: building pagodas; accommodating visiting monks; cooking; apportioning distributable items; tending elder, senior, and junior monks; and various other tasks. Finally, the Buddha added that a superintendent capable of management should be appointed from among the laypeople. Similar accounts appear in three other Vinaya texts.[83] However, the elder in these variants is identified as Pilindaka. Here the five hundred purity-keepers were not captured bandits, but members of families from a nearby village.[84]

Purity-keepers saved monks from having to perform "unclean" duties, such as money handling and food preparation. They received any money donated to the monks, especially money for robes.[85] They were even known to loan out the belongings of the pagodas (including the pagoda grounds) with interest[86] and to accept monks' "illegitimate" money, trading it for items the monks may have needed.[87] They prepared food[88] and distributed meals, porridge, and fruits.[89] They chopped wood for the beams of the buildings,[90] removed weeds,[91] and handled items that were lost.[92] They were in attendance when monks preached to women to allay any suspicion.[93] *Jingren* were male or female.[94]

In the Vinaya, the status of the purity-keeper's position was between that of a layperson and a novice. These texts would seem to indicate that purity-keepers were usually laypeople; yet their close relationship with monks made them far more involved in temple life than lay followers.[95] At the same time it should be noted that in the Chinese monastic tradition, the purity-keeper, while still untonsured, does indeed leave home and join the order and is therefore considered fully monastic. In *Chanyuan qinggui*, the terms postulant *(tongxing)*, server *(xingzhe)*, and purity-keeper *(jingren)* are used interchangeably; the first term, however, is used only as a title indicating general status, whereas the latter two refer to specific duties. The term "server" was usually used in conjunction with a more specific occupation, such as food delivery server or rectory server. "Purity-keeper" referred only to those who served meals.[96]

Personal Possessions

"Reception of the Precepts," the first section of Fascicle 1, begins by discussing how to prepare for receiving the precepts—that is, for ordination into a monastic order. The text briefly outlines the minimal obligatory belongings of the initiate: three robes, bowls, a sitting mat, and new, clean clothes. The Vinaya texts[97] also indicate that during the ordination process the instructing preceptor must first ensure that the initiate possesses the three robes and bowls before he may begin learning the precepts. The *Four Part Vinaya*[98] includes a story in which a man who had neither bowls nor robes was given full ordination. When he was told to go to the village for alms, he replied that he did not have the necessary bowls or a robe to wear. Thus the Buddha proclaimed the rule that any person without bowls or robes should not be allowed to receive full ordination. The text includes an episode in which a monk borrowed bowls and robes from others to receive full ordination. After the ordination, the owners asked that the bowls and the robes be returned, leaving the monk naked and ashamed. The incident was reported to the Buddha, who then gave the rule that monks should not borrow bowls or robes for ordination.

According to the Vinaya tradition, the three robes must be made of cloth strips sewn together: the *sanghāṭi* robe consists of nine strips of cloth, the *uttarāsaṇga* robe is made from seven, the *antarvāsaka* robe from five. The Vinayas give the following explanation for the origin of strip robes. Once the Buddha pointed to a nearby rice paddy and told his attendant Ānanda that a monk's robe should resemble the pattern of the cultivated rice paddy. He asserted that the disciples of all the Buddhas in the past wore robes patterned after rice paddies. In addition, the Buddha explained, a robe made of separate strips would deter bandits.[99] The monk's robe came to be regarded as the "robe of the merit field."[100] Donations made by laypeople are likened to seeds sown in a rice paddy. Someday this seed will be ready for harvest, just as the donors' merit will eventually reach its fruition.

Rules regarding clothing in *Chanyuan qinggui* constitute some significant departures from Indian customs. Daoxun contrasted the different ways of showing respect in China and India.[101] In India, to expose one shoulder and to bare one's feet is considered a show of respect, while in China respect is shown by dressing as fully as possible, including covering one's head with a scarf and wearing shoes. For communal labor, Chan monks wear a piece of clothing, the *gualuo* ("hanging clothes"), which drapes from the neck. Because it covers both shoulders, the propriety of the *gualuo* was brought into question by both the Lü and the Tiantai schools. The Lü school preferred the more appropriate *kāṣāya*, which covers only the left shoulder. The Tiantai monk Zunshi condemned the *gualuo* with great vehemence, insisting that the garment be burned.[102]

However, Daocheng, the author of *Shishi yaolan*,[103] defended the *guazi* as legitimate monastic dress, citing the authority of the *Mūlasarvāstivāda Vinaya*.[104] He argued that there are three types of five-strip robes mentioned in the Vinaya: upper, middle, and lower. The upper robe is three-arm-lengths long and five-arm-lengths wide. The lower one is half the size of the upper, and any robe that measures between these two sizes is considered a middle robe. According to the *Mūlasarvāstivāda Vinaya*,[105] the Buddha further instructed that there are two additional kinds of five-strip robes—one measuring two arms in length and five in width, the other two arms in length and four in width. The latter two robes are referred to as *shouchi yi;* they should be large enough to cover the three "wheels" of the body, that is, large enough to cover the navel above and the two knees below. Daocheng argued that the size of contemporary *guazi* differs very little from these latter two robes. As long as the *guazi* is made from five strips, has one dimension longer than the other, and is pleated or sewn, it should be considered legitimate apparel and should not be criticized. The *guazi*, he insisted, is worn by Chan monks every day and is in no way a violation of the Vinaya. Moreover, if one cannot wear a *kāṣāya* all the time (for example, during communal labor), it is far better to wear a *guazi* than no form of *kāṣāya* whatsoever.[106]

"Preparation of Personal Effects" in Fascicle 1 enumerates the "equipment of Dao," items a monk must bring with him upon entering the monastery. Each item has a specific reason for being required—originating in the Vinaya or in Chinese secular law. Among the required belongings, for example, is the "mountain hat." The episode in which permission to wear hats is granted appears in *Mahāsāṅghika Vinaya*.[107] After completing a summer retreat at Stupa Mountain,[108] Elder Aniruddha went to pay homage to the Buddha, who was sojourning in Śrāvastī. Aniruddha arrived with his clothes soiled and complained that because monks were not allowed to use umbrellas, he was soaked by rain whenever he walked for alms. From that moment on the Buddha allowed monks to use umbrellas made of bark, leaf, or bamboo. The practice of wearing hats most likely evolved from the use of bamboo umbrellas.

Chanyuan qinggui also lists a small pure water vessel among a monk's required equipment.[109] The concept of dividing items or subjects into two categories—pure and soiled (or impure)—is prevalent throughout the Vinaya texts. The *Four Part Vinaya*[110] relates a story in which a number of monks, after traveling without water for some time, arrived at last at a spring. They drank the water immediately, being too thirsty to consider whether or not the water contained insects. Consequently, they were criticized for the taking of life. The Buddha then set forth the rule that monks should carry two bottles, one "pure", the other "soiled."[111] Yijing stipulated that the "pure" bottle be made of pottery or porcelain and the "soiled" one of copper or iron.[112] The water in the "pure" bottle was to be drunk during the "improper" time (afternoon); the water held in other vessels was to be used during the "proper" time (morning). The water in the "soiled" bottle was to be used after visiting the toilet.

Two other examples of the pure/soiled distinction for objects appear in Daoxuan's works. The part of the ladle that scoops up water was regarded as pure while the part used as the handle was soiled.[113] The upper two-thirds of the outside surface of a bowl was considered pure while the remaining part was soiled.[114] In "Packing One's Belongings" the walking stick is also divided into two parts—the "pure" head, which is the end without twigs, and the "soiled" head, the end with twigs. The concept of purity and impurity (or pollution) can be traced back to not only the early Buddhist Vinaya, but also Indian social custom. Indian society, or more specifically Indian Brahmanized society, has a deeply rooted tradition of bifurcating all things into categories of "pure" and "polluted." Indian Buddhism adopted these concepts of purity and pollution from its native land.[115]

It is worth noting that the strainer, one of the monk's six necessities, does not appear in *Chanyuan qinggui*. *Chixiu Baizhang qinggui*[116] mentions that in the first year of Chongning (1102), Zongze, the author of *Chanyuan qinggui*, devised a large strainer and attached it to the wooden threshold beside the wells at his Hongji monastery as well as his other monasteries.

Rituals of Indian Origin

Circumambulating the hall with burning incense, a ceremony called *xingxiang*, is an extremely important ritual in *Chanyuan qinggui*. Daoxuan's *Xingshi chao*[117] gives a detailed description of *xingxiang* and claims that the ritual in China can be traced back to the time of Daoan. In *Chanyuan qinggui*, this ceremony is followed by the recitation of verses. Doaxuan[118] pointed to the instruction given in the *Four Part Vinaya* that monks should perform the verse after the meal. Yijing[119] noted that during his travels in India and South Asia he observed no prayers before the meal. In China, however, it was Master Daoan who began the practice of circumambulating with burning incense and chanting the verse before the meal. Doaxuan himself considered this change to be appropriate and adopted the same routine for the Chinese Lü school. *Xingxiang* also became a ritual performed by the imperial family and aristocrats during visits to monasteries. When an emperor or empress passed away, the ceremony of offering incense for the national mourning *(guoji xingxiang)*[120] was considered a crucial ritual.

Another ritual that recurs throughout *Chanyuan qinggui* is the custom of *chuli sanbai*,[121] that is, placing a folded sitting mat on the floor in front of oneself and bowing down, touching one's forehead to the sitting mat three times. Yijing pointed out that the sitting mat was not originally used for the bowing gesture.[122] The practice of displaying the sitting mat on the floor before bowing does not appear in the Vinaya texts and generally was not practiced in India. However, Daoxuan's work *Xinghu lüyi* suggests that in the Chinese Lü school the sitting mat was used for bowing down. One should take out and unfold the sitting mat during meals [for bowing]; and after bowing down one should collect one's sitting mat before ascending the platform to take one's seat.[123] *Lüyuan shigui*, the later monastic code of the Lü school compiled in 1325 and adopted from the Chan codes, omits this practice of *chuli* altogether, asserting that the sole purpose of the sitting mat is to protect the body and the clothes from becoming soiled. Thus, according to *Lüyuan shigui*,[124] the practice of *chuli* goes against the intent of the Vinaya.

Was the use of the sitting mat for prostration adopted from traditional Chinese practice? The section "The Evolution of Decorum" in *Sengshi lüe*[125] informs us that "in the past, when foreign monks [from India and Central Asia][126] arrived here [China], they unfolded their sitting mats and bowed down on the top of them." This implies that the custom was originally brought from India. Allowing that Yijing's travel route was through South Asia to parts of eastern India, and assuming that *Sengshi lüe's* information is reliable and there is no source for this practice in China, we can infer that the custom was most likely introduced from North India (also known as the Western Region). It should be remembered that the *Mūlasarvāstivada Vinaya*, which Yijing translated into Chinese, prevailed in North India, and that *Sengshi lüe*, compiled by Zanning, should be used cautiously.

Sengshi lüe goes on to explain the reason for *chuli:* "Later, to prevent excessive formalities, a senior monk, when seeing [a junior] unfolding his sitting mat, would immediately move to make a greeting. Thus the junior would unfold his sitting mat and attempt to bow a second time, only to be stopped by the senior once again. Accordingly, attempting to unfold one's sitting mat and starting to bow came to be considered the fulfilment of the proper courtesy."[127]

"Overnight Residence" in Fascicle 1 includes appropriate phrases for the visitor and host monks to exchange when meeting. In his record,[128] Yijing reminded us that the Buddha taught welcoming monks to greet guest monks with *"Shanlai"*[129] (literally, "well come"). In India, at the time when Yijing was a traveler there, it was the custom that whenever a guest monk visited, whether he was an acquaintance, a friend, or a disciple, the host monk had to greet him by saying "Welcome." The guest monks would wait for this greeting and then reply "Most welcome!"[130] If a host monk did not comply with this rule, he would have violated not only monastic regulations,[131] but also the Vinaya itself. Whatever the guest monk's status, he was given the same greeting.

"Entering the Abbot's Quarters" describes the procedure for entering the abbot's quarters for instruction. *Zuting shiyuan*[132] indicates that the practice of entering the room to ask for instruction had been carried out since the time of the Buddha, as is recorded in the Chinese *Agama*. The exact passage referred to can be found in *Epidamo dapiposha lun,*[133] which relates a story in which the Buddha announced to the monks that he would retreat for two months for meditation. During this period, the monks would be excused from instruction, as the Buddha did not want to be disturbed by visits of any sort save food deliveries and the cleaning of his dwelling. Thus from this text it can clearly be inferred that entering the Buddha's room had already become a regular practice. Dōchū, however, adopted Dahui's argument that the practice of entering a master's room for instruction began in the eighth century with the monk Mazu (709–788).[134] But according to Yijing (635–713), when he was an adolescent, he would enter the room of his teacher, Huizhi, for instruction.[135]

Fascicle 2 includes a section describing the procedure for an abbot's visits to the assembly quarters. The *Mahāsāṇghika Vinaya* indicates that the Buddha visited the monks' quarters *(sengfang)* every five days.[136] There were five purposes for the Buddha's regular visits to the monks' quarters: to discern whether the śrāvaka disciples were engaged in worldly affairs; to discern whether the monks were involved in secular discussions; to discern whether they were indulging in sleep, which hindered the practice of meditation; to visit ailing disciples; and to inspire joy in the junior monks and novices by the example of his own dignified demeanor.

Chanyuan qinggui includes many regulations about bathing, and one of the administrative positions described in Fascicle 4 is the office of bath master. In *Wenshi xiyu zhongseng jing,*[137] which provides valuable information on the bathing practices of Indian monks and their belief in its salutary effects, the Buddha stipulated that seven things should be provided at the bath house: fuel, pure water, bean pod soap, ointment for massage, ashes for body powder, willow twigs for toothbrushes, and underwear. After bathing, monks were able to cure themselves of seven kinds of sickness, and donors of the bathhouse supplies would accrue seven kinds of meritorious karma. In China, monks opened their bathhouses to the general public, believing that the promotion of public health was one of their duties.[138]

Structure of the Monastery

The Sangha hall was the most important place in the monastery in the life of a monk.[139] Most scholars translate *sengtang* as "monks' hall." I here adopt Foulk's translation, "sangha hall," since Dōgen pointed out that "the principal buildings within a monastery are the Buddha shrine, Dharma hall, and Sangha hall."[140] As is evident in *Chanyuan qinggui,* monks not only meditate and receive the abbot's regular sermon in this hall, but they also take their two meals and sleep there. This building was generally located in the west section of the monastery complex and placed directly across from the storage hall[141] in the east section. The Sangha hall was usually designed with platforms arranged in rows and was large enough to accommodate thousands of people. The prominent monastery Tiantongshan had one such hall. Its Sangha hall, which was initially built by

Hongzhi Zhengjue in 1132–1134, was "200 feet in length and 16 *zhang* [160 feet] in width."[142] In the center of the hall, a statue of Bodhisattva Mañjuśrī was enshrined as the Holy Monk.[143]

The Sangha hall was also referred to as the "cloud hall,"[144] where monks were said to gather like accumulating clouds,[145] or where those who traveled like the "clouds and the water" come to meditate. It was also known as the "Place for Choosing Buddhas,"[146] where those who were candidates to become Buddhas could be found. It is worth noting that in some prominent monasteries there was more than one Sangha hall within the monastic compound.

From Daoxuan's works[147] we see that monasteries of the Lü school during the Tang dynasty did not include a particular building called the "Sangha hall" that served as the center of monastic life. It seems that monks of the Lü school slept in a dormitory,[148] ate in a dining hall,[149] and attended lectures in a lecture hall.[150] A question we can consider here is when did monks begin sleeping in the Sangha hall? *Chanyuan qinggui* clearly shows that Chan monks in the Song slept in the Sangha hall; however, *Chanyuan qinggui* is not the earliest document showing the construction and function of this building. The Tiantai monastic regulations *Tianzhusi shifang zhuchiyi*,[151] compiled by Zunshi several decades before *Chanyuan qinggui*, shows that the Sangha hall was central to monks' lives. The practice of sleeping in a Sangha hall may have begun sometime between the time of Daoxuan (596–677) and that of Zunshi (964–1032). The Sangha hall was adopted by all schools. In the Lü monastic code *Lüyuan shigui*,[152] we see monks of the Yuan dynasty sleeping and eating in the Sangha hall. The monastic code attributed to Baizhang, *Chanmen guishi*,[153] seems to indicate that the institution of the Sangha hall was Baizhang's invention. However, *Chanmen guishi* was written later in the Song dynasty, and therefore cannot be used as evidence that Baizhang established the Sangha hall and the practice of sleeping within it.

In the assembly quarters, desks were available for studying. In addition to reading, monks took their break for tea here before resting in the Sangha hall. Formal tea ceremonies were also held in the assembly quarters and infrequently used personal belongings were stored here. Judging by later texts as well as the practices in modern monasteries, one can assume that the assembly quarters came to function first and foremost as a study room or monastery library. However, in *Chanyuan qinggui*, we find that the place sanctioned for reading and storing sutras was not the assembly quarters, but the sutra-reading hall.[154]

Chanyuan qinggui notes that upon entering the Sangha hall, the new arrivals bow before the image of the Holy Monk.[155] Yijing stated[156] that monks who lived during the time of the Buddha were allowed to sleep in the same room with him, so it was not inappropriate for monks to maintain an image of the Buddha in their sleeping quarters. He observed that in India and South Asia, a holy statue was enshrined inside the Sangha residence and placed either in a window or in a shrine. This statue was meant to represent the image of the Buddha. The term "Holy Monk" occurs in Yijing's diary:[157] During the meal offering, after the monks have washed their hands and feet and are standing before the assembly, the donors first make an offering to the Holy Monk. During the ritual of the eulogy, after the sutra master has descended from his "lion seat," the most senior monk pays homage first to the "lion seat" and then to the Holy Monk. Yijing did not specify precisely who the Holy Monk was.

Similarly *Chanyuan qinggui* does not identify this image, and none of the later monastic codes[158] clarifies the meaning of the term "Holy Monk." However, in the Chinese Lü school the Holy Monk clearly represents the arhat Piṇḍola. Daoxuan's *Xingshi chao*[159] notes that the seat of the Holy Monk should be decorated in accordance with the instructions given in *Qing Bintoulu fa*.[160] The custom of placing Piṇḍola in the dining hall is said to have begun with Daoan (312–385).[161]

Fayuan zhulin[162] includes a section entitled "Holy Monk" that states that physical depictions of the Holy Monk did not appear until the Taishi era (465–471) of the Liu Song dynasty and were first created by Shi Fayuan at Zhengshengsi and by Shi Fajing at Zhengxisi. This text also includes the episode taken from the *Ten Section Vinaya* describing Piṇḍola's punishment by the Buddha as well as the instruction given in *Qing Bitoulu fa jing*. According to the commentary of Fazang (643–712) to the *Brahma Net Sutra*,[163] all the Hinayanist temples in India treat Piṇḍola as the senior seat (that is, the representative of monks), while in the Mahayanist temples Mañjuśrī takes the senior seat. In China the image of Piṇḍola enshrined in the refectory of all monasteries was replaced by that of Mañjuśrī when the Tantric monk Amoghavajra petitioned the emperor to support the Mahayana teachings.[164]

The Holy Monk in the Sangha hall is also thought to be Kauṇḍinya, the first disciple of the Buddha. This belief is based on the fact that ordination seniority has always played the deciding role in the arrangement of monks' seating. As *Chixiu Baizhang qinggui*[165] indicates, the post indicating the places of monks who took residence in

Sangha hall for the summer retreat[166] listed Kauṇḍinya before the abbot and the assembly of monks. From this Dōchū inferred that Kauṇḍinya is one of the best candidates for the Holy Monk in the Sangha hall.[167] A second source that offers the same hypothesis is *Keizan shingi*,[168] a Japanese monastic code compiled in 1268. This code contains a diagram of ordination seniority identical to that used by the Tiantongshan temples that identifies the Holy Monk as Kauṇḍinya. *Keizan shingi* therefore concludes that the Holy Monk at Tiantongshan must also have been Kauṇḍinya.[169] (Some caution must be exercized regarding the identity of the Holy Monk. There is no explicit evidence in Dōgen's writing that indicates the Holy Monk was Mañjuśrī. The modern claim that the Holy Monk is Mañjuśrī, therefore, may be a later interpretation based on the source pertaining to Amoghavajra's petition.)

The Dharma hall *(fatang)* was used by the abbot when he expounded the Dharma during *shangtang* (held four times a month) and when the inauguration of a new abbot took place. *Fo benxing jijing* discusses the establishment of the Dharma hall.[170] Initially monks lectured outside in open areas, where they were susceptible to cold and heat. The Buddha gave them permission to build roofs over their heads and later walls to protect themselves from dust. When he saw that the floor inside was not level, the Buddha told the monks to make it level and to keep it neat and clean.

The importance assigned to the Dharma hall in the traditional Chan monastery surpasses even that of the Buddha shrine. *Jingde chuandeng lu* states that when Baizhang, who established an independent Chan school, built his monastery, "there was no Buddha shrine on the grounds, only a Dharma hall."[171] The Buddha shrine came to be considered less important because the abbot was thought to be the representative of all Buddhas and patriarchs and honored as a manifestation of the Buddha in the present.

According to *Wujia zhengzong zan*,[172] the Chan monk Deshan Xuanjian (or Jianxing (782?–865)[173] dismantled the Buddha hall shrine but maintained the Dharma hall in every monastery where he served as abbot. Nevertheless, we will see that the Buddha shrine was never disposed of entirely. In later Chan monastic complexes, the Buddha hall continued to be built in the center location. As previously mentioned, Dōgen took the position that the Buddha shrine, Dharma hall, and Sangha hall should all be regarded as principal buildings within the monastery.[174]

Communal Labor

Fascicle 4 includes a description of the duties of the chief gardener, and *Chanyuan qinggui* makes it clear that farming was crucial to the monastery's operation. Although farming is technically a violation of the precepts, a number of accounts in the Vinayas indicate that the monks of the time cultivated fruits and vegetables. The *Four Part Vinaya*[175] records an instance in which a group of monks who had planted vegetables later became unsure of the correctness of their actions and, not daring to eat them, went first to the Buddha to seek advice. The Buddha told them that since the vegetables had grown by themselves, the monks were allowed to eat them. Again later, when the monks replanted these vegetables in other areas, the Buddha once more allowed them to eat, explaining that the vegetables had in a sense been reborn. The Buddha gave explicit permission for monks to plant and eat cucumbers, sugar cane, grapes, pears, *harītakī, pixile, āmalaka* fruit, ginger, and long peppers. The *Five Part Vinaya* indicates that during times of famine, the Buddha allowed monks to plant fruits and vegetables.[176]

To avoid of being called social parasites (mostly by Confucians), Chinese Buddhist monks began farming as a means of self-support. As is evident in the biographies of eminent monks, farming was never thought to detract in any way from a monk's honor.[177] The later monastic code *Lüyuan shigui* reveals that monks of the Lü school engaged in agriculture and horticulture.[178]

The principle of communal service can be found as early as the Vinaya. The *Five Part Vinaya*[179] relates a story in which a house, donated to monks, was flooded by water. Each monk concentrated on bailing out water from his own room and protecting his own furniture. As none of the monks thought to protect the vacant rooms from flooding, the entire house was eventually inundated, and the monks were forced to escape. The donor of the house complained that the monks were negligent, fleeing so readily. In response, the Buddha ruled that henceforward, when there are fires or floods, monks should shout and strike the signal for everyone to come to the rescue. Any monk that did not rush to aid of others was guilty of *duṣkṛta* (evil deeds).

In the *Mulāsarvāstivāola Vinaya*,[180] it is recorded that an old monk, having heard the Buddha preach on the merits of sweeping, decided to give up meditation and chanting and dedicated himself wholly to sweeping the ground. Meanwhile, after overhearing the Buddha tell an administrator that it was best for young monks to spend their time in meditation and chanting, the young monks of this monastery refused to sweep, deeming this chore inferior to more spiritual pursuits. Thus the administrator was unable to ensure that the floors were adequately swept. Seeing this, the Buddha ordered all monks to take part in sweeping the grounds. Thenceforth, on the eighth and fifteenth of each month, the administrator struck the bell to gather all members of the Sangha to sweep the ground. Dōchū remarked that abbots in the past regarded this custom of striking the bell to summon everyone to work, first recorded in this Vinaya, as the beginning of communal labor in the Chan monastery.[181]

Influences of Chinese Culture

In addition to a rich inheritance from the Vinayas, close study of *Chanyuan qinggui* yields another discovery: its incorporation of Chinese governmental policies and traditional Chinese etiquette based on Confucian ideology. Many of the rules and regulations were clearly created specifically to accommodate Chinese social and cultural norms. Given these additions, one is compelled to ask whether they merely demonstrate the inevitable infiltration of Chinese norms into Chan practices based on Indian Vinaya, or if the Chan school as represented by *Chanyuan qinggui* was self-consciously calling into question the legitimacy of a purely Indian Vinaya by creating a more Sinicized Vinaya.

State Control of Chinese Buddhism[182]

The Song regulated Buddhism in China in ways that were unknown in India: through the issuance and sale of tonsure certificates, the ban on traveling without a government permit, secular supervision of the selection of abbots, systematization of clerical offices, and government policies that subjected the clergy to secular laws above and beyond its own monastic regulations. This section examines the policies of the Song government regarding Buddhism. It focuses on the way in which the regulations of *Chanyuan qinggui* were supplemented by the Song edict *Qingyuan tiaofa shilei* (henceforth *Qingyuan fa*),[183] especially by the chapter *Dao Shi men* (Chapter on Daoism and Buddhism). This text provides us with a wealth of information about the government's attitude towards Buddhism and enhances our understanding of monastic life during the Song.

Registration of Clergy and the Issue and Sale of Tonsure Certificates

To bring the clergy under the supervision of the state, the Song government required monks to register, which allowed the authorities to control the number of tonsured individuals in any given region. This policy is said to have been initiated during the Tang in the seventeenth year of Kaiyuan (729), when Emperor Xuan ordered all monks and nuns to register with the government every three years. Two copies of each register were made, one for the Department of Sacrifices and one for the local government.[184] Later, during the Five Dynasties period, the court of the Post-Zhou emperor (r. 923–936) supplemented the comprehensive three-year registration *(quanzhang)* with an annual registration *(cizhang)*, which recorded only the newly ordained clergy each year. The Song government adopted the system instituted by the Post-Zhou, requiring the local prefect, the imperial court, and the Department of Sacrifices to each keep one copy of both the annual registration and the three-year registration.[185] Even probationary postulants, most of whom were untonsured teenagers, were required to register. In contrast to ordained monks, the postulants were not exempt from taxes[186] and were therefore eager to be tonsured as soon as possible. In Song China the tonsuring of monks was no longer under the authority of the monastery, and each postulant was forced to wait for official permission to pass through the cumbersome state tonsure system *(gongdu zhi)*, which allocated slots by region.[187] Any cleric not registered in accordance with the governmental edict was forcibly laicized.[188]

Scholars have traditionally identified the sixth year of Tianbao (747), two decades after Emperor Xuan's registration edict, as the year when tonsure certificates were first issued.[189] Yamazaki Hiroshi and Moroto Tatsuo question this date, however, arguing that the custom predated the imposition of government registration. (They do not offer an alternative date.)[190] Under the Tang the tonsure certificate was a prerequisite for a postulant obtaining a position in a Chinese monastery. This custom would persist throughout Chinese history. In fact, the requirements for the certificate became more and more stringent over the years, as the authorities relied increasingly on the regulation of certificates to control the Buddhist clergy.

The Song-era *Chanyuan qinggui* describes the procedure for obtaining a certificate as follows: "The server [that is, postulant] must first apply for and receive a certificate of tonsure from the government. Once he has received the document, he then places the certificate inside a double-layered box, which he presents to the abbot, the administrators, and the chief officers of the temple where he wishes to take up residence, bowing down and thanking each of them three times. This is the procedure to request the tonsure."[191]

The tonsure certificate was a source of revenue for the government; beginning with the Song most of the clergy were required to pay a fee for the document, a policy that became one of the greatest burdens on the Song Buddhist community. When certificates were first issued by the Tang court, members of the clergy had to pass rigorous sutra examinations,[192] thus ensuring a minimum level of proficiency in Buddhist scholarship in the monastic community. Over time, these standards were lost when the document came to be bought and sold on the open market. Although it was long believed that the sale of tonsure certificates began under the Song, evidence of this practice can be traced as far back as the reigns of emperors Zhong and Rui (684) of the Tang dynasty.[193] Nevertheless, it was during the Song period that the market for tonsure certificates flourished. The state's practice of selling tonsure certificates (which bestowed on the recipient a considerable tax exemption) became a makeshift remedy for a fiscal crisis brought about by the government's extensive military campaigns.

Beginning in 1067, tonsure certificates were divided into two categories: certificates with the recipients' names already written on them *(jiming dudie)* and blank certificates which could be filled in by the owner *(kongming dudie)*.[194] The former were issued only to those who had passed examinations (as before) or were given as favors by the imperial family; the latter were simply sold to the public by central and local government officials.[195] During the Northern Song period, the number of certificates sold on the open market fluctuated in accordance with the government's needs, their sale sometimes banned, at other times encouraged. However, as the Southern Song increasingly diverted its resources to finance wars with neighboring tribes, the need for immediate funds flooded the market with certificates, reaching a peak under the emperors Gao (r. 1127–1162) and Xiao (r. 1163–1189). It is estimated that within one nine-year period (1161–1169) the government sold more than 120,000 certificates.[196] Income from the sale of tonsure certificates throughout the Song played no less a role in government finances than the collection of taxes on salt and commerce.[197]

The price of blank certificates fluctuated greatly, generally increasing from year to year. Eventually, inflation drove the price to the point where a postulant of humble or even average social station could not afford to take the tonsure. Many monasteries were compelled to take up collections for their postulants, soliciting donations from laypeople for the specific purpose of setting up an endowment fund so that the interest could be used to buy tonsure certificates. It is clear that taking the tonsure was by no means a simple process and an undertaking far beyond the financial means of most individuals.[198] Despite the growing difficulty of procuring certificates, the numbers in circulation increased steadily, contributing to a steep decline in the cohesivenes and overall ethical and religious standards of the monastic community. *Chanyuan qinggui* bears witness to the excesses generated under these circumstances when it warns monastic fundraisers to resist the temptation to embezzle monies for personal purchases of titulary or tonsure certificates or for the tonsuring of postulants as their own disciples.[199]

In addition to the price of the tonsure certificate, which itself could be as much as one hundred thousand coins,[200] the government imposed additional fees. According to *Qingyuan fa*, "When a postulant applies for a tonsure certificate or buys a blank certificate, he must pay 'tonsure money' *(piti qian)* in the amount of one string of coins *(yiguan)*.[201] Once payment has been received and approved by a government official, the certificate is granted. At this time the postulant must pay an additional 'writing fee' *(mifei qian)*[202] of one string of coins."[203] Postulants obtaining certificates through examination or imperial grant were still required to pay the above fees totaling two strings of coins, whereas those purchasing blank certificates paid the two fees as well as the price of the certificate.

The government required monks to pay a separate (and undoubtedly less expensive) annual registration fee, referred to as *gongzhang qianwu* in *Chanyuan qinggui*.[204] The Yuan monastic code *Chixiu Baizhang qinggui* reveals that in the Song dynasty, "Buddhist and Daoist clergy registered with the government every year and paid 'money for exemption from adult service obligations' *(mianding qian)*." In return, the government would issue an exemption certificate,[205] which a monk was required to carry on his person when traveling[206] in addition to his personal effects and his ordination certificate. It is often thought that the issuing of the *mianding qian* began in the fifteenth year of the Shaoxing era (1145).[207] Given that it is mentioned in *Chanyuan qinggui* (compiled in 1103), we have proof that the actual collection of annual registration fees far predates the government edict that officially endorsed the practice.

Although membership in the clergy exempted one from state labor obligations, the lot of the monk during the Song period was not without its difficulties. Postulants were compelled to save a great deal of money before they could purchase tonsure certificates, the poorest among them waiting sometimes twenty years before obtaining the document. And once they had received the certificate, they were still legally bound to pay two strings of coins in fees. Until a postulant could save this large amount, he was not exempt from taxes. Thus, while it is a common perception that monks were all given tax-exempt status, a considerable number of them—those awaiting tonsure—continued to pay full taxes, and even those tonsured were subject to an annual exemption fee.

After receiving tonsure, the postulant graduated to the status of novice. Upon full ordination, he would be issued an ordination certificate *(jiedie)* by the Department of Sacrifice. At the same time, a document entitled "The Six Awarenesses" *(liunian)*[208] containing the signatures of the ordination preceptors was issued by the monastery. These three documents—the tonsure certificate, the ordination certificate, and "The Six Awarenesses"—were the standard papers needed to apply for travel permits.[209]

Issuing Travel Permits

Chanyuan qinggui provides detailed examples of the format used by clerics when applying to the government for travel permits *(panping shi)* and for extensions of the permit *(piping shi)*. The instructions stipulate that the cleric must "present his tonsure certificate, 'The Six Awarenesses' document, and his ordination certificate to the appropriate office for inspection to receive a permit for pilgrimage travel."[210] *Qingyuan fa* indicates that a reference from a superior was also necessary. Any Buddhist monk (or Daoist priest) who wished to travel beyond the boundaries of his local prefect had to have a superior vouch for him. The superior referred to here would have been the traveling monk's teacher or, if this was not feasible, the abbot of the monastery to be visited.[211] After presenting the documents to the local authorities, the monk was issued a permit that strictly prescribed the limits of his itinerary. This permit was to be kept on the monk's person during the entire journey and, along with the tonsure and ordination certificates, served as the standard form of identification. If a monk were to be found without these documents, or with forged papers, he would summarily be placed in the custody of the local government.[212]

The travel permit clearly stated the monk's destination, the trip's duration, where he would be lodged, and any incidental areas of travel. *Qingyuan fa* explains that the maximum permissible length of a journey was usually ninety days, but in cases where a monk had to travel more than one thousand miles, the trip could be extended to half a year. If a monk's return was unavoidably delayed for more than thirty days, he could receive special permission to prolong his travel by petitioning the local government.[213] The rules concerning the petition to extend a journey are given in *Chanyuan qinggui*.[214] If a traveler desired to prolong his stay in a monastery, he had to exchange his original permit for a new one. The traveler had to proceed directly and without delay to his destination; along the way, he was not allowed to stay at any one inn or lodging for more than a single night unless he had fallen ill.[215] *Qingyuan fa* prohibited travel in the buffer zones between areas under Song control and enemy territories.[216]

The procedure for gaining entrance to a monastery is described in *Qingyuan fa*. Within three days after a monk's arrival at a monastery, an administrator must ask for the traveler's ordination certificate and travel permit, verify their authenticity, and transfer them to the local government. The travel permit was then destroyed.[217] According to *Chanyuan qinggui*, it was the duty of the rector *(weinuo)* to inspect the certificates and permits, as well as any government documents, such as master title certificates. (The rector was also charged with confiscating these documents when a monk died, and it was his responsibility to collect the annual registration fees.) After inspection, the rector handed the traveler's documents to the prior *(kusi)*, who, in turn, submitted them to the local government.[218] A visiting monk who wished to return to his place of origin would be required to apply for a new permit.

Bureaucratic policies regulating travel were strictly enforced; as *Qingyuan fa* makes clear, any infraction of the rules carried with it a harsh punishment. For example, if a teacher's letter of recommendation was found to be a forgery, the possessor would be caned. Similarly, a caning would be given to any traveling monk who had failed to register at a monastery or who had not yet received full ordination. Any monk discovered beyond the borders of his district or outside the confines of his permit destination would be laicized; a monk found traveling without any permit would first be caned one hundred times and then laicized.[219] The severity of these punishments is ample evidence of the importance placed by the Song government on controlling the mobility of the Buddhist clergy.[220] Both *Chanyuan qinggui* and *Qingyuan fa* reveal in painstaking detail the extent to which a monk's every move was scrutinized by secular authorities.

Granting the Title of Master

A monk's chances of obtaining a higher position in his home monastery's administration increased if he traveled to other monasteries, and such activity could even contribute to his becoming abbot. A simpler way of increasing his fame and expanding his career opportunities was to acquire an honorific title bestowed by the government. The Song government came to realize that it could use the "granting" of honorific titles to increase revenue, so it offered two types of official recognition: the bestowal of a purple robe and the granting of the title of master.

It is recorded in *Sengshi lüe* that the practice of bestowing purple robes began with Empress Wu (r. 684–704), who gave purple-colored robes to Falang and eight other monks for their "retranslation" of the *Great Clouds Sutra,* thereby smoothing her way to the throne.[221] The granting of the title of master *(dashi)* is believed to have begun in 870, the eleventh year of the Xiantong era, during the reign of the Tang Emperor Yi .[222] Even before this time, however, a special title (other than *dashi)* had been given to the monk Louyue by the Emperor Wu (r. 502–547) of the Liang dynasty.[223] Both practices were maintained by succeeding dynasties as a means of showing favor to the clergy.

When these titles were first instituted, they were a universally respected acknowledgement of an individual's virtue, wisdom, or career achievement. In the early Song period (969–979), the government endeavored to maintain the integrity of the title of master by requiring candidates to pass examinations on the sutras, vinayas, and commentaries at the imperial court. Those who passed such exams were known as *"shoubiao seng,"* that is, "monks who have gained audience with the emperor by their own hands."[224] Over the years, the examination system was quietly abandoned and replaced by personal recommendation. Candidates could be recommended by the imperial family, by the nobility, even by high-ranking officials and monk-officers. It was not long before this practice became corrupt, and by the eleventh century the title of master was being bought and sold alongside the certificates of tonsure. The first clearly recorded sale of the title in the Song dynasty is dated 1071, but one can assume that this practice began when certificates of tonsure were first sold in 1067.[225] As with the tonsure certificates, the title of master had become a commodity to the fund the government's war effort.

Since the title of master carried no tax benefits, its market price was far lower than that of the blank tonsure certificate, often no more than one-tenth the price. The price of the title, which had to be renewed yearly like the annual registration fee, varied according to the number of characters written on the certificate: the more characters, the greater the prestige and, accordingly, the greater its monetary worth. Titles could contain as few as two characters or as many as ten. The price also varied according to the sectarian affiliation of the recipient. For example, in 1145 a monk ordained in the Lü or Tiantai school who wished to purchase a two-character master title had to pay six strings of coins. Eight strings were required for a four-character title, nine strings for a six-character title. A monk of the Chan tradition, however, was required to pay only three strings of coins for a two-character title, four strings for a four-character title, and six strings for a six-character title. Daoist priests, who could also purchase such titles, paid roughly the same price as Chan monks, except for them a six-character title was even less expensive at only five strings of coins.[226]

At the same time that these titles were being bought and sold, it is believed that they continued to be granted by imperial decree. No doubt such royal favors had lost much of their original prestige. The corruption surrounding the conferral of monastic titles was a phenomenon that proved offensive not only to the general public, but also to many within the Buddhist community. For instance, Dōgen's master, Rujing, railed against a system in which monks who had bought their tonsure certificates to begin with were now paying the government large sums of money for master titles in hopes of eventually attaining the rank of abbot.[227]

Election of a New Abbot in a Public or Private Monastery

As we have seen, the Song government kept tight control over the status and mobility of an individual monk. It also closely regulated general protocol within monasteries, especially public monasteries. The election of an abbot is a prime example of a procedure carefully dictated by Song legal edicts.

Buddhist monasteries of the Song period fell into two categories: the public, or "ten directions," monastery *(shifang cha)* and the private monastery, or "successive cloister" *(jiayi yuan)*. The two were distinguished by their different systems of succession. Public monasteries invited renowned senior monks to serve as abbots, and there was no limit on their sectarian affiliations; in other words, succession was not based on a master-disciple relationship, but rather was open to all meritorious candidates.[228] In the private monastery, sometimes referred to as the "cloister of disciple tonsuring" *(dudi yuan)*, the abbot appointed one of his own tonsured disciples (or his Dharma brother) as the next abbot; thus transmission was based on direct succession.[229]

According to *Qingyuan fa,* when a vacancy for the position of abbot occurred in a public Buddhist monastery, the administration of the local prefecture entrusted its own clerical officials in the local department of Sangha rectifiers *(sengzheng si)* with the task of assembling the heads of the public monasteries or temples in that prefect to select a monk to fill the vacancy. Candidates were to be of senior status, possessing great virtue and cultivation that commanded wide respect. The clerical officials then reported their selection to the prefectural government, where the candidates were either approved or rejected. If the clerical officials were unable to locate a suitable candidate, they were to expand their search to include monks in neighboring prefects.[230]

The system is discussed in *Chanyuan qinggui.* After the demise of an abbot, "the appointment of a new abbot is then discussed and the administrators issue letters to neighboring monasteries to explain the situation and ask for recommendations. Senior monks from surrounding monasteries and monk-officials may suggest candidates, but if their recommendations are not agreed on by the assembly, the administrators must meet with a government official, explain the situation, and ask for an alternative. If the government entrusts the monastery with the power to select unilaterally an abbot, the monastery should do so quickly to avoid having the abbot's position vacant for an extended period of time.[231]

Qingyuan fa also prohibits the establishment of retirement hermitages within the grounds of the monastery,[232] a policy intended to prevent retired abbots from exercising continued influence over the selection of future abbots. *Chanyuan qinggui,* once again reflecting state concerns, echoes this prohibition, and adds that incumbent abbots should not use their position to construct such a hermitage.[233]

The election of an abbot of a private temple as described in *Qingyuan fa* provides a sharp contrast to the procedures followed in public monasteries. This selection process is not mentioned in *Chanyuan qinggui,* a text intended solely for use at public monasteries.) *Qingyuan fa* divides private monasteries into two categories on the basis of the line of succession: "horizontal," with succession accorded to the former abbot's monastic siblings (that is, monks of the same generation); and "vertical," with the abbacy passing to those disciples directly under the former abbot.[234] If the abbot of a "horizontal" monastery passed away or was compelled to retire, a senior monk from within the monastery who was eligible and recommended by the entire assembly would be assigned the position. If there were no qualified candidates in the current abbot's generation, only then would the abbot's tonsured disciple or the abbot's brother's tonsured disciple be chosen as successor.[235] In monasteries that operated on the system of "vertical" inheritance, the abbot's direct disciple succeeded him. If in such a monastery there was no qualified disciple, then one of the abbot's monastic brothers was chosen.[236]

The details of succession seem even more restrictive when one considers that the only monks eligible for an abbacy were the abbot's brothers or disciples who were at the temple at the time the vacancy arose, or those who were traveling on official monastery business for less than half a year and who could return to the monastery promptly. From these eligible candidates the new abbot was selected on the basis of seniority. Those monks who had been away from the temple for a year or more, even if on temple business, as well as those who had been gone for less than half a year for personal reasons, were not considered eligible. The purpose of this rule was to prevent monks long absent from the monastery from suddenly appearing at the time of a vacancy with unmerited aspirations of becoming abbot.[237]

Conversion from Public to Private Status and Vice Versa

The Song government looked far more favorably on public monasteries, which were more easily supervised, than on private ones. Regulations contained in Song edicts made conversion from private to public status a painless process, whereas conversion from public to private was so arduous as to be virtually prohibited.

Qingyuan fa explicitly encourages private monasteries to become public, explaining that when there is no one to succeed to the abbacy of a private temple, or when a private temple is in a state of ruin with little hope of recovery, then conversion to a public institution may take place without any impediment whatsoever on the part of the state.[238] Conversion in the opposite direction, however, is considered nothing less than criminal. According to this Song edict, if the chiefs or disciples of a monastery or temple that had become a public institution arbitrarily entered into litigation to change their institution back into a private hereditary monastery, the institution's successor, that is, the candidate for the post of abbot (most likely the one responsible for the conversion request) would be punished with a caning of one hundred strokes. If a public monastery were to choose its successor unilaterally from among its own members without first requesting permission from the government (thereby effectively acting as a private institution) the number of strokes would double or triple.[239] Any official who allowed such clandestines activities to take place, whether out of negligence or corruption, would receive the same punishment of two to three hundred cane strokes.[240]

It was not only state pressure that led many monasteries to choose new abbots through elections rather than inheritance, that is, to convert their selection system to that of a public monastery. Elections helped to ensure an abbot of high quality. A highly respected abbot brought prestige to a monastery as a whole, which in turn brought in more monks and nuns. Thus many monasteries seeking to grow in stature and size converted to public status of their own accord. Such conversions were prevalent among Chan temples and other schools of the Song era as well, such as the Lü and the Tiantai.

The public system did have some disadvantages. The transition between abbots was a period of potential instability. Establishing a new abbot could result in drastic change: the sudden institution of new rules or the abolishing of old ones. Or squabbles could arise over what possessions the retiring abbot was allowed to take with him. Such problems probably did occur, since *Chanyuan qinggui* takes pains to describe transition procedures to avoid these difficulties: "With the help of administrators, the retiring abbot must clearly write down all monies belonging to the monastery and any donations designated for the Sangha membership in the income records. A list of communal items used in the abbot's office must be transferred properly, along with the income record, all of which is then closed with the monastic seal. The abbot then asks the administrators to appoint someone to safeguard the abbot's quarters and the transferred items."[241]

The public monastery system, dependent as it was on the government's approval, ultimately proved too susceptible to corruption, prompting a reconversion movement to private status that gradually gained momentum during the Southern Song.[242] By this time, the government's conversion regulations had ceased to exert any prohibitive influence on the Buddhist community.

A third category of monastic institution from the Song was "Five Mountains and Ten Monasteries" *(wushan shicha)*. These were some of the most prestigious monasteries in the land, and the emperor appointed their abbots directly.[243] A fourth, and final, category consisted of those monasteries founded by laypeople, usually members of the nobility, who donated their own estates for the building of "merit cloisters" *(gongde yuan)* to render their land tax exampt. In such cases, the abbot was chosen directly by the lay members from the population of neighboring monasteries.[244]

The System of Cleric Officials

One of the Chinese government's most significant acts was the creation of an official hierarchy within Buddhist monasteries. Certain monks were selected as "officials" representing the government and were entrusted with overseeing the Buddhist community. This system of cleric officials began very early during the Post-Qin (393–416), when Yao Chang (330–393) appointed the monk Senglüe as Sangha rectifier *(sengzheng)*.[245] Although the system and its titles varied with each dynasty, the use of cleric officials remained firmly in place, declining only gradually over time, until the Qing dynasty (1644–1911).[246]

In the Song period, the Department of Sangha Recorder *(senglu si)* was part of the central government located in the capital; departments known as Sangha Rectifiers *(sengzheng si)* were instituted at the local level in each circuit. During this time clerical officials were selected from among those erudite monks who had passed the sutra examinations. The various positions in the central government department were Sangha recorders *(senglu)*, assistant Sangha recorders *(fu senglu)*, chief seats of the sutras, chief seats of the treatises *(jinglun shouzuo)*, and secretaries *(jianyi)*. Within the local Sangha rectifier departments, the cleric officials were given the titles Sangha rectifier, assistant Sangha rectifier *(fu sengzheng)*, and Sangha judge *(sengpan)*. In those areas where Buddhism was flourishing, the position metropolitan Sangha rectifier *(du sengzheng)* was added at the local level.[247]

In two of the most prestigious Buddhist monasteries of the time, Wutaishan and Tiantaishan (where each monastic complex was a collection of many individual sectarian temples), the government appointed separate clerical officials for each district. The Wutaishan system was called the Department of Sangha Rectifiers for the Ten Temples *(shisi sengzheng si)*, within which the positions of a Sangha rectifier and several assistant Sangha rectifiers were installed.[248] The Tiantaishan had its own metropolitan Sangha rectifier, Sangha rectifier, assistant Sangha rectifier, and Sangha administrator *(sengsi)*.[249]

Clerical officials were intended to serve as mediators between the government and the Buddhist community. In this capacity, they supervised novices' sutra examinations,[250] novices' ordinations,[251] the registration of clergy,[252] the granting of purple robes and master titles,[253] the selection of abbots,[254] the changing of a monastery's status (from public to private, or vice versa),[255] and monks' travel.[256] The clerical officials in turn were supervised by a separate division of the government. The title and nature of this supervisory division varied from period to period. In general, before 1078 (the first year of the Yuanfeng era), supervisors were called commissioners of good works *(gongde shi);* from 1078 to the end of the Northern Song period, the division was designated the Court for State Ceremonials *(honglu si);* and during the Southern Song it was referred to as the Department of Sacrifices.[257] Takao asserts that the commissioners of good works and the Court for State Ceremonials may not have exercised direct power over local clerical officals; not until the Southern Song period did the Department of Sacrifices control the registration of all monks and nuns.[258]

Clearly, many aspects of life in Buddhist monasteries of the Song were under close governmental supervision, especially the ordination process, the election of abbots, and the mobility of travelers. The threat of punishment for any infraction of a state regulation in monastic life should not be underestimated; the penalty for an offense as minor as traveling without a permit was forced laicization. Such a policy could only have been initiated by secular authorities. Vinaya regulations called for defrocking only if a monk committed one of the four gravest offenses: sexual intercourse, murder, theft, and fraudulent claims to enlightenment. In addition to the rigorous rules prescribed by the Vinaya and the monastic codes, monks in Song China were subject to the same state laws that bound all lay citizens.

Influence of Confucian Rituals on Monastic Practice

One of the major influences on the composition of early Buddhist monastic codes was Chinese cultural customs which, in turn, were heavily imbued with the ideals and practices of Confucianism. In adopting many aspects of governmental protocol, the Buddhist monastery came to function as a microcosm of the imperial court, with the role of the abbot analogous to that of the emperor. The hierarchical organization of monastic administrators was borrowed directly from the Chinese military and civil service. The rules of decorum for the highly ritualized monastic tea ceremony have their precedents in Confucian literature, and worship of the ancient legendary emperors as national deities also found its way into ceremonies held in Buddhist monasteries. There can be little doubt that Chinese Buddhism borrowed many of its practices from Chinese society, whose social institutions, religious concepts, and ritual protocol can be traced largely to the ancient Confucianist scriptures known as the *Three Rites (Sanli)*, or the *Canon of Rites (Lijing)*.

The three works that make up this canonical Confucianist collection are *Zhouli* (Ceremonial of the Zhou Dynasty), *Yili* (Book of Etiquette and Ceremonials), and *Liji* (The Book of Rites). The first, *Zhouli*, describes the imperial system of officials and their titles. The second, *Yili*, relates the proper etiquette for numerous civil and social occasions, such as adulthood ceremonies, marriage ceremonies, social visits, district symposia, local and national archery meetings, banquets, the sending of envoys, and dinners sponsored for the commissioner. The third (and chronologically last) text, *Liji*, records a number of dialogues concerning political philosophy between Confucius and his disciples and contemporaries.[259] Thus all aspects of Confucian society are laid out in these three works: *Zhouli* describes the civil and military hierarchy surrounding the emperor; *Yili* provides concrete guidelines for correct social behavior for both the gentry and commoners; and *Liji* puts forth political ideals for the ruler, who governs a country, and for the individual, who governs himself.

Imperial System and the Monastic Practice

If we carefully examine the physical layout of a Song Buddhist monastery, paying special attention to the arrangement of details concerning the abbot, we see that it closely resembles the imperial court. The abbot's residence is modeled after the private quarters of the emperor, which is discussed in the Confucian *Book of Rites*. In most monasteries, the abbot's quarters *(fangzhang)* were built behind the Dharma hall, the two buildings bridged by an intermediary chamber known as the *qintang*. The abbot gave public sermons in the Dharma hall on formal occasions, received visitors and conducted more private sermons in the *qintang*,[260] and retired to the rearmost quarters to sleep—an arrangement that was largely adopted from imperial custom. The character *qin* was originally used to refer to the rear part of an imperial ancestral temple, a meaning clearly explained by the annotation to the *Liji:* "The front part of the ancestral shrine is called the *miao;* the rear part is called the *qin.*"[261] More detailed information is given in the commentary: "The *miao* is where deities are received; it is considered a place of honor and therefore it is located in the front. The *qin* is where the ancestral clothing is kept; it is considered inferior and therefore it is in the rear. Attached to the east and west sides of the *miao* are two chambers, separated by partitions; the *qin,* however, is just one large room."[262]

Liji indicates that the emperor's bedroom was called *xiaoqin;* the hall outside his bedroom used for meetings with high-ranking ministers was referred to as *luqin.* The functions of the two chambers are made clear in the following description of daily imperial life: "(The ministers and officers) entered (the palace) as soon as they could distinguish the dawning light, and the ruler came out daily (to the first court, inside the Khū gate [*zhumen*]), and received them. (After this audience), he retired and went to the great chamber [*luqin*] to listen to their proposals about the measures of government. He employed men to see whether the great officers (were all withdrawn); and when they had left, he repaired to the small chamber [*xiaoqin*] and put off his (court) robes."[263]

The origins of the monastic building known as the patriarch hall can be traced to Confucian ancestral practices. Referred to as *zhentang* (hall of patriarchal pictures), it was located in the western part of the compound behind the Dharma hall and symmetrical to the earth hall. In the patriarch hall, also called the "hall of principles" *(gangji tang),* the Bodhidharma statue was placed in the center; on its left were the second patriarch, Huike; the founding abbot; and the abbots of the second, fourth, sixth, and eighth generations. On the statue's right were Baizhang and the abbots of the first, third, fifth, seventh, and ninth generations.[264] The arrangement is very much like the placement of statues in a traditional Chinese ancestral temple as recorded in *Liji:* "(The ancestral temple of) the Son of Heaven embraced seven fanes (or smaller temples), three on the left and three on the right, and that of his great ancestor (fronting the south)—in all, seven."[265] This system of ancestor worship, which arose in the Zhou dynasty, placed the primal ancestor in the center. Shrines representing the even-numbered generations were placed on the left and were called *zhao;* those of the odd-numbered generations were placed on the right and called *mu.*[266]

The patriarch hall was not built solely for decoration; it was also used as the site of memorial services. Although *Chanyuan qinggui* does not provide any detailed information about the hall, we can learn much about the building through the later monastic code *Beiyong qinggui*, which closely describes the memorial services held in the patriarch hall for Bodhidharma, Baizhang, the founding abbots, and former abbots.[267]

As previously mentioned, the administrative system of the Song monastery was clearly modeled after the Chinese governmental system. This can be seen in both the hierarchical structure of the monastic staff and in the practice of the abbot ascending to the high seat in the Dharma hall to preach every five days. *Chanyuan qinggui* indicates that the monastic administrative staff (with the exclusion of the abbot) was divided into two categories: administrators *(zhishi)* and chief officers *(toushou)*. The later Yuan text *Chixiu Baizhang qinggui* divides the staff into two two sections: the east *(dongxu)* and the west *(xixu)*.[268] This binary system was adopted from a similar one used in the central government system, which divided official into two branches, civilian and military. Even the custom of administrators and chief officers forming two lines on either side of the Dharma hall as the abbot ascends the platform closely resembles the positions of military officers and civilian officials during an audience with the emperor in the imperial palace.

The abbot ascended the platform in the Dharma hall to give his sermon six times a month: on the first, fifth, tenth, fifteenth, twentieth, and twenty-fifth.[269] This custom can be traced to one practiced by Chinese government officials (more specifically military officers of the fifth grade or above), who made official visits to the emperor every five days. The *Xin Tangshu* states:[270]

Civilian and military officials of the ninth grade or above as well as the offspring of the two princes *(liangwang hou)* hold an audience with the emperor on the new moon and full moon days of each month. Civilian officials of the fifth grade or above, auxiliary officials of the two departments *(liangsheng gongfeng guan)*, investigating censors *(jiancha yushi)*, bureau vice-directors *(yuanwai lang)*, and Erudites of the Chamberlain for Ceremonials *(taichang boshi)* hold audiences on a daily basis. Thus these latter positions are referred to as "officials of frequent audience" *(changcan guan)*. Military officials of the third grade or above hold audience every third day [that is, on the third, sixth, ninth, thirteenth, sixteenth, nineteenth, twenty-third, twenty-sixth, and twenty-ninth; nine days total]; thus, these positions are referred to as "officials of nine audiences" *(jiucan guan)*. Military officials of the fifth grade or above and those posted on guard *(zhechong dangfan)* hold audiences every fifth day and are thus called "officials of six audiences" *(liucan guan).*

The Monastic Tea Ceremony and Yili

From the Song monastic code *Chanyuan qinggui* it is evident that the tea ceremony, held for a variety of occasions, was considered a major component of social life inside the Chinese monastery. The abbot and the prior *(jianyuan)* held tea services to commemorate the transfer of duties from old to new administrators or from old to new chief officers. At the commencement and closing of the summer retreat, the abbot, the prior (as the chief of administrators), and the chief seat of the Sangha hall *(shouzuo,* as the leading position among the chief officers) all sponsored tea ceremonies in the Sangha hall. The abbot also held a tea service during visits by government officers.

The tea service was sponsored not only by the highest-ranking administrators, but by the junior monks as well. Even those who were not members of the administrative staff were responsible for holding a tea ceremony for the abbot and administrators. The abbot's Dharma heirs and select disciples *(rushi dizi)* also sponsored a tea ceremony for the abbot. Generally speaking, tea ceremonies were of great importance because they helped acquaint all members of the assembly with administrators. They were so frequent that descriptions of ceremony procedures, down to the minutest detail, constitute a central part of *Chanyuan qinggui* and all subsequent monastic codes.

During the Song dynasty the tea service was not unique to the Chan monastery. It was a crucial part of social life, secular and monastic, throughout China. The early Buddhist community simply adopted a custom already popular in secular society. Due to the development of commerce and industry as well as the growing trend toward urbanization, people in the Song enjoyed a far greater level of material comfort than their predecessors. The drinking of tea was no longer a privilege of the aristocracy, but a habit among the common people. This "democratization" of tea has attracted the interest of several scholars. In his excellent article on the prevalence of tea drinking in Song China, Japanese scholar Mizuno Masaaki demonstrates how the drinking of tea came to permeate people's daily lives. He asserts that tea drinking, which had become quite popular by the end of the Tang, was transformed into a complex and refined ritual during the Song period. Tea products were the preferred offering to the emperor, and they, in turn, were his favorite gift to others. Tea had become an indispensable item, as much a daily staple as rice and salt even in the countryside.[271] Consequently, Mizuno holds that the tea service in Chinese Buddhist monasteries came about because of the general social prevalence of tea drinking, pointing out that in time many temples even began to grow tea on their estates for their own use or for trade.[272] Lü and Tiantai monastic codes of the later Yuan contain sections describing the protocol for the tea ceremony, an indication that other schools were affected by the prevailing tea culture and carried out practices similar to those but lined in Chan regulations.

Tea was not the only drink provided at tea ceremonies; monks were also offered *tang* ("sweetened drink"). More than simply hot sugar water, *tang* was brewed with various kinds of herbs, fruits, beans, and the like.[273] A confection made from herbs, nuts, and fruits and always taken with tea or *tang* was *chayao*. The herbal confection and *tang* were consumed daily throughout China during the Song. The ingredients and variations of the sweetened drink and confection have been studied by Tanaka Misa, who concludes that the traditional Chinese conception of food as medicine originated with these two items.[274]

Although Buddhist monks adopted the the drinking of tea from secular society, the monastic tea service undoubtedly came to influence the practice outside the monastery. Any visitor to a temple would have been treated to the sweetened drink and witnessed the skillful serving of tea. Thus the monastery helped promote ritualized tea drinking, a custom that ultimately extended beyond its walls. It may even have been directly involved in the widespread distribution of tea throughout China.

As we have noted, tea ceremonies were held on a wide variety of occasions, and *Chanyuan qinggui* provides us with seven examples. Studying the descriptions of these seven ceremonies, we see that the basic protocol remains the same, with only slight variations to suit the given occasion. The extremely meticulous tea service etiquette found in the monastic regulations is missing in the original Vinaya; it is an invention of Chinese Buddhism that reflects a culture rooted in classical Confucian works, especially *Yili*.

Chanyuan qinggui offers many examples of "humble expressions" used during the tea ceremony. These ritualized verbal exchanges were made at auspicious moments between members of the monastery. Characterized by hyperbole and extreme deference, their self-deprecating nature is evident in the following expressions used by an abbot as tea or sweetened drink is being offered to a visiting government official: "We would now like to offer our low-grade tea (or low-grade sweetened drink) and we will follow all of Official X's instructions." Only after permission was obtained from the official could the tea be served. If the official offered a compliment, the abbot's standard reply was, "This low-grade tea is merely a token of our sincerity. It is not worthy for you to touch."[275] At the end of a tea ceremony sponsored by a prior or chief seat, the host thanked the abbot by saying, "Today our humble low-grade tea (or inferior sweetened drink) has received your grace, master, for out of kindness you have stooped to attend; and for this we are extremely grateful."[276] Similarly, following a ceremony sponsored by the assembly, a representative host expresses the assembly's gratitude with the words, "Today's tea (or sweetened drink) is served specially for X and Y. The tea is of a low grade and the seats are uncomfortable. Despite these things, you came anyway. For this I am extremely grateful." As a show of gratitude to the other guests, the host continues: "Today the tea (or sweetened drink) was served especially for X and Y. I am afraid this ceremony was not worth the trouble you [that is, the other guests] have taken to accompany them."[277]

Such formalized expressions of humility and indebtedness have clear precedents in the Confucian book of protocol, *Yili*, which offers dialogue containing similar language. Here a duke invites foreign dignitaries to a banquet:[278]

> To this the [messengers of the] guests reply: "Our unworthy prince is a feudatory of yours, so let your prince not incur disgrace by conferring benefits on us mere messengers. Your servants venture to decline."
>
> The invitation is extended to them [that is, the guests, through envoys] in the following form: "Our unworthy prince has some inferior wine, and, wishing your honors to spend a little time with him, he sends me to invite you."
>
> The messenger [of the host] then replies: "My unworthy prince insists on saying that the wine is of poor quality, and sends me to press the invitation on your honors."
>
> To which the [messengers of the] guests reply: "Our unworthy prince is a feudatory of yours, and your prince should not demean himself by showing kindness to mere messengers. Your servants venture to persist in declining."
>
> The messenger [of the host] again replies: "My unworthy prince persists in saying the wine is of no quality, and he sends me to urge his invitation on you."
>
> They then answer: "As we have failed to secure permission to decline, dare we do other than accept?"

From this brief exchange we can discern rules of decorum that would later become standardized within the monastery. These unspoken rules include the deprecation of anything referring to one's personal estate, as well as a pattern of two humble refusals to attend an affair, under the pretense of unworthiness, followed by a seemingly reluctant acquiescence. An example of these highly rhetorical exchanges, so typical of Confucian etiquette, occurs in *Chanyuan qinggui* when a candidate humbly refuses to accept an abbacy out of respect for the soliciting monastery. Only after the envoys come with a third pressing invitation does the abbot accept the new appointment.[279]

According to *Chanyuan qinggui*, members of the Sangha were instructed on how to bow properly and where to walk during a tea ceremony, both exercises in humility. Once again, we find this same sense of protocol described in *Yili*. During a tea ceremony held in the Sangha hall, the master of ceremonies (*xing fashi ren;* literally, "the person who presides over the service")[280] performs the ritual in the following manner:[281]

After the midday meal, the bell is struck in front of the Sangha hall. Everyone is seated, and the master of ceremonies stands on the south [left] side of the front gate, facing the Holy Monk. With his hands clasped, the master of ceremonies slowly bows and, leaving his position, comes up to the Holy Monk and again bows. Having done this, he stands before the incense burner, bows, opens the incense case, and with his left hand lifts up the incense. Having completed this, he steps back slightly, bows again, goes to the rear door, and bows to the guest of honor. He then turns to the south, approaches the Holy Monk, and bows. He turns north, bows to the abbot, circumambulates the hall, and goes to the first seat on the north [right] side of the rear door. Bending his body, he bows, moves to the first seat on the south [left] side and bows again. If the master of ceremonies moves to the outside section of the hall, he should bow first to the right-hand section then to the left, reenter the hall, and approach the Holy Monk. Once he has done this, he bows, returns to his original position, bows again, and remains standing with hands clasped.

The same meticulous courtesy is apparent in this excerpt describing the offering of wine to a guest of honor from the chapter "The Banquet" in *Yili:*[282]

The master of ceremonies walks to where he can wash his cup and stands to the south of the vessel, facing northwest. The guest of honor then descends, and, standing to the west of the westernmost steps, faces east. The master of ceremonies then begs pardon for the undeserved honor of his company, and the guest replies in the proper fashion. Then the master of ceremonies, facing north, washes his hands and, sitting down, takes the drinking cup and washes it. The guest advances slightly and declines the honor [of accepting the drink]. The master of ceremonies, still sitting, places the drinking cup in the basket and, rising, responds with the appropriate words, whereupon the guest returns to his seat. When the master of ceremonies finishes the washing, the guest, with a salute, ascends [the platform] followed by the master of ceremonies. The guest bows in acknowledgment of the washing, and the master of ceremonies, standing on the guest's right, lays down the drinking cup and responds with a bow.

Clearly, the protocol for the tea ceremony depicted in Buddhist codes reflects the practices described in Confucian works, which, in turn, stem from the rituals carried out in the imperial court and among families of nobility. In fact, a great deal of monastic ritual may have been taken directly from the highest levels of Chinese society, as many of the most renowned monks were sponsored by the court or by aristocrats and perhaps influenced by their benefactors. At the same time, members of the gentry often paid social calls or extended visits to monasteries, and their presence may have had an effect on the customs of daily monastic life.

Chinese Deity Worship and Festival Celebrations

Chanyuan qinggui indicates that on the day before the summer retreat (the fourteenth day of the fourth month), monks were summoned before the earth hall for chanting. They prayed for the protection of the Flame Emperor *(yandi),* one of the traditional Chinese deities. The rector led the chanting with the following words: "I venture to say, the summer breeze now blows through the fields and the Flame Emperor reigns over the region. When the Dharma King [the Buddha] 'prohibits the feet' *(jinzu)* [that is, prohibits traveling during the summer retreat], it is time for the children of Śākya[monks and nuns] to protect all living creatures. I respectfully summon the assembly to gather solemnly at the spirit shrine *(lingci)* to chant the great name of ten thousand virtues *(wande hongming)* and transfer the merit to the rulers of all the halls, and to pray that they protect the monastery, allowing for a peaceful retreat."[283]

On the day before the closing of the summer retreat (the fourteenth day of the seventh month), the monks prayed to the White Emperor *(baidi)*. They chanted, "The golden wind now blows through the fields and the White Emperor reigns over the region. When the King of Enlightenment [the Buddha] brings the summer retreat to a close, it is the time of the completion of the Dharma year. We have reached the ninth ten-day period of the summer[284] without difficulty and all the assembly are safe. Let us chant the great names of all the Buddhas and repay our indebtedness to the rulers of all the halls."[285]

The Flame Emperor and the White Emperor are both included among the Five Heavenly Emperors *(wu tiandi)* worshiped by the Chinese since ancient times. *Zhouli* mentions them: "The platforms for worshiping the Five Emperors were erected in the outskirts of the city."[286] The annotator Zheng Xuan provided this explanation:[287]

> The Blue Emperor is named Ling Weiyang and is also worshiped under the name Taihao; the Red Emperor is named Chi Biaonu and is also worshiped under the name Yandi; the Yellow Emperor is named Han Shuniu and is also worshiped under the name Huangdi; the White Emperor is named Bai Zhaoju and is also worshiped under the name Shaohao; the Black Emperor is named Zhi Guangji and is also worshiped under the name Zhuanxu.[288]

Taihao (Fuxi shi), Yandi (Shennong shi), Huangdi, Shaohao, and Zhuanxu are the legendary emperors of ancient China. An annotation to *Zhouli* written by Jia Gongyan gives a list of the five emperors and their directions: the Blue Emperor is in the east; the Red Emperor is in the south; the Yellow Emperor is in the center; the White Emperor is in the west; and the Black Emperor is in the north.[289] The South Emperor is in charge of the summer period. According to *Liji*, throughout the summer months the reigning ruler is the Flame Emperor and its attending spirit is Zhurong;[290] autumn is the time of Shaohao, the White Emperor;[291] winter is ruled over by the Yellow Emperor;[292] and the months of spring are the time of Dahao (Taihao).[293]

In addition to its own religious holidays, the Buddhist community celebrated the popular secular festivals. In Chinese tradition the lunar New Year[294] and the winter solstice are major festivals. The excitement surrounding the New Year celebrations in the Song capital is recorded in *Dongjing menghua lu:* "The Kaifeng government suspended its usual prohibition of gambling for the duration of three days. Starting at daybreak, the gentry and common people greeted and congratulated each other. In the streets and lanes, people sang and shouted out their bets, which could be anything—food, livestock, fruit, nuts, or even charcoal."[295] The winter solstice was an even greater event: "The winter solstice celebrations in the eleventh lunar month reached their peak in the capital. People would spend their savings or even take out loans just to appear in new clothes for the holiday. They would prepare feasts, worship ancestors, gamble (the government again suspended its prohibition), and greet each other with congratulations as during the New Year."[296]

Buddhist monasteries adopted these two traditional events and in conjunction with the commencement and closing of the summer retreat, they constituted the four major monastic festivals. Not surprisingly, the celebration of the two traditional holidays within the monastery differed from what occurred in the streets of the capital. During the day, the abbot held a tea or sweetened-drink ceremony for the administrators and the chief officers and invited the assembly. The junior monks and other novices went to greet the abbot before the early meal, while the rest of the assembly met him after his sermon in the Dharma hall. At day's end, all Sangha members followed the abbot as he visited the various halls.[297]

Other traditional Chinese festivals, such as *Duanwu* (the fifth day of the fifth month),[298] *Qixi* (the seventh day of the seventh month),[299] and *Chongjiu* (the ninth day of the ninth month),[300] were celebrated at the monastery.[301] On these days the temples held eggplant-roasting feasts. The monastic code *Chixiu Baizhang qinggui* informs us that on the day of the *Duanwu* festival, the temple served specially made calamus herbal tea *(changpu cha)* in the Sangha hall, and *zhuyu cha* was served on the day of *Chongjiu*.[302]

Conclusion

In translating and annotating *Chanyuan qinggui*, I have found that most of the elements of the work reach back much further in time than scholars have suspected. The purpose of my extensive annotations is to demonstrate the great degree to which the Vinaya serves as a source for *Chanyuan qinggui* and other Chan regulations. For example, the Chan emphasis on seniority of ordination as the key factor in determining seating arrangements or the order of monks during their various activities has its origin in the Vinaya. The use of special objects to maintain vigilance during meditation in the Sangha hall and of a signal instrument to summon the assembly are both found in the Vinaya. Chan rituals and ceremonies such as the auctioning of a deceased monk's possessions, the offering of food to all sentient beings, and the burning of incense while circumambulating the hall, likewise all have clear precedents in the Vinaya. Even the use of four nesting bowls at mealtimes, often thought to be unique to the Chan monastery, can be found in the original Vinaya texts.

Many of the Chan practices described in *Chanyuan qinggui* can also be linked to the Lü school. The works of Lü master Daoxuan reveal that some important Chan customs were commonly practiced in the Lü school and had been carried out for much longer than historians had assumed. Because Daoxuan himself was largely preserving practices codified more than two hundred years before by Daoan, through his works we can discern indirectly how many Chan monastic practices, many of them still carried out today, can be traced as far back as the fourth century. We see, for example, that the octagonal hammer with its pillar stand, which sits in the center of the Sangha hall in Chan monasteries, is not a Chan invention, but a device used long before by Daoxuan, who, in turn, inherited it from Daoan. The five contemplations and other verses chanted by Chan monks during the Tang and Song are described in Daoxuan's *Xingshi chao*, and these, too, can be traced back to Daoan's time.

Much of this information contradicts longstanding ideas about the role of *Chanyuan qinggui* in the Chan school. I am in agreement with many modern scholars who have challenged the belief that Baizhang's work signaled an era of Chan independence. I do not, however, share some of their other conclusions, which are based on insufficient evidence. A few have argued that the Chan school did not come into being with Baizhang's code and that its customs and traditions, many of which are found in the early records of the Tiantai school, predate any alleged innovation by Baizhang. Having thus downplayed the importance of Baizhang's work from an evolutionary perspective, these scholars go on to deny the existence of any monastic code written by him, basing their arguments on the fact that his code is neither mentioned in the historical documents of the time, nor in the works of his disciples or contemporaries. In contradistinction to this conclusion, I argue that an absence of evidence is not in itself evidence of an absence, and by way of analogy I cite the case of Zongze, whose authorship of *Chanyuan qinggui* is incontrovertible, despite the fact that the code is not mentioned in any of the numerous documents concerned with his life and work.

While the methodological focus of scholars who argue that Baizhang's code never existed has centered on a broad comparison of Chan and Tiantai texts, I have endeavored to examine Chan regulations in light of Chinese Vinaya translations and commentaries. Since early historians viewed Chan codes as a declaration of independence from the Lü school, I have attempted to examine the differences and similarities between these two schools. My method, therefore, has been to trace the regulations and practices laid out in *Chanyuan qinggui* back to the first Chinese translations of Vinaya texts and to works written by those Chinese monks prior to Baizhang who advocated adherence to the Vinaya monastic practices. My aim in consulting the earliest documents available was to provide a detailed comparative analysis of *Chanyuan qinggui*.

It is crucial to note that *Chanyuan qinggui* and the Chan regulations that followed it also included elements foreign to the original Vinaya texts, elements incorporated from Chinese governmental policies and traditional Chinese etiquette. As such, an examination of the Song legal edict *Qingyuan fa* can provide us with a greater understanding of travel permit restrictions, the sale of tonsure and master title certificates, the conversion of private monasteries to public, and the election of the abbots in *Chanyuan qinggui*. Popular Chinese customs also made their mark on *Chanyuan qinggui:* protocol associated with the Chan tea ceremony, for example, is by and large a direct imitation of the model presented in the Confucian *Book of Rites*. The physical layout of the abbot's quarters and the Dharma hall, as well as the ritual associated with the abbot's sermon in the Dharma hall are plainly appropriated from the customs and practices of China's imperial courts. In short, after a thorough investigation of Chan monastic rules, we gain a clear sense of both their Vinaya origins and their adaptation of Chinese cultural and social practices.

PART TWO

Text

3.

The Author and His Work

Zongze

Chanyuan qinggui was compiled during the Northern Song (960–1127) by the Chan monk Changlu Zongze (?–1107?),[1] about whom very little is known for certain. The earliest biography of Zongze is found in *Jianzhong Jingguo xudeng lu*, which, although written during his lifetime, yields few biographical details. All later Chan texts that mention Zongze rely on this first text and offer no new information. Pure Land texts portray Zongze in quite a different light, but they too offer little biographical information. Following the same pattern used in the Chan works, the earliest of the Pure Land texts to mention Zongze, *Lushan lianzong baojian*, establishes a model that all the subsequent Pure Land works follow. Considering the Chan and Pure Land works together, we can construct a portrait of Zongze, from which three important facts emerge: first, he was a member of the Yunmen lineage, the most influential Chan school of the time; second, he was a learned advocate of Pure Land thought and practice and proclaimed by Zongxiao (1151–1214), the author of *Lebang wenlei*, as Pure Land's fifth great teacher after Huiyuan, the school's first patriarch; third, he is remembered for his exalted sense of filial piety.

Zongze lost his father (whose surname was Sun) when he was young, so he was raised by his mother, who depended on a brother for support. After an early period of Confucian studies, Zongze turned to Buddhism at the urging of Yuanfeng Qingman, a monk in the Yunmen lineage. At the age of twenty-nine, Zongze was tonsured at the Yunmen temple of Fayun Faxiu (1027–1090) and later studied under Changlu Yingfu (no dates available), Faxiu's Dharma brother. For many years Zongze was unable to make any significant progress toward enlightenment, until one day, just as he was stepping onto the monastery stairs, he experienced a sudden awakening, a breakthrough that he described in a poem that won the immediate approbation of his teacher, Yingfu.

The following genealogy shows Zongze as a member of the seventh generation after the founding of the Yunmen sect:

Yunmen Wenyan, founder (864–949)
|
Xianglin Chengyuan (908–987)
|
Zhimen Guangzuo (d. 1031)
|
Xuedou Chongxian (980–1052)
|
Tianyi Yihuai (993–1064)
|
Changlu Yingfu (n.d.)
|
Changlu Zongze (?–1107?)

Given patronage by the government official Yang Wei (1044–1112) and favored by the court, Zongze was presented with the honorific title of *Cijue Dashi* (Master of Compassion and Enlightenment). In his preface to the collection of Zongze's writings *Chanlu Ze Chanshi wenji xu*, Yuanzhao describes Zongze as having presided over the abbacies of three separate monasteries[2] but does not specify which three. In *Yakuchū Zennen Shingi*, the annotations to *Chanyuan qinggui*, Japanese scholars have identified these three monasteries, in chronological order, as Hongji Chanyuan (in present-day Zhengding county, Hebei province), Chongfu Chansi, and Changlusi on the Yangtze River.[3] But several questions arise when one examines these assertions more closely. First, the Japanese scholar Shiina Kōyū has asserted that the gazetteer of Liuhe county identifies Chongfu Chansi and Changlusi as one and the same monastery, located in present-day Liuhe county, Jiangsu province.[4] If we take this statement to be accurate, that is, if these two monasteries are one and the same, there still remains the question of the identity of the third temple mentioned by Yuanzhao. After closely studying the contents of the Liuhe County Gazetteer on which Shiina bases his claim, I found no such correlation of the Chongfu Chansi and Changlusi monasteries. It may be that the name Chongfu Chansi refers to a separate temple, but this remains unresolved.

The chronology proposed by *Yakuchū Zennen Shingi* is also problematic. In some of Zongze's biographies, we are told that from 1086 to 1094 Zongze resided in the Changlusi, where he is known to have furnished a home for his mother in the east room next to the abbot's quarters. Later, during the compilation of *Chanyuan qinggui* in 1103 (or perhaps as early as 1099), Zongze was serving as abbot of Hongji Chanyuan. This last date would lead us to believe that Zongze's term as abbot at Honji Chanyuan was chronologically later than his abbacy at Changlusi and was most likely his last abbacy, for, as we will soon see, Zongze could not have passed away long after 1103. However, in his preface to the *Golden Light Sutra (Jinguangming jing xu),*[5] written at the early date of 1081, Zongze identifies himself already as the abbot of Hongji Chanyuan. If we assume this date to be correct, then Zongze must have been the abbot of the Hongji Chanyuan in 1081—that is, *before* his abbacy at the Changlu Temple. It may be that Zongze served twice as abbot of Hongji Chanyuan, before and after his abbacy at Changlusi, a hypothesis that would make Yuanzhao's mention of three abbacies a slightly erroneous summation. Yet it may simply be that the title "Abbot of Hongji Chanyuan" was no more than a later scribal addition to the original 1081 document, a retrospective "correction."

While the exact dates of Zongze's life are unknown, the biography of Xuechao Fayi (1084–1158)[6] informs us that Fayi studied with the elder Zongze when he was seventeen, that is, in the year 1100. Fayi writes that after a brief period, Zongze passed away and Fayi left to study with Chan master Tongzhao in 1107. Thus we can deduce that Zongze's death must have occurred at some point between 1103, when he is known to have been working on *Chanyuan qinggui,* and roughly 1107, when Fayi left to study elsewhere. This conclusion is also supported by the preface to Zongze's discourse record, *Cijue Chanshi yulu,* which was compiled as a posthumous tribute by Zongze's disciples in 1109.[7]

The existing information is not completely clear as to Zongze's birthplace. Chan literature asserts that Zongze was born in Luozhou Yongnian (present-day Hebei province);[8] Pure Land texts, edited later, state that he was born in Xiangyang. Among the Chan texts, *Jianzhong Jingguo xudeng lu* was written in 1101 by Foguo Weibai, a contemporary of Zongze and the Dharma heir of Faxiu. As Weibai was closest to Zongze in terms of time and Dharma lineage, we can perhaps give the most credence to his version of the facts. Furthermore, Luozhou is corroborated by Yuanzhao in his preface to Zongze's analects, written soon after Zongze's death.

Although Zongze belonged to the lineage of Chan Buddhism, he became widely known as an advocate of the Pure Land school. He was representative of an emerging trend that blended Chan and Pure Land teachings, a phenomenon which became prevalent during the Song era. Zongze held that "the recitation of Amitābha Buddha's name does not hinder the contemplation of Chan; just as the contemplation of Chan does not hinder the recitation of Amitābha Buddha's name. While these two ways may seem divergent, ultimately they are one and the same path." Zongze condemned the mutual casting of aspersions by advocates of the Chan and Pure Land schools, asserting that "Pure Land is in one's own mind and Amitābha Buddha is in one's own self-nature"[9] and that "to recite the name Amitābha is to think of him without thought, to be born in the Pure Land without rebirth."[10] Thus the true samadhi, or focal point, of Pure Land thought is to be "one who recites Amitābha's name the entire day but does not shun the principle of nonthought [that is, nonrecitation]; one who eagerly awaits rebirth in the Pure Land but does not shun the teaching of nonbirth."[11] Within his Chan monastery, Zongze organized a subgroup under the name *Lianhua shenghui* (Holy Assembly of the Lotus) for those dedicated to the recitation of Amitābha's name. We can assume that Zongze took as his model the organization established by Huiyuan, who founded a society for his students dedicated to the practices of Pure Land. However, one cannot pinpoint an exact precedent for Zongzhe's more general ideas of Chan and Pure Land, since copractices such as this were fast becoming the hallmark of Song Buddhism, especially within the Fayan and Yunmen lineages.

The section of Zongze's *Chanyuan qinggui* devoted to clerical funerals reveals the influence of Pure Land thought and practice. In this chapter, the dying monk is encouraged to dedicate himself to the recitation of Amitābha's name and vow to be reborn in the western Pure Land,[12] and all the funeral rituals are accompanied by the ten recitations of Amitābha's name *(shinian)*.[13] Those who chant before the dying monk are told to "begin with the praising of Amitābha's name," after which the text goes on to describe the method of chanting: "The rector then announces to the assembly, 'For Bhikṣu X we chant at length the names of Amitābha Buddha and the bodhisattvas in the western Pure Land, that is, the four holy names.' The merit of the chant is then transferred to the dying monk."

Zongze teaches his followers to recite Amitābha's name continuously, either verbally or through silent concentration, throughout the entire day. In his essays *Lianhua shenghui luwen* (Essay on the Holy Assembly of the Lotus) and *Nianfo fangtui fangbian wen* (Essay on the Recitation of the Buddha's Name as the Means to Avoid Regression), he urges monks to recite the name of Amitābha one hundred, one thousand, or as many as ten thousand times in succession, channeling the merit gained by this practice toward being reborn in the Pure Land.[14]

Biographies of Zongze[15] remark that the master's dedication to the Pure Land was so intense that even bodhisattvas attested to it. Reportedly Zongze once dreamt that a thirty-year-old man came to him, asking to join his Great Lotus Assembly, and that when Zongze asked his name, he replied "Puhui." After he had registered for the society, the young man added that his brother would also like to join. When Zongze inquired as to the brother's name, he answered "Puxian" and suddenly disappeared. Upon awakening, Zongze informed the senior monks, who explained to him that in the *Avataṃsaka Sutra* bodhisattvas named Puhui and Puxian make a vow to propagate the Dharma.[16] With great joy, Zongze interpreted his dream as a sign of encouragement and assistance from these two bodhisattvas, and accordingly, from that time forward, he listed Puhui and Puxian as the leaders of his Holy Assembly of the Lotus.

Zongze, in his assimilation of Chan and Pure Land ideas, was part of a larger trend that became one of the most widespread phenomena of Song-era Buddhism. When Zongze opines "Pure Land is one's own mind and Amitābha is our own self-nature," he is actually quoting from the earlier work of Yongming Yanshou (904–975), the pioneer advocate of Chan and Pure Land integration in the Song period. In his *Wanshan tonggui ji*, Yanshou explains the sentence "Pure Land is in one's own mind" by citing *Da fangguang Rulai busiyi jingjie jing:*[17]

> All the Buddhas in all three ages do not have corporeal existence, but rather to know them depends on one's own mind. Once a bodhisattva can realize that all the Buddhas and Dharmas are merely the "measure of the mind" *(xinliang),* he will attain the state of "great endurance to follow the right direction" *(suishun ren),* and he will enter the first stage in which he abandons his body and is instantly reborn in [Akṣobhya's] World of Wondrous Joy *(miaoxi)* in the east, or in [Amitābha's] Pure Land of Bliss in the west. Therefore, one must recognize the nature and power of the mind before he can reach the realization that "Pure Land is in one's own mind."

Yanshou, like Zongze, advocated the practice of ten recitations of Amitābha's name. He argued that the merit of the ten recitations can extinguish a lifetime of bad karma. Citing from sutra and commentary, he explained the importance of this ritual with an analogy: one hundred large stones may not sink into the ocean if they are put onboard a great ship, but even the tiniest of pebbles, unsupported, will sink into the water; similarly, one who has accumulated bad karma and does not know to recite Amitābha's name will surely fall into hell. Likewise, Yanshou taught that concentrating on a noble thought at the moment of death was enough to eradicate even the greatest amount of bad karma.[18] His assertion that "Pure Land is in one's own mind" *(weixin jingtu)* and his teaching of the ten recitations of Amitābha's name became the hallmarks of the many Song monks who sought to assimilate Pure Land thought into the Chan teachings. Among these were a great many members of the Fayan and Yunmen sects. Yanshou himself belonged to the Fayan sect, whereas Zongze was of the Yunmen lineage. Even Zongze's predecessor, Tianyi Yihuai,[19] and Yihuai's disciple, Huilin Zongben,[20] were renowned for their Chan and Pure Land practices, indicating a long line of ideological succession.

The assimilation of Pure Land into Chan Buddhism was adopted by monks of other Chan sects, including Wuxin (1044–1115) of the Huanglong line[21] and Zhenxie Qingliao (1088–1151) of the Caodong line.[22] In the end, Chan monks were not the only ones to assimilate Pure Land practices into their tradition. Monks of the Tiantai school, such as Siming Zhili, Zunshi, and Zongxiao, as well as many in the Lü school, such as Yuanzhao and Jile Jiedu, were endeavoring to make the same kind of systemic integrations.[23]

The Pure Land practitioner Zongxiao is often cited as having referred to Zongze as the fifth great teacher after Huiyuan, the first patriarch of the Pure Land school—an accolade that should be regarded with some skepticism. In the past, scholars have been apt to paraphrase this description too loosely, designating Zongze as the fifth patriarch of the Pure Land lineage. Such a reading is erroneous on two counts. Zongxiao calls Zongze a "great teacher," not a "patriarch." Furthermore, whether teacher or patriarch, Zongze is the fifth *after* Huiyuan, not including Huiyuan.[24] Thus it can only be correct to say that Zongxiao identifies Zongze as the sixth great teacher of the Pure Land school.[25]

Zongze was known to be intensely devoted to his mother. In his biography, it is recorded that after accepting the abbacy of the

Changlu Temple, he invited his mother to live in the chamber adjoining his. Zongze cared for his mother's physical well-being and her spiritual health as well, encouraging her to dedicate herself to the recitation of the Amitābha Buddha's name. After seven years, his mother peacefully passed away, appearing the day before her death in her son's dreams to tell him that she had a vision in which ten nuns were waiting to receive her. In the dream, Zongze reassured his mother that this was a sure sign of her rebirth in the Pure Land.[26]

To express his ideas on the subject of filial piety, Zongze wrote an essay consisting of one hundred and twenty articles entitled *Quanxiao wen* (Admonition of Filial Piety), in which he distinguishes between notions of "mundane filial piety" and "supermundane filial piety." He explained that attending to a parent's material welfare is "mundane filial piety," whereas attending to the spiritual education of a parent (teaching him or her to recite the name of Amitābha and to focus on being reborn in the Pure Land) is "supermundane filial piety." Zongze asserts that the former is the lesser of the two, for it benefits the parent only for the duration of one lifetime.[27] He instructed his readers to arrange for their parents' last moments: to prepare beforehand a prayer describing their good deeds, which is to be read to them frequently in time of illness to fill their minds with serenity and joy. During the final moments, the image of Amitābha should be placed in front of them and incense should be burned while they lie or sit facing west. They should then be led in the chanting of Amitābha's name in time to the striking of a small bell, with no other cries or laments to interrupt their concentration.[28]

Chanyuan qinggui is the only complete work by Zongze still extant. In 1096 Zongze compiled a four-fascicle liturgical text pertaining to the Water-land ritual *(Shuilu fahui)*, only the preface of which remains.[29] As was the custom, his discourse record was written down by his attendants, under the title *Cijue Chanshi yulu*. This work is known to have existed as late as the first half of this century, although its present whereabouts are unknown.[30] Zongze's analects, *Weijiang ji*, have also been lost but are often quoted in other works, with the result that much of its content has been preserved indirectly.[31] Yuanzhao's preface to the collection of Zongze's writings, as mentioned before, has come down to us, and it is this preface that describes the writings as a collection of didactic essays intended for both monastics and the laity. Finally, Zongze wrote a great number of essays on Pure Land teachings that were published separately and have largely been preserved in the Pure Land canon.

Existing Editions

In the section of *Chanyuan qinggui* that I have called "Chanting" *(nian-song)*, Zongze gives the time of his writing as the second year of Yuanfu (1099).[32] The work's preface is dated 1103, the second year of Chongning, which has led some to call this prefatory work *Chong-ning qinggui*. Thus we can say with some certainty that *Chanyuan qinggui* must have been completed some time between 1099 and 1103. Not long after its completion, still early in the twelfth century, *Chanyuan qinggui* was taken to Japan, where the following six editions are known to exist:[33]

1. Kyū Iwasaki Bunko edition, preserved in Tōyō Bunko
2. Gozan edition, preserved in Daitōkyū Bunko
3. Kanazawa Bunko edition
4. Hōei edition, reprinted in 1709
5. Kansei edition, reprinted with punctuation in 1796
6. Kōrai edition, in the possession of Professor Kosaka Kiyū of Komazawa University

The Kyū Iwazaki Bunko and Gozan editions are all but identical in content, as are the Kansei and Hōei editions. Thus we can identify four primary editions: the Kyū Iwazaki Bunkō, the Kanazawa Bunko, the Hōei, and the Kōrai. Versions 1, 3, and 4 are known collectively as the "circulating edition" *(genkōhon)*, and all three are based on the same text, *Chongdiao buzhu Chanyuan qinggui* (Reprint of the Revised *Chanyuan qinggui*), a copy completed by Yu Xiang in the second year of the Jiatai era in the Southern Song (1202).[34] The Kōrai edition is a copy of a version reprinted in the second year of the Baoyou era (1254), which in turn was known to be a close copy of a version completed in the first year of the Zhenghe era (1111), that is, only eight years after the first publication of *Chanyuan qinggui*. As the Kōrai edition is based (albeit indirectly) on the version closest in time to the original work, we can consider it closest in content to the first *Chanyuan qinggui*. After comparing the Kōrai edition with the "circulating edition" based on the 1202 reprint, we find differences of not only vocabulary, but also overall structure.[35]

Five supplementary essays appear in the "circulating edition" but not in the Kōrai: *Zuochan yi* (Manual of Meditation),[36] *Zijingwen* (Essay on Self-Admonition), *Yibai ershi wen* (One Hundred Twenty Questions for [Self-Reflection]), *Quan tanxin* (Admonition to the Laity), and *Zhaiseng yi* (Method for the Sponsoring of the Monastic Feast). The authenticity of some of these essays can be attested to by

Zongze's contemporary Yuanzhao. Not long after Zongze's death, Yuanzhao wrote a preface to Zongze's analects, in which he listed Zongze's writings, among them three of the above five articles: *Zuochan yi, Zijingwen,* and *Yibai ershi wen.* He does not list *Quan tanxin* and *Zaiseng yi.* However, a text entitled *Zaijia xingyi* (Etiquette for the Laity) is included, which, judging by its title, is probably very close to or even identical to *Quan tanxin.*

Two basic explanations for the discrepancy between the "circulating edition" and the Kōrai edition are possible: either the five supplementary essays were added to the 1202 reprint (the Southern Song edition) or the compilers of the text that became the Kōrai edition chose to omit the essays at an early stage. Kosaka Kiyū believes that the five essays were included at the time Zongze finished the compilation in 1103.[37] Yanagida Seizan, however, thinks that at that time one of the five, *Zuochan yi,* was not included in *Chanyuan qinggui.*[38] He believes that Eisai's (1141–1215) citations of Zongze's *Zuochan yi* were based on *Dazang yilan ji,* a text compiled by Chen Shi prior to 1157 that includes abbreviated excerpts from *Zuochan yi.*[39]

But when we compare Eisai's citations of *Zuochan yi*[40] with the *Zuochan yi* found in the "circulating edition,"[41] we find that the former omits a number of details concerning meditation posture contained in the latter. Obviously the version of *Chanyuan qinggui* seen by Eisai during his travels in China between 1187 and 1191 would have predated the 1202 reprint on which the "circulating edition" is based. The textual variances between these two versions of *Zuochan yi* can be explained in one of three ways: Eisai's citations represent the original text of the essay to which more details were added for the 1202 reprint; the citations themselves are an intentional abridgement of the original; or Eisai based his work on some unknown intermediary text that drew selectively from the original *Zuochan yi.* Yanagida believes that *Dazang yilan ji* may have been the intermediary text, since it would have been available to Eisai at the time of his writing.

However, when we compare three versions of *Zuochan yi*—Eisai's citations, the version in the "circulating edition," and the version in *Dazang yilan ji*[42]—we see that Eisai's citations are far more abbreviated in nature than *Dazang yilan ji,* and that the section concerning meditation posture missing from Eisai is included in *Dazang yilan ji.* It is possible that Eisai simply drew directly from *Zuochan yi,* for Eisai was not averse to summarizing the contents of an original document. Scholars question whether Zongze's *Zuochan yi* ever circulated independently.[43] Since we are not sure whether Eisai cited *Zuochan yi* directly from *Chanyuan qinggui* or from *Dazang yilan*, we cannot conclude that *Zuochan yi*, along with the other four essays, was not collected in the original version of *Chanyuan qinggui* before the 1202 version. The omission of five essays from the Kōrai edition remains unexplained.

The only commentary on *Chanyuan qinggui* is a recent work entitled *Yakuchū Zennen shingi*, written by Kagamishima Genryū, Satō Tatsugen, and Kosaka Kiyū. This commentary relies on the Hōei edition and makes note of any variations (such as alternate characters) in editions 1, 2, 3, and 6 listed above. For my own translation of *Chanyuan qinggui*, I am heavily indebted to this valuable comparative analysis.

Synopsis

The text of *Chanyuan qinggui* is divided into a preface and seven fascicles. The brief preface states the text's purpose: to establish a complete, definitive set of rules for monasteries of the Chan school of Buddhism. It bemoans the proliferation of different sects of Buddhism within China and the numerous and sometimes conflicting sets of rules accompanying the development of each different sect. *Chanyuan qinggui* is an attempt to compile a set of rules that encompasses not only practices and laws familiar to its author, but also those attested to by "virtuous and knowledgeable monks."

Of the seven fascicles that follow, the first is the longest. It comprises the rules for the most basic activities of the monastic life, focusing on regulations that a monk first entering a monastery would need to know right away. Foremost among these are the guidelines for receiving and upholding the precepts. The longest section in the fascicle is a detailed description of the protocols at mealtimes, a tremendously important part of everyday life in the monastery. Other sections in Fascicle 1 enumerate a monk's belongings (clothing, bowls, and so on) and the proper procedures for packing and carrying them; the protocols for taking up permanent and temporary residence within a monastery; and proper behavior at tea ceremonies and when approaching the monastery's abbot for instruction.

With Fascicle 2, the focus shifts to more specific topics. It includes the correct procedures for announcing and giving sermons, initiating chanting sessions, opening and closing the summer retreat, and receiving venerable visitors. It also contains the regulations for making appointments to administrative offices within the monastery. Fascicle 3 outlines the responsibilities of several of these offices, including those of the prior, the rector, the cook, and the director of the library. Fascicle 4 continues in this vein, covering the duties of the lesser offices.

Fascicle 5 begins with the description of the responsibilities of fundraisers and the procedures for resigning from administrative offices. The bulk of this fascicle, however, is devoted to the procedures for conducting various types of tea ceremonies. Fascicle 6 also discusses tea ceremony protocol before turning to other activities, such as burning incense, giving thanks, reading the sutra, and delivering letters. Fascicle 7 covers proper use of the toilet, funerals, and appointments to honorary positions. Lastly, it addresses the office of the abbot in detail, an administrative post not covered along with the others in Fascicles 3 and 4. Separate sections outline the procedures for a new abbot's entrance into a monastery and an abbot's funeral and retirement.

4.

Chanyuan qinggui
in Translation

Preface

Compiled by Zongze, Master Chuanfa Cijue, and Abbot of the Hongji Public Chan Monastery in the Zhending Prefecture.[1]

[3] The following is in regard to Chan monastic precedents. Although in principle two different sets of Vinaya should not exist, there is a particular tradition[2] in the school of Chan[3] that stands apart from the general, common regulations. This tradition holds that for those individuals who enjoy the fruits of Dharma on the way to enlightenment, who are extraordinarily pure and exalted, the general precepts need not apply. But for those monks who have not attained such lofty qualities, neglecting the Vinaya is much like coming up against a wall[4] and, it can be said, this neglect will result in a loss of respect in the eyes of others. Therefore, we have consulted with virtuous and knowledgeable monks[5] and have collected texts from all directions in order to complement what we already see and hear,[6] listing everything in outline form with subtitles. Alas, the phenomenon of Shaolin[7] can already be compared to the wounding of healthy flesh that grows infected.[8] The introduction of new regulations and the establishment of Chan monasteries by the Chan Master Baizhang can be regarded similarly. Further problems have been created by the spread of monasteries to all regions, numerous even to the point of intolerability. Regulations have expanded accordingly, causing complications and problems to increase as well. However, in order to sanctify the temple and raise the Dharma banner[9] there should not be a lack of regulations in the monastery. Regarding the bodhisattva threefold pure precepts[10] and the seven categories[11] of the śrāvaka precepts,[12] one might ask why the established laws must focus on such complicated details. The Buddha established new teachings only when a given situation required it. It is our wish that the novice pay great heed to these regulations, and as for virtuous senior monks, we hope to have the fortune to present these rules to you for your approval. This preface written on the fifteenth day of the eighth month in the second year of Chongning [1103 c.e.].

Prefatory Note to the Reprint: When this text was first published it gained great popularity. Unfortunately, the woodblock characters have since been worn down to the point of illegibility. We now present for circulation a new carving using larger characters. We hope that collectors of such texts will grant us the honor of inspecting this new edition. Written in the *renxu* year of Jiatai [1202 c.e.] by Yuba[13] to propagate the teaching and to sincerely solicit comment.

Fascicle One

Reception of the Precepts

[13] All the Buddhas of the three ages[1] say, "One must leave home and join a monastic order to attain Buddhahood." The twenty-eight patriarchs of the Western Heaven and the six patriarchs of the Land of the Tang[2] who transmitted the seal of the Buddha mind were all sramanas.[3] If one solemnly purifies oneself by observing the Vinaya, then one can become an influential paragon of virtue in all Three Realms.[4] Therefore, both meditation and the quest for the truth[5] begin with receiving the precepts. If one cannot abstain from error and avert evil, how can one become a Buddha or a patriarch?

To receive the precepts, the future monk must prepare three robes,[6] bowls, a sitting mat,[7] and new, clean clothes. If he has no new clothes, he should at least wash all his clothes before ascending the ordination platform. It is not permissible to borrow the robes or the bowls.[8] During the ordination ceremony, he must concentrate and should not let his mind wander to other subjects. For someone who is on the way to Buddhahood, imitating the manner of the Buddha, upholding the Buddha's precepts, and receiving the Buddha's joy[9] are not trivial, insignificant matters. How can he undertake these activities lightly? If his robes and bowls are borrowed, then, although he ascends the ordination platform to receive the precepts, he cannot truly obtain them. If he does not obtain the precepts, then all his life he will be a person without the precepts, he enters the Gate of Emptiness[10] as an impostor who usurps the donors' offerings. If beginners, who are unfamiliar with the law and precepts, are not given instructions (told not to borrow robes and bowls, and so forth) by a teacher, then they will also be caught in the trap of living as impostors. And so now, with bitter mouth, humbly imploring, I dare to wish that you will inscribe this caveat in your minds. After receiving the śrāvaka precepts, the initiates should receive the bodhisattva precepts:[11] This is the gradual path of entering the Dharma.

Upholding the Precepts

[16] After a monk has received the precepts, he must always uphold them. A monk would rather die with the law than live without the law.[12] The Hinayana precepts listed in the *Four Part Vinaya* are:[13] four "defeats,"[14] thirteen "formal meetings,"[15] two "undetermined offenses,"[16] thirty "forfeitures,"[17] ninety "expiations,"[18] four "confes-

sions,"[19] one hundred "myriad infractions to learn,"[20] and seven "methods of adjudicating disputes."[21] The Mahayana precepts in the *Brahma Net Sutra* include ten major offenses and forty-eight minor offenses.[22] Every monk must study and memorize them so he can chant them fluently. He must know what to obey and what constitutes an offense, when exceptions can or cannot be made.[23] He must follow the Golden Voice and the Holy Words given by the Buddha alone, not commonplace people. Prohibited foods should not be eaten. (For example, onions, leeks, scallions, garlic, chives,[24] wine, meat,[25] fish, rabbit, cake made with milk,[26] cheese, maggot larvae,[27] pig fat, and goat fat—all of these items should not be eaten. Even in times of sickness, a monk should sacrifice his body even to the end of his life, rather than consume wine or meat and destroy the precepts.) Nor should foods be consumed at the wrong time, that is, in the afternoon. (For example, light snacks, "medicine stone,"[28] fruit, rice soup, bean soup, and vegetable juice—any food not consumed at the midday meal or early meal[29] is considered untimely food.) The evils of wealth and sensuality are more dangerous than a poisonous snake[30] and should be greatly avoided. The monk should be compassionate and he should think of every sentient being as a newborn infant.[31] His words must be true, and his thoughts and speech should be in harmony. He must study the Mahayana teachings and develop the inspiration for great dedication and deeds. When the *śīla* are pure, that is, when the precepts are obeyed, the Dharma will become manifest. If the skin did not exist, then where would the hair be placed?[32] Therefore, in the sutra it is written that the precepts must be rigorously upheld as though one were protecting a precious gem.[33]

Preparation of Personal Effects

[20] Before a monk comes to the monastery he must prepare his personal effects:[34] a mountain hat,[35] a walking stick,[36] a precept knife,[37] a tonsure certificate canister,[38] a bag for his bowls,[39] a sack for his shoes (inside which is placed a cloth used to wipe the feet), a pillow,[40] "bell-mouth" shoes,[41] the cloth wrap used to protect the lower legs,[42] the cloths used for the front and rear knapsacks,[43] a white silk wrapping cloth,[44] a cloth belt,[45] a "pillow sack,"[46] a dust cover, a small cover made from tree oil, a larger cover made from persimmon oil,[47] a bed sheet,[48] a quilt,[49] three clean towels (one to cover the quilt, one for eating, and one for general use), a small pure water vessel,[50] a bath towel, a skirt for bathing,[51] and a lock and key for his storage compartment.[52] Possessing items such as tea vessels or additional clothing depends on the monk's financial position.

Packing One's Belongings[53]

[22] Inside the front knapsack are placed the monk's robes (which are covered with a handkerchief and wrapped in a sitting mat), the short gown,[54] a lined jacket, and a vest. These "pure" clothes are placed in the front knapsack. The rear knapsack holds all "soiled" items,[55] the bedsheet, cotton clothes, and undergarments, which should be wrapped first in the white silk cloth. Then inside the pillow sack are stuffed the bathing towel and bathing skirt. The Holy Image, the sutra, and the tea vessels are placed inside the hat.[56]

[23] To properly pack the rest of his belongings, the monk should tie his skirt over his short gown, put the front knapsack over this, and tie his pillow sack to the knapsack. Then the rear knapsack is put on, after which the bowl bag is placed over the right shoulder, hanging under the left armpit, with the mouth of the bowl against the body.[57] The shoe sack is slung over the left shoulder and hangs under the right armpit. Then the knife is inserted under the skirt below the right armpit,[58] and the certificate canister is inserted under the skirt below the left armpit. (The certificate bag [canister] is hung by a cord or a ribbon over the shoulder and fastened to the waist by a belt. It will be easier if the monk hangs, secures, and properly adjusts the bag before putting on the rear knapsack.) He then puts on and ties his cloth belt and inserts the pillow, tea canister, and water vessel under the belt to the right and left of the front knapsack.

To properly don the hat, the right hand should be placed under the brim, and the hat lifted up, turned, and placed on the head. It is best that the hat is placed level; it should not lean front to back or side to side. **[24]** To remove the hat, the right hand should be lifted up to turn the hat and lower it. The same hand is used to hold the hat by the brim and keep it by the right shoulder. The following illustrates the proper way to hold the walking stick. The handle of the stick with twigs on it is considered the "soiled head," while the end with no twigs is the "pure head."[59] This pure head should be kept in front of the body while walking and should be held in the right hand. When a monk doffs his hat, the walking stick should be in the left palm. If he should encounter someone on the road, he should use his left hand to hold the stick, take off his hat with his right hand, and pull the hat and the top of the stick close to his chest in order to bow with his hands clasped and his body slightly bent.[60] When departing from a monastery, once he has said farewell to his fellow monks, the monk may don his hat only when he is beyond the eaves of the Triple Gate.[61]

[25] When entering a monastery, a monk must doff his hat outside the eaves of the Triple Gate. He should carry his walking stick in his left hand and let the top end drop. With his right hand he should carry his hat against the front of his right shoulder. If he should encounter a fellow monk within the monastery grounds, he merely pulls his hat in front of his chest to show respect. If he is taking up residence in the monastery, he should go to the south platform (on the left side) in front of the Sangha hall.[62] There he takes off his hat and places it on the platform before putting his walking stick on the top of the end of the platform[63] with the pure head pointing to the north. He takes out his water vessel, tea canister, and pillow and places them inside the hat. Then he unties his cloth belt and also puts it inside the hat. He places the shoe sack on the floor and puts the bowl bag in front of the hat. He then unties the rear knapsack and the pillow sack and places them on the platform. He takes off his front knapsack and places it inside the hat or on top of the rear knapsack, taking out the *kāṣāya* (his three robes)[64] and the sitting mat. He places the pillow, cloth belt, pillow sack, and front knapsack into the rear knapsack and ties it shut. Having done this, he carries a clean towel and his shoe bag to the rear washstand[65] to wash his feet. He then puts on his socks and bell-mouth shoes and returns to the Sangha hall, placing the shoe bag containing the straw traveling shoes under the platform. He should use the towel to clean his hands before he puts on his *kāṣāya*. He puts his certificate of ordination inside his sleeve. He then visits the rectory[66] to meet with[67] the rector[68] and takes up residence.[69] If there is a storage compartment in the Sangha hall, the monk can collect all his luggage, place it in the compartment, and lock it, with the exception of his hat and stick, which are returned to the assembly quarters.[70] If there is no storage compartment in the Sangha hall, then, after visiting the assembly quarters for the greeting,[71] he follows the director of the assembly quarters and the chief seat of the assembly quarters,[72] who will show him where he may put his things. After meeting the chief of the assembly quarters and the chief seat, he places his bowls and quilt in the Sangha hall. His tea canister and words[73] he leaves on a desk in the assembly quarters.

Overnight Residence

[27] Once a guest monk has entered the gate of the monastery, he first inquires where the overnight quarters[74] are located. After he has entered the hall of overnight residence and unpacked, he gets himself ready[75] to see the guest quarters.[76] He announces, "Temporary visit," and the guest master[77] comes out for them to perform *chuli sanbai* to each other.[78] The guest monk's words indicating a temporary stay are: "Passing by on this occasion I am most fortunate to be met by you." The guest master's reply is: "Taking the road up mountains and across streams, you have journeyed here with great difficulty." Later the guest master goes to the hall of residence to return the courtesy[79] of the guest's visit. If the guest meets with the abbot, the guest master must still go to the guest lodging to return the courtesy. If a guest decides to take up residence on a permanent basis, after one or two days he goes to visit the rectory.

Taking Up Residence

[28] The new arrivals should get themselves ready and place their certificates inside their sleeves. (If there are more than two people arriving, the person well versed in monastic custom or senior to the others in ordination should be selected as the group leader.)[80] The newcomers then go to the rectory to meet with the rector, first finding the server[81] and having him report to the rector, saying, "New arrivals visiting." When the arrivals and the rector see each other, they do *chuli sanbai*. Once tea has been served and consumed, the newcomers stand up and step forward, saying, "We have been drawn to this monastery's spiritual tradition.[82] On this occasion we have traveled here to remain at your side, and we greatly hope for your compassion." The rector replies, "The monastery will receive many fortunes by your esteemed arrival." All the newcomers present their certificates to the rector in order of ordination seniority. Once the rector has collected the certificates, and placed them in the trunk, the arrivals *chuli* one time, saying, "On this occasion we have received many fortunes by your warm treatment and for this we owe you our gratitude." The rector bows once and replies, "The treatment here is very strict. I hope that you will let the Buddhist teaching guide your thoughts." At this time no sweetened drink[83] is served. The rector escorts the new arrivals out of his office, saying, "Please, Venerable Seniors,[84] return to the hall and take up residence."

[29] The new arrivals enter the Sangha hall through the south [lefthand] side of the front door and go before the Holy Monk,[85] with the group leader walking at the north [right] end of the procession. They stand in their positions, fully unfold their sitting mats, and bow down three times. They then pick up their sitting mats and, starting from the place of the chief seat[86] in the Sangha hall, they circumambulate the hall once, returning to the Holy Monk, before whom they bow. They then

take their seats in order, beginning with the second seat from the lead seat[87] of the platform to the south [left] of the front door. The rector records information about all the arrivals in the "platform register"[88] in order of ordination seniority. When this is finished, he has a server carrying the chest containing the certificates [30] follow him into the hall. (In some monasteries the rector first burns incense before the Holy Monk.) The new arrivals stand up and, remaining in front of the platform, bow to each other. The rector returns the certificates to them in order. He goes to the lead seat of the platform, faces southeast, and does *chuli* once. The new arrivals do the same. The rector then arranges for the monks to take up residence in order of ordination seniority and both sides perform *chuli* once to each other. The rector should always occupy the "upper arm."[89] (If the monks and the rector are standing to the north [right] of the front door, the rector faces northeast. If they are standing to the south [left] of the front door, the rector faces southeast. If they stand north of the rear door, then the rector faces northwest. If they are south of the rear door, then the rector faces southwest.) Once all the monks have taken up residence, the rector exits the hall. (In some monasteries the rector exits through the front door; in others, he exits through the rear door.) The new arrivals escort the rector out of the hall. (If the rector exits through the rear door, the new arrivals should not step beyond the threshold; if he exits through the front door, the new arrivals should escort him beyond the doorway.) Before he leaves, the rector says, "Please, Venerable Senior X, Venerable Senior Y, et cetera, go to X quarters to 'take off your robes,'[90] that is, to take your rest." He then bows and leaves.

[31] The visitors return to the assembly quarters and seek out the chief of the assembly quarters, announcing, "New arrivals visiting." Once they meet him, they do *chuli sanbai* to each other. After the tea is served, all the monks, beginning with the group leader, stand up and step forward, saying, "The rector has instructed us to enter these superior quarters and remain by your side." After this, the chief of the assembly quarters discerns all the details of their ordination seniority and assigns each of them, starting from the group leader, to a particular platform and reading desk. Then they all do *chuli* one time to each other. The newcomers stand in their positions and bow before the holy statue.[91] Next, they circumambulate the hall and seek out the chief seat. Once they have found him, everyone does *chuli sanbai* to each other. They then gather their luggage and ask the chief of the assembly quarters and chief seat to make long-term arrangements.

[32] The newcomers go to the abbot's office[92] to see the attendant[93] and, without bowing down, say, "We newcomers pay homage to the ab-

bot. We wish to trouble you, attendant, to convey this to the abbot."
(If the abbot is visiting with guests or resting, then the attendant should detain
the guests, offering them tea or sweetened drink. If there is no reason for delay,
then there is no need for tea.) The attendant **[33]** asks, "Are you, Venerable Seniors, select disciples or Dharma relatives?[94] If none of the
monks is a select disciple or Dharma relative, then all the monks enter simultaneously to meet the abbot. If some of them are select disciples, they must wait until the other newcomers have finished their
greeting before they meet with the abbot.[95] The attendant addresses
the abbot, saying: "X number of newcomers, among whom are X
number of select disciples and X number of Dharma relatives, have
come to pay homage to you." He then leads them in to see the abbot.
The newcomers do *liangzhan sanli*.[96] Those Dharma relatives who are
senior to the abbot must also do *liangzhan sanli* to the abbot as a courtesy.[97] However, the abbot should not accept this courtesy and should not do
chuli. The abbot should merely say, "Soon I will visit your hall of residence and
pay homage." The senior monks should be assigned to superior lodging, which
the abbot will visit to return the courtesy. If those monks senior to the abbot are
very close [Dharma relatives, for example], then the abbot fully unfolds his sitting mat and bows down nine times.[98] If he is refused in this courtesy, then he
need only do *liangzhan sanli*. If this, too, is refused, then he should simply do
chuli sanbai. If these Dharma relatives are somewhat more distantly related, the
abbot will do *liangzhan sanli* or *chuli sanbai*. If they are the abbot's direct Dharma
relatives, then, whether they are senior or junior to the abbot, the administrators,[99] the chief officers,[100] junior monks,[101] and servers all extend a greeting to
them. The select disciples and the junior Dharma relatives all fully unfold their sitting mats and bow down nine times or do *liangzhan sanbai*. Then the group leader slightly bends his body and steps forward,
saying, "We are drawn to the abbot's virtuous reputation.[102] Today
we have been granted the opportunity to see the abbot's venerable
visage. For this, we are extremely joyous." He then withdraws and
returns to his original position. The group leader unfolds his sitting
mat again, extends the appropriate seasonal greeting,[103] and then continues, "I humbly wish on your honorable body and your daily life
ten thousand fortunes." (The various seasonal greetings are: first month—
first spring, still cold; second month—second spring, gradually becoming warm;
third month—third spring, very warm; fourth month—first summer, gradually
becoming hot; fifth month—second summer, poisonously hot; sixth month—third
summer, extremely hot; seventh month—first autumn, still hot; eighth month—
second autumn, gradually becoming cool; ninth month—third autumn, frosty
and cool; tenth month—first winter, gradually becoming cold; eleventh month—

second winter, rigidly cold; twelfth month—third winter, extremely cold.) The select disciples then say, "We have not been treated to the abbot's compassionate instruction for a long time, but today we are granted the opportunity of seeing your venerable visage." The Dharma relatives say, "We have not received the abbot's Dharma protection for a long time, but today we are granted the opportunity of seeing your venerable visage. For this we are extremely joyous." The seasonal greeting that follows is the same as above.

[35] After the service of tea and sweetened drink, the new arrivals meet with the attendant, the prior,[104] the chief seat, the scribe,[105] the sutra curator,[106] and the guest master, saying, "On this occasion we are most fortunate to have the opportunity of being by your side." They then extend a brief seasonal greeting and all present *chuli sanbai* to each other. If one of the newcomers has previously been a temporary guest, he does not have to bow down when he comes to the guest master's quarters. The newcomers also greet those monks who are staying in the monastery for meditation on an extended basis.[107] If the bath master[108] holds a major tea ceremony,[109] it will be possible for the newcomers to meet him. At these ceremonies, they meet with fellow monks in the same lineage and bow down to each other. For three days, they remain in the assembly quarters or in the Sangha hall and wait to be summoned to these ceremonies. They should not wander about the monastery, forcing others to look for them. Rather, they should rise early in the morning to prevent those people who come to summon them from waking up others. (In some monasteries, when the abbot, administrators, and chief officers visit the newcomers' hall of residence to return the courtesy, the newcomers merely bow and withdraw without sitting. When the administrators and chief officers visit, they stand in guest positions—only the abbot may stand in the host position. The newcomers step outside the door of their hall to greet them and to see them off.) If a newcomer needs to leave the monastery, he must first fulfill the Sangha hall regulations; according to these he must remain in the monastery for at least half a month.[110] During this period he must attend the "enter-the-hall" tea ceremony[111] or the chanting in the shrine during the holy festivals.[112] Before he leaves he must inform the chief of the assembly quarters and his neighbors to the right and left of him in the Sangha hall.

[37] When people renowned for their virtue[113] come to the monastery to take up residence, the abbot, the rector, and the guest master escort them to individual lodgings.[114] If monks of slightly lower standing come to the monastery, they are escorted by the rector. If they

have already taken up residence in the assembly quarters, they are moved from the assembly quarters to individual accommodations. Those monks retiring from the positions of prior,[115] chief seat, and library director are assigned to individual lodgings. They should extend their gratitude to the abbot for their lodgings either by fully unfolding their sitting mats and bowing down or by performing *liangzhan sanbai* or *chuli sanbai*. The form of courtesy chosen depends on the situation. Next they give thanks to the rector—some bow, some do *chuli sanbai*. On the day of moving, they go to the abbot's quarters[116] and the rectory to return their residence.[117] The courtesy extended at this point depends on the situation, as above. The lock and key must be presented to the rector in person before moving.

[38] If the new arrivals have previously served as administrators, chief officers, or fundraisers[118] in this monastery, then they take up residence in the retired quarters.[119] Administrative officers from other monasteries,[120] personages renowned for their virtue, those with official titles, and those known as national masters[121] should take up residence in the superior quarters.[122] If there are more than two monks arriving, they need not visit the abbot's quarters individually to thank him before returning to their hall of residence but may do so as a group. If, before the end of the summer retreat[123] (that is, before fulfilling the requirement of the Sangha hall regulations), a monk has to leave due to an emergency, he must report to the rector to ask for leave; if he leaves without permission he will be subject to the monastery's penalty. If a monk should ask for leave to travel in the mountains for more than half a month, then he must present his certificate and follow the Sangha hall regulations again when he returns.[124]

[39] The application for a traveling permit[125] is written as follows:

"Monastery X [monk's monastery of origin]. Brown (or purple) robe.[126] Monk X [monk's name]. The following official document[127] registered in year X, owned by Monk X, and acquired at Monastery Y [monk's current or most recent monastery of residence]. I now carry with me my tonsure certificate, the document of "Six Awarenesses,"[128] and my ordination certificate to present to this office[129] for inspection. I hereby wish to apply for a permit[130] in order to travel to location X[131] for a pilgrimage. I humbly beg Government Official X to deign to carry out this request. I humbly await Your orders (or instructions). Sincerely written in year X, in month X (and stamped with the monastic seal) on day X, by X (give all appropriate titles here, such as Abbot of Temple X)."

[41] The application for modification or extension of the pass-port[132] is written as follows:

> Initial information is given in the same format as above, after which the application continues: "I, Monk X, humbly beg Your permission for the following undertaking. Previously I applied for a travel passport in month X, on day X, in location X, for permission to make a pilgrimage to location Y, but due to weather (or disease) I was unable to make the journey. I fear violating the passport expiration date and so I humbly beg Your permission to modify this document. I dare not act without Your permission, so I humbly await Your instructions. Written sincerely in year X, in month X (without the monastic seal), on day X, by X (give all appropriate titles here, such as Abbot of Temple X)."

Attendance at Meals

[42] The seating for meals should be arranged according to ordination seniority. In the early morning, after the breaking of silence when all first rise from sleep[133] and before the three strikes of the bell signaling mealtime, the monks sit in their dining seats[134] and wait for three long sequences of the striking of the metal sheet.[135] When they have heard the end of the third sequence,[136] they stand up and take down their bowls, which hang on the pillars behind them. (Previously it was the rule that the monks should not wait until after the third sequence [that is, they must take down their bowls before the end of the third sequence]). They then place their bowls before them on the side of their upper shoulder.[137] After the wooden fish[138] is struck, no monk is allowed to enter the hall. Those who enter from the front should use the south [left-hand] side door,[139] stepping through with the right [left] foot.[140] To show respect for the abbot, they do not enter through the north [right-hand] side door.[141] Those who enter from the rear door and sit in the upper section[142] use the north [right-hand] side and step in with the left foot. Those who enter from the rear door and sit in the lower section[143] use the south [left-hand] side and step in with the right foot. The entering monks bow before the Holy Monk and take their seats.

[43] Before ascending his platform,[144] the monk should first bow to his neighbors. Then, using his right hand to gather the material of his left sleeve, he presses the left sleeve under his armpit.[145] He then uses his left hand to gather the right sleeve and slightly lifts it up. Next, he uses both hands to pull up the front of his *kāṣāya* and holds it up with his left hand. He then mounts the step at the foot of the platform,[146] sits on the edge of platform,[147] and removes his shoes and neatly places them aside. Using his right hand for support, he first pulls his left leg onto the platform and then his right leg.[148] He should lift up his body and sit upright, with his left leg on top of his right leg. He should use his *kāṣāya* to cover his knees and should not expose his undergarments.[149] He should not let his robes drape over the edge of the platform.[150] He must sit back so as to allow a space on the platform in front of him roughly large enough for one bowl to preserve the purity of this area. (The space in front of the platform is used for three things: first, it is where the *kāṣāya* is placed; second, it is where the bowls are displayed; and third, the monk sleeps with his head in this direction— therefore, this space is called the place of three purities.)[151]

[44] The prior, the rector, the superintendent,[152] and the attendants are in the outer section of the hall on the right-hand side. The guest master, the bath master, the coal master,[153] the itinerant preacher,[154] and the director of the infirmary[155] are in the outer section of the hall on the left-hand side. Three drum sequences are struck to indicate that the abbot is approaching the hall. The administrators and chief officers bow to the abbot from their positions. After the bell in front of the Sangha hall is rung, the assembly descends from the platforms. The abbot enters the hall, bows to the Holy Monk, and then bows with the assembly simultaneously. The abbot then assumes his position, but before he sits down he bows once again. Thereafter the assembly may ascend the platforms. The attendants and novices[156] who have followed the abbot into the hall now exit the hall and stand in line outside. They wait there until the monks have taken their seats, at which time they all bow simultaneously; an attendant enters the hall, moves the table in front of the abbot, bows, and exits. Then the rector enters the hall, bows before the Holy Monk, burns incense, and stands beside the octagonal stand with a hammer.[157] At this point, the monks display their bowls. (In the Hongji tradition,[158] there is an additional strike of the hammer, and the rector announces, "All present will now chant the Heart Sutra three times and then transfer the merit of this chant to X [donors' names]." Various other monasteries add a hammer strike only when they offer the "Earth Porridge.")[159]

[46] The following is the procedure for the feasts arranged for auspicious or inauspicious occasions. After circumambulating the Sangha hall with burning incense,[160] the donor genuflects in the hall with the incense burner in his hands. The rector strikes the hammer one time and speaks. He begins by reciting a verse, which may be one of the following: "I pay homage to the Bhagavat,[161]/ To the perfect sutra, / And to the Mahayana bodhisattvas, / For their merit is beyond conception;" Or "The treasures of the Buddha, the Dharma, and the Sangha / Comprise the most wondrous field; / Whenever one takes refuge in this field, / Reward is ever manifest;" Or "If the water is clear, the autumn moon will be reflected; / If one prays with great sincerity, one's merit field will grow, / For the Enlightened Buddha / Is the only true place of refuge." While the rector stands beside the hammer, it may be more advisable not to chant a long verse. The rector then continues, "This morning a feast has been arranged for donor X, and so here in cloud hall (the Sangha hall) I shall now respectfully read a prayer[162] on the donor's behalf. I beg the Buddha's compassionate witness." After reading the prayer, the rector continues, "Now that this prayer has been given, I wish that the unbiased Holy Eyes of the Buddhas will bestow their clear and illuminating vision on me to discern my sincerity. Now we must depend on the venerable assembly to begin the chanting." After some time they start the chanting with "The Pure Dharma Body."[163] If the rector strikes too quickly with the hammer, it is as if he strikes the Buddha's feet. If he strikes too slowly, it is as if he strikes the Buddha's head.[164]

[48] The following is the procedure for feasts arranged on a regular basis. The rector strikes with the hammer and announces, "We gaze upward and wish that the Three Treasures might grant us their wise approval." There is no need for further prayer to the Buddha. A short time after the "ten recitations of Buddhas,"[165] the hammer is struck once and the chief seat offers food. During the porridge,[166] all present chant, "This porridge has Ten Benefits.[167] / These benefits accrue to the practitioners. / As a reward for this meal, the donor will ascend to heaven, / And attain final happiness." Then they chant, "This porridge is exceedingly great medicine, / And shall satisfy hunger and quench thirst. / Both donor and receiver shall become pure and tranquil, / And shall attain the ultimate thruth." During the midday meal, the monks chant, "The food with three virtues and six tastes[168] / Is offered to the Buddha and the monks. / The human and heavenly beings in this Dharma realm, / Receive the offering as well." The words praising the rice are: "The donor and the receiver / Shall obtain the "Five Endurances,"[169] / physical appearance, strength, longevity, mental peacefulness, / And unhindered eloquence." All the aforementioned words are chanted in full, loud voices. After the offering of food has begun, the server who announces each course[170] enters the hall. (The meal announcements should be in a clear voice, and the names of the courses must not be misspoken. If there is any error, the proper custom of receiving the food cannot be carried out, and the server must make the announcement again. If the food is served too quickly, the monks being served will be in undue haste. If the food is served too slowly, the monks will have to wait between courses and will grow restless.) Once the food has

been distributed, the rector strikes with the hammer once more. The chief seat then presses his hands together in honor of the food[171] and all the monks engage in contemplation. After the contemplation, the assembly begins to eat. Behind the screen to the rear of the Holy Monk, the rector turns to bow to the chief seat to invite him to have the donated money distributed, and then returns to his position, where he strikes with the hammer again as a signal to the chief seat to begin distributing the money. The announcement is made, "The material goods given by the donors and the Dharma offered by the monks / Are completely equal. / The perfection of *dāna* [offering] / Is accomplished." The supply master[172] or the rector then distributes the donation[173] to one person at a time. The money should be placed in front of each monk gently to show respect. The monks press their hands together[174] while receiving the money. Throughout the feast, they should try not to steal any glances at the donations. Moreover, they are forbidden to make noise by throwing their money onto their seats. They should wait until the end of the feast before taking the donations.

[50] To correctly display a nest of bowls, the monk should first bow and untie his cloth bundle.[175] He takes out the bowl wiper[176] and folds the cloth into a small shape. He then takes out his spoon and chopstick bag and places them horizontally, close in front of him. Next the clean towel[177] is used to cover the knees, after which the cloth bundle is completely opened and the three corners closest to him are folded over and neatly joined together at the center, while the far corner is allowed to drape over the edge of the platform. He then uses both hands to unfold the mat.[178] With his right hand facing down, he holds the corner of the mat closest to him on the right side and places it over the top of the bowls in front of him. Then, with the left hand facing up, he reaches under the mat to pick up the bowls and places them on the left side of the mat. Using the fingertips of both hands, he takes out the three smaller bowls[179] stacked together and places them on the mat one at a time without making any noise. If his seat is narrow, he should display only three of his bowls. He then opens the bag to take out his spoon and chopsticks.[180] (When removing these items, he should take out the chopsticks first. When replacing them, he should put the spoon in first.) He places the chopsticks and spoon horizontally behind the first bowl, with the handles to the side of his upper shoulder. The brush[181] he places on the edge of the mat to the side of the lower shoulder with the handle facing out. He then waits for the offering of food to all sentient beings.[182]

[52] The serving should be done by the purity-keepers;[183] monks

should not serve themselves with their own hands.[184] The purity-keeper must serve the food skillfully in accordance with custom. Foods such as soup and porridge should not be allowed to soil the monks' hands or the rims and sides of the bowls. Two or three dabs of the ladle should be used to dispense the food. The purity-keepers serve food only intermittently; while waiting (when not serving), they bend their bodies and place their hands together in front of their chests. The quantity of food meted out depends on each person's request.

To correctly receive the food, the monk should hold the bowl with both hands and lower his hands close to the mat. The bowl should be held level.[185] The monk should gauge the amount of food served him; he should not request too much and leave unfinished food. He must wait until the food has been distributed and the rector has struck with the hammer[186] before he lifts up his bowl to make the offering. After the hammer has struck, he presses his hands together in honor of the food and performs the five contemplations:[187] one, to ponder the effort necessary to supply this food and to appreciate its origins; two, to reflect on one's own virtue being insufficient to receive the offering; three, to protect the mind's integrity, to depart from error, and, as a general principle, to avoid being greedy; four, at the same time to consider the food as medicine and bodily nourishment, preventing emaciation; five, to receive this food as necessary for attaining enlightenment. After this comes the offering of food to all sentient beings. **[53]** (Before the completion of the five contemplations the food cannot be considered one's own portion and therefore cannot be offered to sentient beings.) While the monks perform the offering of food to all sentient beings, they chant a verse: "All spirit beings and deities, / Now I offer you this food. / May this food be spread in all ten directions / For all spirit beings and deities to share."[188]

[54] When eating, the monk brings the bowl to his mouth and not his mouth to the bowl.[189] The top half of the outside of the bowl is considered pure, while the bottom half is considered soiled.[190] The thumb is placed inside the bowl, on its rim, and the second and third fingers are placed outside, on the bottom, while the fourth and fifth are not used at all.[191] The method of holding smaller bowls is the same. When lifting or placing the bowls, or when picking up the spoon or chopsticks, the monk should not make any noise. The following rules were written in the *Four Part Vinaya*.[192] The mind should be righteous to receive the food.[193] Soup and rice can be served only up to the rim of the bowl.[194] Soup and rice should be eaten together[195] and eaten in order,[196] and the monk must not stir or pick at his food before eating it.[197] Unless the monk is ill, he may not request extra or special soup and rice.[198] He must not use his rice to cover his broth and then request more.[199] He must not compare his own food with the food in his neighbor's bowl and hold a grudge in his mind.[200] His mind should be focused on the food in his own bowl.[201] Food should not be eaten in large clumps,[202] and the monk should not open his mouth in anticipation of each bite.[203] The monk should not talk with food in his mouth.[204] He should not roll the rice into balls to throw into his mouth.[205] He should not spill rice onto the floor.[206] He should not chew with his cheeks bulging full[207] and he should not make noise when he chews.[208] He should not make inhaling noises,[209] lick his food,[210] or wave his hands as he eats.[211] He is not allowed to spill rice[212] or hold the eating vessels with soiled hands.[213] All of the above rules are written in the Vinayas and must be followed.

[55] The monk should not scratch his head while eating lest his dandruff fall into his bowl. He should not shift his body back and forth, scratch his knees, sit squatting, stretch and gape, or make noise blowing his nose. If he needs to sneeze he should cover his nose[214] and if he wants to pick his teeth he should cover his mouth. Fibrous vegetable stalks and fruit pits or stones should be placed hidden behind the bowls so as to avoid displeasing a neighbor. Even when a neighbor has leftover food in his bowls or an extra piece of fruit and offers it, the monk should not accept it. If his neighbor is especially bothered by drafts, he should not use a fan. If he himself is bothered by drafts, he should ask permission from the rector to eat outside the hall. If he has a need of any sort, he should gesture silently and should not beckon the server in a loud voice. After he has finished eating, if there is anything left in his bowl he should use the bowl wiper to clean it and then eat it. When he receives the water, the monk should wash the largest bowl first and then the other bowls in order from largest to smallest. He should not wash the smaller bowls inside the large bowl. He then wipes the bowls to [56] dry them. In addition, the spoon and chopsticks should be washed and placed inside their bag. The water for the bowls should not spill onto the floor around the platform. The mantra[215] pronounced while the water from the bowls is poured out is *"Om mahorase svāhā."* The two thumbs are used to stack all the bowls inside each other. With the left hand facing up, the monk puts the bowls into the center of the cloth. Then with the right hand facing down, he holds the corner of the mat closest to him on the right side and puts it on top of the bowls. He then folds the mat and places it back on top of the bowls. Next he picks up the corner of the cloth closest to the body to cover the bowls. Then he pulls

the corner of the cloth draped over the end of the platform toward himself to cover the bowls. He folds the clean towel and places it, together with the bag containing the spoon and chopsticks and the bowl brush, on top of the now covered bowls and covers them with the bowl wiper. After the monks have put their bundles back in order, when they hear the hammer strike to exit the hall, they will all chant the verse for the completion of the meal: "After the meal, the body is full of physical energy / And quakes with a power like the heroes,[216] which permeates all ten directions in the past, present, and future.[217] / One can now revert causes and transform effects[218] and therefore one need no longer be preoccupied with one's inabilities. / Let all sentient beings obtain supernatural power through this strength."

[58] Now the abbot exits the hall and each monk stands up and hangs his bowls, making sure the bowls and his residential unit are neat and in order. He squats down and crouches on the platform. Holding the back of his clothes with his left hand, he slowly slides over the edge of the platform and lets his feet drop to the ground; he should not step off the platform from a standing position. When a grand tea ceremony[219] is held in the hall, the custom of entering and exiting the hall and ascending and descending from the platform is the same as above. If, after the early meal, there is to be a hiatus from the abbot's regularly scheduled sermon,[220] the abbot exits the hall and the bell is struck three times. If there is to be a morning sermon, there is no need to strike the bell. If the abbot will be ascending the platform in the Dharma hall to acknowledge the feast host,[221] then after the three strikes, the bell must be struck again. After a grand tea ceremony, the abbot bows before the Holy Monk and exits. The bell is then struck three times as a signal for all to exit the hall. If the prior or the chief seat sponsors a major tea ceremony in the hall, then, after escorting the abbot out, the host returns to the hall, stands before the Holy Monk and bows first to the right section and then to the left. When the teacups and stands[222] have been collected, the bell is rung three times as a signal to exit the hall. At this point, the assembly can descend from their platforms. The manner of exiting the hall is the same as that of entering.

Attending the Tea Ceremony

[59] When the monastery holds a special tea ceremony,[223] it is a very solemn occasion; those invited should not be arrogant or careless. After being invited, the monks should remember to go to Hall X first, then to Hall Y, and then to Hall Z.[224] When they hear the drum and

board signal, they should leave for the ceremony in good time to arrive early, and they should remember their seating positions so as to prevent undue haste, misunderstandings, or any commotion.

[60] At a tea ceremony sponsored by the abbot,[225] the assembly is summoned and the attendant bows to the guests of honor to invite them to enter. Following the chief seat into the hall, the monks stand in their positions. Once the abbot has greeted them, the monks gather their *kāṣāya* and take their seats calmly and peacefully. After removing their shoes, they should not place them haphazardly. When they withdraw their legs, they should not make any noise with the chair. They should sit upright, with straight bodies, and they should not lean on the backs of their chairs. The *kāṣāya* should cover their knees, and the sitting mat should be draped in front over the edge of the platform. They should clasp their hands solemnly and greet the abbot. The monks should always use their short gowns to cover their sleeves and should not expose their wrists. When the weather is hot, each monk may clasp his hands outside his sleeves. When the weather is cold he may clasp his hands inside the sleeves, using the thumb of his right hand to hold down the left sleeve and the second finger of his left hand to hold the right sleeve. The attendant bows, burns incense, and generally presides over the service on behalf of the abbot; the guests of honor, therefore, should treat him with respect and prudence. The monks calmly pick up their teacups and stand holding them with both hands in front of their chests. They should neither drop their hands too low nor raise them too high. It is most desirous for each monk, observing his neighbors to the right and left, to hold his teacup at the same level.

[61] First, the guests of honor should look to the master and greet him, greet their neighbors to the right and left, and then have tea. The guests should not blow on their tea and should be careful not to drop their teacups. They should not slurp or make any noises. When they pick up and put down their tea with each sip, the teacups and tea stands should not clink together loudly. If the teacups are put down first, they should be placed behind the tray. The teacups should be placed in order, not haphazardly. The right hand should be used to pick up the confection[226] and to hold it. The guests wait until they have all been assigned their places and have greeted each other before eating. They should not throw the confection into their mouths or chew loudly. When the ceremony has ended and the guests leave their seats, they should calmly lower their feet, bow, and follow the assembly to the exit. The guests of honor **[62]** come forward one or two steps and bow to the host to extend their gratitude for the tea. When exiting, they must walk in a dignified and orderly manner; they must not walk too fast, take large steps, shuffle their feet, or make noise on the floor. If the host sees the guests off, the guests should turn to bow to show their respect before withdrawing. They should then go to the storage hall[227] and other quarters in their proper order to continue the ceremonies.

[63] If a monk is invited to a tea ceremony sponsored by the abbot but cannot attend because of an abrupt illness or the need to urinate or defecate, he should ask someone attending the ceremony to inform the attendant and he should have his seat removed. If the abbot were to expel from the monastery every transgressor, exhaustively enforcing all the regulations,[228] then there would be no assembly at all. The abbot should not grimace and show his anger to the assembly. (At the tea ceremonies sponsored by new arrivals, held in order of seniority at the assembly quarters,[229] as well as tea ceremonies held in various other quarters, those attending should not laugh or talk.)

Invitation to Give Instruction on the Causes and Conditions of Attaining Enlightenment[230]

[64] In some monasteries, the abbot's instruction is held after half a month of training in the hall and, in other monasteries, it follows the tea ceremonies and lasts one or two days. When the instruction is scheduled, however, depends on the abbot's discretion. Before they may enter the abbot's quarters, the assembly of monks must meet with the abbot's attendant to request an audience with their master. Only after the attendant has informed the abbot do the monks enter the abbot's quarters. Beginning with the group leader, all the monks face north, standing motionless while one at a time they light incense. Then the group leader steps forward and bows to the abbot, after which he moves to the southwest corner of the abbot's seat, bows, and says, "For us, X [group leader's name] and fellow monks, the questions of life and death are extremely significant. All things are impermanent and fleeting. So we humbly request the abbot's compassion to give us instruction on the causes and conditions of attaining enlightenment." If the abbot assents, the group leader returns to his position and together with the rest of the assembly fully unfolds his sitting mat and bows down three times. The monks then pick up their sitting mats and move to the west side of the abbot's seat where they face east, bow one at a time, and remain standing.

[65] After the request for instruction, all the monks, beginning with

the group leader, return to their positions, fully unfold their sitting mats, prostrate themselves three times, bow, and leave. (In some monasteries they bow down three times to make the invitation, and six times to show their gratitude, for a total of nine prostrations. In other monasteries they bow down six times to make the invitation and six times to show their gratitude, for a total of twelve prostrations. The monks' words of invitation are: "We humbly request the abbot's compassion in granting his permission. We are extremely joyous." The monks' words of gratitude are: "We, X [group leader's name] and fellow monks, are most fortunate in this life to have received the abbot's compassionate permission to receive his instruction on the causes and conditions of attaining enlightenment. We are extremely grateful.") After descending from the abbot's quarters, the assembly goes to the attendant's quarters to extend its gratitude to him. In some monasteries, the monks will perform *chuli* once to each other; in others, they merely bow. (In some monasteries, once the assembly is standing motionless, the group leader alone burns incense to extend the invitation and returns to his position, where he and the assembly fully unfold their sitting mats, prostrate themselves three times, and bow. Then the assembly as a whole turns to extend their invitation. After this invitation, the monks, beginning with the group leader, all burn incense one at a time, face the abbot while standing in their own positions, fully unfold their sitting mats, and prostrate themselves three times. In some monasteries this is done six times). Execution of the above procedure depends on each school's tradition. The monks must inquire of the attendant as to the proper protocol and should then proceed accordingly. They should not insist upon their own methods, thereby earning the abbot's disdain. (If among those monks who have recently taken up residence there is a monk who has met the abbot and has entered the abbot's room before,[231] then he must burn incense, inform the abbot that this is not his first time, and ask the abbot for permission to stay, saying, "I beg the abbot's compassion in allowing me to enter his room as I have done previously." If he receives permission to enter he should fully unfold his sitting mat and bow down three times, saying, "I humbly receive your kindness in granting me permission and I am extremely grateful." He then withdraws, bowing down three more times. If the abbot exempts him from this last courtesy, then he simply unfolds his sitting mat and performs only the first three bows.)

Entering the Abbot's Quarters[232]

[66] Appointments to meet with the abbot in his quarters are sometimes arranged section by section[233] or quarter by quarter. Sometimes they are scheduled for every other day or fixed on a certain day, with some appointments in the morning and some in the evening. What-

ever arrangement is chosen depends on the abbot.²³⁴ When the time comes for the monks to enter the abbot's quarters, the attendant has the server put incense into the incense case and arrange the cushions used for bowing in the center of the room. (In some monasteries it is not necessary to bow down and therefore the cushions need not be set out.) Once this is done, the attendant informs the abbot. When the abbot gives instructions for the monks to enter his quarters, a placard is suspended outside, reading, "Enter the Room." To summon the assembly, in some monasteries the drum is beaten, in still others the board is struck or the "Enter the Room" placard is struck. The abbot takes his seat inside his quarters while his attendant stands outside the abbot's quarters on the east side with his hands clasped. When a group begins to gather and stands waiting outside the abbot's quarters, in some monasteries they form a single line and face east, in others they form two lines and face each other. The attendant enters the abbot's quarters and bows to the abbot in the center of the room, goes to the east side of the abbot's seat, and stands behind the incense table. He then faces south, bows, lifts up the incense with his left hand, and bows again. Having done this, he returns to the center of the room, faces the abbot, and bows. He then exits the quarters, approaches the assembly, and bows to invite them to enter. After this the attendant returns to his own quarters.

[67] As each monk enters the abbot's quarters he should turn his body slightly and bow. Outside the quarters, the assembly stands with hands clasped, moving forward in order one by one. It is not permissible to disrupt the assembly's peace of mind by cutting in line. Each monk should enter the abbot's quarters stepping with his left foot through the right-hand door.²³⁵ He should bow facing the abbot and move with hands clasped to the southwest corner of the abbot's seat, where he bows again and remains standing. To begin his inquiry, he first bows, and then reveals the subject of his query.²³⁶ He should not be long-winded or speak of worldly or trivial matters and detain the assembly. After he has revealed his question and received the abbot's reply, he bows, steps back facing the abbot, and bows down again. (In some monasteries one bow suffices; in others the monk bows three times. In still others he fully unfolds his sitting mat or does *chuli.*) He then turns around to the east [to his right] to exit. He should step with his left foot through the left-hand door to avoid a collision with the monk entering next. Having exited the abbot's quarters, he faces the direction of the abbot and bows. He then approaches the assembly, bows, and exits the hall. In those monasteries where the monks form two

lines, the assembly enters the hall in double file, and each line goes to the opposite wall where they turn to face east and west to face each other. The monks enter the abbot's quarters from each line in alternating order. (In some monasteries the entering monk and the abbot discuss the previous koan,[237] or they engage in conversation,[238] or the monk asks for further instruction.[239] Separate times are allocated for these three methods of inquiry. In other monasteries, any or all of the three methods are employed in one session.)

[68] After all the monks have finished consulting with the abbot, the attendant enters the quarters, rolls up the cushion, and withdraws. (As a courtesy, when entering the quarters, the monk is supposed to burn incense. To properly burn the incense he should enter the abbot's quarters facing the center, bow, and move to the incense table with hands clasped. There he should stand facing south, bow again to the abbot, lift up the incense with his right hand, and then move toward the center to bow and remain at the corner of the abbot's seat. However, because this practice lengthens the time for each monk and therefore detains the waiting assembly, it is no longer done. In some monasteries, a cushion is set up outside the door where the monks bow down one at a time and withdraw. This custom is an attempt to avoid delaying the assembly. The monk entering the abbot's quarters should wear clean clothes, without stains or dirt. His manner should be within the bounds of proper decorum, and his movements should be easy and calm as a show of respect for the abbot.) The abbot should inform the attendant that unless there is an urgent guest or some important business, the attendant should not interrupt the abbot while the monks are entering his quarters. The abbot should also order the attendant not to talk, make any noise, or create a disruption among the assembly during the interview.

Fascicle Two

Ascending the Seat in the Dharma Hall[1]

[71] On the fixed dates[2] when the abbot is to ascend the seat in the Dharma hall to give the morning sermon,[3] there is no hiatus from the abbot's scheduled sermon after the early morning meal. At dawn, after the signal for the "opening of the quiet" is given, the chief seat leads the assembly to the Sangha hall. When the first drum sequence is heard, the chief seat and the assembly enter the Dharma hall.[4] They stand single file in "wild geese formation"[5] in order of seniority, each with his side to the center position. The position closest to the Dharma seat is the most senior. The chief seat, the scribe, the sutra curator, the guest master, and the bath master form their own row in front of the assembly, standing in order. The remaining chief officers simply take their positions among the assembly. The retired elderly abbots[6] take their seats in front of the chief seat, leaving two empty positions between them and him. These retired elderly abbots stand facing south, but with their sides turned slightly to the center. At the sound of the second drum sequence, the four administrators[7] enter the hall, walking in order of their respective ranks. They stand at their "bowing mats"[8] by the Dharma hall door on the south side and face the Dharma seat. The prior takes his position on the east side of the hall.

[72] When the postulants[9] hear the first sequence, they form a row in front of the storage hall[10] and stand waiting. At the second sequence they follow the administrators into the Dharma hall to attend the sermon. Inside the Dharma hall, they bow to all present and move to the east side of the hall where they stand facing the west. The position farthest to the north should be the most senior position. The postulants attending the sermon must wear shoes and socks. At the third sequence, the attendant informs the abbot that it is time to enter. Everyone bows simultaneously to the abbot, and the abbot ascends the Dharma seat[11] and stands in front of the *chan* chair.[12] First **[73]** the attendant bows. The attendant who carries the incense[13] now ascends the Dharma seat on the east side not far from the seat and stands facing the west with his side to the center. Then the chief seat and the assembly turn to face the Dharma seat, bow, and return to their positions. The administrators then step forward and bow, standing opposite and facing the chief seat. The one standing closest to the Dharma seat is the most senior. Then the novices and the postulants turn to face the Dharma seat, bow, and return to stand in their positions. In the tradition of Lushan Yuantong,[14] the postulants enter the Dharma hall single file, bow, and stand in the east section divided into three rows. The administrators then bow and remain standing. At this point the three rows of postulants, beginning with the southernmost position, walk one after the other toward the Dharma seat and stand in an east-west row in front of the abbot. After they bow again, the easternmost position leads the postulants back to their original positions in three rows on the east side of the hall, where they bow once more and remain standing. The guest master leads the donors[15] to stand in front of the administrators.[16] The administrators,[17] as well as the assembly, remain standing in the straight line with their sides to the center, listening to the abbot's sermon. When the abbot descends from the Dharma platform to exit the Dharma hall after the sermon, all those present bow simultaneously and, beginning with the chief seat, enter and circumambulate the Sangha hall. Everyone then remains standing in the Sangha hall until the abbot enters.[18] Then the administrators circumambulate the hall.

[74] If the monastery serves tea after the sermon, the abbot sits in his position and the administrators stand outside the door. After the tea is finished, the abbot stands up and the bell to exit the hall[19] is rung. If there is no tea, the administrators circumambulate the hall and exit, merely waiting for the abbot's bow before withdrawing. Sometimes, after the three strikes of the bell to exit, the abbot ascends the platform inside the hall. In the morning, according to custom, there is a break from the sermon; but if the abbot is scheduled to preach, then after the sermon there is no circumambulation of the Sangha hall.[20]

[75] Whenever the abbot ascends the seat in the Dharma hall, all must attend, with the exception of the chief of the assembly quarters and the Sangha hall monitor.[21] Whoever violates this rule will suffer the monastery's penalty. It is best to avoid this offense. If a monk is detained because of some other business or an emergency, and not due to his own indolence, then he may arrive a little late. But if the abbot has already ascended his seat in the Dharma hall, the monk should not enter, and he should avoid letting the abbot see him. All those who attend the sermon should not wear hats or sleevelike cowls,[22] including the abbot. If a person should ask an unintendedly amusing question, no one should burst out laughing or even break a slight smile. They should maintain a demeanor of sincerity and solemnity while listening to the abbot's profound teaching.

Chanting

[76] On each day of the month ending in a three or an eight, after the midday meal the server in the rectory[23] informs the abbot that

there is to be chanting and hangs the poster announcing this event. When the time comes, the server prepares, scatters water, sweeps, and arranges the incense and the lighting in the Sangha hall, in the great shrine,[24] and in the earth hall[25] before striking the bell to summon the assembly. The assembly and the administrators congregate, and the abbot burns incense, moving from the earth hall to the great shrine to the Sangha hall. Only in front of the Buddha statue does he perform three prostrations. The abbot, the administrators, and other members of the assembly take their positions on the right-hand side. On the left-hand side are the chief seat and those in his section. The rector strikes the bell seven times[26] and leads the chanting.

[77] On the third, thirteenth, and twenty-third of each month the monks chant, "May the spirit of the emperor live forever, / And may the Dao of the emperor forever flourish. / Let the sun of the Buddha grow brighter, / And let the wheel of Dharma eternally turn. / May the guardian deities of the monastery[27] and the guardian deities of the earth[28]/ Protect the Dharma and comfort all humans, / And may the donors from the ten directions/ Increase their merit and wisdom. // For all these hopes we chant: 'Pure Dharma Body'"[29] On the eighth, eighteenth, and twenty-eighth of each month they chant, "We announce to all that from the day the great master Tathāgata[30] entered *parinirvāṇa* until this day—the second year of Yuanfu[31] in the imperial Song—it has been 2047 years. (Add one year for each year that passes.) Another day has passed, / And our lives have been reduced commensurately; / We are like fish trapped in water that is slowly dwindling. / How can there be any pleasure at all in such an existence?[32]/ One must live vigorously, / As if one's head were on fire and needed to be extinguished immediately. / Simply contemplate the impermanence of all things / And take care to avoid idle delay. // May the guardian deities of the monastery and the earth / Protect the Dharma and comfort all humans, / And may the donors from ten directions / Increase their merit and wisdom. // For all these hopes the monks chant: 'The Pure Dharma Body.'"

[78] When the chanting has ended, the abbot goes to his position first. Beginning with the chief seat, the assembly circumambulates the hall and remains standing. The attendants follow the assembly in circumambulating the hall until they reach the left-hand side of the front door, where they stand in the empty spaces at the head of the section. The administrators form a single file and follow the end of the line. The novices do not circumambulate but stand outside the hall facing the Holy Monk. When the administrators and abbot exit,

the novices bend their bodies to bow to them. The temporary arrivals[33] follow the assembly and stand inside the rear door. The retired elderly abbots, if they have taken up residence, stand next to the chief seat. If they have not taken up residence, they stand in the guest section, which is on the north [right-hand] side of the rear door, facing the abbot. After their circumambulation, the assembly returns to the assembly quarters, bows, and has sweetened drinks. They then enter the Sangha hall, display their mats,[34] and lower the door of the compartment.[35] If the monastery is located in the mountains or the forest, the big bell is struck. When the abbot has exited the shrine, the rector is left in charge of the bell. The assembly bows and continues to chant.

Informal Sermon[36]

[79] Every five days the abbot ascends the platform in the Dharma hall to inspire the monks to rise up, filled with the doctrine of the school's traditions.[37] On those days of the month ending in a three or an eight, there is chanting to repay the dragons and the heavenly beings. The monks invite the abbot to give instruction on the profound teachings and to explain the links between the present and the past.[38] The informal sermon concerns the admonitions peculiar to the monastery[39] and discipline. The informal sermon is conducted as follows: In the "early night,"[40] the bell is struck and seats are arranged in the abbot's front hall.[41] The administrators and the abbot's disciples are summoned. The master abbot and his audience engage in debate[42] just as in the morning sermon.

[80] During the informal sermon, in addition to the *tichang*,[43] all inappropriate behavior—from the administrators and chief officers down to the novices and postulants—no matter how insignificant, should be discussed and brought into accordance with the monastic precepts.[44] Each of the so-called "chiefs of the monastery"[45] must take responsibility for his own section. The chiefs should not confuse their respective duties and should always seek out peaceful relations. The chief seat must remain in the Sangha hall from morning until evening, arriving at the morning sermon and the two daily meals before the others. Unless there is an urgent need to mobilize the assembly, the administrators should perform their duties themselves, utilizing their own best talents to help the monastery flourish. Although the assembly and the administrators may interact as guests and hosts for the time being, at some distant point in their lives the former administrators may come to regard former assembly members as their teachers.[46] Therefore present-day administrators should

not become complacent about their previous achievements or hard work and develop arrogance and idleness within themselves. Even the fellow monks in the cloud hall should practice diligently day and night, always asking questions. The monks should sculpt and polish each other. They should fully understand the regulations and know the workings of the monastery by rote.

[81] When a monk travels to visit other monasteries,[47] he should pack and carry his own luggage on his person. But, if he is delivering a letter for his monastery and is not merely on personal business, he may also carry a cagelike trunk. Once he has performed his duty he must return to his own monastery without delay. If the monk stays overnight in a private residence, he should not use the opportunity to soak his clothes.[48] When traveling on the road, he should not let his arms hang down or swing his body from side to side. He should not have a springy gait, and when resting he should not sit in a squatting position or stand with arms akimbo. His demeanor should not be arrogant or wild, and he should not speak with the use of his hands. When walking, he should step heel first. His gaze should be solemn and respectable, and his eyes should be fixed no more than eight feet[49] in front of him. Inside any monastic hall, the monk should not cross in front of the Holy Monk or the center platform[50] and should not walk on the passage from the right section to the left, or vice versa.[51] When reciting a sutra or mantra, it is better to chant silently and to avoid making noise with the prayer beads.

[81] At the time of the morning sermon and the evening invitation to instruction,[52] the monk should simply clasp his hands in a dignified manner. Under his short garment he should wear undergarments so as not to expose the body.[53] His "bell-mouth" shoes should be worn correctly with socks. Straw sandals are permissible without socks, but the bottom edge of the pants must not be allowed to hang loosely: it should be bound.[54] When sitting, the monk should withdraw his legs; he should always pull up his clothes before taking a seat; and he should clasp his hands in front of his chest with the right palm on top. When pressing the hands together to bow, the fingers of each hand should be contiguous and the palms should be touching. It is inappropriate to read the sutra dressed only in *chayi*[55]— with the *kāṣāya* draped over the left arm—or *guazi*.[56] When a monk blows his nose, spits, defecates, or urinates, how can he do so facing the direction of the pagoda? When sleeping, the monk should lie on his right-hand side with his head on his right palm and with his left hand placed on his left hip as though carrying a knife.[57] While at-

tending a sermon he should stand in a straight line with his fellow monks with his side to the center, listening to the sermon carefully. The monk's bedding and clothes should always be kept neat and orderly. He should not arbitrarily remove any mattress that does not belong to him. His mattress and comforter should be displayed and folded with care and mindfulness. He should not ascend his platform with his back to the other monks lest he should be ridiculed for it. He should not stand or walk on his platform: this practice is incorrect. Before he lies down to sleep, his *kāṣāya* should be placed nearby— specifically, next to his pillow, folded, and covered with a clean towel. Before going to sleep he should not remove the clothes from his upper body in case of an emergency, such as a robbery. When sitting on his platform, he should not lean his head against the wall panel[58] behind him. When walking in the corridor, he should avoid laughing or talking too loudly.

[83] The following is inappropriate behavior in the monastery: congregating in the hall; shuffling one's feet after nightfall; releasing the curtain noisily behind oneself as one enters or exits instead of quietly returning it;[59] making noise with the bucket and ladle while washing; making noises while blowing one's nose or spitting, which would disturb the assembly of purity;[60] making medicine pills; leaning on the railing in the venerable shrines;[61] being publicly naked at the bathhouse; taking on duties in excess of those required by one's position, thereby interfering with the affairs of the monastery as a whole; spreading gossip; creating unnecessary complications out of simple situations; not being sincere or mournful during the funeral of a deceased monk; inflating the value of auctioned items when serving as auctioneer; not following the precepts[62] for one's spiritual cultivation; vying for the more honorable seat during assemblies (the seating should be arranged according to ordination seniority); never being satisfied with the meals and talking only of those offered at other monasteries; failing to attend tea ceremonies after being invited; complaining about the abbot's insufficient courtesy; appropriating property that has been temporarily entrusted to one's care; and becoming overly friendly with the younger generation while scorning the venerable and virtuous elders.

[84] Monks leave their home temple masters[63] and parents and travel far away to practice meditation and seek enlightenment. If such a monk has a body and mind without the Dharma, how can he transcend the secular and enter the sacred? Even if a monk has some partial understanding of the world and considers himself learned, this

is not a reason for him to turn up his nose arrogantly.[64] And even if a monk really has studied widely and has become rather erudite, it is still fitting for him to keep his feet on the ground. If someone[65] fears the knife and evades the arrow,[66] if he will not take on the monastery's burdens, if he is not willing to live and die at the same time as his fellow monks—then it can be said that he is ungrateful to his virtuous predecessors. Whenever a person is leaving his home, traveling, entering the assembly, practicing meditation, partaking of meals, drinking tea or sweetened drink, attending the morning service and evening instruction—at all times he must follow the regulations of the assembly in his words, his actions, and his demeanor. The abbot should educate and lead his disciples[67] with a patient hand.[68] If he keeps his mouth sealed, then the profound principles will fall to the ground.[69] When a member of the younger generation receives the Dharma medicine,[70] he should carve it into his bone and inscribe it in his heart. He should try his utmost to cultivate even the smallest traces of goodness and should endeavor to remedy even the slightest imperfections. All of the above principles are the very reason the informal sermon is given.

Commencement of the Summer Retreat[71]

[85] If an itinerant monk wishes to go on a monastery's summer retreat, he must take up residence in that monastery half a month in advance. This principle ensures that he will not be in haste for the welcoming tea ceremony.[72]

[86] On the fourteenth day of the fourth month, after the midday meal, the poster announcing the chanting[73] is put up. In the evening the administrators prepare incense, flowers, and other items needed for the service[74] in front of the earth hall to summon the assembly to the chanting. The words recited by the rector before the chanting are: "I venture to say, the summer breeze now blows through the fields and the Flame Emperor[75] reigns over the region. When the Dharma King 'prohibits the feet,'[76] it is the time for the children of Śākya[77] to protect all living creatures. I respectfully summon the assembly to gather solemnly at the spirit shrine to chant the great name of ten thousand virtues[78] and transfer this merit[79] to the rulers of all the halls[80] in all monasteries, and to pray that they protect the monastery, allowing for a peaceful retreat. Now we must depend on the venerable assembly to chant at length." After the chanting, the rector continues, "Let us transfer the merit of chanting to the dragon and the deities, that is, to the earth guardians who protect the right Dharma. We humbly wish that the light of the deities will develop this merit, help the monastery to flourish, and give the blessing of selflessness.

Now we must depend on the venerable assembly[81] to chant again. 'All the Buddhas in all ten directions.'"[82] Briefly the Dharma instruments are played as the monks chant, after which the drum is struck and they leave for the Sangha hall. The administrator has the server wait until he hears the announcement of the second chanting service[83] before he strikes the drum. The rector prepares beforehand the diagram indicating the monks' seniority,[84] at which time fragrant flowers are offered. (All of this is arranged in front of the Sangha hall.) All those present circumambulate the hall in order and sit in their own positions. One of the administrators presides over the service. Originally the prior presided over the service, with the rector substituting when the prior was unavailable. Before the chanting, a poster should be presented to the chief seat to invite him as well as the assembly. The poster should read: "Tonight the priory will sponsor a tea ceremony in cloud hall[85] especially for the chief seat and the assembly, simply to symbolize the commencement of the summer retreat.[86] I humbly wish that you will all kindly descend to provide us with your illuminating company. Sincerely written by Prior Bhikṣu X et al."

[88] On the day of the fifteenth, before the early meal, the administrators, chief officers, junior monks, and the abbot's Dharma relatives come to the abbot's quarters to greet him. If the abbot relieves them of this formality the night before, they need not come. After the abbot ascends the platform in the Dharma hall, the administrators step forward and do *liangzhan sanli*. For the first bow they unfold their sitting mats, saying, "As this retreat disallows the use of feet,[87] we shall be afforded the opportunity to tend the abbot's towel and water vessel.[88] We hope to depend on the abbot's Dharma power for support, and we hope there will be no difficulties." The administrators again unfold their sitting mats, extend the seasonal greeting, and perform *chuli sanbai*. The abbot replies by saying: "We are most fortunate to have this opportunity to participate in a retreat together. I hope to depend on your Dharma power to foresee and alleviate all difficulties." The greetings of the chief seat and the assembly follow this same pattern. Next the chief seat and the assembly do *liangzhan sanli* before the abbot while the junior monks, the attendants, the postulants, the abbot's Dharma relatives, and the novices stand to one side so as to avoid performing this courtesy at the same time. When everyone has finished this courtesy, the administrators return to the storage hall and stand in the host position. The chief seat leads the assembly into the priory to greet the administrator with a *chuli sanbai*. At this point the junior monks, the attendant, the Dharma relatives, and others go to the Dharma hall to pay homage to the abbot. Then the chief seat stands before

the Sangha hall facing south while the assembly faces north. They do *chuli sanbai* to each other, circumambulate the hall in order of ordination seniority, and remain standing. The administrators then enter the hall, approach the Holy Monk, fully unfold their sitting mats, prostrate themselves three times, stand up, and do *chuli sanbai* before the chief seat. The assembly bows down in return, and the administrators circumambulate the hall and exit. The abbot enters the hall burning incense, fully unfolds his sitting mat, bows down three times, and stands up. At this time the junior monks conceal themselves, standing behind the Holy Monk, thus shielding themselves from inadvertently being the object of the abbot's bow. The Dharma relatives follow the assembly. In front of the chief seat the abbot will do *chuli* again, and the assembly will do a prostration in response and circumambulate the hall in the same manner indicated above. The junior monks wait until the assembly stands up from the prostration before standing in their positions and waiting to bow.

[89] The abbot exits the hall, and all bow down to each other three times, beginning with the chief seat, saying, "We are most fortunate to have this opportunity to make a retreat together. I fear that my thoughts, words, and deeds[89] are inferior, and so I beg your compassion." Then everyone, beginning with the chief seat, returns to their hall of residence. If this hall is the assembly quarters, then all beginning with the director and chief seat of the assembly quarters do *chuli sanbai* to each other. The words of gratitude exchanged are the same as those in the Sangha hall. Then the abbot visits each quarter one at a time, beginning with the storage hall. The assembly follows him **[90]** and escorts him to the abbot's quarters and retires. All the monks then greet each other at their own discretion. The abbot's office, priory, and chief seat in order sponsor tea ceremonies in the Sangha hall. The abbot's office sponsors a tea ceremony for the administrators and the chief officers, inviting the chief seat and the assembly to accompany them.

[90] The next day is the special tea ceremony sponsored by the priory for the scribe, the chief officers, and those under them. The chief seat and the assembly are invited to accompany them. After this, the chief seat sponsors a tea ceremony in the Sangha hall for the administrators and the chief officers, inviting the assembly to accompany them. The rest of the officers, beginning with the rector and followed, for example, by one of the chief officers, the retired senior abbots, and the chief seat emeritus,[90] sponsor tea ceremonies for the administrators or chief officers in their own quarters.

Closing of the Summer Retreat[91]

[91] On the fourteenth day of the seventh month, in the evening, there is chanting and sweetened drink is served. On the following day, the ascending of the platform in the hall, the greetings, the visiting of various quarters, and the tea ceremonies—all is done in the same manner as the commencement of the summer retreat. Only the words on the posters are different. For example, the poster written by the prior is the same except for a small modification: "To symbolize the closing of the summer retreat." The monks then chant in front of the earth hall. The rector's words are: "I venture to say, the golden wind now blows through the fields and the White Emperor[92] reigns over the region. When the King of Enlightenment[93] brings the summer retreat to a close, it is the time of the completion of the Dharma year. We have reached the ninth ten-day period[94] of the summer without difficulty, and all the assembly are safe. Let us chant the great names of all Buddhas and repay our indebtedness to the rulers of all halls. Now we must depend on the assembly." (The remaining words are the same as those given for the commencement of the summer retreat.) The words of gratitude given by the administrators are: "It is with humble joy that we acknowledge that the Dharma year has been completed without any difficulty. This is due to the protection of the abbot's power of Dao. For this we are extremely grateful." The abbot's words of gratitude in response are: "We must give thanks for the Dharma power of X [person's name] and of others now that this Dharma year is complete. For this I am extremely grateful." The words of gratitude from the chief seat and the assembly of the Sangha hall as well as from the director of the assembly quarters and those below him are as follows: "On this ninth ten-day period of summer we have come to depend on each other. I fear that my thoughts, words, and deeds are inferior. For having disturbed the assembly I humbly beg your compassion." Then the administrators and chief officers make the announcement: "Those brothers who wish to travel must wait until the tea ceremony has ended. Only then may they go where they wish." If there is an emergency or some other urgent business, this rule may be suspended.

Winter Solstice and New Year Greetings

[92] If the abbot wishes to exempt the assembly from the festival greeting, then he must post this information in front of the Sangha hall the day before the festival. That evening the prior serves sweetened drink[95] in the Sangha hall. The poster for the winter solstice greeting includes the phrase "Simply to symbolize our congratulations on the winter solstice." The poster for the New Year greeting includes

the line "Simply to symbolize our congratulations on the changing of the year."
The beginning and end of these posters read the same as the posters described
above. The abbot then announces his sponsorship of a tea ceremony
in the Sangha hall. The words of the poster announcing this ceremony are
the same as above. The next day the abbot sponsors tea in his own quarters especially for the administrators and the chief officers, and all
the assembly are invited to accompany them. The next day the administrators hold a tea ceremony in the priory especially for the chief
seat and those under him. Then all the officers in order, beginning
with the chief seat and the rector, have special tea ceremonies in their
respective halls of residence. If the abbot does not exempt the assembly from
the winter solstice or New Year greeting, then before the early meal the junior
monks and the others must go to greet the abbot. After the abbot ascends the
platform in the Dharma hall, the assembly greets him and visits the various halls.

Abbot's Visit to the Assembly Quarters[96]

[93] In the Sangha hall a poster is hung to announce a visit to the
assembly quarters.[97] The director and chief seat of the assembly quarters arrange the seats, incense, flowers, and tea or sweetened drink
in the assembly quarters and wait for the abbot to arrive, at which
time they strike the board to summon the assembly. The monks stand
in a line in order outside the assembly quarters, facing the door of
the quarters to bow when the abbot appears. They then follow the
abbot into the quarters. The director of the assembly quarters burns
incense, and the assembly bows to the abbot, after which tea or sweetened drink is served. After the abbot has given his sermon,[98] at the
point when he stands up, the director of the assembly quarters steps
forward, unfolds his sitting mat, and extends his gratitude with the
words, "We humbly receive the abbot's Dharma-riding[99] visit, and for this we
are extremely grateful." They then extend to the abbot a seasonal greeting. If the
abbot does not accept their bowing, then the assembly merely bows
and escorts him out of the quarters. If it is not the occasion of the commencement or closing of the summer retreat, a full moon, or a new moon day,
then it is not necessary to escort the abbot outside and follow him to the various
quarters.

Reception of a Senior Venerable

[94] When a venerable senior monk[100] visits the monastery, all the
monks should gather in advance at the mountain gate to greet him
when he arrives. All those present, together with the guest, enter the
Dharma hall, where the abbot, the administrators, and the assembly

greet the guest in order of seniority. After the greeting, they escort the senior venerable to the guest lodging.[101] The guest then meets with the abbot. If he is not to stay at the guest lodging, he meets with the abbot immediately. The abbot then accompanies the guest in visiting all the quarters. They return to the abbot's quarters, have sweetened drink, and the guest is dismissed. The abbot later goes to the guest lodging to extend his gratitude. If the guest and the abbot are not Dharma relatives, they exchange letters of self-introduction.[102] That evening, the night sermon is given by the venerable guest. The next day the guest ascends the platform in the Dharma hall and there is a special feast. If the guest is of the same seniority as the abbot or the abbot's juniors, then the procedure depends on the particular situation. The method for receiving government officials is as follows. Only when a circuit supervisor[103] or a district magistrate[104] arrives should the entire assembly be mobilized to receive them. The administrators wait outside the triple gate; the chief seat and those under him wait inside the triple gate (thus the superior monks are outside). When seeing off officials, the chief seat and the assembly form a line beginning with the superior monks inside the gate. They should stand in an orderly fashion with no one standing out of line. When government officials are being greeted or seen off, the abbot remains in the Dharma hall.

Appointment of the Administrators (zhishi)

[96] The administrative section[105] includes the prior (in some places it also includes the assistant prior),[106] the rector, the cook,[107] and the superintendent. When a new appointment is needed, the abbot invites the administrators, the chief officers, the retired staff,[108] and the senior retired staff[109] to have tea. After the tea the abbot makes his request, saying, "Administrator X has announced his retirement. Now I must impose on you all to deliberate on this matter. I know of no candidate for the post of administrator, implying the question, 'Does anyone know of a suitable candidate?'" He asks again, and then a third time, for candidate suggestions. When there are no replies, the abbot says, "In that case I should like to nominate X for the position of administrator. What is your opinion on this suggestion?" When everyone consents to the appointment, the abbot sends his attendant to invite X and his acquaintances. The attendant invites the proper guests one at a time. Tea is served once more, after which the abbot stands up, saying, "Administrator X has announced his retirement. This position cannot be left vacant, so I should like to appoint (for

example) Chief Seat X to the position of administrator. I hope everyone will cordially welcome his appointment. It is my wish that there
be no objections: Think first and foremost of the Dharma."

[97] After the appointment, the new administrator does *liangzhan
sanli* to the abbot. First, he unfolds his sitting mat, saying, "I, newly ordained,
have hastily come to the monastery; everything here is unfamiliar to me, and so
to receive your exceedingly generous appointment I am extremely awestruck."
He unfolds the sitting mat a second time and extends a seasonal greeting, saying, "I humbly wish on your honorable body and your daily life ten thousand fortunes."[110] He then does chuli sanbai. Then all the administrators congratulate the abbot by performing *liangzhan sanli.* **[98]** They unfold
their sitting mats, saying, "It is the great fortune of the monastery and it gives us
great joy that the newly appointed Administrator X has received your kind decree. We are extremely elated." They unfold their sitting mats, extend a seasonal
greeting, and do *chuli* as above. Next, by way of mutual *chuli sanbai*, one
by one they all congratulate the new administrator, who thanks them
in return. His words of gratitude are: "I am extremely ashamed to stain the honor
of your recommendation." And then the words of congratulation from the other
administrators: "Your capabilities are so great that you could carry all the burden of the assembly's work. Knowing this we have reason to celebrate." A chair
is moved to the abbot and placed facing the center, after which sweetened drink is served. When the abbot is prepared to announce the
new appointment, the bell is rung to summon the assembly into the
hall, where the monks remain sitting. The rector burns incense before the Holy Monk and privately informs the abbot. The rector then
circumambulates the hall, bows, and strikes with the hammer once,
saying, "I announce to you all, Former Administrator X has made
known his retirement and this position cannot remain vacant. We
have received the abbot's kind decree to appoint Senior X[111] as administrator. I announce this to you with all sincerity." The rector
strikes the hammer once, and the administrators, the chief officers,
the retired staff, and the senior retired staff approach the new administrator to elicit his consent.

[99] After receiving his appointment, the new administrator does
liangzhan sanli to the abbot. The words of gratitude are the same as above.
The rector strikes with the hammer once, saying, "And now we are
able to appoint X to the position of administrator. I announce this
with all sincerity," and then strikes once more. The guest master leads
the new administrator before the Holy Monk, and the administrator
fully unfolds his sitting mat and bows down three times. He then folds
his sitting mat before the chief seat and does *chuli sanbai*. The as-

sembly bows in return, after which the guest master escorts the new administrator to circumambulate the hall and exit. The rector then makes the announcement, "Now I should like to invite the assembly to escort the administrator into the storage hall." If it is the rector who is being appointed, the guest master or the abbot's first attendant makes the announcement: "Now I should like to invite the assembly to escort the rector into the rectory." Then all the assembly, beginning with the abbot, escort him into the storage hall or the rectory. The abbot assumes the center seat and is approached by the new rector, who does *liangzhan sanli* to him and escorts him to the exit. The rector then returns to his position and exchanges *chuli sanbai* with his colleagues, the chief seat, and the assembly, after which he escorts the assembly to the exit. The attendant to the rector then collects the new rector's clothes and quilts, places them in a trunk, and returns to the rectory to make arrangements. The guest master then leads the new rector on visits to the various quarters. They visit the abbot's quarters first, where they sit in a prearranged way and have sweetened drink. Here the senior retired staff accompany them. After all the quarters have been visited in order, the former administrator transfers[112] the records of money and silk[113] to the new one while the abbot, other administrators, and chief officers are present. On the same day or the next, the new administrator sponsors a tea ceremony and then withdraws.

[101] The next day the priory holds a special feast. The newly appointed administrator should act in accordance with the old customs and not alter his duties or powers or inflate his own importance. If he should have his own idea for a change in policy, he must wait to consult the abbot and his colleagues courteously, and if it is deemed feasible he may carry it out. If his proposal is not agreed on, he should halt his plans. He should not violate public opinion by indulging his own ideas and disturb the assembly. The day after the feast, the abbot holds a special tea ceremony in the Sangha hall for the new and old administrators. The poster for the tea ceremony reads as follows: "This morning after the meal, the abbot will sponsor a special tea ceremony to extend gratitude to the new and old administrators X [their specific positions] in the cloud hall. The chief seat and the assembly are also invited to descend and join us in their illuminating company. This day X of month X. Respectfully written by Attendant X." The poster for this ceremony is posted outside the Dharma hall on the right-hand side. The new prior waits for the abbot and the chief seat to finish their tea ceremony before entering the hall and holding a tea ceremony for the chief seat and the assembly. The poster for the tea ceremony reads as follows: "This morning after the meal

the priory will sponsor a special tea ceremony for the chief seat and the assembly in the cloud hall. All administrators are invited to accompany them. I humbly ask that you all kindly descend to provide us with your illuminating company. This month X, day X. Respectfully written by Administrator Bhikṣu X." Before the midday meal, the new administrator prepares a box and carries in it a poster for the tea ceremony, presenting it to the chief seat, saying, "It is my honor to inform[114] you, Chief Seat, that this morning after the meal a tea ceremony will be held in the hall. Therefore I humbly request your kindness to descend to attend." Sometimes he does *chuli sanbai* (this action is performed only when inviting senior monks who have been abbots or chief seats), sometimes he merely bows and exits. He then has the server place the poster for the tea ceremony outside the Dharma hall on the left-hand side. He has the servers invite the chief officers from all quarters and goes himself to the abbot's office, where he does *liang-zhan sanbai*. First, he unfolds the sitting mat, saying, "This morning after the meal a tea ceremony will be sponsored in the hall specially for the chief seat. I respectfully invite you, Master,[115] and the assembly to provide him with your company. I humbly beg your kindness to give your assent." He then unfolds the sitting mat a second time to extend the seasonal greeting and then does *chuli sanbai*. The new administrator invites his colleagues to enter the hall and accompany the assembly. The next day the special shift[116] from old to new administrators and from old to new chief officers in the storage hall takes place, and the chief seat and the assembly are invited to be present. Then one by one tea ceremonies are sponsored by the administrator, the chief seat, and the chief officers for the new and old administrators. If the assistant prior, the cook, or the superintendent is in the storage hall, or if the rector is in the rectory, he also holds a tea ceremony. Only the abbot, the prior, and the chief seat will enter the hall for the tea ceremony.

Fascicle Three

Prior (jianyuan)[1]

[105] The prior manages various affairs of the monastery, including supplies and petitions to government officials, greeting such officials, the ceremony performed by the assembly of circumambulating the hall with incense, visits to donors, extending congratulations and condolences, financial loans, the annual budget, monitoring of grain storage, bookkeeping, and providing for meals year by year. The prior is entrusted with the purchase of grain as well as the making of vinegar and pastes and sauces according to the season. He should carefully tend to the production of oil and grinding. He must organize feasts for monastic assemblies with the utmost skill and effort. He must show attentive hospitality to guests from all four directions. The winter solstice feast, the New Year feast, the retreat-ending feast, the retreat-commencement feast, and the eggplant-roasting feasts[2] (which are held on the occasions of Duanwu, the Qixi, and the Chongjiu),[3] the ceremony commemorating the first and last days of the use of the heating stove,[4] the Laba Festival,[5] and the feast marking the middle of the second month[6] are managed by the prior, provided that the given ceremony is within the means of the monastic budget. If a festival requires work beyond his capabilities, the prior enlists the aid of others. He manages minor or routine affairs unilaterally, but for greater matters and for those cases where the reputation of the monastery may be at stake,[7] he consults the administrators and the chief officers and reports back to the abbot before carrying them out. He gently counsels monks (except the abbot) who have violated the regulations or betrayed the customs (no matter how great or small the infraction) rather than remain silent or chastise them with exceedingly harsh words. The prior should instruct postulants beforehand with skill and expediency to prevent such incidents and should not beat or whip them indiscriminately after a transgression has been committed. If punishment is called for, he should carry it out[8] openly before the assembly in the storage hall; the punishment should not exceed twenty strokes. The prior should be prudent in regard to unexpected events. For a server to be expelled from the monastery,[9] his offense must be severe, and he should be questioned first and must admit to the crime. The prior should report the offense to the abbot, who alone can rule on the expulsion. The final decision is not the responsibility of the prior. If inappropriate behavior does occur, the monastery should prevent the matter from attracting investigations by government officials.[10] In se-

lecting positions such as the traveling fundraiser,[11] the director of the farming village,[12] the coal master, the paste master,[13] the porridge master,[14] the traveling *Prajna Sutra* preacher,[15] the traveling *Avataṃsaka Sutra* preacher,[16] **[106]** the bath master, the water master,[17] the head gardener,[18] the mill master,[19] and the lamp master[20] to assist the chief officers, the prior should consult the abbot, leaving ample time for the appointment decision, and should not delay. When donors visit the monastery, the prior must arrange their seating and entertain them in a proper and courteous fashion. When there is a great feast the prior must consult the administrators and the chief officers beforehand to prevent any possible oversight.

[109] Such is the essential virtue of the prior: he should respect those who are capable and honorable, embrace the masses in general, be in harmony with his superiors, be friendly with his subordinates, and peacefully coexist with his colleagues. He should strive to please everyone. He should not use his position to slight or neglect others. He should not act according to personal whim, making others uncomfortable. If he is not sick or entertaining guests, the prior should be in attendance at the hall. One of his chief duties is to ensure that the servers deliver the food[21] properly at the two daily meals. When the priory is low in funds, it is the prior's responsibility to replenish the accounts; he should not approach the abbot or appeal to the assembly. If a given colleague is especially capable or virtuous, the prior should praise his worthiness before others. If a staff member is slow in his duties or if his personal behavior seems suspicious, the prior should tell him in private in hopes that this alone will inspire him to reform. If the prior maintains these virtues, the resulting harmony will make the Dharma last forever. When a staff member[22] commits a great offense and causes harm to the monastery, it is appropriate for the prior to inform the abbot in private. As to most quotidian activities of his staff, he should simply observe the general progress and passively await positive results.

Rector (weinuo)[23]

[110] The Sanskrit term *karma-dāna* is translated into Chinese as one who brings joy to the assembly.[24] All matters concerning the members of the Sangha are the responsibility of the rector. The rector should be diligent and sincere in his courtesy toward the newly arrived monks who take up residence in the Sangha hall. He is to specially select the best lodging available for those administrative officials who come from other monasteries[25] and for those personages renowned for their virtue. In determining the seniority of retired abbots, the rector should rely on their certificates of appointment[26] and their inauguration documents[27] so he can arrange their dining seats in the three leading positions of each platform section, excluding the position of chief seat in the Sangha hall. Worthies from every direction should be assigned by the rector to the same category of honor and be placed in the first three seats in order of their seniority by years of ordination. Each winter and summer, the rector is in charge of changing the mattresses, replacing the cool and the warm reed screens, hanging and taking down the curtains, and turning the stove on or off. He should prepare the registration list for the summer retreat[28] in advance. He must also tend to the lamps and the incense in the Sangha hall and must clean the various liturgical vessels before the assembly enters the hall. He often supervises the Holy Monk's attendant,[29] the servers of the rector, and the food-delivering servers.[30] He prepares or sets up the dormitory gate, the windows, the mosquito nets,[31] and the miscellaneous movable items in the hall. Frequently he must take special care to see that they are kept in order. The rector reports to the priory and the superintendent to replace such items when needed. **[111]** The rector must cooperate with the head of the infirmary in giving meals to sick monks, supplying mosquito nets, and delegating tasks to the hospital servers. He must make sure the sick are not left unattended.

[112] Low-ranking officers,[32] such as the abbot's attendant,[33] the attendant to the Holy Monk, the director of the hall of longevity,[34] the stove master,[35] the chief of the assembly quarters, the chief seat, the chief of the hospice pavilion,[36] and the director of the great shrine,[37] are appointed by the rector. If, however, donations to the shrines and pavilions are large and unmanageably distributed due to an inordinate number of pilgrims visiting each location, then for efficiency's sake these positions should be appointed by the abbot. If any person in the Sangha hall should commit a serious offense, the rector should report the matter to the abbot and that person should be expelled from the monastery.[38] If the transgression is slight, the rector should merely transfer the person to other quarters.[39] If there is a quarrel among members of the Sangha hall, the rector should with every possible courtesy try to bring about a reconciliation. In such a dispute, if the two refuse to yield to each other, then, according to the rule, they should be punished.[40] If any personal belongings are reported missing and the owner[41] insists on a search, the rector must announce to the assembly a search of the hall. If the missing item cannot be found, then the individual who made the false claim must be expelled or be transferred to another quarter. If the lost item is not valuable, the rector should try to assuage the owner to avoid a commotion among the assembly that could halt all progress in the monastery. The money donated to the Holy Monk is to be used only for acquiring incense, lamps, and liturgical vessels.[42] The money should not be used for other purposes. The rector takes the money from the collection box and allocates it to the *tangsi*, tallying the amount along with the Holy Monk attendant.

[113] The rector must wait for instructions from the government supervisor to post the list of monks' seniority.[43] Monks' curriculum vitae[44] and ordination certificates are to be collected and inspected by the rector. Following traditional custom, the rector also collects the registration fees.[45] Although the collection of the official certificates is the task of the priory and could be carried out unilaterally, it is more appropriate and can be done in greater detail by the rector. The rector should examine each certificate for authenticity without haste when a monk is to take up residence in the monastery. [114] He is in charge of preparing the report to the government officials regarding sick monks, the managing of funerals for deceased monks,[46] the auction of deceased monks' property,[47] and the confiscation of deceased monks' ordination certificates, certificates of the purple robe, and certificates of title within the government. The rector must then give these reports to the prior, who in turn will give them to the government. He should not violate government regulations.

[114] When the rector recites a prayer or strikes with the mallet,[48] he must be careful to do so clearly so as to generate good thoughts in the minds of the donors. The tea ceremony[49] for newly arrived monks must be conducted by the rector with special care and no lack of courtesy. When there are newly arrived monks, the rector gives the list of their ordination seniority to the attendants, the administrators, and the chief officers, [115] and he assigns the new monks a residence in the hall. One of the rector's most important duties is to know the order of ordination. (The record should read: "Newcomer *Senior* X, ordained in X year, next in seniority after monk X.") The rector has each of the assembly quarters prepare two lists, one being a register of the monks' names in each section,[50] the other recording the order of ordination,[51] both of which should be continually updated. Additionally, among the rector's important duties are knowing without error the correct seating for the tea ceremony and determining the

rotation of the directors of the assembly quarters to avoid any disturbances at assemblies. Whenever the monks are summoned to communal labor,[52] all must work except the chief of the assembly hall
and the Sangha hall monitor. If without reason the abbot does not
attend the work session, the rector has the abbot's attendant expelled
from the monastery, unless the abbot is sick or entertaining officials
and guests.

Cook (dianzuo)[53]

[116] The cook is in charge of all the assembly's meals. He must exercise his mind with Dao and must always vary the menu so that everyone will receive enjoyment. He should not waste monastery food, and
he should make sure there is no disorder in the kitchen. In selecting
his kitchen help, he should choose people who are capable and assign them to appropriate positions. His orders should not be so severe so as to oppress his assistants, and yet not so lax that they will
not fulfill their duties. During food preparation the cook must personally make sure the food is natural, carefully prepared, and clean.
In buying the ingredients for a meal or choosing the menu, he must
consult the prior in advance. Sauces, vinegar, and pickled vegetables
are the responsibility of the cook, who must be careful not to miss
the appropriate seasons for making them. In addition, he must tend
the oven fires, lighting and extinguishing them at the proper times. The
cook should mete out benefits and tasks to everyone equally. For the
tasks that require cooperation with the prior, the superintendent, and
the chief of storage,[54] the cook should consult all three and should
not claim more than his share of the power and duties. Whenever
stoves, pots, or miscellaneous cookware are broken or become worn,
he must replace them. He must teach the kitchen servers how to follow the regulations, such as the proper way of serving food[55] in the
Sangha hall or delivering food[56] to various quarters. He must acquaint
them with proper etiquette so that, for example, when they encounter
teachers or senior monks, they stand aside and bow. The cook should
select quick-witted servers to deliver food to the abbot's office, the
administrators, and the chief officers. He must closely watch the
servers to every quarter and carefully discern which workers are in-
competent or remiss. If an administrator or chief officer decides to
keep a particular server on his own staff, the cook should respect his
decision and not insist on rotating the server. The cook eats his food
in the kitchen, but what he eats must not differ from the food served
to the assembly. After preparing a meal, the cook faces the direction

of the Sangha hall, burns incense, and worships. After completing this he can distribute the food to everyone.

Superintendent (zhisui)⁵⁷

[119] The superintendent is in charge of all manual labor. He oversees any construction, such as the replacement, repair, and decoration of gates, doors, windows, walls, and any movable items. He supervises the mill, the cultivated land, the farmhouse, and the oil workshop, as well as the stables, saddles, horses, boats, and other vehicles. He cleans the monastery, plans the farming, patrols the mountain gate, prevents robberies, assigns work to the laborers, and rotates the tenants.⁵⁸ He should be loyal and diligent, know the proper time for each enterprise, and he should be aware of each situation. For large construction projects and big tasks, he should ask the abbot for help with the planning, and then consult his colleagues, rather than simply exercising his own will.

Completion of an Administrator's Term

[120] When a staff member has finished his year of service, he enters the abbot's quarters in the evening to report his resignation. He does *chuli* three times then leaves. The next morning during breakfast, after the rector has struck the stand with the mallet, the staff member enters by the rear door. When the rector strikes the stand, the staff member says (for example), "Bhikṣu X [his own name]. In the past I received the abbot's kind decree allowing me the privilege of entering the priory in the service of X position. But now the power of my mind is exhausted, so I am announcing to you that I am ready to return to the Sangha hall. I say this with all sincerity." The stand is struck once more, and the former administrator turns from the Holy Monk to approach the abbot and does *liangzhan sanli*. The abbot then has the attendant remove the dining table, paying homage to the monk in return. After this, he approaches the Holy Monk, fully unfolds his sitting mat, and bows down three times. He then circles the hall, exits, and does *chuli* three times to his colleagues outside.

[121] After the abbot, the administrators, and the chief seat have selected a new staff member, they escort the former staff member into the Sangha hall to take up residence. There he will do *chuli* three times before the abbot, who then along with the administrators and the chief seat accompanies him to the assembly quarters, where he will once more do *liangzhan sanli* to the abbot. The retired staff member then escorts the abbot, the administrators, and the chief seat to the

door. When they have left, he will bow to the assembly, which is then dismissed. Then he and the new staff member tour the various quarters together. After a lesser tea ceremony, he will return to his own quarters, where there will be a major tea ceremony for him, his new replacement, and his old colleagues.

Appointment of the Chief Officers (toushou)[59]

[122] The chief officers include the chief seat of the Sangha hall, the scribe, the director of the library, the guest master, and the bath master. The appointing of monks to these positions is the same as for the appointing of administrators discussed previously. The appointees are escorted to their quarters by their fellow monks and led before the abbot, where they do *liangzhan sanbai*. They then escort the abbot out of the assembly quarters and do *chuli* three times to all their fellow monks. After this, the guest master takes them to visit each of the quarters, just as was done for the administrators. Then follow three days of lesser tea ceremonies and feasts held for all five positions, just as for the chief seat. The abbot sponsors a formal tea ceremony in the Sangha hall. (The poster announcing the tea ceremony[60] is, from beginning to end, the same as the aforementioned poster [used in the appointment of administrators], with one revision: "Specially held for the new chief seat to extend the courtesy of congratulations." [If the former chief seat will also be present, the revision should read, "Specially held for the new and former chief seat to extend the courtesies of congratulations and gratitude."] The administrators and the assembly are also invited to provide their illuminating company.")

[123] The next day, the chief seat holds a major tea ceremony in the hall for the scribe (if the scribe is not being replaced, then the ceremony is held for the next rank of chief officers) and the assembly. The invitation letter reads as follows: "For Chief Seat Bhikṣu X to open and receive. This morning, after the early meal, a major tea ceremony will be held in the cloud hall specially for the scribe and the assembly. I should also like to invite all the administrators to join us. I hope to be fortunate enough to receive your kind assent to descend to illuminate our ceremony. X month, X day. Written by (his appropriate title given here) X." The envelope reads, "This letter is to invite the scribe and the assembly. Sincerely, sealed by (his appropriate title given here) X." This letter should be glued inside a small box. After the invitation is finished, the poster should be placed on the south [left] side of the Sangha hall door. Next, the abbot should be invited to enter the hall to accompany the guests. Before the meal, the chief seat should have the server invite the administrators and the chief officers. After the meal, the long striking of the board summons the assembly. The chief seat stands before the Holy Monk, burns incense, fully unfolds his sitting mat, bows down

three times, circumambulates the hall once, exits the hall, and bows to the monks in the outer section of the hall. In this outer section he simply sits with the prior and the rector to have his meal. He will still announce to the assembly that the scribe will perform the prayer before the meal[61] on his behalf. A major tea ceremony for those appointed by the abbot, such as the scribe, the director of the library, the bath master, the water master, the traveling preacher, and the coal master, is held in their respective sections. For those appointed by the rector, such as the abbot's attendant, the Holy Monk's attendant, the director of the shrine, the director of the infirmary, the latrine attendant, and the stove master, the monastery sponsors a three-day lesser tea ceremony. For those appointed by the director of the library (the sutra curator,[62] the traveling precentor),[63] the monastery sponsors a lesser tea ceremony as mentioned above.

Chief Seat (shouzuo)

[124] The chief seat sets a good example for all the monks and detects and deals with any infractions of the monastic code. In the Sangha hall, the placement of the seats and monks' belongings,[64] the hanging and displaying of bowls, and the consumption of porridge, rice, tea, or sweetened drink must be done [125] quietly, unobtrusively, and in unison. Whenever inappropriate behavior occurs in the Sangha hall, the chief seat announces it to the assembly before the meal in soft language. His words should be simple and direct. The chief seat should not eat in a hasty manner and should provide cordial company for all the monks. He must not finish his meal first, fold his arms, and stare at the others, thus forcing them to eat quickly. If the food is prepared inappropriately or if the service is unbalanced— now too slow, now too fast—the chief seat should point out the problem to the people in charge of such things. His most important task is to ensure that it is peaceful and pleasant for everyone in the Sangha hall.

[125] Before a break in the abbot's schedule of sermons, the chief seat enters the Sangha hall, burns incense before the Holy Monk, and sits at his place. The Sangha hall server makes an announcement in each of the quarters, saying, "The chief seat is now sitting in the hall." (In the Huilin lineage,[65] the server strikes a board three times in front of the assembly quarters to announce this to the public.) All the monks then enter the hall and sit in their places, facing each other. The Sangha hall server first informs the abbot that the assembly is ready, then hangs the *fangcan* ["No sermon"][66] poster, rolling up the screen in the front of the hall. The server bows before the chief seat and whispers, "*He-*

shang fangcan." [The abbot is giving no sermon today.][67] Then he bows before the Holy Monk, stands up, and cries out, *"Fangcan!"* and the bell to signal a break from the abbot's sermon is struck. All the assembly display their mattresses and let down the screens covering their compartments. Finishing this, they return to the assembly quarters, bow, and can have sweetened drink at their own discretion. Or, if they are returning to the quarters chanting, they bow and have their drink first. When they finish this they return to the hall to display their mattresses and let down the screens covering their compartments. The window screen is to be lowered when the bell is struck at sunset and rolled up the next morning when the sky becomes light. In the hall, the monks are prohibited from rolling up their mattresses, folding their comforters, or rolling up their screens before *kaijing* so as not to disturb others. After breakfast, that is, after *kaijing*, or before hiatus from the scheduled sermon in the evening, the monks are not allowed to unroll their mattresses, cover themselves with their comforters, and go to sleep. In the morning, **[126]** after the long sequence of the boards and the three strikes that immediately follow signaling breakfast, the monks may take down their bowls. When entering the hall while chanting the names of the Buddhas, the monks should not cover their heads. At the end of the striking with the mallet, after the distribution of food into the bowls of each monk, the chief seat will do *yishi*,[68] clasping his hands with lowered head in an expression of gratitude for the food before him. After this, he leads the contemplation, and after the contemplation he placidly offers food to all sentient beings. All the monks wait until the chief seat starts to eat before they begin. After they finish the meal they hang their bowls and step down from the platform. They must do so calmly and without haste. It is the chief seat's duty to observe closely and give instructions pertaining to all of the above.

Scribe (shuzhuang)

[127] The scribe[69] is in charge of writing all letters and prayers in the monastery. His characters should be precise and his language consistent. His envelopes should be folded correctly. His writing should be comprehensible to superiors and to inferiors,[70] to people with evil minds and to those with pure minds,[71] to monks and to lay people.[72] He must not issue any letter without due consideration, especially when corresponding with government officials. Each year he should prepare the letters for fundraising beforehand and should be ready for any unexpected scribal demands. He should carefully inspect each letter to insure accuracy and to avoid any error in envelope folding or any omission of a donor's name or title. When writing letters on behalf of the monastery, he should use the monastery's pen and paper. When writing on the abbot's behalf, the abbot's pen and paper should be used. If the scribe is writing his own personal letter, he should not appropriate monastic property. Although it may be light like dust, it can accumulate to become a mountain.[73] It is far better to refrain from misappropriation. The scribe should not neglect the courtesy of having a lesser tea ceremony for newcomers. The posters for the announcement board beside the monastic gate and the prayers for the feasts should be made by him with a dedicated mind and should be written correctly. He should read widely—ancient and modern correspondence, poetry, and prose—to improve his knowledge. If the language used by the scribe is refined and elegant and the style is well suited to the message, then a letter transmitting a message a thousand miles away can still represent the glory of the assembly.[74] He must not use pen and ink to spite or intimidate his colleagues with no consideration for the Dharma. Monks Chanyue[75] and Qiji[76] may have obtained the title of poet-monk; Jia Dao[77] and Huixiu[78] may have abandoned the monastery to become secular officials—but was this their intention when they became monks?

Director of the Library (zangzhu)

[129] The director of the library takes care of the golden scripture, sets up the desk for reading sutra, and prepares the tea, the sweetened drink, the oil and the fire, the incense, and the candles. He appoints the director of the shrine, selects the traveling precentor, and assists people in the assembly quarters and in the sutra hall. The procedure for requesting the use of a desk for the reading of sutras is as follows: first, one must go to the chief seat in the sutra hall[79] and ascertain whether there are any desks available for use; then, if any desks are available, one must go to the director of the library and inform him; finally, after the tea, the director of the library leads those wanting to study to the desks in the sutra-reading hall, and they all do *chuli* to each other once. After the director of the library has been escorted out, those wishing to read must unfold their sitting mats, place them on the floor before the holy statue,[80] and bow down three times. They must then stand up and do *chuli* one time to the chief seat. They will then circumambulate the hall once and meet the sutra curator to request a time to read the sutras. It is not necessary to bow down. The next day, after everyone has gotten up and before the

evening hiatus from the abbot's sermon, the sutra curator strikes the bell for the reading of the sutras.[81] He checks the sutras first and then gives them to the readers. The monks who are reading the sutras must burn incense in the sutra hall and worship solemnly. While holding the sutras in their hands, the monks must not talk or laugh with others. The desk should not have sutras piled up on it, and there should be no pens, ink, miscellaneous stationery items, or Chan literature alongside the sutras. The readers should personally light the lamp flame, add oil, and extinguish the lamp, in a courteous and meticulous manner to avoid any desecration of the holy teaching. They must not entertain guests in the hall, and should someone come to visit, they must simply clasp their hands silently and return to their quarters. The readers must not talk to people outside the hall window lest they disturb others. Inappropriate times for reading the sutras include cloudy or humid days, when one's hands are not dried sufficiently, when sitting close to open flame, or when under direct sun.

[131] When returning the sutra, one must not bind it too tightly so as to damage it or too loosely so that pages fall out of order. One must not lean on the desk, pressing on the sutra with the elbows, or hold the ribbon that binds the sutra in one's mouth. To properly open the sutra one must use two hands to hold the outer cover. The left hand should be faceup and the right hand facedown, with the two hands directly opposite each other on either side of the book. The sutra should be placed on the desk without making a sound. To properly close the sutra, the right hand should be faceup and the left hand facedown. Bring the two hands together to close the sutra carefully. Opening the sutra, folding the string, closing the sutra, tying the ribbon: each of these actions has its own prescribed method. One should ask the chief seat in the sutra-reading hall and those who are familiar with these practices for specific instruction. While sitting at the desk, one should not tie or untie one's clothing, sew clothes,[82] or look for lice. If a monk does not know a certain word, he should look it up in a dictionary.[83] If he still has questions, he can inquire of others. However, if he asks too frequently he may disturb others. If he must step away from the desk for a moment, he must cover the sutra. He should not cover it with a folded *kāṣāya*. While reading sutra one should adjust the body and sit up straight. One should not make any sound or move the lips. While reading, one should not let the mind wander to unrelated topics. During the evening at the time of *kaijing*, the sutra reader should return the lamp and follow all the others in retiring to the Sangha hall. He should not delay in return-

ing the lamp when the others do, thereby perturbing the chief seat. In the evening, the monks should remove the *xiadeng* board,[84] used for extinguishing the lamps, and add more oil. If a monk has some business to attend to and cannot return to the hall to continue reading the sutra, he should entrust the person at the next desk with the removal of his *xiadeng* board. When vacating the desk, the sutra reader should first report to the chief seat and the director of the library in the sutra-reading hall and have the sutra returned to its proper storage place. The monk should carry this out in whatever way they suggest. It is the responsibility of the library director to educate the assembly concerning all the aforementioned rules. If any individual is negligent with regard to these rules, the director of the library should give him insightful instruction. The director of the library should keep all income and expense records separate and in clear order, and need only ask the abbot for his seal of approval.

Fascicle Four

Guest Master (zhike)

[135] When government officials, lay patrons, venerable seniors, clerical officials,[1] or people from any direction renowned for their virtue come to the monastery, the guest master first has his server inform the abbot's office and then leads the guests himself to see the abbot. The guest master is also in charge of the guests' accommodations. If the guests are regular visitors, the guest master shows them to the guest seats and simply offers them tea or sweetened drink. If the guests would like to visit the abbot's office, priory, or one of the various quarters, the guest master has his server take them. The guest master must keep bedding, mosquito nets, and various movable items in order in the dormitory for overnight guests. The guest master should treat monks[2] who stay overnight with gentleness and solicitude.[3] When lay patrons come to donate money for feasts, simply to visit, or to offer incense,[4] they should always be escorted by the guest master. With visiting guests, the guest master should be respectful and sincere and should not speak impetuously about insignificant things. He must praise the master, the administrators, and the chief officers with true words and say good things about all the assembly. Word of unpleasant matters at home need not be spread outside.

Supply Master (kutou)

[136] The supply master is in charge of such things as the monastery's savings, grain, income, expenses, and annual budget. He must record immediately and clearly all monies received and payments made. He should know how much vegetable stock, rice, and wheat remain in supply. He should stay apprised of these amounts and should purchase more when appropriate. Once every ten days, the supply master reckons the accounts and together with the administrators stamps it with his approval. Once a month the account totals are given to the abbot for his signature. [137] The supply master should not arbitrarily hide precious items such as silver and gold. He should know the amount of currency in the accounts and must not loan it to anyone without permission. If the master or his colleagues make unreasonable requests for money, the supply master is not obliged to comply and should stand his ground. All the monastery's money down to the last cent is the property of all monks from all directions. How can the supply master make use of these

funds according to his own selfish whims? Unless the monastery has permitted him to loan monies to a lay patron or to a powerful government official who has protected the Dharma, the supply master should not lend monastic property to anyone capriciously. When considering a loan of grain or money, unless it is to be a strict loan to the master or a colleague who can reimburse the monastery from his own accounts, the supply master should not lend out monastic property without good reason. The supply master's server should be mentally astute and able to understand mathematical calculations. The supply master should entrust this position to one who is upright and incorruptible, whose words and actions correspond, and whose virtue is publicly recognized.

[138] When a monastery is located in the mountains or in a remote area somewhat distant from the city, the supply master is obliged to make sure that all the necessities used by monks (such as medicine, honey, tea, and paper) are stored in adequate supply. If the monks or postulants ask him to buy these necessities with excessive frequency, the supply master should maintain the mind of Dao and should not lose patience. There must never be a lack of provisions for those monks who have fallen ill. Whenever the supply master needs to buy medicine, he should do so without delay to meet the demands of the situation. If any leaks are discovered in the food storage containers, if this food becomes infested with birds or mice, or if the grain is in danger of rotting due to heat and humidity, the supply master must protect this monastic property and move the food to a better location. If the food has been stored improperly, it is the supply master's responsibility to report this to a colleague and remedy the situation.

Bath Master (yuzhu)

[139] The day before setting up the bath,[5] the bath master scrubs down the bathhouse and begins boiling water. On the day of the bath, before mealtime, he posts the announcement for the "opening of the baths," the "rinsing of sweat," or the "cleaning of the hair."[6] In the bathhouse, the bath master decorates the area designated for the Holy Ones,[7] sets out clean towels, incense, flowers, lamps, and candles, and prepares "wind medicine"[8] and tea sets for all the monks. After the midday meal, he signals the readiness of the baths by striking the board. Then the bath master escorts the donors into the bathhouse to burn incense, worship, and invite the Holy Ones to enter the water.[9]

After waiting a moment for the Holy Ones to bathe, the bath master invites all the monks by striking the bell[10] and drum. The first two sessions are for the general assembly of monks, the next for the servers, the fourth and last is reserved for the abbot and the administrators. The correct procedure for striking the board in the bathhouse is as follows: the first strike signals hot water, the second indicates cooler water, and the third indicates that the bath is full.

[140] The following are the rules for entering the bath: The senior monks go to the upper hall and the junior monks go to the lower hall. Everyone must bring his own clean towel and basin. While bathing, the monks should not be naked, and they should preserve a sense of modesty.[11] They should not laugh or talk loudly or make noise with their buckets and ladles. They should not spit or blow their noses, thus polluting the water. They cannot wash their clothes in the bath or hang them over the fire to dry out the lice. They must not enter the bath barefoot. They must not contaminate the pure water passage or the bath water in any way. The monks should respect each other and yield to their superiors. They should not behave unceremoniously with one another. If some violation of the regulations occurs, the bath master should try to reprimand the monks in an instructional manner, with soft words rather than an angry face and risk offending the assembly. The bath master must prepare the bath in accordance with the seasonal schedule and cannot be remiss in his duties. On any given bath day he must be present to tend the fire and the candles in the proper fashion and to clean the bathhouse. Having finished this, he may rest. The account books for the bathhouse need only the stamp of approval from the abbot's office.

Street Fundraisers (jiefang), Water Master (shuitou), Coal Master (tantou), and the Avataṃsaka Sutra Preacher (huayantou)[12]

[141] Certain officers of the monastery are entrusted with the task of leaving the monastery to encourage potential lay patrons to "cultivate their fields of merit" by giving to the monastery. Within the monastery these monks help other monks to nurture the fruit of Dao. These positions include the fundraiser for porridge, the fundraiser for rice and wheat, the fundraiser for vegetables, the fundraiser for paste, the water master, the coal master,[13] the lamp master, the Avataṃsaka Sutra preacher, the Prajna Sutra preacher,[14] the sutra preacher,[15] and the Amitābha Sutra preacher.[16] [142] If these monks' actions do not correspond to the deeds of the Holy Ones and if they

do not exercise their own minds of Dao, how can they repay the hopes of the people whose donations they collect?

Mill Master (motou)

[143] The duty of the mill master[17] is as follows. It is preferable for the drip sieve to be fine in order to sift out the small pebbles. The dust sifter has no holes and is for coarser products; therefore, it is used only to wash away dust. When using the drip sieve, a fan mechanism[18] is used at the same time. The dust sifter must be struck three hundred times. New wheat does not have to be rinsed, but inferior wheat should be washed. To wash this inferior wheat, mix two pecks[19] of wheat with eight pecks of unwashed dry wheat and place in the shade. During the ninth month of the year, three pecks should be washed, increasing the amount washed by one peck each month until the twelfth month, when six pecks should be washed. During the first month of the year, five pecks should be washed, decreasing the amount washed by one peck each month, so that in the fourth month only two pecks are washed. Mixing the wheat with a little moisture and storing it overnight so that in the morning the consistency is neither dry nor wet—this is the crucial method. As the saying goes, "For the coarse product, the dust sifter; for the fine product, the drip sieve; and rinse the wheat according to the four seasons."

The mill master must monitor the moisture of the wheat, increase or decrease the amount to be washed, and place the wheat in the shade. If the wheat is too dry or too wet, it will be somewhat difficult to produce flour. As part of the first and second steps in the procedure, the wheat must be ground into a fine consistency or else it will be difficult to obtain flour. Also part of the first and second steps, the wheat must be steamed. The third step is to moisten the flour, and the fourth and fifth steps are to wash and rewash the flour. The finest sifter[20] should be used in the open position and should not be stepped on with the foot. The millstone should be covered with a cloth skirt to protect it from dust. Animal waste should not accumulate around the stone. The animal tracks should be kept dry and flat. The beasts of burden should be fed twice a day. One should not be remiss in watering and feeding grass to the animals at the proper times. During the summer, the days are longer, so it is easier for the animals to become thirsty; therefore, they can be watered an extra time. The animal's collar should be flat and even, and the bridle should be neat and untangled. Care should be taken that the harness is tied well to avoid rubbing or chafing. If an animal becomes sick, it should be treated as soon as possible. When the animals become fatigued, they should be allowed to rest. The mill master should work diligently to inspire the spiritual mind in his servers and workers.

Chief Gardener (yuantou)[21]

[145] The duty of the chief gardener[22] is to fertilize the crops, erect boundaries between fields, sow the seed, cultivate the sprouts, irrigate the crops, and eliminate weeds—all of which must be done in a timely fashion. The chief gardener should consult experts in these matters for assistance. He must gauge the seasonal weather conditions to guarantee that there will be vegetables in supply all year round. He must give the best vegetables to the assembly and can sell only what remains as surplus. He must continually repair or replace his tools[23] and should try to maintain harmonious relations with the cook. Generally speaking, in the beginning of spring he should plant lettuce, turnips, and plantains. Before the festival of Hanshi,[24] he should plant eggplant, gourd, cucumber, senna, gumbo, and basil. Radishes are to be planted in the middle of the fifth month, cucumbers in the middle of sixth month, and cole and spinach in the middle of the seventh month.

Director of the Farming Village (zhuangzhu)[25]

[146] The following are the duties of the director of the farming village.[26] He must oversee the semiannual taxes paid to the government.[27] Ploughing the soil, sowing seeds, hoeing weeds, harvesting, grafting, building dikes, and collecting fertilizer—all of these activities must be done by him at the appropriate times. He should personally make sure his subordinates maintain and clearly mark the field boundaries. He should see that the animals are fed well and that the whipping of the animals is minimized. He should help the tenants[28] settle in the village and select good families. He should arrange for the seamstresses to work in an open, conspicuous place so as to avoid any suspicion. The records of grain and income should be kept in a precise fashion, and wine, meat, or onions should never be allowed to enter the monastery. The director of the farming village should not become engaged in the material expansion of his enterprise.[29] He should delegate responsibilities in an expedient manner to his servers and workers. He must skillfully arbitrate between the south and [147] the north during disagreements among the villagers.

He should exercise prudence so as not to hire poor workers or allow indolence.

Monks who come to stay overnight in the village should be treated with respect and sincerity; however, the director should not use the monastery's money to offer gifts to monks from all directions.[30] If a cow or a mule should suddenly die, it must be buried deep in the ground. The horns and skin should be removed immediately and sent to the government.[31] The director of the farming village should not wait until government officials personally come to inquire about the livestock. If villagers allow the animals to trample the fields or invade the grain supply, the director of the farming village should only reiterate the rules to the villagers and give instructions not to let it happen again. He must not beat them, shout at them, or complain to government officials. After the fall harvest, the director of the farming village and the tenants divide the yield among themselves and estimate the total crops.[32] The records kept should be precise and clear; however, when conflict does arise, the director should make concessions to people from all directions.[33] If there is need for repair or construction, the director should notify the administrators in the monastery beforehand.

Monastery's External Agent (xieyuanzhu)

[148] The duty of the monastery's external agent[34] is to trade the monastery's grain. He must also keep abreast of the latest changes or replacements of county officials, seek out news of any governmental pronouncements, and report back to the monastery. He sometimes collects donations and occasionally he entertains donors who have come from far away.

Director of the Infirmary (yanshou tangzhu)[35]

[149] The monastery should hire a person with a broad mind, who is patient in all matters, who always maintains the mind of Dao, who will comfort a sick monk, and who knows the repercussions of the law of cause and effect to be director of the temple's infirmary, the hall of longevity. Supplies for the infirmary, such as firewood, coal, rice, flour, oil, salt, pickled vegetables, tea, medicinal herbs, ginger, dates, black plums, and other miscellaneous items, must be obtained from the devotees by the director of the infirmary. If the director of the infirmary is incapable of acquiring all of these, the monastery will furnish only the rice, flour, oil, and coal. When a sick monk **[150]** comes to the hall for recuperation and recovery, the director of the infirmary has his server make up a bed and make all other preparations in the proper fashion. He must cook the medicinal herbs, offer meals, inquire from time to time as to the patient's well-being, and make the sick monk feel as comfortable as possible. If the patient begins to suffer or becomes irritable, if he rejects his medicine or meals for the slightest of reasons, if he starts to moan or scream, or if he begins to defecate in an unhygienic manner, the director of the infirmary must continue to care for him with sympathy and should not allow feelings of disgust or aversion to enter his mind. If the patient wants wine in which to cook or soak his medicinal herbs, or if he wants fish, meat, onions, or scallions to nourish his body, the director of the infirmary must educate the patient about the law of cause and effect and the prohibition of these items by the precepts to strengthen the righteousness of the patient's mind and keep him from indulging in evil thoughts. He must severely prohibit the food servers, the barbers, and the seamsters from smuggling wine or meat into the infirmary. (If medicinal herbs must be blended with wine, they can be soaked outside the monastery, or the wine may be mixed with an herbal paste to make pills. The cooking of onions with medicine or the blending of medicine with animal liver, kidney, fish, or any meat is not permissible, not to mention the direct, unrestrained consumption of these foods.)

[151] As long as the sick monk is strong enough to move about and can still take meals, the director of the infirmary must persuade him to remain a vegetarian and refrain from violating the precepts. The woks and pots in the infirmary cannot be used to boil cloth; such an action would prevent them from being usable for others. The director of the infirmary cannot accept into the infirmary, or give meals to, people who have not come for recuperation. (In some monasteries, a strict log of the number of patients in the infirmary is kept, and this record is consulted when supplies and donations one requested from the priory.) When a patient becomes critically ill, the director of the infirmary should notify the rectory to keep abreast of his condition and should remove the sick man to the pavilion of the critically ill. (If the critically ill patient's eyes of Dao are not clear and sharp [that is, if he has not yet attained a higher state], the director of the infirmary should encourage him to concentrate on the name of the Amitābha Buddha and to hope for rebirth in the Pure Land. If he can, it is best for the director of the infirmary to lead his colleagues in chanting and striking the bell to help the dying man's concentration.) Among the Eight Merit Fields, attending to the sick is first and foremost.[36] (The Eight Merit Fields are: the Buddha, Dharma, and Sangha [which are considered

as one], father, mother, teachers, the poor, bridge building, well digging, and attending to the sick.)[37] When those monks who wander about without roots like duckweed on the water become ill, who will give them sympathy? They will recover only if they can depend on the compassion of their fellow monks. The director of the infirmary's task is extremely important; how can he undertake it without the utmost sincerity?

Latrine Attendant[38] (jingtou)

[152] In accordance with his duties, the latrine attendant lights the lamp at the fifth *geng*,[39] and when the sun rises he collects the bamboo spatulas[40] and wash towels and places them in water to soak. Then he must wash the latrines and sweep the floor, replacing the bamboo spatulas, the wash towels, the ashes, [153] and the bean pod soap. He then cleans the hand- and face-washing hut.[41] After the meal, he washes the bamboo spatulas and towels. Having finished this,[42] he boils water and adds oil. He must ensure that there is a continuous supply of hot water so as not to trouble the minds of the assembly. The latrine attendant carries out that which many people consider the most burdensome and disagreeable occupation. One can say that by performing this task, the latrine attendant is practicing merit. His bad karma cannot remain unextinguished or unredeemed; his merit cannot but gain in stature. How can his fellow monks enter the latrines with arms folded idly without feeling ashamed?

Shrine Director (dianzhu), *Bell Master* (zhongtou), *et cetera*

[154] The shrine director, the pavilion director, the pagoda director,[43] the director of the arhat hall,[44] the director of the Water-land hall,[45] the director of the hall of patriarchal pictures,[46] and the bell master are charged with dusting their respective shrines, displaying the liturgical vessels, cleaning up as required, arranging the incense and lamps, and spreading the cushions after the abbot's sermon in time for everyone to worship. In the book entitled *Fufazang yinyuan zhuan*,[47] the King of Zha in the land of Kaśmīra[48] died and was reborn as a thousand-headed fish, whereupon his heads were continually being severed one at a time by a great wheel of swords. The pain the former king felt was beyond description, but each time he heard the sound of a bell, the swords did not descend, providing him with temporary relief.[49] Therefore, the striking of the bell in the morning and the evening is a practice not lacking in Buddhist significance. (The monk

Shi Zhixing (588–632) in the *Biography of Eminent Monks, Second Series,* strikes the bell in the proper fashion and the sound of the bell vibrates to hell, where suffering beings are relieved.)[50]

Holy Monk's Attendant (shengseng shizhe)[51]

[155] The Holy Monk's attendant is required to set out the offerings of food, tea, incense, lamp, and candles to the Holy Monk. He should work with the server to the rectory in sweeping the Sangha hall, dusting the sutra closets and desks, and arranging the liturgical vessels. After offering money to the Holy Monk, during mealtime, the Holy Monk's attendant collects the donations for the Holy Monk and puts them into the collection pail. (The collection pail is hung on the pillar next to the chief seat's position. The Holy Monk's attendant briefly shows the donations to the chief seat and deposits them in the pail.) At the close of each of the two meals, he is also in charge of striking with the mallet to signal the monks' egress from the hall. (He must wait until the abbot, who is the first to exit, returns his bowl to its proper place before striking this signal, and he then withdraws to stand behind the Holy Monk to avoid obstructing the abbot's bowing to the assembly.) [156] The Holy Monk receives clothing and monetary gifts as donations. With the exception of robes and money, which the attendant collects with the rector and tallies in the records, all donations are entrusted solely to the Holy Monk's attendant. These include handkerchiefs, needles, thread, tea, medicine, and money given specifically for the reading of the sutra or for *jieyuan,* small donations given for the sake of the common bond among all living things.[52]

Stove Master (lutou)[53]

[157] Although the stove master is officially appointed by the rector, he is chosen by the monks in charge of coal.[54] On the first day of the tenth month he lights the heating stove, and on the first day of the second month he extinguishes it. He prepares the stove before the break from abbot's sermon and adds coal each morning before breakfast. Gauging the room temperature at all times, he adds or removes coal to maintain the desired heat. When the weather is warm, adding too much coal is a waste of donated fuel; when the weather is freezing, adding too little will leave the assembly cold. The stove master should always sweep out the soot from the stoves. When fellow monks gather around the stove, they should yield to each other and not crowd or shove. They should not draw out the ashes, poke at the fire, make noise with the fire tongs, or chatter idly. They should

not take advantage of the fire for personal household chores without permission.

Sangha Hall Monitor (zhitang)

[158] The rotation procedure for assigning the positions of Sangha hall monitor[55] begins with the second sleeping seat,[56] excluding the chief seat, in the upper section of the Sangha hall and moves one sleeping seat at a time in a circle. The monitor's task is to protect all the monks' personal effects. In the morning, after the long strikes of the board, when the monks have assembled for the meal, the previous day's monitor approaches the senior monk[57] on duty that day, holding the placard indicating "Monitor." He bows and says, "Senior, you are on duty today." He then hands him the placard, bows again, and returns to his seat. (If it is the case that one's eating seat[58] is not located near one's sleeping seat,[59] then the previous day's monitor should remember who occupies the sleeping seat next in line. If the previous day's monitor does not know where his successor takes his meals—for example, if the successor does not eat in the same Sangha hall—he should seek him out in a patient manner. Even if the successor is seated immediately to the side of the monk who has completed his shift, the previous day's monitor should descend from the platform to hand over the placard. The one who receives does not descend from the platform but merely performs a half bow in acceptance.) The monitor must always remain in the Sangha hall and keep watch over the upper and lower sections. If he has other business to attend to, he should entrust a close and reliable fellow monk with the duty temporarily.

The monitor should not attend ceremonies in the Dharma hall. He should not accept invitations for chanting at the infirmary or outside the monastery, and he should not join tea ceremonies at any location. If the entire assembly is leaving the monastery, the monitor can leave his post only when the rector has given instructions to lock the hall. Until then, he cannot be away from his appointed position. After the break from abbot's sermon, he is relieved of his duty. If a loss occurs in the hall before this break, it is the monitor's responsibility. (Thus, the break from the abbot's sermon marks the outer limit of the watch.)[60] If a monk wants to open a closet to retrieve his belongings, he must first inform the monitor. If the person does not report to him beforehand, the monitor should confront and question him. After the break from the abbot's sermon and before *kaijing*, fellow monks are not allowed to open any closet to take items out, but putting their belongings into the closet is permissible. If anyone is seen violating this rule, his neighbor and other surrounding monks should try to stop him. Monks should not attempt to evade the monitor's authority or change their sleeping place without prior permission, thereby potentially disturbing the other monks' peace of mind.

Director of the Assembly Quarters (liaozhu)[61]

[160] The director of the assembly quarters is appointed according to a rotating schedule determined by the monks' chronological seniority in entering the assembly quarters. Some monasteries have terms of duty for one month, some for half a month, some for ten days. Each director of the assembly quarters takes care of the belongings of all the monks in his respective hall. He is accountable for the transfer of all miscellaneous movable items (as well as an inventory list) to his sucessor. He arranges tea services for newcomers and the formal tea ceremonies for the former and new staff. He is in charge of the stove and coal in the assembly quarters and should keep cold and hot water in supply. His duty is to clean the hall and serve his fellow monks in a respectful, diligent, and tireless manner. If anyone in the hall violates the rules, the director of the assembly quarters should approach him with soft language rather than loudly commanding or scolding him, which would disturb the assembly. If some item is needed, the director of the assembly quarters should make use of the time when the abbot is visiting the assembly quarters to tactfully report what is needed. But he should not make such a request without good reason. The monks should not use the water containers to wash or boil lice from their clothes.[62] The director of the assembly quarters should prohibit solicitors and unauthorized people from entering the hall to prevent theft.

Chief Seat of the Assembly Quarters (liao shouzuo)

[161] The person appointed as the chief seat of the assembly quarters should be a senior monk of great virtue, who has lived in the monastery for a long time, and is familiar with monastic etiquette. He should take up residence in the assembly quarters to guard the monks' personal effects in conjunction with the director of the assembly quarters.[63] These two should also greet newcomers. (To avoid unnecessary bother, they should offer only one portion of incense, medicine, and tea to each newcomer.) Should fellow monks fall to quarreling, it is the duty of the chief seat, along with the director of the assembly quarters, to placate them. They should not allow any monks into the assembly quarters before *kaijing*. After the break from the abbot's sermon, they should not allow monks to enter the storage room and

arbitrarily open the trunks. Monks are allowed to open the trunks only in case of emergency (for instance, to procure medicine or to obtain clothes during a sudden cold spell) and then only after informing the chief seat or the director of the assembly quarters. The chief seat should not allow people uninvited by the rector to remain in the assembly quarters.

Abbot's Attendant (tangtou shizhe)

[162] If an abbot's attendant needs to be appointed, he should be young and physically strong, his words should be precise and clear, he should be righteous in the observance of the precepts, and he should be especially quick-witted; then everything in the abbot's office will be accomplished with natural ease. The formal tea ceremony and **[163]** the lesser tea ceremony should be held according to seasonal protocol. If the attendant ensures that the visiting guests' stay is pleasant and enjoyable, then the Senior One [the abbot] can propagate the Dao undisturbed. Although the abbot's attendants are appointed by the rector, they must first be selected by the abbot.

[163] On the occasion of a formal tea ceremony, the duty of the "outside" attendant[64] is to inform the abbot beforehand, to hang a poster inviting the guests, and then to arrange the seating. The burning of incense, general protocol, personal behavior—all must be conducted according to proper etiquette. For the scheduling of the abbot's meetings with guests, the attendant should determine the most propitious opportunities, should inform the abbot at the right time, and should make cordial inquiries as to the availability of both parties. The following tasks are all the charge of the "outside" attendant: presenting letters requesting an appointment to the master [abbot], asking the scribe to reply to these letters, **[164]** arranging for newcomers to meet with the abbot and participate in the welcoming tea ceremony with him, forwarding requests for sermons to the abbot, escorting monks who enter the abbot's room for instruction, scheduling the chanting and the break from the abbot's sermon, and preparing the list of seats in order of ordination seniority of the monks who will attend the summer retreat.[65]

[164] The "inside" attendant tends to the abbot's robes and bowls, his records of expenditure and income, and the public items used by the abbot. He takes care of the abbot's tea, paper, and pen, as well as his winter and summer clothes, all of which should be kept in proper order and should never be in short supply. If any item is needed, the inside attendant should inform the abbot beforehand. If the atten-

dant wants to auction the abbot's personal effects after the abbot's death, he should do so with the rector's cooperation.

[165] Although the duties of the "outside" and "inside" attendants are distinct, the two should work in harmony with each other. For instance, the task of serving tea to the abbot should not be assigned solely to one or the other attendant, lest one resent fulfiling this task more or less often than the other. At night when parting from the abbot, or while greeting him before the early meal, the attendants should ask the abbot whether there will be any tea ceremony or other business to attend to the next day (or that day). Outside of their duties, the attendants should not engage in gossip about the administrators, chief officers, or members of the assembly. They should not repeat the abbot's private words to any other monk. While entertaining guests or conducting any business, the attendants' every action should be based on the principle of serving the master as well as the public assembly, and in general they should not be afraid to take on a great deal of work. They should not discuss any perceived fault of the abbot in his absence. And they should not take on the role of the abbot by passing judgment on others or praising or criticizing members of the assembly. The attendants should always perform their duties with respect and diligence, they should serve the monastery with prudence in all matters, and they should be careful not to disturb the abbot's peace of mind.

Fascicle Five

Fundraiser (huazhu)

[167] Fundraisers are selected either when a list of the names of pre-fectures and districts to which fundraisers are to be sent is posted in the attendants' quarters,[1] asking for volunteers, or directly by the ad-ministrators and the chief officers. The procedure for appointing the fundraiser is the same as that used for appointing the chief officers. Once the fundraiser has entered the hall of residence to prepare for his journey,[2] he should assemble all the necessary letters and docu-ments, tea and medicine, and those items asked for by donors. He must be meticulous and focused at all times. During the transfer tea ceremony, wherein the former fundraiser is officially replaced by the new one, the new fundraiser should inquire about the events of the previous year. The fundraiser should request the abbot's personal let-ters to prospective donors or letters in general at the proper time be-fore he departs. If he must carry items that are subject to tax,[3] he should have ready a clear record of his tax payments. He must choose skillful and careful people for his porters and servers. He should keep all monies in his personal charge and should not rely on his porters or servers in this regard, lest they be tempted by thoughts of betrayal. If the fundraiser should meet a venerable senior, that is, the abbot of another monastery, he should bow down to him after presenting him with a letter. If he should meet a respectable government official, he should present both his self-introductory letter and a letter from his monastery.

[168] Before visiting donors, the fundraiser should inspect his self-introductory letter, forms of identification,[4] and other letters to in-sure they are free from error. At this time, he should also prepare tea and any other items required to greet donors. He should be patient and use gentle words when giving instruction. If donors should in-quire about the monastery's state of affairs, he must answer truly and without thoughtless exaggeration. He should not depend on the power and authority of government officials. He must not become involved in any situation beyond the scope of his immediate busi-ness, especially if it could delay his return or prevent his turning over the position to next year's replacement. Since the fundraiser is se-lected by the monastery to "hold the bowl"[5] on behalf of all his fel-low monks, he must exert his entire mind and strength to expand the annual list of donors.[6] He may take a short break only if he becomes ill and needs to recuperate. **[169]** He should not merely travel in the mountains.[7] Even if attending summer retreats does not hinder his fundraising progress, it still detracts from the accomplishment of his duties. The fundraiser must wait until he has completed his donation collections, presented his list to the monastery, and returned to the assembly before he can resume personal activities. The names and titles of the donors should not be carelessly lost or omitted. Donated items or money should be collected and recorded in a precise fashion. (The devotees' donations are meant for the field of merit,[8] and only foolish people who create bad karma would consider them their own money or possessions. Some fundraisers may spend the money on wine and women; some may save it for personal use; some may use it to buy a certificate granting tonsure or the title of master;[9] some may use it to have a novice tonsured. Such people do not understand that every penny of this money belongs to the body of monks as a whole. Even if a thousand Buddhas were to appear at once, people who behaved in this manner would not be allowed to repent.[10] Before they can ascend to heaven they must first descend into hell. Thus the people in charge of such things should follow the honest path of incorruptibility.)

[170] The memento[11] brought from the region visited by the fundraiser and given to the abbot, and the souvenir[12] given to the administrators and the chief officers, must be chosen according to the customs of previous years, to the way people have done it in the past. The gift should not be excessive, thus distorting the custom. However, if a lavish present is given by a donor then no harm will result. When the fundraiser is far away from the Chan monastery, visiting the houses of devotees and families of donors, everywhere besieged by secular people, he may gradually find himself living a secular life. He should, therefore, always keep in mind the need to return to the monastery as soon as possible to practice the Dao. He should not allow himself to drift about outside the monastery, falling into matters involving money or women. He must remain extremely vigilant with himself. The monastery must inquire as to the day of his departure to observe the custom of seeing off the fundraiser. The day before he leaves, the monastery should prepare a tea ceremony and a feast. On the day of departure the abbot should ascend his seat in the Dharma hall and recite a verse to encourage the fundraiser's spiritual mind and then escort him to the gate of the monastery. The chief officers must also attend his farewell tea ceremony.

[171] When the fundraiser returns to the monastery, he gives a brief greeting. (The administrators, the chief officers, the retired staff, and his fellow monk acquaintances visit the guest lodge to express their gratitude and joy now that he has returned safely.) The fundraiser then carefully unpacks

and prepares the donated items and money. Having finished this, he seals the list of donors[13] and the travel log,[14] together with the inventory of donations.[15] He must maintain these items meticulously to prevent losing any part of them, and if he is questioned when handing them over he must answer honestly. The model for the donation inventory is as follows: "I, Bhikṣu X, fundraiser for this monastery, received in the past the abbot's kind decree and traveled to X location to ask for donations, such as *senggong*, et cetera.[16] I now present the following list: I obtained X number of donations for *senggong* in the total amount of X *qian*.[17] I obtained X number of donations for *luohan* in the total amount of X *qian*. I obtained X number of donations for *zhou* in the total amount of X *qian*. Deducted from the above donations are X number of X items in the total amount of X *qian*. Also paid for were tea greetings and general travel expenses in the total amount of X *qian*. Subtracting the above expenses, the remaining balance totals X *qian*. The aforementioned donations are meager in number, but I bow down and beg the abbot, the administrators, the chief officers, and the body of monks to accept them. The above statement is presented with all sincerity. Written by Bhikṣu X, fundraiser for this monastery, in the year X, in X month, on X day." At the end of the statement this postscript is added: "Previously I borrowed money from the monastery in the amount of X *qian*. Now I return this money along with the donation inventory" and the list of gifts for the abbot. (The model for the list of gifts for the abbot is as follows: "I, Bhikṣu-in-training X, have brought X number of X items and would like to sincerely present to you, the abbot, these mere mementos. Now I bow down and beg you kindly to accept them. The above statement is presented with all sincerity. Written by Bhikṣu-in-training X in the year X, in X month, on X day." If he is a junior monk novice of fewer than ten years, then he should refer to himself as "Xiaoshi Bhikṣu X.") He places the papers in a trunk and informs the administrators that he is ready to present the donation documents.

[172] First, the donated items are brought to the Dharma hall and put on display. The rectory informs everyone of this fact, while in the center of the Dharma hall a chair is placed and beside it a stand for incense. Then the drum is struck to summon the assembly. The abbot stands in front of the chair and his attendant burns incense. All those assembled simply bow in their places because the donated items are visibly placed before them. The guest master will then make the proper announcements. The guest master comes forward and faces the abbot, bows, and says, "Fundraiser X returning from Circuit X presents the donations." Then he escorts the fundraiser [173] before the abbot to bow and remain standing. The guest master takes the inventory of donations out of the trunk and gives it to the fundraiser, who then presents it to the abbot. The fundraiser then bows, steps back, and stands

aside. The abbot passes the inventory through the scented smoke of the incense, symbolically offering it to the Buddha, and hands it to his attendant. The attendant gives it to the scribe or the rector or the guest master, who reads it to the assembly. When he has finished, the fundraiser comes forward, faces the abbot, bows, and remains standing. The guest master then takes the list of mementos from the trunk and gives it to the fundraiser, who then presents it to the abbot. The fundraiser then bows, steps back, and stands aside. Without waving it over the incense, the abbot hands it directly to his attendant. The attendant then gives it to the scribe or the rector or the guest master to read. When he has finished this, the fundraiser thanks the abbot by doing *liangzhan sanbai*. After the first unfolding of the sitting mat the fundraiser states, "These donated items are so very insignificant. I fear I now will offend you in offering them." After the second unfolding of the sitting mat, he expresses a seasonal greeting and then does *chuli* three times. Next the administrators congratulate the abbot. The chief seat and the assembly congratulate the abbot and they all do *liangzhan sanli* before him. The congratulatory words are as follows: "The fundraiser was able to return without difficulty. We bow down and consider this cause for great celebration. We are most joyous." Then the abbot congratulates the assembly in return. The junior monks should withdraw at this time to avoid being the object of the abbot's homage. The chief seat, the assembly, and the administrators then congratulate each other by doing *chuli* three times. Their congratulatory words are as follows: "The fundraiser was able to return without difficulty. We bow down and consider this cause for great celebration."

[174] After this ceremony the abbot returns to his quarters, and the chief seat and the assembly (and the rest) return to their seats in the Sangha hall. The guest master escorts the fundraiser to the Sangha hall to stand before the Holy Monk, where the fundraiser fully unfolds his sitting mat and bows down three times. The fundraiser then stands up in front of the chief seat and does *chuli* three times, saying to him, "On this occasion I was able to seek donations without difficulties because I depended on the protection of the chief seat and the assembly through the power of Dharma." Beginning with the chief seat, all return the bow to him. The chief seat says, "The assembly is so happy that you have begged alms[18] for us and have now returned. The donations are plentiful and we are extremely grateful." The guest master then leads the fundraiser in circumambulating and exiting the hall. They then go to the abbot's office, where the fundraiser fully unfolds the sitting mat and bows down nine times. After bowing the first three times, he says to him, "On this occasion I was able to seek donations without encountering difficulties because I depended on the protection of the abbot through the power of the Dao. For this I am extremely

grateful." After bowing another three times he offers a seasonal greeting, bows three more times, and stands up. All those present take their seats and sweetened soup is served. The new and former fundraisers should be invited, accompanied by some of the senior, retired staff—fewer than twenty people in all. Next the guest master leads the fundraiser to visit the assembly quarters. In the assembly quarters the director and the chief seat will treat him to tea ceremonies and special feasts for three days. Then, without taking up residence in the Sangha hall, the fundraiser is led by the rector to stay in the rear chambers of the assembly quarters. (In some monasteries, the next day the abbot will ascend his seat in the Dharma hall and express his gratitude. In other monasteries, the abbot ascends his seat after the presentation of the donated items and before the formal greeting. In still other monasteries the fundraiser will first sponsor a feast, after which the abbot ascends his seat in the Dharma hall. If the abbot is not invited to ascend his seat in the Dharma hall, there is no need for him to do so.)

Completion of a Chief Officer's Term

[176] When the chief officer appointed by the abbot's office reaches his term limit of a year, he should resign in an expedient manner. Before the early meal he should visit the abbot's quarters for consultation, do *chuli* three times, and then withdraw. Those lesser chief officers appointed by the rectory, who have no term limits, should go to the rector to resign. Those chief officers appointed to serve under the director of the library should go to the library director to resign. When the six chief officers appointed by the abbot resign, the abbot sponsors a tea ceremony. The abbot, accompanied by the rector, guest master, et cetera, escorts the chief officers to their individual lodgings. The chief officers then do *liangzhan sanbai* and escort the abbot out. To the others the chief officers simply bow. The chief officers of lower rank than these six[19] enter the hall of retirement[20] and take up residence[21] there. The rector alone invites them to a tea ceremony and accompanies them to the hall of residence, where the special tea ceremonies and feasts last for three days. For the chief officers appointed to serve under the director of the library, the monastery sponsors the feast, and the library director should also entertain them. Only the director and the chief seat of the assembly quarters do not sponsor any tea ceremonies.

The Tea Ceremony Sponsored by the Abbot's Office

[177] At the time of the night sermon or before the early meal, the attendant informs the abbot saying, "Tomorrow (or, after the midday meal) a tea ceremony[22] is going to be held for X." Before the mid-

day meal the attendant supervises the servers in the preparation of hot water vessels (the water should be replaced and boiled), the teacups and stands, the tea trays (which should be washed and polished), the scented flowers, the seats, the "medicines,"[23] the seating chart, and the low-grade tea.[24] Once all these things are prepared, the invitations are carefully made. When inviting a guest, the attendant should bow repeatedly, saying, "The abbot is going to hold a tea ceremony for X after the midday meal. When you hear the sound of the drum please come to attend." He then bows again and withdraws. His manner should be dignified and not mirthful or insincere. (On the occasion of a special sweetened soup service, the abbot should also be informed the previous night or before the midday meal. After the midday meal, the attendant should supervise the servers in the preparation of the cups and stands, the sweetened soup, et cetera, as above. The invitation should be worded: "Tonight, after the break from the sermon, the abbot will host a sweetened soup service for X.")

[179] After the meal, the attendant goes to the abbot's quarters and prepares the incense holder and the seats. Once the water vessels as well as the teacups and stands have been tended to, and the server has displayed the tea in the proper fashion (the incense stand is for the incense burner only; the incense case, the confection case, and the teacups should be placed separately elsewhere), the attendant should inform the abbot, and the tea drum is struck. (If the tea is not fully prepared before the drum is struck, the assembly will have to sit too long and will become irritated. When the attendant from the storage hall strikes the drum or when the members of any residence strike the board, they must know not to strike too early.) All the guests assemble, and the attendant enters and greets them. (Only then is the drum no longer struck.) The guests enter the hall and take their seats in order, beginning with the chief seat. (In the case of a late guest, the attendant should send someone to collect him. The chief virtue, however, is to avoid disturbing the abbot's peace of mind; the attendant should not act with excessive haste.) The attendant should wait until everyone has gathered before he invites the abbot to enter. (If any guest is absent, the attendant must wait for instructions from the abbot. Then he may withdraw the extra chair. If the abbot does not give any instructions, the attendant cannot withdraw the chair on his own initiative. Even if a guest is absent or the ceremony is not proceeding properly, the abbot should not show any expression of his emotions to those assembled lest he should make the guests uncomfortable.) However, it is permissible for the abbot to come out beforehand, stand in front of his chair, and wait for the assembly while the attendant greets the arriving guests. When the guests and the host are all standing in place, the attendant, who stands in the northeast corner of the

banquet hall, steps forward and bows to invite the guests to be seated. The attendant then invites the guests to burn incense and bow in order of rank from senior to junior. The attendant responds to this courtesy and bows on behalf of the abbot. The invited guests should perform this one by one, each with a demeanor of respect and sincerity, not with arrogance or carelessness. After some time has passed, more incense should be lit.

[180] To properly burn the incense, the attendant should stand beside the incense table, face east toward the abbot, bow, open the incense case, and lift up the incense. He should lift up the case with both hands, and then use the right hand to place it into the palm of his left hand. He then uses his right hand to lift the lid off the case and place it on the incense stand. With the right hand again, he lifts up the incense and faces the guest of honor, then places the incense in the burner and lets it burn. He uses his right hand to replace the lid and uses both hands to return the case to the incense stand. He must do all this gently and carefully, without making any noise or letting the case fall to the ground. After this, he need not bow, but should simply adjust his sitting mat and clasp his hands. He then approaches the guest of honor and bows. (In some monasteries, after the guests have taken their seats, the attendant will stand beside the abbot and "invite the sitting mat" and "invite the incense."[25] [This is done to show solemn courtesy on the occasion. However, here[26] the attendant stands beside the incense stand and bows to the abbot to symbolize the courtesy of "inviting the incense."] The attendant then turns and stands with his hands clasped. First he invites the guests to have tea and then he bows to encourage them to have more tea. Next he burns incense and invites them to have still more tea. After this, the confections are presented, and the attendant invites the guests to eat them. Then he invites the guests to have tea again and bows once more to persuade them. After the tea is over the attendant will step forward and bow. He then has someone collect the teacups and stands. Finally he bows and departs from his post. (The attendant instructs a server beforehand to be ready so that as soon as the guests stand up, he can immediately move the chair of the abbot. The guest of honor then comes forward one or two steps toward the abbot, bows in gratitude for the offered tea, and withdraws. The abbot then escorts all the guests to the door and each guest turns to bow to the abbot as he leaves. The attendant instructs the servers to remove all the chairs, seat cushions, fans, napkins, and the incense stand tablecloth. They clear away the tea, teacups, and stands, check to see that all items are accounted for, and wash everything. The attendant and servers then have tea themselves, after which they are free to do as they like. They should always avoid troubling the abbot and should simply respect his instructions.)

[182] If the prefect of the monastery's own prefecture, the super-

visor of its circuit, or the magistrate of its district comes to the monastery, the entire assembly must go out to greet him and to see him off. The abbot will be the host. If the magistrate is of the monastery's own district, the abbot must personally come out to greet him, but if he is not then the abbot need not do so. After his attendant has lit the incense, the abbot stands up, saying, "We would now like to offer our low-grade tea (or low-grade sweetened drink) and we will follow all of Official X's instructions." Only when they have obtained the official's permission can they begin serving tea. If he should receive a compliment from the government official, the abbot should merely say, "This low-grade tea is only to show our sincerity. It is not worthy of your touch." All the officials who come to the monastery should be treated equally to tea and food. If an official asks about things unrelated to the Dharma, it is not necessary to respond in special detail. When a lay patron or donor or an official visits, incense need only be burnt once, and the attendant should merely bow to the abbot. The custom is to serve just one round of tea and one sweetened drink. Should the abbot summon his attendant to serve another tea or sweetened drink, the attendant need not light more incense. (When a lay patron visits the monastery, only one tea and one sweetened drink need be served, and it is not necessary to burn incense.)

[183] The abbot should not arbitrarily invite monks to tea. But if a tea ceremony is called together suddenly, the attendant should have a server arrange the seats, incense, tea, and confections, and after this the attendant may invite the guests. When the guests and the host are seated, the attendant will face the center, bow, and light the incense using his right hand to lift it up. The attendant then steps back and bows to everyone. If a higher-grade tea is served, then sweetened drink should not be offered. If the guests have sat for a long time and more sweetened drink is requested, the attendant need not light more incense. For newcomers, temporary guests, or monks from other monasteries, the attendant should burn incense only once, bow to everyone, and serve only one tea and one sweetened drink. (If the attendant is meeting an official for the first time, he should greet him with solemnity and need not avoid doing so in front of the abbot. But if the guests are monks or lay people who are frequent visitors, the attendant should not greet them in the abbot's presence.)

The Tea Ceremony Held in the Sangha Hall

[184] To summon the assembly to a tea ceremony in the Sangha hall, the abbot's office and the priory should use an invitation poster called the *bang,* and the chief seat should use a smaller poster called the

zhuang,[27] both of which are kept by the server in a box. The abbot's attendant, the prior, or the chief seat first presents the *bang* or the *zhuang* to the guest(s) of honor, and after this invitation he will post it on one of the doors of the Sangha hall entrances. (The abbot's *bang* will be posted on the right-hand door, the administrator's or chief seat's on the left.) The prior or chief seat will go to the abbot's quarters to cordially invite the abbot. After the long striking of the board, all the monks will assemble and enter the hall. The attendant, the prior, or the chief seat lights the incense, fully unfolds his sitting mat, bows three times, circumambulates the hall, and invites the assembled monks to the tea ceremony.

[184] After the midday meal, the bell is struck in front of the Sangha hall. Everyone is seated, and the person who presides over the Dharma[28] stands on the south [left] side of the front gate, facing the Holy Monk. With his hands clasped, he slowly bows and, leaving his position, comes up to the Holy Monk and bows again. [185] Having done this, he stands before the incense burner, bows, opens the incense case, and with his left hand lifts up the incense. Having completed this, he steps back slightly, bows again, goes to the rear door, and bows to the guest of honor. He then turns to face the south, approaches the Holy Monk, and bows. He turns north, bows to the abbot, circumambulates the hall, and goes to the first seat on the north [right] side of the rear door. Bending his body, he bows, moves to the first seat on the south [left] side, and bows again. If the host moves to the outside section of the hall, he should bow first to the right-hand section, then to the left, reenter the hall, and approach the Holy Monk. Once he has done this, he bows, returns to his original position, bows again, and remains standing with hands clasped.

[185] After the tea is poured, the host should have the sweetened drink served. He goes to the front and bows to the guest of honor, inviting him to drink the tea first. Then the water vessel is brought out, and the host circumambulates the hall to encourage everyone to have more tea. As with the first round of tea, he bows and circumambulates the hall, but now he does not burn more incense. After the tea drinking is finished, the guest of honor's cup is removed and the assembly place their cups on the platform, remaining seated with their hands clasped. As described above, the host again burns incense and bows to the guest of honor. Having done this, he goes before the Holy Monk and fully unfolds his sitting mat, bowing down three times. He circumambulates the hall once and stands in his position. After the confections are presented, the host steps forward,

bows, and invites the guests to partake of the confections. Then tea and sweetened drink are served once more, and the host bows again to invite the guests to have more tea. If the water vessel is again presented, the host just as before will bow and circumambulate the hall to encourage the guests to have more tea. When the tea drinking has finished, the host will resume his position.

[186] If the abbot's attendant is the one presiding, then, when the tea drinking is over, he must first bow as the teacups and stands are collected and removed. Then the guest of honor stands before the abbot and unfolds his sitting mat, saying, "I am extremely grateful to receive this special tea ceremony from the abbot now." He then unfolds the sitting mat a second time and offers a seasonal greeting, saying, "I humbly wish on your honorable body and your daily life ten thousand fortunes." He does *chuli* three times and escorts the abbot out of the hall. The attendant then stands before the Holy Monk and bows to the right section and then to the left. After this is completed, the bell to exit the hall is struck.

[187] If the prior or chief seat sponsors the tea ceremony, then, when the tea drinking is over, the abbot's cup is collected first, and all the administrators (or the chief seat) take their place before the abbot, unfold their sitting mats, and say, "Today our humble low-grade tea (or "Today our inferior sweetened drink") has received your grace, abbot, for out of kindness you have lowered yourself to come to us: for this we are extremely grateful." They unfold their sitting mats a second time and express a seasonal greeting, saying, "We humbly wish on your honorable body and your daily life ten thousand fortunes." They then do *chuli* three times. After the third bow, the abbot need not bow in return but should simply bow to the assembly and express a parting courtesy. After this courtesy, the administrators (or the chief seat) escort the abbot out of the hall. The person who presides over the ceremony then reenters the hall and, standing in front of the Holy Monk, bows to the right section and then to the left. At this point all the cups are collected, the host bows again, and the bell to exit the hall is struck. The chief seat exits the hall, and outside he and the administrators do *chuli* three times to each other. If the chief seat is host and the scribe is guest of honor, then the scribe must also exit the hall first, and outside he and the chief seat do *chuli* three times to each other, whereupon all are dismissed.

[188] The Poster for the Abbot's Tea Party Beginning the Summer Retreat reads: "This morning after breakfast, the abbot will sponsor a tea ceremony in the cloud hall. This tea ceremony is to be held especially for the chief

seat and the assembly, and symbolizes the commencement of the summer retreat. In addition, all administrators are invited to provide their illuminating company. Today is X day of X month. Respectfully written by Attendant X."

The Poster for the Abbot's Tea Party Ending the Summer Retreat: For this poster the beginning and the end read the same as above. Only the middle phrase is changed to "symbolizes the ending of the summer retreat."

The Poster for the Prior's Tea Party Beginning the Summer Retreat reads: "This morning after breakfast, the prior will sponsor a tea ceremony in the cloud hall. This tea ceremony is to be held especially for the chief seat and the assembly, and symbolizes the commencement of the summer retreat. I humbly wish you all will kindly condescend to come. Today is X day of X month. Respectfully written by Prior Bhikṣu X."

The Poster for the Prior's Tea Ceremony Ending the Summer Retreat: For this poster the beginning and the end read the same as above. Only the middle phrase is changed to "symbolizes the ending of the summer retreat."

The Letter for the Chief Seat's Tea Ceremony Beginning the Summer Retreat reads: "Chief Seat Bhikṣu X, addressed to X who may open and receive this letter. This morning after breakfast, I will sponsor a tea ceremony in the cloud hall. This tea ceremony is to be held especially for the scribe and the assembly, and symbolizes the commencement of the summer retreat. Moreover, all administrators are invited. I humbly wish you all will kindly condescend to come. X day of X month. Written by Chief Seat Bhikṣu X." On the outside of the envelope is written: "By this letter I invite the scribe and the assembly. Sincerely sealed by Chief Seat Bhikṣu X."

The Letter for the Chief Seat's Tea Ceremony Ending the Summer Retreat: For this letter the beginning and the end read the same as above. Only the middle phrase is changed to "symbolizes the ending of the summer retreat." The poster for the tea ceremony sponsored by the abbot for the new and former administrators and chief seats and the poster for the tea ceremony sponsored by the administrators and chief seat have already been discussed in the section on the appointment of administrators and chief officers.

The Tea Ceremony Hosted by the Administrators or the Chief Officers

[189] The tea ceremony hosted by the administrators or the chief officers begins after the striking of the board. The host stands in his position to greet the assembly and makes sure everyone is seated. Then the host himself is seated, and after a short time he can withdraw his legs and sit in the lotus position.[29] After another brief interval the host stands up, bows, and leaves his position to burn incense. He lifts up the incense with the right hand. He then bows to the guests of honor and returns to the side of his seat, where he bows to everyone. The host should not bow in front of his seat at this point. **[190]** He returns to his position, bows, and sits down. After the server has poured out two or three cups while making his way around the table, the host lifts his cup to greet the guest of honor (he need only greet the leader of the assembly) and those seated to the right and left of him. Then everyone begins drinking the tea. After drinking (if, as is sometimes done, any cups are to be removed at this point, only the host's cup may be collected), the host stands up, bows, leaves his position to burn incense, returns to his seat, and bows in the manner mentioned before. Next, the confections are presented, and all are invited to eat. Then the guests are invited to have more tea. When the tea drinking is done, the teacups are collected. When this is finished, the host bows, stands up, and sees the guests to the door. When the director sponsors a tea ceremony in the assembly quarters for the assembly, he invites the chief seat of his assembly quarters to be the guest of honor and presides over the ceremony himself. When a special tea ceremony for newcomers is held, the practice should be the same as the ceremony for the administrators. Nonincumbent chief officers should not invite administrators to have tea lest they should hinder public duties or arouse suspicion.

[191] The custom for the prior and all the chief officers in welcoming newcomers is to serve tea after the morning meal and to serve sweetened drink and make one offering of incense after the evening break from the abbot's sermon. But if sweetened drink is not to be served in the evening, then it may be served immediately following the morning tea without the guests leaving their seats.

The Tea Ceremony in the Assembly Quarters
Hosted by the Senior Monks

[192] According to the custom for the tea ceremony in the assembly quarters sponsored by the senior monks, the host burns incense and bows first to the director and then to each person in the director's section and then, starting from the chief seat, to each person in the chief seat's section. After this, the tea is poured and later the host circumambulates the hall to encourage the guests to have more tea. After a short time, he comes forward and bows, saying, "The tea is of a low grade. Please forgive us for not changing the teacups in the course of the ceremony." Having said this, he burns incense and again invites the guests to have tea. He circumambulates the hall again and

bows. Next the confections are served, and then more tea is poured, after which the guests are encouraged to have still more tea. (The above two instances, when the host burns incense and bows to the guests as well as the display of gratitude at the end of the ceremony, should be done in sequence according to the guests' seniority. For the second encouragement to drink, the bow and circumambulation may simply be omitted. For the first encouragement it is sufficient to bow once, first to the right section and then to the left.) The host thanks his guests for coming by saying, "Today our low-grade tea was specially received by the director of the assembly quarters, the chief seat, and the assembly when you kindly agreed to descend to our hall." He then does *chuli* three times and circumambulates the hall once while the teacups are removed. Then he bows and stands up. If other senior monks would like to invite guests to an informal tea ceremony, then, when all the monks are sitting in the assembly quarters, the sponsor burns one stick of incense, saying, "Someday we would like to respectfully invite the director of the assembly quarters, the chief seat, and the assembly to come for tea. We humbly hope you will kindly descend to our hall." He then does *chuli* three times, circumambulates the hall, and bows. On the day of the tea ceremony, the sponsor will preside.

The Tea Ceremony Hosted by the Assembly

[193] For morning tea ceremonies, invitations should be extended the preceding day. For tea ceremonies after the midday meal, invitations should be made that morning. For evening sweetened drink, invitations should be made after the midday meal. If respectable senior monks (for instance, the chief seat emeritus, senior monks from other monasteries, or elder monks of the same lineage, such as the host's teacher's elder or junior colleagues or the host's own senior colleagues) are being invited, then one must fully unfold the sitting mat and bow down three times. If the guest should refuse such an honor, then it is sufficient to do *chuli* three times. If respectable monks of the next rank in seniority (for instance, fellow monks with higher ordination seniority and virtue) are being invited, then one should do *chuli* three times. If fellow monks of equal seniority (or, in the same lineage, junior monks or the disciples of fellow monks) are being invited, one need only bow.

[194] The host arranges the seats, incense, flowers, and seating chart at the proper time, and stands at the door to greet the guests. When the guests have taken their seats, he bows, saying, "Please withdraw your legs."[30] He then burns incense and bows to the guest of honor. Having done this, he bows and says, "Please put aside your sitting mats."[31] On exceedingly warm summer days he says, "Please

feel free to use your fans." On very cold winter days he says, "Please feel free to cover your heads." Then three to five rounds of tea and sweetened drink are served. The host bows and says, "Please partake of the tea and sweetened drink first." Next the water vessel is presented, and the host bows before the guest of honor, and bows again to encourage everyone to have more tea. Then, after the teacups have been removed, he burns incense and bows to the guest of honor. (If the teacups are not removed, the host will announce, "The tea is of a low grade. Please forgive us for not changing the teacups in the course of the ceremony." If the sweetened drink cups are not removed, the host will announce, "This sweetened drink is inferior. Please forgive us for not changing the sweetened drink cups in the course of the ceremony.") Next, the confections are served, after which the host says, "Please partake of the confections." Then tea and sweetened drink are served again, and the guests are encouraged in the aforementioned manner to drink more tea. After the tea, the host shows his gratitude by saying, "Today's tea (or "Today's sweetened drink") is served specially for X and Y. The tea is of a low grade and the seats are uncomfortable. Despite these things, you came anyway. For this I am extremely grateful." For the most respectable senior monks, the host should fully unfold his sitting mat and bow down three times. In the evening, before or after the break from the sermon schedule, he should go to these monks' residences to extend his gratitude. For respectable monks of the next rank in seniority as well as for fellow monks, he should show his gratitude by saying, "Today the tea (or sweetened drink) was served especially for X and Y. This ceremony is not worth the trouble you have taken to accompany them." The host should then do *chuli* twice, saying, "For fear of bothering you in the evening I dare not go to your quarters to extend my gratitude." He bows once, then everyone bows to each other. After a short time, the host bows and the teacups are collected. The host then bows once more, leaves his position, and goes to the door to see the guests off.

The Tea Ceremony Hosted by the Assembly for the Elder Monks of the Same Lineage

[196] If, when a tea ceremony is being held for elder monks of the same lineage (such as the host's teacher, the teacher's elder or junior colleagues, or the host's own senior colleagues), the seats in the host's quarters are deemed uncomfortable and bothersome to the assembly, then the assembly quarters should be used. The invitation procedure has been discussed above. If there is only one guest of honor, then

the director of the assembly quarters sits in the center seat, and a seat is placed next to him for the guest of honor. After the guests are seated, the host turns to face the center and, using his left hand, lifts up the incense. He approaches the seats of the director of the assembly quarters and guest of honor and, facing them, bows down. If there are two or more guests of honor, then these seats are placed facing the director of the assembly quarters. The host lifts up the incense with his left hand and bows down at the edge of the banquet area. The words expressed, the host's demeanor, and everything else are identical to the customs for the tea ceremony in honor of the abbot, except that, after bowing down, standing up, and stepping forward to bow (the host does not have to greet the guest of honor before he stands up), the host must do *chuli* three times at the edge of the banquet area and bow to the company one by one to express his gratitude. He then stands outside the door to see the guests off. At night, the host will visit the senior monk in his quarters to thank him. He then goes to the director of the assembly quarters and bows to express his gratitude. If the ceremony is held in the host's own quarters, then the guest of honor will sit in the center seat, burn the incense, and bow down from that location. After both parties have agreed to allow the assembly to use the hall for the tea ceremony, the director of the assembly quarters should find some pretext to avoid attending. He should not increase the complexity of the ritual with his presence, for his status would demand that he occupy the center position, making it inconvenient for the host, who must then regard him as the most senior figure, bowing to him at each step, et cetera.

Fascicle Six

The Tea Ceremony in the Abbot's Honor
Sponsored by Dharma Relatives or Select Disciples

[199] In the morning, the prospective host should prepare himself and go first to the abbot's attendant, saying, "I wish to trouble you to inform the abbot that it is our desire to sponsor a tea ceremony in honor of the abbot after the meal in the abbot's quarters." The attendant informs the abbot and then leads the host to meet him. After the host bows, he says to the abbot, "Please, Venerable Teacher, be seated." If the abbot is already seated, it is not necessary to invite him to sit. The host fully unfolds his sitting mat and bows down three times. He then bends forward, saying, "This morning after the early meal, we would like to hold a tea ceremony in your honor in your quarters. We humbly beg your kindness in giving us permission." The abbot replies, "I will follow your order with all sincerity. You need not bow down." Whether or not the abbot bows down in response depends on the host's seniority. The host then bows down three times. Some may further extend the courtesy by fully unfolding the sitting mat and bowing down three times; others may simply unfold the sitting mat once. The choice depends on the host's seniority. After this, the host does *chuli* three times. Then the host bows and withdraws. He must consult with the attendant to arrange the seating and the seating chart. It is then his obligation to invite the other guests. The host should choose the company from among senior chief officers and senior monks of the same lineage as well as from senior retired staff.

[200] After the meal, the host should go to the abbot's quarters to prepare the incense, tea, confections, teacups, stands, and water vessels, and to make sure that nothing is left unprepared. Next, the guests assemble. (The drum should not be struck to summon the guests.)[1] The host greets them and has them take their seats. When the correct number of guests have arrived, the host enters the abbot's room to invite him to take the center seat. Once the abbot has withdrawn his legs, the host steps forward and bows. He then turns to the west, passes by the east side of the incense stand to face the southwest corner of the banquet area, and bows. Having done this, he clasps his hands and stands with his side to the center seat. This posture of deference to the abbot indicates the host's actual guest status within the abbot's quarters. If the abbot himself is hosting the tea ceremony, then his attendant burns the incense and stands in the southeast corner of the banquet area on the host's behalf. The host should wait until everyone is seated and settled, and then slowly bow. He leaves his position and goes to the side of the incense table, where

he remains standing. He bows to the abbot and uses his left hand to lift up the incense. After replacing the lid of the incense case, without bowing, he clasps his hands, passes the east side of the incense stand, and turns to the north facing the abbot. He bows, returns to his original position, bows again, and remains standing. After the tea has been poured for everyone, three to five cups of sweetened drink are served. The host comes forward to bow (this is the initial invitation to drink tea) and steps back to remain standing in his original position. The water vessels are then presented. (On those occasions when the host is sponsoring the tea ceremony for his own teacher or for senior monks of his teacher's generation, the attendant pours the sweetened drink, and the host should personally offer the tea to show sincerity and respect.) The host steps before the abbot to bow and encourage him to have more tea. He then returns to his position and remains standing. After the tea drinking has ended, the teacups are removed. If the attendant has personally poured the tea, then he should personally collect the cups as well. Waiting until the teacups and stands are dealt with, the host should then burn incense as before and, facing the abbot, fully unfold his sitting mat and bow down three times. He then comes forward and bends his body, saying, "I would like to prolong your most honorable[2] visit to offer you more of our low-grade tea. For this I humbly beg your kind permission." The host bows down three more times to withdraw. Or the host may fully unfold his sitting mat, immediately express the above invitation, and then withdraw by again bowing down three times. The abbot replies, "I have already received your most diligent hospitality. There is no need for you to persist." Whether or not the abbot bows in response depends on the host's seniority. Waiting until the abbot has withdrawn his legs, the host bows, returns to his seat, and remains standing. After the confections are served, the host will step forward and bow (that is, invite the assembly to partake of the confections). The host then steps back to his position and remains standing. Three to five cups of tea and sweetened drink are served (the host may personally pour the tea) and the host bows to invite the guests to drink. The water vessel is then presented, and the host steps forward to bow in order to encourage the guests to drink more tea. He then returns to his position and remains standing.

[202] Once the tea drinking has ended, the abbot's teacup should be collected first. Sometimes the host may personally collect this cup. The host then fully unfolds his sitting mat and bows down three times before the abbot, saying, "Today the abbot has kindly descended to receive our low-grade tea. For this I am extremely grateful." The abbot replies, "I am extremely grateful for your moving hospitality and the tea you have served." Whether or not

the abbot bows in return depends on the host's seniority. The host then withdraws, after bowing down three times. However, it is also possible for
the host to unfold fully the sitting mat, step forward, partially bow with
bent body, utter the same words as above, and withdraw, bowing down
three times. If the abbot does not bow in reply to the host's bow, then
the host steps forward, bows, and, having done this, withdraws to the
west side and stands with hands clasped and his side turned to the center. The abbot then gets up from his chair, takes leave of the assembly,
and returns to his room. (At this time the assembly need not stand up.) The
host escorts the abbot to his door, bows, and withdraws. If the abbot
wishes to bow in return, he must do so during the host's third bow but
before the host rises. If the abbot does not bow in return, he merely
presses his hands together and bows to take leave of the assembly. If
the administrators or the chief officers host the tea ceremony for the abbot in the
Sangha hall, the procedure will be the same. Without withdrawing, the host
escorts the abbot back to his room, bows, and then returns to his original position, where he remains standing. There he thanks the assembly, saying, "Today's low-grade tea was especially for the abbot. But I am extremely grateful to have received the kind company of those present." He then
does *chuli* three times and bows standing in his position. After the
teacups have been collected, he bows and stands up to see the guests
off. He escorts them only one or two steps beyond the banquet area,
as it is not proper for a guest to see off other guests.[3] The host then
goes to the attendant's quarters to extend his gratitude.

The Procedure for Burning Incense
during the Tea Ceremony in the Assembly's Honor

[203] The procedure for the grand tea ceremony held in the Sangha
hall in honor of the assembly is as follows: Before the meal the host
enters the hall and offers only one stick of incense to signal the invitation. After the meal, tea is served or, in the evening, sweetened drink is
served. Before the first round of tea, two sticks of incense should be
offered. Before the second round, one stick will suffice. When the abbot's quarters, the priory, and the other quarters hold tea ceremonies in their own
halls, they follow all of these incense-burning practices with the exception of the
invitation procedure. For ceremonies not held in the assembly's honor,
only one stick of incense should be offered.

The Presentation of Feasts

[204] To sponsor a feast, the host must first extend the invitation before the meal. When it is time, the long striking of the board will sum-

mon the guests. When all the guests have taken their seats, the host enters and approaches the table, where he bows to the guest of honor. He then moves to the edge of the banquet area, where he bows to the rest of the guests. After the food has been presented, the host burns incense and bows to the guest of honor. Later a money offering is made to each of the monks present, after which the host approaches the guest of honor and bows as before. If the abbot is sponsoring the feast, then his attendant will preside as host over the ceremony. If the prior is the sponsor, then the priory section's host representative will preside over the ceremony.

Giving Thanks for the Tea Ceremony

[205] The procedure for giving thanks after a feast or tea ceremony sponsored by the abbot's quarters depends on the status of the guest of honor. If the guest of honor is lower in seniority than the abbot, he should go to the abbot's quarters, fully unfold his sitting mat, and bow down three times. If the abbot refuses to accept this gesture, the guest of honor may simply do *chuli* three times. If the guest of honor is of the same generation as the abbot or the abbot's senior, then in the evening he should go to the abbot's quarters and extend his gratitude by saying, "Today I have received special treatment in the form of your tea ceremony, for which I am extremely grateful." This is in accordance with the ancient adage, "The guest thanks the host for the tea but not for the food." The practice of bowing down depends on the particular situation. If the tea ceremony is sponsored by the administrators or the chief officers, the guest of honor need not go to their quarters to express his gratitude. If the tea ceremony is sponsored by a monk of the guest of honor's generation, then the guest of honor should go to express his gratitude before or after the break from the abbot's sermon.

The Reading of the Sutra

[206] On those occasions when a donor sponsors a sutra reading by the assembly in the library[4] or the Dharma hall, the superintendent arranges the chairs and desks. The cook sends food servers to help, while the director of the library prepares tea, incense, flowers, lamps, and candles. The rector then posts a list of those invited to read in order of ordination seniority and composes a chart allocating the sutra and arranging the seating. He must also invite the *ācāryas*, one to preside over the Dharma service[5] and one to lead the chanting.[6] The scribe writes the prayers to begin and end the ceremony and

makes the poster announcing the sutra reading. The sutra curator then takes out the sutras and displays them.

[207] When the time comes, the rector rings the bell, and everyone assembles and sits in their assigned seats for the reading of the sutra. The presiding *ācārya* blows the conch and strikes the gong. The guest master meticulously checks to verify that all is in order before leading in the donor to offer incense. The donor then kneels down carrying a small incense holder. The rector offers his praise of the ceremony, reads the initial prayer, and recites the Buddhas' names, after which the chanting *ācārya* leads the chanting. When the chanting is finished, everyone opens the sutra. If any monks are ill, recuperating from an illness, or attending to business outside the monastery, the rector will keep their share of the money and wait for them to return to the Sangha hall or to their section of the monastery and assign them sutras to read. This remuneration is extremely beneficial. If an ailing monk requests the money being saved for him to read sutra later, the rector must give it to him. If there are sutras, that is, donated funds, left over after the initial distribution, the extra sutras should be assigned according to the sutra-reading seniority list. If a donor wishes to offer a feast on the last day of the sutra reading, the rector should read the final prayer at that time. All the money donated by the donors for sutra reading is collected and distributed by the rector. **[208]** Money is first deducted from the total to pay the postulants, the rector who recites the prayer, the scribe who writes it down; the library sutra curator who provides the incense, candles, and tea drink; the guest master who leads the incense offering; the presiding *ācārya,* and the chanting *ācārya.* The remaining funds are then counted and distributed to the readers. The prior is in charge of the service in general and he should show hospitality to the donors. The director of the library provides tea and sweetened drink for everyone and teaches them to cherish and protect the Holy Teaching.

[209] The proper way to read the sutra is illustrated in the section on the library director. The sutra should always be read with special care. If a monk cannot read the sutra, he should voluntarily approach the rectory to withdraw his name from the list. Once the sutra has been received, it should be read in the correct manner. It is better to finish reading sooner rather than later; this not only promptly fulfills the donor's wishes, but also prevents any lingering obligations.

The Grand Feast Sponsored by the Donor

[209] When a donor visits the monastery to sponsor a grand feast to commemorate an auspicious or grave occasion,[7] the prior should ascertain how many monks and lay people from outside the monastery are coming, as well as how much money is to be offered to the monks. He then informs the abbot and consults the cook to arrange the courses and prepare the ingredients. The superintendent sets up the tables and chairs either in the priory or in the Dharma hall. The amount of incense, flowers, and decorated curtains to be used depends on the financial resources of the donor. The scribe composes a prayer appropriate for the occasion. It is the rector's duty to arrange the seating chart.

[210] The abbot sits in the center seat. (If the abbot is absent from the monastery, the prior takes his place.) The chief seat sits with the abbot in the front at the center. (If a respectable senior monk is present, he sits with the abbot at the center, and the chief seat sits on the abbot's left-hand side.) The rest of the monks sit in order of seniority, beginning with the director of the library. The donors and lay people are seated in their assigned section. The prior, the rector, and the superintendent sit near the drum. The rest of the chief officers and the senior monks of virtue are seated according to their seniority. If the guests sit in two rows placed far apart, they are seated facing each other. Even if the two rows are placed close to each other, on the same platform, the guests face each other. The most senior monks are seated in order, beginning from the south end.

[211] The wooden fish[8] is struck to assemble the guests, and the bell is rung for the guests to take their seats. The guests and host bow and enter the hall together. Music is played before the holy statue while the guest master checks to verify that all is in order and leads in the donors to offer incense. The donors offer incense from the abbot's seat to the southeast corner of the banquet area, from the center of the banquet[9] to the southwest corner of the banquet area, and then to all the others in as expedient a manner as possible.

[211] When the offering of incense is completed, the donor genuflects before the holy statue carrying a small incense holder. After the presiding *ācārya* chants and the rector reads the prayer and recites the names of the Ten Buddhas, the donors take their positions. If the Dharma instruments are not played after the incense offering, then the head of the Dharma service is selected to chant the *Gongjing tou*[10] ("We all respect and faithfully bow down to the eternal Three Treasures"— the first line and title by which people refer to this chant)[11] and recite the Buddha's name until the incense offering is finished. Then begins the chanting of the *Rulai fan*[12] (which begins, "The Magnificent Body of the *Tathāgata*" and ends with "Therefore I take refuge and faithfully bow down to the

eternal Three Treasures"),[13] after which the donor kneels down before the incense holder while the rector reads the prayer and recites the Buddha's name. The donors are then seated in the aforementioned manner. If instruments are not played, then there need not be any recitation of the Buddha's name or reading of prayers. The rector strikes the bell and recites the *Gongjing tou*. When the donor has finished offering the incense, he genuflects before the holy statue, carrying a small incense holder. **[212]** The rector chants the *Rulai fan*, expresses the purpose of the feast, chants again, and then the donors are seated and the bell is struck to call order.

[213] The bell is struck once more and the chief seat presents the food, offers incense, and announces that eating may begin. During the Grand Feast, the server does not make announcements. Instead he stands outside the banquet area after each course is served. The bell is again struck once, and the assembly clasp their hands for a moment of silent contemplation, after which the food is offered to all sentient beings. After the food is eaten, the rector strikes the bell and the chief seat distributes the money to the monks. (Sometimes the donor distributes the money, sometimes the administrator does it on the behalf of the chief seat.) When the feast has ended, the head of the Dharma service or the rector strikes the bell, chanting, "Though placed in this world, one's mind is in the emptiness."[14] He then reads a brief excerpt from the prayer, explaining the purpose of the feast and thereby transfering the merit. Next, the names of the Ten Buddhas are chanted, the bell is struck, and all present stand up. In some monasteries, the bell is rung twice, first to signal the chanting of verses to end the feast, and a second time to dismiss the guests. It is better to hold the Grand Feast early in the day because it is not appropriate to eat after noon.

Egress and Entrance

[214] If, after the early meal, the assembly leaves the monastery on some business—to attend a feast, chant, or greet venerable seniors—then the rector must make the announcement before the early meal. If they are to leave after the midday meal, then the rector must make the announcement during the midday meal.

[215] The procedure for making the announcement in the hall[15] is as follows: After the food has been distributed, or after the money has been distributed, the rector strikes once with the hammer, saying, "I now announce to you that this morning after the meal you will hear the sound of the bell. You should prepare your demeanor and personal effects, for you are invited to attend a feast at X location.

All chief officers in their respective quarters should roll up the curtains on their doors and attend. This I announce with all sincerity." The rector strikes with the hammer once more, bows before the Holy Monk, bows before the abbot, and circumambulates the hall once. If there are monks in the outer section of the hall, he should also bow to them (excepting those in the rear hall which is a separate section behind the Sangha hall).

[215] When it is time to leave, the bell is rung to summon the entire monastery to assemble at the mountain gate. The abbot leads the procession and behind him are the chief seat, the scribe, the director of the library, the guest master, the bath master, the senior retired staff, and the assembly, marching in order of ordination seniority. Behind the assembly are the superintendent, the cook, the rector, and the prior. The procession should be an orderly single file with no monk losing his place. Those walking should not gaze about to the right and left, talk, make jokes, chant loudly, or swing their arms. The arms should remain clasped in the front.

[216] Once they have arrived at their destination, the monks may calmly remove their hats. They should wait until the abbot, administrators, chief officers, and the assembly have gathered together before greeting the donor and taking their seats. They should be solemn and quiet to inspire the donor's piety. If anyone should need to relieve himself, he should not simply remove and fold his *kāṣāya*, place it on his desk, and leave the group. Rather he should take leave of the assembly first, remove his *kāṣāya* outside, and leave it in a clean place. After he is finished, he should wash his hands, put his *kāṣāya* back on, and return to the group. The chief virtue is to avoid disturbing the assembly of purity. When the donor is making preparations or offering incense or money, the monks should remain mindful and should not receive such offerings arrogantly or absentmindedly. They should not be looking at the donor's books or paintings or playing with children. No matter how pleasant or interesting the surroundings, the monks should not become distracted.

[217] After the feast, every monk should follow the abbot in returning to the monastery. No monk should remain behind to conduct business (such as buying clothes or medicinal herbs, visiting other donors, sightseeing, visiting a teacher-monk at another monastery, or any number of reasons too numerous to list) lest he should become the target of ridicule. If he does indeed have business to attend to, he should wait for another day and ask the rector's permission to leave. On those occasions when the monastery leaves to attend a chanting service or to greet the ar-

rival of an honorable senior, the procedure follows this same general outline. Whether or not the chief officers of the respective quarters receive permission to leave depends on the given situation.

Signals to the Assembly

[217] Whenever the bell, drum, or fish-shaped board is struck, the monks must know what they are expected to do. At the fifth *geng*,[16] the big bell is tolled as a signal for the monks to wake up and rise from bed. The ringing of the small bell in front of the kitchen signifies the "opening of small quietness."[17] (The server who delivers food to each quarter and the lamp attendant[18] **[218]** must rise before the others.) The cloud-shaped metal sheet[19] is struck for the "opening of big quietness."[20] (All the monks rise at the same time, and only then can they fold their comforters and roll up their mosquito nets.) Striking the long board tells the monks to take down their bowls (all the monks having formed a line outside the hall before entering at the same time), and striking the wooden fish[21] is the signal for the gathered assembly to be seated quietly. Late arrivals are not allowed to enter the hall. Three striking sequences on the drum is the signal for the abbot to go to the Sangha hall, while the striking of the small bell in front of the Sangha hall[22] tells the monks to descend from their bed platforms and wait to bow to the abbot.

[219] At the beginning of the morning meal, the rector strikes an octagonal stand inside the Sangha hall once with the hammer as a signal for the monks to display their bowls. Following the sound of the striking hammer, the Heart Sutra is chanted three times. The rector strikes once more to signal the preparation of the porridge. (Sometimes praise is also given and a prayer recited.) The hammer's striking ten times begins the chanting of the names of the Ten Buddhas. The rector then strikes once with the hammer for the chief seat to distribute more porridge. The hammer strikes once again for the final meting out of the porridge. After the morning meal has ended, the hammer is struck once for the monks to exit the hall. After the abbot has exited the hall, all the monks may hang up their bowls.

[219] The small bell in front of the Sangha hall is struck three times to signal a break from the morning sermon schedule. If there is to be no hiatus, then the drum inside the hall will be struck for the abbot to ascend the center platform in the hall. When the sermon and tea service are finished, the small bell in front of the Sangha hall is rung three times for all monks to descend from their bed platforms. At the time of the midday meal, when three strikes of the board are heard, the monks take down their bowls. Then the big bell is rung to announce the beginning of the meal. (For monasteries inside the city, the bell is rung first and then three sequences of the drum are given. Monasteries in the mountains or forest give three sequences of the drum first and then ring the bell.) The other signals—such as those given with the long board, the wooden fish, the small bell in front of the Sangha hall, the rector's hammer—and that used for exiting the hall after the meal, all are sounded according to the same procedure as the early meal. Only in the case of a donor feast is the hammer struck an additional time: once after the distribution of food as usual, and once more to signal the offering of money.

[220] When the striking of the drum in the abbot's office or priory, or the striking of the board in any given quarters, is heard, all the monks assemble to attend the tea ceremony at the location indicated by the signal. If the drum in front of the kitchen is heard, it is the summons for all monks to begin communal work. The bell in front of the Sangha hall is rung for the reception of respected officials or appointed administrators or for the funerals of deceased monks. The drum in the bathhouse[23] is struck to signal the "opening of the baths" or the "rinsing of sweat." When the bell in front of the Sangha hall is rung three times in the evening, there will be no night sermon. On the third and eighth days,[24] the big bell or the small bell in front of the Sangha hall is rung for chanting. All monasteries inside the city strike the small bell to summon the assembly to recite the Buddha's name. The monasteries in the mountains or forests strike the big bell first to summon the assembly, then strike the small bell for the recitation of the Buddha's name. The sound of the big bell at sunset means the servers must go to the shrine for chanting. When the drum inside the hall is heard, there will be an informal sermon. From morning until evening the bell and drum work together. Not only are they reminders for the assembly, but they themselves continuously preach the Dharma. So you, honorable people in the monastery, each of you should know the proper times for each activity.

[221] For the first wake-up call, the board is struck three times, each strike being progressively louder and stronger. The small bell in front of the kitchen is then given rolling strikes; the sound should be smooth, progressing from slow to tight and from heavy to light. This is considered one complete sequence. After the end of the second sequence, there follows one sharp strike and then three slow strikes of the board. For the general wake-up call, the method is the same as for the first call, but only one long sequence is struck.

When striking the long board or the wooden fish, a light hand should be used to initiate the sound. The strikes then gradually grow louder and stronger and the sound should be smooth. The tempo then speeds and slows intermittently, while the strikes become lighter then heavier, respectively. After the first sequence there is a pause. It is most important that the beats be precise so that the listener will not be confused. The third sequence ends with a sharp strike, followed by three slow strikes.

When striking the drum to signal the abbot's ascending the platform in the Dharma hall to give an informal sermon, the face of the drum should first be tested by striking lightly three times. Then the sequence begins with a heavy hand and slow beats. The tempo then speeds and slows intermittently, while the strikes become lighter then heavier, respectively. The sound then rises smoothly, with the strikes closer together and muffled, producing a rumbling like the first thunder in spring. The first sequence should be longer than usual, with a short pause at the end. During the second sequence, the beats should be even closer together. At the end of this sequence there is no pause, and the third sequence begins immediately. The drum is then hit continually until the abbot ascends his seat, at which time the drumming stops, followed only by three strikes with the two sticks.

When striking the drum to announce the early and midday meals, three sequences are given—that is, the same pattern as when the abbot ascends the platform except the tempo is quicker. When striking the drum to announce the opening of the baths, a tea ceremony, or a work period, one long sequence is given. A second and third sequence need not follow. When ringing the bell in front of the Sangha hall to signal entrance into the hall, a light hand is used to begin. Then the ringing gradually becomes louder and stronger until the abbot enters the hall, and the ringing stops. When ringing the bell to announce a break from the sermon, the board is struck three times, followed by two slow strikes. When ringing the bell to announce chanting, the method is the same as for the first wake-up call. After the abbot has entered the hall, offered incense, and is standing in the front section of the hall, the rector stops ringing the bell. When the assembly has finished chanting the Ten Buddhas' names, the rector strikes the bell twice and stops. When ringing the bell to signal the descent from the platform, the board is not struck and the bell is rung twice at continual intervals. When ringing the bell during the reception or farewell of important personages, during the appointment of administrators, and during funerals, only one sequence is necessary.

Before the rector strikes with the hammer, he must first bow. He then uses his right hand to grasp the handle and lifts up the hammer. He holds the head of the hammer against the surface of the octagonal stand, with the head pointing toward his body. He extends two fingers of his left hand and touches them to a corner of the hammer's head before he begins slowly turning the handle as he strikes the stand. He then lowers the two fingers against a corner of the stand. While the stand is being struck, the hammer should not be lifted more than five inches from the stand and, once it is struck in one particular area, it should always be struck in that area.

When tolling the big bell, the bell should first be tested with three strikes using a light hand. Then the bell is struck slowly eighteen times. Then follow eighteen more strikes at a faster rate. All together there are three sequences of faster strikes, each preceded by three sequences of slower strikes, totaling 108 strikes. The server on duty must offer incense, bow down, and recite the verse before striking the bell. The verse recited reads, "When they hear the toll of the monastery bell, those beings of the Three Paths[25] and the Eight Difficulties[26] are momentarily relieved of their sufferings, and all sentient beings in the Dharma realm attain enlightenment." After this verse is recited, all suffering immediately stops.

[223] The drums inside the halls are in the attendants' care. The drum in the priory is the prior's responsibility. The cook is in charge of the board signaling early and midday meals, the wooden fish, and the small bell and cloud-shaped metal sheet for the opening of quietness. The small bell in front of the Sangha hall is cared for by the rector. If there is no bell master, the big bell is also in the rector's charge. The cook should supervise the servers who strike the bells. If the aforementioned bells and drums are not struck in the correct manner—that is, too softly or too loudly, too quickly or too slowly—the striker must be taught that it is best to maintain a sense of harmony and smoothness.

The Delivery of Letters

[224] When a special envoy[27] arrives at the monastery with a letter announcing a lineage inheritance,[28] with an abbot's will,[29] or with a letter announcing the appointment of a new abbot,[30] the guest master should make arrangements for his visit. The procedure in the Dharma hall is the same as when the fundraiser presents the statement of donated items. When the scribe has finished making the announcements, the envoy will do *liangzhan sanbai* before the abbot. (He first unfolds the sitting mat, saying, "By delivering this special letter I am afforded the opportunity of seeing your honorable face. I am extremely honored." He then unfolds the sitting mat again to extend a seasonal greeting and to do *chuli* three times.) After this, the administrators, chief officers, and assembly express to the abbot their congratulations or consolations. (For the appointment of a new abbot, this last action of congratulation or consolation is not necessary.)

[225] The chief seat and the assembly stand before the Sangha hall, where they arrange the incense table. (The chief seat stands outside

by the right-hand door in the leading position, and all the monks stand in a row on the left-hand side.) The special envoy hands the letter to the chief seat, who passes it through the incense smoke and hands it to the rector to read aloud. After this is done, the special envoy steps forward to bow to the chief seat and then withdraws to remain standing. Then the chief seat and the assembly enter the Dharma hall, where they stand waiting. The special envoy enters the hall in the manner described in the section that discusses the fundraiser's entrance. The letter and the envelope are posted on the outside of the left-hand door. The guest master leads the special envoy into the storage hall. The letter is presented to the prior, who then passes it through the incense smoke and hands it to the rector to read it aloud. After this is done, a greeting tea ceremony is held. (When the letter in question is a routine letter of lineage inheritance, a will, or a letter announcing the retirement of the abbot,[31] it is simply delivered to the abbot's quarters. When the letter is from the abbot himself, it should be delivered to the chief seat's quarters. When the letter is from the chief seat and the assembly, it is posted on the outside door of the left-hand section. When a letter is delivered to the prior in the storage hall, and for all of the situations listed above,[32] the rector need not read the letter aloud to the assembly.) After the delivery of the letter and tea ceremony (if appropriate), the guest master escorts the envoy to each quarter of the monastery. (If a fundraiser or novice of fewer than ten years visits the honorable senior [the abbot] to deliver a letter, he must present the letter first before bowing.)

The Issuing of Letters

[226] When a letter is written, the characters should be precise and consistent. The writing should be logical and coherent, and the envelope should be sealed in the correct fashion. Such a letter will inspire benevolence and respect in the mind of the reader. If the letter is written in a hasty or absentminded manner, it will only waste paper and ink and will hinder the attaining of enlightenment. If the letter is to be sent to a government official, the author should encourage him to be lenient and to protect the Dharma and the monastery. When an official judgment involving the monastery is pending,[33] the author should request that minor transgressions be overlooked, or, if there has been a gross offense on the part of a particular monk, the author should encourage the official to protect the kāṣāya.[34] When writing a letter to a fellow monk, the author should encourage him to meditate, chant, burn incense, and realize the universal state of impermanence. When addressing a letter to an honorable senior

monk, the author should write that he prays the senior monk is able to carry his burdens, endure his sufferings, propagate the Dharma, and benefit all sentient beings. When writing to a donor, the author should encourage the donor to practice charity and cultivate merit. In all the letters mentioned above it is best not to write excessively about secular matters. The writing should be simple and succinct, but inspirational. After the letter is sealed, it should be passed through incense smoke before being delivered. **[227]** (If a letter is not urgent or absolutely necessary, it should not be sent; it is unsuitable to issue letters arbitrarily.)

Received Letters

[228] If a letter is received from the most respectable among monks, the receiver should pass the letter through the incense smoke and pay homage by facing the direction of the sender. After this courtesy, he himself should open the letter. If a letter is received from a monk of the second highest rank, the receiver should pass the letter through the incense smoke and open it himself. If the letter received is from a monk of equal rank, the receiver has the attendant or server open the seal. (The receiver should open the seal at one end and gently take out the letter. He should not tear the envelope, which would be considered not only insincere, but indelicate.) After the letter has been read, it should be put in its proper place. The receiver should maintain feelings of gratitude and should not regard the letter as something insignificant. If a letter is received from an official, it should be read with sincerity. After reading it, the receiver should immediately chant and pray for the official's merit and wisdom.

The Abbot's Hiatus from Sangha Hall Residency Due to Illness

[229] If the abbot is taking medicine for more than a routine sickness and for more than three days, he should withdraw from his quarters to receive treatment and have his attendant inform the chief seat or the administrators. If the prior, an administrator, or any of the chief officers should fall ill, he should have the server who routinely delivers food inform the rector and should request leave to stay in the infirmary to recuperate. (In some monasteries the infirmary is referred to as *Shengxing tang*, the "hall of contemplating the suffering resulting from the law of impermanence.")[35] If the illness is not of a serious nature and will not impede the performance of his duties, he should remain in his own quarters to recuperate. If the sickness continues, he should ask the abbot to appoint a replacement.

[230] Once the abbot has recovered from his illness, he ascends the platform in the Dharma hall to thank the assembly for their concern. He then descends from his seat as the administrators, chief seat, and assembly greet him by doing *liangzhan sanli*. The abbot's words of gratitude are as follows: "Because I have improperly maintained my health, I have had to impose on you. Fortunately, I have received your Dharma power and so was able to recover." Then follows the reply: "We humble monks are so overjoyed to see that the abbot's Dharma health has improved. We are extremely elated." The abbot circumambulates the hall, pays homage before the Holy Monk, and greets the assembly. Next, he returns to his quarters to have tea with the assembly. When an administrator recovers from a sickness and is ready to return to his own quarters, he first expresses his gratitude to the abbot, and then goes to the administrators, the chief officers, and each quarter to exchange greetings. When a monk of the assembly begins to feel ill, he asks the rector (either in person or through a messenger) for leave to recuperate and informs the director of the assembly quarters before entering the infirmary. After he has recovered and is ready to return to the Sangha hall, he first visits the rectory and then goes to the abbot to greet him. The monk's words of gratitude are as follows: "On this occasion I have depended on your Dharma protection and therefore was able to recover. For this I am extremely grateful." The abbot replies: "I am pleased that your body has recovered. I am most overjoyed." Next the monk visits the administrators and chief officers' quarters and bows. The chief officers next in rank to the abbot decide whether tea should be served; there is no need for a special ceremony.

Fascicle Seven

Using the Toilet

[233] If a monk needs to use the toilet[1] he should do so in good time and not wait until the last moment, allowing internal pressures to compel unseemly haste.[2] He should first fold his *kāṣāya* and place it on his desk or on the clean pole, and bow before leaving.[3] He then puts on his *guazi*[4] and places a clean towel over his left arm. He should not pass through the main shrine on the way to the latrine. When he reaches the latrine, he hangs his *guazi* and towel over the clean pole outside the latrine. He then rolls up his underskirt, folds his short gown, and places them on the pole in front of the latrine. He places the short gown on top of the underskirt and ties them together with his belt, which serves to identify his belongings;[5] this will also prevent his clothes from falling to the ground. He carries the water vessel with his right hand and, entering the latrine, removes his shoes and lays them side by side. He softly pulls the door to close it and lowers the vessel with his hand. Before relieving himself he should snap his fingers three times to warn the ghosts who feed on excretment.[6] He should not be dirty with mucous or spit, scattering it about, and he should not make excessive noise.[7] He should not use the bamboo spatulas to draw on the floor, door, or walls,[8] and he should not talk to or make jokes with the people next door.

[235] When cleaning oneself, it is better to use cold water, for hot water can lead to "the intestinal wind."[9] Holding the water vessel with his right hand (and protecting his thumb and index finger), the monk uses the water with his left hand. He should be careful not to splash the water and pollute the floor or soil the edges around the toilet. He should not use more than one section of bamboo spatula.[10] Some people, after using the bamboo spatulas, will wash them before leaving. To wash his hands he should use ashes first and then dirt. He then goes to the washing stand behind the latrine and uses the bean pod soap,[11] washing up to his elbows. He also rinses his mouth. (According to the Vinaya,[12] he should chew a willow twig to clean his mouth.) He returns to retrieve his *guazi* and clean towel, bows, and puts on his *kāṣāya*. The Vinaya states that if a monk is not clean or fully washed, he cannot sit on the monks' platform bed, bow to the Three Treasures,[13] or receive bows from others.[14] When a monk arrives at the door of the latrine and senses that someone is inside, he should not cough, snap his fingers, or talk to make the person hurry.[15] If he is in the latrine himself and realizes that someone is waiting outside, he should try to finish as soon as possible. (At such times washing the bamboo spatulas would be inappropriate.)[16] If the monk is going to the place for urination, he should roll up his clothes, should squat down close to the toilet, and should not spit, blow his nose, or talk.[17] He should always yield to senior monks.[18] (According to the Vinaya, the monk must also wash himself after urination or be guilty of the offense of uncleanliness mentioned above.)[19]

The Monk's Funeral

[237] If a monk becomes seriously ill, the director of the hall of longevity must consult the rector, the prior, the chief seat, the library director, the scribe, and the guest master, and together they take down the patient's will and transfer his ordination certificate and personal effects to the rectory for safe keeping. The chief seat seals this box of belongings and keeps the key himself; the rector[20] reports the situation to the officials. If the illness becomes critical, the administrators must inform the officials once again. If the monk passes away, the administrators must report the death to the officials and ask for permission to conduct a funeral. The deceased's ordination certificate, purple robe, or certificate of master title must be turned in to the government within three days of the monk's death.

[238] As soon as a monk dies, he should be bathed, his head should be shaved, and he should be dressed in a *guazi*. His body should be placed in a sitting position in a large vessel set in a small shrine and positioned in front of the hall of longevity. Fragrant flowers should be arranged as an offering, and a white banner should be made, on which a verse pertaining to the law of impermanence is written. "Mourning flowers for the Buddha"[21] should be placed on the shrine and the following should be written on a tablet: "The spirit of the late honorable monk X." The assembly is then summoned for chanting. That night, a service is held to chant precepts to transfer merit to the deceased. The last farewell[22] is held the next day, in the morning or after the midday meal.

[238] On the day of the funeral, the rector strikes one blow with the hammer after the distribution of porridge or money, and announces, "After this early meal (or midday meal) the assembly will hear the sound of the bell. All monks should prepare themselves to attend the funeral. With the exception of the chief officers of each quarter, everyone must be present. This I announce with all sincerity." He then strikes the hammer once more, bows before the Holy Monk, bows to the abbot, and circumambulates the hall once. If there are monks in the outer section, he must bow to them as well, excepting

the monks in the rear section. At the appropriate time, the bell is rung and all assemble before the shrine containing the deceased. Then each person present, one at a time beginning with the abbot, offers incense. After the rector finishes the chanting, the drum is struck and the shrine is lifted to begin the procession. **[239]** The assembly follows, some holding the banner, some holding the bell or the incense burner and incense stand for the service. The administrators in the priory should have sent a few servers beforehand to help with preparations. The superintendent leads the procession of shrine bearers and prepares the firewood before the altar. The superintendent takes care of all the particulars of the funeral rite. When the procession has arrived at the pagoda area, everyone offers incense in turn, beginning with the abbot, while the Dharma instruments are played, chanting is performed, and a fire is lit. The abbot should then read a few verses of Dharma words. Everyone then chants the name of the Amitābha Buddha ten times. The playing of the Dharma instruments and chanting continue, after which the assembly is dismissed. Whether chanting follows the reading of the sutra depends on the discretion of the abbot.

[240] If the funeral takes place in a city, the monks should go and return in single file. They should not laugh or jest; rather they should remain silent, mentally reciting the name of the Buddha and the mantra and transfering the merit to the deceased. All the monks should leave together and return together; no monk should remain behind. If a monk has some business to attend to, he should ask the rector for leave at another time. The next day the director of the hall of longevity and the rector perform the service and collect the ashes, placing them in the pagoda of "the universe"[23] or spreading them over water.

[240] A placard is hung announcing the auction of the deceased monk's possessions[24] to the assembly. While the bell is rung, everyone enters the hall. First, there is chanting for the deceased monk,[25] then the chief seat is invited to examine the seal of the deceased's property before opening it in front of the assembly.[26] The possessions should be displayed in the hall before the bell is rung. The items are auctioned one at a time,[27] after which the rector again leads the chanting. The abbot or the administrators should not be allowed to preside over the auction. The payments made by the rector for the funeral, using funds raised by the auction, should be reasonable and within customary limits. **[241]** He should not arbitrarily spend unusually large amounts. In addition to the funeral expenses, money is needed to pay the assembly for the chanting of the sutras, to distribute to the temporary visitors who have come to attend the farewell funeral, and to give to those who attend the auction; thus, the surplus funds are divided into these three equal amounts. This method of dividing funds resembles the distribution procedure used when a lay patron sponsors a sutra reading: after initial expenses, donations are meted out in equal parts to all participants. If there are many possessions to be auctioned, part of the net proceeds should be used to sponsor a feast. On the seventh day after the death,[28] the assembly is summoned to chant the sutras and mantras. At this point the rector [?] announces the expenses; a full account should be written down and posted at the rear of the hall for all to see. (The accounts placard should receive the seals of approval of all administrators as testimony to all that there have been no misappropriations.)

[242] Other than the enlightenment that comes with spiritual cultivation, which is the chief goal for all those who have renounced the world, monks should seek to acquire nothing but their clothes and a bowl. They should not accumulate property, which leads to avarice. A monk should prevent the possibility that, on the day of the auction after his death, the assembly will sit too long and become distressed because of the excessive number of belongings to be auctioned. It is equally improper to bequeath nothing, not even one's clothes and bowl, for to do so places the burden on the monastery of paying the funeral expenses out of its own coffers. The purpose of the auction is to create an atmosphere that supersedes the deceased's material attachments,[29] as well as to help those present develop a feeling of kinship with the deceased's spirit. The auctioneer should not announce beforehand that items will be auctioned cheaply and then, at the time of the auction, set higher prices. If the possessions are priced too high, this may disturb the mood of the assembly and elicit ridicule. When the rector presides over an auction, he should know the proper price of each item. New items, old items, and broken items should be clearly identified as such. The rector should base his asking price on an item's actual worth. (Some items may be raised in price, others lowered, and still others left unaltered: in each case, the rector should make the proper adjustment.) Even if there is a lack of bids and the asking price remains far lower than the worth of an item, the item should still be sold. If bids are rising too high, the rector should warn the bidders: "You should exercise greater caution. You may regret your bid afterward, and it cannot be changed." This will avoid disturbing the mood of the assembly and prevent any potential incidents. To avoid suspi-

cion, neither the possessions of the assembly nor the monastery's property may be auctioned at the same time as the deceased monk's belongings. Only when monastic property or the property of the abbot's office has already been scheduled for auction can it be added to the list of items to be sold.[30]

[243] *Chanting for a Sick Monk*

After he has praised the Buddha, the rector begins, "This morning, the ailing Bhikṣu X, in order to release the grievances of many past lives and to repent of the sins he has accumulated over the aeons, must now exercise great sincerity and rely on the assembly of purity to chant the Holy Names in the hope of expelling his misfortunes. Let him now depend on our deeply pious chanting of 'Pure Dharma Body.'" After the chanting, the merit accrued is transferred to the ailing monk. The rector continues, "We humbly wish that Bhikṣu X will be of one pure mind, that the four great elements that constitute his body[31] will be at rest, and that his physical life as well as his life of wisdom will be extended. May his corporeal body and his Dharma body be strong." If a monk is terminally ill, the assembly aids the sick monk in performing the ten recitations of the name of Amitābha Buddha.[32] The chanting that follows begins with the praising of Amitābha Buddha. The rector then announces to the assembly. "For Bhikṣu X we chant at length the names of Amitābha Buddha and the bodhisattvas of the Western Pure Land: the Four Holy Names."[33] The merit of this chant is then transferred to the infirm monk. The rector continues, "We humbly wish that Bhikṣu X, whose connections to the living have not yet ended, will recover as soon as possible. Since his great life has reached the point of no return, we hope that he will be reborn in the place of peaceful sustenance."[34] The assembly again chants the Four Holy Names, after which they encourage the dying monk to pacify his mind and purify his thoughts to keep them from wandering into secular matters like unruly vines.

[244] *Chanting before the Shrine*

As soon as the deceased monk has been placed in the shrine, the rectory asks the assembly to gather before the shrine when they hear the bell. Following the abbot, the administrators, chief officers, and the director of the infirmary offer incense one at a time. The rector strikes the bell and praises the Buddha, after which he says, "Life and death fade into endless alternations; heat and cold change eternally, one into the other.[35] Life comes like a lightning strike across the distant sky; it ends like a wave that subsides into the vast sea. On this day we commemorate the deceased Bhikṣu X, whose karma in this world has ended. His great life is suddenly altered. To understand the impermanence of all phenomena, to enter nirvana—this is true happiness.[36] So we, with great sincerity, rely upon the assembly to come solemnly before the shrine and chant the Great Names of All the Holy Ones to lift this pure spirit to the Pure Land. Now we depend on the assembly to chant 'Pure Dharma Body.'" The merit of the chanting is transfered to the deceased, and then the rector continues, "We humbly desire that the deceased's spirit will transcend to the pure realm and that his karma will fade into dust. May his lotus flower bloom in the 'highest class.'[37] May he receive the Buddha's prediction that this has been his last life before attaining Buddhahood."[38] The rector goes on, "Now we should like to trouble the venerable assembly to chant 'Ten Directions, Three Ages.'"[39]

[245] *Chanting as the Shrine Is Lifted*

The words spoken before the shrine is lifted are: "Now we should like to carry this shrine to the location of the great cremation ceremony. We must depend on the venerable assembly to chant the Great Names of All the Holy Ones to enable the deceased's spirit to climb up to the path of enlightenment." After the Buddha's name has been recited ten times, the procession begins.

[245] *The Ten Recitations before the Pagoda*

The words spoken in front of the pagoda are: "As the deceased Bhiksu X has inevitably succumbed to annihilation, we now, in accordance with the law, must cremate his body. Let us burn this body, which has propagated the Dharma for one hundred years, and its spirit will enter the road toward *nirvana*.[40] We must depend on the venerable assembly to assist in this process." After the ten recitations, the rector says, "By chanting the Holy Names, we have assisted this spirit to be reborn in the Pure Land. We hope with all sincerity that the mirror of wisdom will spread its light and the wind of genuineness will diffuse its glory.[41] In the Bodhi garden the flower of enlightenment blooms; in the ocean of Dharma nature the mind polluted by secular things is cleansed. **[246]** We now pour three libations and burn incense in a single holder to assist the spirit to ascend on its journey to the clouds and to pay homage to the Holy Assembly."

[246] The chanting before the auction is as follows: After the assembly is summoned, the rector strikes the bell once, saying, "When the floating cloud disperses, its moving shadow is cast no more; and when the candle stub is finished, the flame, too, is extinguished. Through this auction we illustrate this notion of impermanence. We must now depend on the venerable assembly to assist the spirit of the deceased Bhiksu X to be reborn in the Pure Land." Then the chanting of "Pure Dharma Body" begins. The rector strikes the bell again and says, "This auction is conducted according to traditional custom. If a purchased item is deemed too new, too old, too short, or too long, it is the purchaser's responsibility. The purchaser should have the correct number of coins ready[42] (some use only 77, others 75 instead of the standard string of 100)⁴³ and he should be careful that his money does not have 'new tin' mixed in with it.⁴⁴ After the sound of the bell signaling that an item has been officially sold, the buyer should not express any regret. I announce this with all sincerity." When the auction has finished, the rector announces, "The merit performed by the assembly through this chanting and auction will now be transfered to the late X and will help his spirit to be reborn in the Pure Land. Now I should like to trouble the assembly to recite the names of the Buddhas of ten directions of the past, present, and future." The assembly should then recite the names of the Buddhas with sincerity and should not laugh, talk, or fight among themselves.

[247] The tea ceremony that follows the recitation of the Vinaya and the tea ceremony that follows the auction are the responsibility of the prior. According to the Vinaya, neither the body of the deceased nor the deceased's clothes or possessions should pass under the Buddha's pagoda. The corpse should not be cremated beneath the Buddha pagoda.⁴⁵

*Appointment of the Chief Seat Emeritus*⁴⁶

[248] If a retired abbot, chief seat, or library director has the approval of the assembly, he may be named chief seat emeritus. The incumbent abbot ascends his seat in the Dharma hall and announces the appointment of the chief seat emeritus. The administrators and the assembly then visit the chief seat emeritus candidate's hall of residence to extend a cordial invitation to him. The wording of the invitation should be: "The assembly has been hoping for your instruction for a long time. We humbly desire that you kindly consent to our request." If the retired monk does not accept the position, he does not bow in return and replies, "I cannot save myself—how can I help others?" If he gives his consent, he returns the courtesy, bowing immediately, and answers, "Since you have invited me with such persistence, I dare not continue to refuse." The monk then goes to the abbot's quarters to express his gratitude. Here proper etiquette depends on the relative positions of those involved. If the chief seat emeritus is of higher seniority than the incumbent abbot, he thanks the abbot by saying, "Initially I intended to avoid all contact to conceal my shortcomings, but now that I have received your recommendation, I dare not object." The abbot replies, "Your elephant-riding (that is, most honorable) visit shall make the wheel of Dharma spin eternally. Although it is inappropriate to bother you with such an appointment, please think first and foremost of the Dharma." If the chief seat emeritus was of the same seniority ranking as the abbot, then his words of gratitude are as follows: "I had planned to cul-

tivate myself and had wondered how I can be of benefit to others. Because your superior decree cannot be refused, I must accept but still feel greatly humbled." The abbot replies, "Although it is inappropriate to bother you with such an appointment, please think first and foremost of the Dharma." If the chief seat emeritus is famous, with a virtue known in all ten directions, or if he is a junior monk still in training, he thanks the abbot by saying, "I have received the abbot's instruction and the assembly's request and so, although I do not have any deep attainment in my spiritual practice, I dare not persist in refusing. I am extremely disconcerted yet grateful." The abbot replies, "Since you yet have surplus light to give, please think first and foremost of the Dharma." The chief seat emeritus visits the administrators to extend his gratitude, and the next day the abbot sponsors a special tea ceremony in the priory. Whether a feast is held depends on the discretion of the abbot.

Appointment of the Honorable Senior—the Abbot

[250] It is recommended that one person from the priory or rectory be selected as an envoy to invite the new abbot, as well as one of the chief officers and several of the retired staff and senior monks—all of whom should be mentally capable, knowledgeable about the monastery, and familiar with etiquette. The money for travel expenses and luggage should be obtained, and a sedan chair, boat, or other mode of transportation should be prepared. In addition, the envoys should assemble documents from the monastery and local officials: the monastery's tea ceremony poster and letters from monk-officers, senior monks of other monasteries, someone writing on behalf of all the donors, retired officials, the retiring abbot (writing to the district of his own monastery as well as to the district of his replacement) and other officials. All of these items must be prepared with care and correctly packed. One monk should be in charge of items such as money and the financial records. He should be neither extravagant nor excessively frugal in spending. The envoys should avoid inspections by government officials and should refrain from ostentation or conspicuous preparations; it is better to travel unannounced.

[251] One of the envoys should be sent ahead to the district of the prospective abbot to deliver the documents to the local government officials. All the other envoys take up residence at the prospective abbot's monastery and stay there while awaiting an official response. If the officials of this district refuse to release the abbot, the envoys should request a response letter asking these officials to explain their refusal. Then one of the envoys should return to his home district with this response letter; meanwhile, the other envoys should not re-

turn until word is received from home. If the envoys waiting at the prospective abbot's monastery receive a letter from their own district officials urging them to make a second request for release of the abbot, the envoys should go to the officials of that district and ask again for the abbot to be discharged. If there is no letter from their own district officials asking them to make a second request, they may return home to their own monastery. If the officials of the prospective abbot's district allow the abbot's release, then the envoys present their invitation at his monastery in accordance with proper etiquette. The envoys should first meet and consult with the temple administrators. They then meet with the abbot for a greeting tea ceremony. After the tea is served, the letter of invitation is cordially presented. The envoys should repeat their invitation three times, each time with mindfulness and diligence. The abbot may accept only after the third invitation. (Whenever Chan Master Fayun Yuantong received an invitation, he would wait until envoys had been sent to him three times before accepting.)[47]

The Letter of Appointment Received by the Abbot Candidate

[252] If an incumbent abbot is given a letter inviting him to become abbot at another monastery, the envoys should go to the abbot's quarters and invite him three times. Even if the abbot has accepted the invitation and the drum is struck and the assembly summoned, still he must make a show of refusing the invitation and must claim to accept only because he has no choice. The letter of invitation is passed through the incense smoke (at this point Dharma verses should be recited), after which the rector reads it aloud to the assembly. The abbot ascends his seat to propagate the Dharma[48] and then descends to perform *liangzhan sanli* out of gratitude to the administrators, the chief seat, and the assembly, who congratulate him in return. The words of congratulation are: "It is a great honor that you are ascending to a more prestigious monastery. This news has brought intense joy to the monastery and has given your patriarchs and teachers cause for paternal pride. Heaven and earth shall celebrate together and we are extremely elated." The abbot's words of gratitude are: "Without permission I recklessly accepted this invitation and have stained the traditions of this school. When I look up I feel ashamed before all heaven; when I look down I feel ashamed before the entire assembly."

[253] If the person to be invited is not an incumbent abbot, the envoys should go to his hall of residence to extend the invitation to him three times. If the candidate accepts the invitation, then the abbot of the monastery ascends his seat to announce the news and, along with the assembly, urges the candidate to accept the outside

appointment. The candidate bows to the abbot and receives a letter from him. If the candidate has not "gone out into the world"[49] in this monastery, then one of the envoys prepares a Dharma robe. After the invitation is read aloud, the envoy presents the robe to the candidate, who passes it through the incense smoke and puts it on. Dharma verses should be recited at this time. However, if the candidate has "gone out into the world,"[50] the robe is not necessary. The candidate faces the Dharma seat and ascends it, reciting Dharma verses. He then gives a sermon, after which he descends and bows to thank the abbot. At this point, candidates sometimes fully unfold their sitting mats and bow down nine times, sometimes they do *liangzhan sanli*. The candidate's words of gratitude are: "Throughout my spiritual career I have looked to the examples of my virtuous predecessors and have felt ashamed when I compared myself to them. However, since three invitations have been made with such insistence, it is difficult for me to refuse this superior decree. I am extremely disconcerted and moved by this appointment." The ensuing words of congratulation from the abbot are: "Since the awl has come out of the bag,[51] it cannot escape the rain.[52] It is most fortunate that you are undertaking this benevolent duty; indeed, it is worthy of celebration." Then the candidate, the administrators, the chief seat, and the assembly do *liangzhan sanli* to thank and congratulate one another. The candidate expresses his gratitude as follows: "Without permission I recklessly accepted this invitation and have stained the traditions of this school. You have bestowed on me too great a compliment. I am extremely grateful." The congratulatory reply is as follows: "It is a joy that you have received this invitation from earthly and heavenly beings, which increases the honor of the light of the Buddhas and the Patriarchs. We are utterly elated."

[254] The newly appointed abbot visits the various quarters of his former monastery to say goodbye. After a day or two the envoys hang a poster announcing a tea ceremony for the new abbot, and the next day they hold a combined feast-tea ceremony. When it is time for him to leave for his new monastery, he may ascend the seat in the Dharma hall to give a small farewell sermon. If the appointee was the incumbent abbot of his former monastery, he should not take any monastic property with him. If money or grain is to be transferred to the next abbot, then it should be made clear what is owned communally and what is owned privately. [255] The abbot should not take the most capable servers with him, removing their names from the monastic registry when he leaves. He should not accept too many farewell banquets from the monastery, and he should consult with others as to how large a retinue will travel with him so as not to create hardship for his former monastery. Three messengers are sent to

deliver messages to his new monastery in advance of his arrival. He prepares all the letters and selects one messenger to deliver them to the officials and to donors to express his gratitude and announce his appointment. He selects two other messengers to travel to his new monastery and make all the preparations. On the day of departure, the new abbot packs his belongings and leaves with his attendants and servers. (If the newly selected candidate is not the incumbent abbot of the monastery, his farewell procession is as follows: The incumbent abbot follows behind the assembly, while the envoys, other monks, and laypeople who wish to say farewell walk behind the new abbot.)

The Newly Appointed Abbot's Entrance to the Monastery

[256] The new abbot should enter his new monastery carrying his luggage with his retinue following behind. If he encounters a welcoming party on the road as he approaches the monastery, he may take off his bamboo hat, put his walking stick aside, and bow; or, using his right hand to hold the brim of his hat, he may bend his body slightly. If he is invited to sit down for tea or drink, he should simply take off his hat and, leaning on his stick for support, sit down without unpacking his luggage. If he is met by senior monks, he may merely bow, saying, "As I am traveling on the road I cannot collect myself to bow down to you." If he is met by officials, he may simply clasp his hands and greet them, saying, "On the road my clothes make it inconvenient to express my respects; I hope I will not offend you." When he has entered the monastery through the mountain main gate, he should burn incense and Dharma verses should be recited. He then unpacks his belongings in front of the Sangha hall and goes to the rear washing stand to wash his feet. He enters the Sangha hall to offer incense before the Holy Monk. His attendants follow him as a group and fully unfold their sitting mats, bowing down three times to the Holy Monk and then circumambulating the hall together once. Then the rector invites the abbot to assume the abbot's seat and does *chuli* three times to him. Once this is done, the abbot takes up residence in the Sangha hall.

After he has established his position in the Sangha hall, the new abbot goes first to the Great Shrine, then to the earth hall of the guardian deities. Next he visits the hall of the patriarchs' pictures. In each location instruments are played, sutras are chanted, and incense is burned. The administrators then invite the new abbot to the abbot's quarters, where he sits in his seat and gives a short speech.[53] After this, the administrators extend their gratitude, and the abbot meets briefly with his guests. The drum is struck, and the abbot as-

cends his seat in the Dharma hall. The procedure for expressing congratulations and gratitude at this location is the same as the procedure for the commencement and closing of the summer retreat.[54] The
words of congratulations are: "We humbly greet your elephant-riding[55] arrival.
We are extremely glad to receive your illumination at the Dharma banquet." The
words of gratitude are: "I regret that I am not a worthy vessel. I have usurped the
leadership of a famous monastery—for this reason I am most abashed." That
evening the abbot delivers an informal sermon. In all, this ceremony
lasts three days. The first morning after the final day of the ceremony,
the abbot pays a courtesy visit to the local officials one at a time. The
abbot also must choose a day for his inauguration ceremony.[56] He
should wait until all of the greetings begin to subside before he hosts
a tea ceremony especially for the envoys and for the retainers who
arrived with him. Officials, donors, retired staff, and senior monks
should also be invited in groups. The retainers should be provided for courteously. The messengers who arrived at the monastery before the others should
have arranged a place for the arriving retinue to stay. After the ceremony, the retainers disperse to the various residential quarters.

The Role of the Abbot

[257] The abbot represents the Buddha in his propagation of the
Dharma, and he sets an example for the administrators; he is therefore called "Transmitter of the Dharma." Abbots are spread across
the land, each occupying his own place and continuing the Buddha's
life of wisdom; they are therefore called "Dwelling and Holding."[57]
They begin the turning of the Dharma wheel, so they are called "those
who have gone out into the world." The abbot inherits the teaching
of his lineage, so he is also known as "Transmitter of the Flame."[58]
He has received the title of "Elder of Benevolent Manifestation."[59] The
abbot resides in the building known as "ten square meters" of the
Golden Grain Tathāgata.[60] He calls himself the "Sprayer of Water and
Sweeper of Floors."[61] His chief duty is to ensure the monastery's purity and strict adherence to the Vinaya. His other duties include providing spiritual cultivation when asked by government officials as well
as praying for the emperor's longevity. The abbot must exercise his
great mind, propagate the great Dharma, harbor great virtue, undertake great action, increase great compassion, accomplish deeds
of great Dharma, and achieve great benefits. [258] The abbot has the
right and authority to make important decisions when they are
called for. With the initial version of the monastic regulations as a
guide, it is still difficult to anticipate potential problems. The abbot's

operating principle should be to enforce the rules of prescription and prohibition in a strict and stern fashion. His outward image may be that of a righteous man, but it is far more important that he be truly respected. He should measure the abilities of the monks he selects to serve on his staff. He should clasp his hands and look up in expectation of a task's being carried out, being careful not to jostle the elbows of others.⁶² The abbot should attempt to streamline the monastic regulations. He should foster elite monks. He should tirelessly give instruction; only then will he be the "eyes of human and heavenly beings."⁶³

The Funeral of the Abbot

[259] When the abbot passes away, his body should be placed in the abbot's quarters and fragrant flowers should be offered. Then verses from the abbot's last instruction should be written on two placards and suspended over the right- and left-hand side of the deceased's devotional shrine. One of the senior monks of the abbot's Dharma lineage should be appointed as "funeral master."⁶⁴ If there is no one of the same Dharma lineage, then an abbot from a neighboring monastery should be invited. Next, the abbot's will should be copied, and messengers should inform the officials, the lay patrons, the monk-officials, the senior monks of neighboring monasteries, the junior Dharma heirs, and monks in the abbot's direct lineage. Different monks are appointed to deliver each of these letters. Three days after the abbot's death, his body is placed in the shrine according to the funeral procedures described above.

[260] When the body is placed in the shrine,⁶⁵ an honorable senior is appointed to lift up the "seat of the spirit." At this point, a few more Dharma verses should be pronounced. The shrine is placed on the west side of the Dharma hall. On the east side the abbot's bed is made, beside which is placed the abbot's hanging stand and daily items. A painting of the abbot is suspended above the Dharma seat. In the Dharma hall, white curtains, white flowers, lamps, candles, and offertory items are used to decorate the devotional shrine. The junior monks stand behind and below the curtain, wearing mourning garments and guarding the shrine. After all the arrangements are made in the Dharma hall, the entire assembly, beginning with the funeral master, bows down to the picture of the abbot. Then the administrators, chief officers, "filial sons,"⁶⁶ and general assembly meet with the funeral master and offer condolences to each other individually. If outside guests come to mourn, the external guest master leads them to the

Dharma hall, and the internal guest master escorts them to offer incense and bow down before the abbot's picture. Then the guests meet
with the funeral master, the administrators, and the chief seat, after
which they approach the curtain to offer condolences to the junior
monks. They return to have tea with the funeral master, and the external guest master escorts them out. If guests bring sacrificial offerings, they are displayed in front of the abbot's picture. If the guests
do not bring with them a person to read the eulogy, then the rector
or the scribe of the monastery reads it. At the farewell funeral, the
big shrine is decorated accordingly, and the picture shrine, the incense shrine, the service, and the flower banner are prepared.

[261] On the day of "lifting up the shrine,"⁶⁷ the monastery should
sponsor a large feast in accordance with its financial capabilities and
should offer more money than usual. When the time arrives, a senior monk should be appointed to lift the shrine up symbolically. At
this point, a few Dharma verses should be read. The filial sons and the servers
circumambulate the shrine, after which they form an escort for the
shrine, following behind the funeral master. The filial sons and the
assembly walk in the center of the road in single file. The officials
and the donors walk on the right- and left-hand sides parallel to the
monks. Nuns and the abbot's blood relations follow at the end of the
farewell procession. When the deceased abbot's body is cremated, a
senior monk is appointed to light the fire. At this point, a few more Dharma
verses should be read. When the ashes are put into a pagoda, a senior
monk is appointed to lower the shrine into the pagoda while more
Dharma verses are read. A second senior monk is appointed to spread
the soil, and again more Dharma verses are read. After this, ten recitations
of the Buddha's name are performed as in the case of a monk's funeral, and the monastery distributes the money offered for the recitations. The monks return to the monastery, and a senior monk is appointed to suspend the picture of the late abbot in the area next to
abbot's front hall, and more Dharma verses are read. Beginning with the
funeral master, each monk bows down before the painting. After this
all monks offer condolences to each other and then all are dismissed.
The administrators, chief officers, filial sons, et cetera, offer incense
before the picture in the morning and evening and offer two meals
a day to the late abbot concurrent with the meals of the assembly.
[262] The assembly waits for a new abbot to arrive at the monastery.
At some point before that day arrives, the painting is removed from
the abbot's front hall and placed in the hall of pictures.

[263] At each stage of the funeral—placing the body in the shrine,

lifting up the shrine, lighting the fire, placing the shrine into the pagoda, spreading the soil, suspending the picture—"milk medicine"[68] should be offered to all who attend the funeral. For his role in the ritual, the funeral master should be paid well. Near the end of the funeral ceremony, the monastery should show its gratitude to the senior monks who have performed the various funerary tasks mentioned above. The appointment of a new abbot is then discussed and the administrators issue letters to neighboring monasteries to explain the situation and ask for recommendations. Senior monks from surrounding monasteries and monk-officials may suggest candidates, but if their recommendations are not agreed on by the assembly, the administrators must meet with a government official, explain the situation, and ask for an alternate. If the government entrusts the monastery with the power to unilaterally select an abbot, the monastery should do so quickly to avoid having the abbot's position vacant for an extended period of time.[69]

Retirement of the Abbot

[264] When the abbot reaches an advanced age or becomes ill, or if there is a particular reason for him to retire, he should not insist on maintaining his position. He should pack his robes, bowls, and personal belongings beforehand. Together with the administrators, the retiring abbot must clearly write down in the income records what belongs to the monastery and what belongs to the monks. The communal items used in the abbot's office must be transferred properly along with the income record, all of which are then sealed with the monastic seal. The abbot then asks the administrators to appoint someone to safeguard the abbot's quarters and the transferred items. This guardian should take up residence in the attendants' quarters. If the abbot owns an excessive number of robes, bowls, and other personal items, he should auction them off before he retires, sponsor a feast for the assembly, and donate a portion of this money to the monastery to avoid any financial offense. The possessions he takes with him into retirement should be only those things he usually carries on his person and other basic possessions. If he has too much luggage, he is likely to be ridiculed or criticized. Gold, silver, silk, and taxed items, as well as any prohibited items,[70] should not be carried by the retired abbot. He should neither give personal letters to government officials nor should he divulge the location of his hermitage.[71] Furthermore, he should not plan his place of retirement beforehand.[72] If the abbot is traveling a great distance from the region where his current monastery is located, he should expediently arrange his travel certificate in advance.

[265] Once everything has been arranged, the retired abbot should have his attendant or a junior monk deliver the letter of retirement. After the letter has been presented, the abbot should avoid contact with members of the monastery and should leave or take up residence in other quarters. After he has retired, he will stay at numerous places as a guest. It is only appropriate for him to bring one attendant and one server; he should not maintain an entourage of followers, thereby imposing on the households and monasteries he visits. When visiting monasteries, he must accept refined as well as coarse food, customs, et cetera; in everything he should follow the practice of the assembly. He should not interfere with monastic affairs or criticize the master, administrators, or chief officers. He should not mention his past role as abbot or previous accomplishments; he should not voice any grievance he may be harboring. If, while visiting a monastery, the host abbot should ask the retired abbot to "ascend the seat" to give a formal sermon or perform a small sermon, he may or may not accept, depending on the situation. Unless the retired abbot is recommended by the host abbot or courteously invited by the administrators and the assembly, he should not **[266]** have monks "enter his room."[73] Once an abbot has retired from his post, it is not appropriate for him to be a constant presence or to take up residence in his former monastery. Relations among people are a highly unstable matter; it is best to be extremely cautious regarding the continuation of former relations. If the retired abbot is ill or convalescencing and therefore cannot move about without difficulty, the choice of whether to leave or remain at the monastery is his; deciding to stay will cause no harm.

Notes

Introduction

1. Here and throughout this book, for the sake of convenience I have opted to use the term "monks." The word most often refers to monks *and* nuns, so it should be read as equivalent to the noun "monastics." I have, at times, also made use of the term "clergy," which I regard as synonymous with "the monastic body," or "Sangha."

2. *senggui*. Here I modify Tsuchihashi Shūkō's classification: *jielü*, *sengzhi*, and *qinggui*. See his "Chūgoku ni okeru kairitsu no kussetsu: sōsei shingi wo chūshin ni," in Tsuchihashi, *Kairitsu no kenkyū* (Kyoto: Nagata Bunshōdō, 1980), 887–924. *Sengzhi* also traditionally refers to governmental law and policy relating to the clergy. To avoid confusion, I refer to those regulations compiled before the Chan Rules of Purity as *senggui*.

3. *qinggui*. This term originally referred only to monastic codes produced by the Chan school; however, after the Song dynasty it was adopted by other monastic schools.

Chapter 1. Evolution of Monastic Regulations in China

1. *DSL* (*T* 54:237c21–23).

2. "Vinaya" literally means "extinction of evil." Thus, by following the rules, or precepts, collected in the Vinaya, one can restrain oneself from doing wrong or evil.

3. Monastics had to embrace a set of rules guiding their behavior and demeanor in the communal life of the monastery. These Vinayas do not occur to an upholder automatically; they are implanted through the transmission from teachers or patriarchs to novices. This occurs during ordination, which also bestows on the postulant the privileges and obligations of the monastic. Ordination usually consists of two steps: first receiving a number of precepts to become a novice, then receiving additional precepts to become a fully ordained monk or nun. Male novices are *śrāmaṇera*, females are *śrāmaṇeri;* monks are *bhikṣu*, nuns *bhikṣuni*. Those under the age of twenty, considered minors, take only the first step. The number of rules varies among the different schools. In the Dharmagupataka school, novices receive 10 precepts, monks an additional 250, nuns 428. The body collecting these precepts for adult monastics is known as a *prāk-*

timokṣa. These *prāktimokṣa* rules can be classified into seven or eight categories according to the degree of offense and punishment a monastic incurs by breaking them.

4. *GSZ* 1 (*T* 50:324c29–325a1).

5. See *Kaiyuan shijiao lu* 1 (*T* 55:486c3–4). *Sengqi jiexin* was lost in the eighth century.

6. 布薩. For English translations of Vinaya terminology, I have consulted I. B. Horner's *The Book of the Discipline: Vinayapiṭaka*, 6 vols. (London: The Pāli Text Society, 1982–1986).

7. *GSZ* 1 (*T* 50:324c27–325a5).

8. *GSZ* 1 (*T* 50:325a2).

9. *T* 54:237c7–10.

10. See Hirakawa Akira, *Rituszō no kenkyū* (Tokyo: Sankibō Busshorin, 1970), 203, and Ōchō Enichi, *Chūgoku Bukkyō no kenkyū* (Kyoto: Hōzōkan, 1958), 26.

11. For a good general introduction to the Vinayas, see "Vinayapiṭaka" in Étienne Lamotte, *History of Indian Buddhism*, trans. Sara Webb-Boin (Louvain: Peeters Press, 1988), 165–178. For an excellent analysis of the formation of the Vinaya of each school, see E. Frauwallner, *The Earliest Vinaya and the Beginnings of Buddhist Literature* (Rome: Is. M.E.O., 1956).

12. Tanmoshi 曇摩侍 is sometimes written Tanmochi 曇摩持.

13. Hirakawa (*Ritsuzō*, 159) believes the translation was done in 383.

14. Hirakawa, *Ritsuzō*, 161.

15. See Yabuki Keiki, *Meisha yoin kaisetsu* (Tokyo: Iwanami Shoten, 1933), 351. Hirakawa (*Ritsuzō*, 167) believes it was translated between 265 and 360 c.e.

16. The exact location of Jibin has changed over time, but scholars long believed that in the fourth to fifth centuries the name indicated the region known as Kaśmīra. Enomoto Fumio argues that during this period Jibin encompassed a wider region that included not only Kaśmīra but Gandhara. See Enomoto Fumio, "Keihin: Indo Bukkyō no ichi chūshinchi no shozai," in *Tsukamoto Keishō kyōju kanreki kinen ronbun shū: Chi no kaikō—Bukkyō to kagaku* (Tokyo: Kōsei Shuppansha, 1993), 259–269. In this text, I have translated the Chinese place name "Jibin" simply as "Kaśmīra."

17. In the biography of Buddhabhadra (*GSZ* 2 [*T* 50:335b13]), Huiyuan defends Buddhabhadra, who had been forced to flee after Kumārajīva's followers blamed him for his disciples' claiming supernatural powers. Tang Yongtong believes that the conflict most likely arose over their differing interpretations and approaches to dhyana (meditation). See Tang's *Han Wei Liangjin Nanbeichao Fojiaoshi* (Reprint, Taipei: Luotuo Chubanshe, 1987), I:307–310.

18. See *SGSZ* 1 (*T* 50:710b22).

19. *GSZ* 2 (*T* 50:333c7).

20. Ui Hakuju, "*Hyakujō shingi* no rekishiteki igi," in *Dōgen Zenji kenkyū* (Tokyo: Dōgen Zenji Sangyōkai, 1941), 36–37; Kawaguchi Kōfū, "Chūgoku Bukkyō ni okeru kairitsu no tenkai," part 1, *BKN* 5 (1971): 134, n.1.

21. Tang, *Fojiaoshi*, 828–829.

22. Tsukamoto Zenryū, *Gisho Shaku-Rōshi no kenkyū* (Tokyo: Daitō Shuppansha, 1974), 162.

23. *GSZ* 9 (*T* 50:387a11–12).

24. *CSJ* 11 (*T* 55:80a29–b1).

25. Shi Hu was the third king of the Later Zhao, one of sixteen countries established by non-Chinese tribes in northern China during the Eastern Jin dynasty. Ran Min was a commander of the Post-Zhao army before he overthrew the king and took the throne, naming his newly created state Dawei 大魏.

26. *CSJ* 11 (*T* 55:80a28–b2).

27. *CSJ* 11 (*T* 55:81b25). See also Ōchō, *Chūgoku Bukkyō*, 75.

28. Fu Jian was king of the Earlier Qin, one of sixteen non-Chinese countries in the north.

29. *CSJ* 11 (*T* 55:80a).

30. "*Sengni guifan fofa xianzhang*" is often given as the title of Daoan's regulations; however, I suspect that it was originally used as a general description of the work's content.

31. *GSZ* 5 (*T* 50:353b24–27).

32. 行香定座上講經上講之法.上講經上講 should be 上經上講. Cf. the same passage in *FYZL* 16 (*T* 53:407a11) and *SXCZ* 1D (*T* 40:232b17).

33. *Zengyi ehan jing* 22 (*T* 2:661c–662a).

34. *DSL* 2 (*T* 54:241c5).

35. *SXC* 1D (*T* 40:36c5–7).

36. See *NBZ* 113:182. For more discussion of the ritual of offering incense, see fasc. 1, n. 160.

37. See Ōchō, *Chūgoku Bukkyō*, 184–185.

38. Ui Hakuju, *Shaku Dōan kenkyū* (1956; reprint, Tokyo: Iwanami Shoten, 1979), 24; Tang, *Fojiaoshi*, 214.

39. See *T* 24:917a12; see also Tang, *Fojiaoshi*, 214.

40. *SXC* (*T* 40:36b19).

41. *YZS* **[72]**.

42. *CSJ* 12 (*T* 55:92b13–14); see also Tang, *Fojiaoshi*, 214.

43. *T* 24:917a16–17.

44. *GSZ* 13 (*T* 50: 417c12–13).

45. See Table 2.

46. 常日六時行道飲食唱食法.

47. Both Daoxuan and Yijing have written on this subject. See Daoxuan's *Shimen guijing yi* 2 (*T* 45:863a) and Yijing's *NJNZ* 3 (*T* 54:225b).

48. *YZS* **[46–47]**.

49. Ui, *Shaku Dōan*, 25. Ui does not cite his sources. I believe the topic is in need of more research.

50. Yijing noted that during his travels in India and South Asia, he observed no practice of prayer before meals. See *NJNZ* 1 (*T* 54:209b3).

51. *SXC* 3C (*T* 40:136b14–16).

52. 布薩差使悔過等法.

53. *SXC* 1D (*T* 40:34b22, 35b11).

54. Almost nothing is known about the biography of Puzhao. See *SXCZ* (*T* 40:232b14–15).

55. *T* 50:353b27–c9.

56. *GSZ* 5 (*T* 50:353b17–22). For the story of Piṇḍola, see *SSL* 37 (*T* 23:

268c28–269b4) and John S. Strong, "The Legend of the Lion-roarer: A Study of the Buddhist Arhat Piṇḍola Bhāradvāja," *Numen* 16, no. 1 (1979): 50–88. For more discussion on the Holy Monk, see "Heritage from the Vinaya Tradition" in Chapter 2.

57. The custom of honoring Piṇḍola was changed during the late Tang dynasty. The Tantric monk Amoghavajra 不空, who came to China from Central Asia, petitioned to the emperor that the image of Piṇḍola enshrined in the refectories of all monasteries be replaced by the image of Mañjuśrī, thus beginning this Mahāyānist tradition. See *Daizong chaozeng Sikong Dabianzheng Guangzhi Sanzang Heshang biaozhi* 2 (*T* 52:837b5–6); see also Stanley Weinstein, *Buddhism under the T'ang* (Cambridge: Cambridge University Press, 1987), 81.

58. *Zengyi ehan jing* 21 (*T* 2:658b26–c14).

59. *GSZ* 5 (*T* 50:352c29–353a3).

60. The transliteration of *ghaṇṭā* (the signal instrument) later became *jianchui* 揵椎 in Yijing's translation. However, as Daoxuan indicates in *SXC* 1A (*T* 40:6c3), this instrument was originally written *jianzhi* 揵稚.

61. As explained by the compiler of *CSJ*, Sengyou 僧祐 (445–518), these two texts were traditionally included in the catalogue of Daoan's works, but by the time of the canonical catalogue's compilation they had been lost, compelling Sengyou to relegate them to the category of "missing works." See *CSJ* 3 (*T* 55: 18b26–27); see also Ōchō, *Chūgoku Bukkyō*, 187.

62. In *Xinbian zhuzong jiaozang zonglu*, a catalogue edited by the Korean monk Yitian 義天 (1055–1101). See *T* 55:1174c10.

63. In *Longxing Fojiao biannian tonglun*, compiled in 1165. See *ZZK* 2B-3-3: 224b15. This statement was adopted in *Fozu lidai tongzai* 6 (*T* 49:524b19–20) and *Shishi jigu lüe* 2 (*T* 49:784b13).

64. *GSZ* 5 (*T* 50:353b27).

65. *GSZ* 5 (*T* 50:356a21–27).

66. *SSL* 53 (*T* 23:396b1–4).

67. *SSL* 8 (*T* 23:61a11). The other three medicines allowed are ghee (*su* 酥), sesame oil (*you* 油), and molasses (*shimi* 石蜜). According to the Pāli Vinaya, there are five medicines available to monks: ghee, fresh butter, oil, honey, and molasses. See Horner, *Discipline*, II:131–132.

68. *SSL* 27 (*T* 23:194a6–7). Also see Horner, *Discipline*, 2:131–132.

69. *SSL* 8 (*T* 23: 60c19–20); *SSL* 26 (*T* 23:185a17–18).

70. *SSL* 26 (*T* 23:185b11–21). Cf. *MSL* 28 (*T* 22:457b18–19).

71. *GSZ* 6 (*T* 50:360b28).

72. *CSJ* 12 (*T* 55:84a).

73. *GSZ* 4 (*T* 50:384c9).

74. *GSZ* 4 (*T* 50:349b28–c1).

75. *CSJ* 12 (*T* 55:84a5), see also *DSL* 2 (*T* 54:241b8).

76. *GSZ* 11 (*T* 50:401b8); *Da Tang neidian lu* lists the work as *Shisong sengni yaoshi jiemo* 十誦僧尼要事羯磨. See *T* 55:261a21.

77. *Da Tang neidian lu* 4 (*T* 55:263b29–c2).

78. *XGSZ* 5 (*T* 50:464b5).

79. *Lidai sanbao ji* 11 (*T* 49:97c2–5).

80. *Weishu* 114, 8:3039.

81. *XGSZ* 21 (*T* 50:608a).

82. *CSJ* 12 (*T* 55:85c22–23).

83. *SXC* 1D (*T* 40:34b).

84. *Guang hongming ji* 28 (*T* 52:324c13–26).

85. In India the first half of the month is regarded as "black," the second half "white." Thus the terms "black" and "white" are used to refer to the new and full moons. See *Da Tang xiyu ji* 2 (*T* 51:875c20–23).

86. *Guoqing bailu* 1 (*T* 46:793c–794a).

87. Ōno Hideto, "Tendai *Kanjin jikihō* no kenkyū" part 2, *Zen kenkyūjo kiyō* 10 (1981): 228.

88. The six realms between which sentient beings transmigrate are heaven, human being, *asura*, animal, hungry ghost, and hell. The six paramitas carried out by a bodhisattva to attain enlightenment are giving, the observance of precepts, forbearance, ceaseless effort, concentration of mind, and wisdom.

89. *Guanxin shifa* (*ZZK* 2-4-1:55c).

90. *T* 46:798c9–799a18.

91. Ikeda Rosan, *Maka shikan kenkyū josetsu* (Tokyo: Daitō Shuppansha, 1986), 271.

92. For some of the Tiantai text titles, I consulted Neal Donner and Daniel B. Stevenson, *The Great Calming and Contemplation* (Honolulu: University of Hawaii Press, 1993).

93. Shioiri Ryōdō points out that Xinxing 信行 (540–594), the founder of the Three-Stage school (*Sanjie jiao* 三階教) and a contemporary of Zhiyi, also edited a text for the ritual of repentance. See his "Shoki Tendaizan no kyōdanteki seikaku," in *Bukkyō kyōdan no shomondai*, ed. Nihon Bukkyō Gakkai (Kyoto: Heirakuji Shoten, 1974), 137.

94. The five texts are *SXC* (compiled in 626 C.E.), *Sifen lüshi pini yichao* (627 C.E.), *Sifen lü biqiu hanzhu jieben* (630 C.E.), *Sifen lü shanbu suiji jiemo* (635 C.E.), and *Sifen biqiuni chao* (645 C.E.).

95. See Kawaguchi Kōfū, "*Shiburitsu gyōjishō* ni arawareta in'yō tenseki no kenkyū," *BKN* 9 (1975): 59.

96. See Daoxuan's *Xuan Lüshi ganying ji* 宣律師感應記, quoted by Daoshi 道世 (?–668?) in *FYZL* 94 (*T* 53:981a8–14). However, this account cannot be found in any of Daoxuan's three extant works regarding revelation from deities; *Lüxiang gantong zhuan* (667 C.E.), *Daoxuan Lüshi gantong lu* (664 C.E.) and *Ji Shenzhou sanbao gantong lu* (664 C.E.). Since Daoshi was not only a contemporary of Daoxuan's but also the latter's colleague in Xuanzang's 玄奘 translation center, Daoshi's statement is probably accurate.

97. *SXC* 2A (*T* 40:49c1–2).

98. See *SXC* 2C (*T* 40:84a9–12); *SXC* 3C (*T* 40:128b3–c10); and *YZS* **[52]**. Daoxuan notes that the contemplations during mealtime can be divided into five categories as in [*Lü ershier*] *Mingliao lun*. However, the exact citation could not be located in the version of *Mingliao lun* collected in *Taisho shinshū daizōkyō* (*T* 24: 665b–73a). Matsuura Shūkō argues that the five contemplations given in *Mingliao lun* were compiled from fragments taken from other sutras or Vinaya texts. The diagram presented by Matsuura shows that the first contemplation was adopted from *Zengyi Ehan jing* 12 (*T* 2:603c29) and the [*Sapoduobu pini*] *Modelejia* 6 (*T* 23:602b6); the second from *PNMJ;* the third from the Vinaya; the fourth from *Zengyi Ehan jing* 12 (*T* 2:604a6), *Bieyi za Ehan jing* 1 (*T* 2:375a28), and the *SSL;* and the fifth from *Zengyi Ehan jing* 12 (*T* 2:604a2) and *Bieyi za Ehan jing* 1

(*T* 2:375a28). See Matsuura Shūkō, *Zenshū kojitsu gemon no kenkyū* (Tokyo: Sankibō Busshorin, 1981), 5.

99. See *SXC* 3D (*T* 40:146b15–20). For a comparison of the use of the hammer and stand, see *YZS* **[221]**.

100. Compare *SXC* 3D (*T* 40:150a9–b15) and *YZS* **[297–318]**.

101. See "Zunshi's Regulations" in this chapter.

102. *T* 45:815c–816b.

103. Tajima Tokuon has advanced two arguments that cast doubt on the authenticity of *Jiaojie xinxue biqiu xinghu lüyi* (*JXXL*). First, Tajima points to the fact that we know this text only through its inclusion in the collection of Daoxuan's works compiled by Yuanzhao under the title *Nanshan Lüshi zhuanji lu* 南山律師撰集錄. To accept Daoxuan's authorship, we must trust Yuanzhao's editorial judgment. Yuanzhao lived and worked during the Song era, separated from the time of Daoxuan by a long period of chaos marked by the Huichang 會昌 suppression of Buddhism (840–846); a time when many records were destroyed or lost, and the constant wars of the Five Dynasties period. It would have been difficult for Yuanzhao to pinpoint the authorship of any text with certainty; thus his decision to attach Daoxuan's name to *JXXL* becomes less credible. Second, we find a text identical to *JXXL* compiled under the title *Xingxiang fa* 行相法 in the collection *Nihon Biku Enchin nittō guhō mokuroku*, a catalogue of Buddhist texts brought to Japan by Enchin 圓珍 (814–891), who traveled in China from 853 to 858. Significantly, the work appearing in this collection bears no mention of Daoxuan as its author. (See *T* 55:1100b29.) What is more, this same work, bearing the same title, is found in another version of Enchin's catalogue, *Chishō Daishi shōrai mokuroku*, with the monk Putong 普通 from the temple Qixia 栖霞 cited as its author. The edition of *Chishō Daishi shōrai mokuroku* used by Tajima is kept in the Tentaigaku kenkyūshitsu 天台學研究室 at Taishō University. The version included in *T* 55:1106a25 gives only the temple name "Qixia." See Tajima Tokuon, "*Kyōkai ritsugi* senjutsusha ni kansuru gimon," *Taishō Daigaku gakuhō* 2 (1927): 97–110.

Hirakawa argues that since the first catalogue, *Nihon Biku Enchin nittō guhō mokuroku*, was compiled in 857 without a preface, the preface included in the second collection, *Chishō Daishi shōrai mokuroku*, compiled in 859, must have been a later addition. Thus Putong's authorship becomes problematic, as he is mentioned only in the later edition. Accordingly, Hirakawa accepts the traditional view that *JXXL* was written by Daoxuan, and on this point I am inclined to agree with him. See Hirakawa Akira, "*Kyōkai shingaku biku gyōgo ritsugi* kaidai," in *Kokuyaku issai kyō*, Shoshū bu 14:2.

104. See Table 2.

105. This text was among those included in the *Chishō Daishi shōrai mokuroku*, *T* 55:1107a2. In the afterword, the text is identified as a reprint based on the version revised by Yuanzhao during the Song.

106. For the story of Candana Kaniṣka, see *Fu fazang yinyuan zhuan* 5, *T* 50:315b5–6. The same story also appears in Daoxuan's *SXC* 1A (*T* 40:6c21–24).

107. See *YZS* **[154]**.

108. See *YZS* **[220]**.

109. For example, see *SGSZ* 10 (*T* 50:770c22) and *Jingde chuandeng lu* (*T* 51:251a6).

110. *Jingde chuandeng lu* (*T* 51:251a).

111. It is worth noting that the term *huazhu* in the later text *Chanyuan qing-gui* refers to the position of fundraiser rather than abbot.

112. For further discussion, see fasc. 1, n. 116.

113. 禪門獨行由百丈之始. From *Jingde chuandeng lu* (*T* 51:251b).

114. 一日不作一日不食.

115. See Martin Collcut, *Five Mountains: The Rinzai Zen Monastic Institution in Medieval Japan* (Cambridge: Harvard University Press, 1981), 137. Collcut refers to Yanagida Seizan, *Chūgoku zenshū shi*, Kōza: Zen 講座-禪 series, no. 3, ed. Nishitani Keiji et al. Tokyo: Chikuma Shobō, 1968), 28. See also Kondō Ryōichi, "*Hyakujō shingi* no seiritsu to sono genkei," *HKDK* 3: 19–48.

116. See Ui Hakuju, "*Hyakujō shingi* no rekishiteki igi," in *Dōgen Zenji kenkyū* (Tokyo: Dōgen Zenji Sangyōkai, 1941), 43; and Narikawa Hōyū's article "*Hyakujō ko shingi* ni tsuite: *Chokki* hensanji ni mita," *IBK* 31, no. 2 (1983): 338. For a contrasting view, see Kondō, "*Hyakujō shingi*," 28. Okimoto Katsumi, challenges Kondō's view and asserts that Baizhang's monastic code was formulated into a text. See "*Hyakujō koki* ni tsuite," *ZBKK* 12 (1980): 51–61.

117. *T* 50:770c–771a.

118. *DSL* 1 (*T* 54:240a–b).

119. *T* 51:250c–251b.

120. *ZZK* 2-16-5:465b–469a.

121. *T* 48:1157c–1158b and *ZZK* 2-16-3:287b–288a.

122. See Ui Hakuju, *Zenshūshi kenkyū*. (Tokyo: Iwanami Shoten, 1939–1943), 2:375–376.

123. See Narikawa, "*Hyakujō ko shingi*," 337.

124. Ui, *Zenshūshi*, 2:277–278.

125. *T* 48:1160a–b. For a helpful annotation to this letter by Dōchū, see his *CHSS*, in Zengaku sōsho edition, ed. Yanagida Seizan (Kyoto: Chūbun Shuppansha, 1979), 8:1030b–38a.

126. *CBQG* (*T* 48:1160a18).

127. *CBQG* (*T* 48:1159b6).

128. Ui, *Zenshūshi*, 2:377–378.

129. Kondō, "*Hakujō shingi*," 19–48.

130. See Griffith Foulk, "Myth, Ritual, and Monastic Practice in Sung Ch'an Buddhism," in *Religion and Society in T'ang and Sung China*, ed. Patricia B. Ebrey and Peter N. Gregory (Honolulu: University of Hawaii Press, 1993), 156–159; see also his "The *Daily Life in the Assembly* (*Ju-chung jih-yung*) and Its Place among Ch'an and Zen Monastic Rules," *The Ten Directions*, Spring/summer 1991, 25.

131. Collected in Yuanzhao's *Zhiyuan ji* (*ZZK* 2-10-4:302b–c).

132. See *Changlu Ze Chanshi wenji xu*, collected in Yuanzhao's *Zhiyuan ji* (*ZZK* 2-10-4:302b–c).

133. The extant biographies of Zongze, in chronological order, are as follows: *Jianzhong Jingguo xudeng lu* 18 (*ZZK* 2B-9-2:133c–134a, edited in 1101); *Lebang wenlei* 3 (*T* 47:193c13–24, edited in 1200); *Jiatai pudeng lu* 5 (*ZZK* 2B-10-1:51b–c, edited in 1202); *Fozu tongji* 27 (*T* 49:278c–279a, edited in 1269); *Lushan lianzong baojian* 4 (*T* 47:324c16–325a7, edited in 1305); *Wudeng huiyuan* 16 (*ZZK* 2B-11-4:317b–o, reprinted in 1364); *Xu chuandeng lu* 12 (*ZZK* 2B-15-3:202c–203a, edited in 1368–1398); *Wudeng yantong* 16 (*ZZK* 2B-12-4:355a–b, edited in 1650); and *Jungtu shengxian lu* 3 (*ZZK* 2B-8-2:126b–127b, edited in 1783).

134. Kondō, *"Hyakujō shingi,"* 22, 28.

135. Kondō, *"Hyakujō shingi,"* 28.

136. See *Tang Hongzhou Baizhangshan gu Huaihai Chanshi taming*, collected in *CBQG* (*T* 48:1157a21–27).

137. The details of this argument are presented in a paper published in a forthcoming Festschrift for Stanley Weinstein.

138. The Chinese Tiantai school was divided into two factions, Shanjia 山家 ("Mountain Host") and Shanwai 山外 ("Mountain Outsider") from the time of the Five Dynasties until the Song dynasty (tenth century). After most Buddhist works were burned during the civil war and persecution at the end of the Tang dynasty, Chinese Buddhists regained Tiantai works from Korea and Japan, thus bringing about a Tiantai revival. The conflict between these two factions centered around differing opinions on the authenticity of Zhiyi's work and the interpretation of his philosophy. Zunshi and his colleague Siming Zhili 四明知禮 (960–1028) were the leaders among the Shanjia faction.

139. *Tianzhusi shifang zhuchi yi* (*ZZK* 2-6-2:153d–154a).

140. The monks in the Tiantai school are "Dharma teachers," while the abbot of the Tiantai monastery is referred to as "the Dharma chief" (*fazhu* 法主).

141. See *ZZK* 2-6-2:153d–155a. The text as it appears in *ZZK* is not divided into paragraphs very carefully. After reparagraphing, there are clearly a total of ten rules.

142. *ZZK* 2-6-2:155a–d.

143. *ZZK* 2-6-2:155d–156a.

144. *ZZK* 2-6-2:156a–d.

145. These two works are collected in one of Zunshi's analects, *Jinyuan ji* 1 (*ZZK* 2-6-2:109a–113).

146. *Jinyuan ji* 1 (*ZZK* 2-6-2:112a).

147. *ZZK* 2-6-2:128a. Only the titles of these texts are listed.

148. *Jinyuan ji* 2 (*ZZK* 2-6-2:116a–120d).

149. However, Daocheng 道誠 cites the Vinayas to defend the legitimacy of the *luozi*. See his *SSYL* 1 (*T* 54:270c). For further discussion, see "Personal Possessions" in Chapter 2.

150. *Klozen gokoku ron* 2 (*T* 80:9b6).

151. There are two English translations of *Eihei shingi*: Ichimura Shohei's *Zen Master Eihei Dōgen's Monastic Regulations* (Woodville, Wash.: North American Institute of Zen and Buddhist Studies, 1993) and Taigen Daniel Leighton and Shohaku Okumura's *Dōgen's Pure Standards for the Zen Community* (Albany: SUNY Press, 1996).

152. Leighton and Okumura, *Dōgen's Pure Standards*, 15.

153. For the textual history of *Eihei shingi*, see Leighton and Okumura, *Dōgen's Pure Standards*, 21–22.

154. In "Sōdai Nit-Chū Bukkyō kōryū shi: *Zennen shingi* to *Eihei shingi*." (*Bukkyō shigaku kenkyū* 19, no. 1 [1977]: 11), Nishio Kenryū endeavors to give the exact number of citations from *Chanyuan qinggui*: twenty-nine in *Eihei shingi* and fifteen in *Shōbōgenzō*. However, many of the borrowings from *Chanyuan qinggui* are not explicit, and Nishio bases his figures on only three of Dōgen's six extant works. Clearly, the extent to which Dōgen borrowed from *Chanyuan qinggui* is far greater than has been acknowledged.

155. See Carl Bielefeldt, *Dōgen's Manuals of Zen Meditation* (Berkeley: University of California Press 1988), 60.

156. As Leighton and Okumura (*Dōgen's Pure Standards*, 21) point out, much of the material in *Eihei shingi* remains incomplete or unedited, thus providing evidence that Dōgen was unable to finish the text before his death.

157. For example, see fasc.1, nn. 140, 147.

158. This text is sometimes referred to as *Riyong* [*xiao*] *qinggui* 日用[小]清規 ([Concise] Pure Regulations for Daily Life), or *Riyong guifan*. 日用規範 (Standards for Daily Life). An English translation of this text with an introduction has been published by T. Griffith Foulk: "The *Daily Life in the Assembly* (*Ju-chung jih-yung*) and Its Place among Ch'an And Zen Monastic Rules." For information on the various versions of this text, see Sakuma Ken'yū, "*Nichiyō shingi* no kenkyū," part 1, *KDBKN* 24 (1991): 93–99.

159. Nothing is known of Zongshou's biography, but one of his discourse records is preserved in *Zengji xu chuandeng lu*, *ZZK* 2B-15-5:389a–b.

160. *ZZK* 2-16-5:497b14.

161. Dōchū refers to the text's preface and postscript, which seems to indicate that he possessed the work. See his *CHSS*, 51c.

162. For the biography of Zhongfeng, see Chun-fang Yu, "Chung-feng Mingpen and Ch'an Buddhism in the Yüan," in *Yüan Thought: Chinese Thought and Religion under the Mongols*, ed. Hok-lam Chan and Wm. Theodore de Bary (New York: Columbia University Press, 1982), 419–477; see also Satō Shūkō, "Gen no Chūhō Myōhon ni tsuite," *SGK* 23 (1981): 231–236.

163. This text is also known as *Xianchun qinggui* 咸淳清規, after the era of its compilation, and as *Wuzhou qinggui* 婺州清規, after its author's place of residence (present-day Zhejian province). It may in fact be identical to the work referred to elsewhere as *Bingyan qinggui* 屏巖清規. See *CHSS*, 51a–b.

164. This text is also referred to as *Zhida qinggui* 至大清規, after the era of its compilation, and as *Zeshan qinggui* 澤山清規, after the author's place of residence (possibly Shanxi province).

165. See the preface of *Beiyong qinggui* (*ZZK* 2-17-1:28d) and its annotation by Dōchū in *CHSS*, 1020d–1026b.

166. Three annotated editions of *Chixiu Baizhang qinggui* were completed by Chinese and Japanese monks. The earliest is entitled *Hyōkujō shingi shō* 百丈清規抄, (1459–1462), also known as *Untō shō* 雲桃抄, a contraction of the names of its two authors, Unshō Ikkei 雲章一慶 (1386–1463) and Tōgen Zuisen 桃源瑞仙 (d. 1489). The second edition is entitled *Chokushū Hyakujō shingi sakei* 敕修百丈清規左觽, annotated by Dōchū. By consulting other sources, Dōchū intended his commentary, written in the years 1699–1700 but published only in 1718, to be comprehensive and definitive. The third work is entitled *Baizhang qinggui zhengyi ji*, written by the Chinese monk Yuanhong Yirun in 1823.

167. Huiji Yuanxi was the one who asked Yishan Liaowan from Baizhang Mountain to revise Baizhang's text of monastic regulation. See "Authenticity of Baizhang's Monastic Code" in this chapter.

168. *ZZK* 2-11-1:1c4.

169. Of course, the Lü school has its own lineage of patriarchs.

170. See *LYSG* (*ZZK* 2-11-1:33b–34a).

171. *JYQG* (*ZZK* 2-6-4:380a–b).

172. *JYQG* (*ZZK* 2-6-4:380b).

173. *JYQG* (*ZZK* 2-6-4:380c–381a).

174. *JYQG* (*ZZK* 2-6-4:381a–c).

175. The reference here is to *Shou pusajie yi shike* 授菩薩戒儀十科, written by Zunshi and collected in the *Jinyuan ji*, *ZZK* 2-6-2:109ra–113vb.

Chapter 2. Genesis of *Chanyuanqinggui*: Continuity and Adaptation

1. *SFL* 17 (*T* 22:678b9–11).

2. *Fanwang jing* (*T* 24:1004b–1009b).

3. Fasc. 1, "Upholding the Precepts," **[16]**.

4. Horner, *Discipline*, 3:245.

5. *SFL* 25 (*T* 22:736c–737b).

6. *SFL* 52 (*T* 22:956b14–19).

7. Horner, *Discipline*, 5:196; 4:271.

8. *Fanwang jing* (*T* 24:1005b6–16).

9. *Lengyan jing* 8 (*T* 19:141c5–8).

10. Fasc. 1, "Upholding the Precepts," **[16]**.

11. *SFL* 42 (*T* 22:866c11–12)

12. *SFL* 42 (*T* 22:872b6–18).

13. *san bujing rou* 三不淨肉.

14. See also Horner, *Discipline*, 1:298.

15. *SFL* 42 (*T* 22:868b10–869a18).

16. *SFL* 59 (*T* 22:1006a19–21).

17. *xiong* 熊 and *pi* 羆.

18. *MSL* 32 (*T* 22:487a23–25).

19. Cf. Horner, *Discipline*, 1:98.

20. *T* 24:1005b6–16.

21. *Niepan jing* 11 (*T* 12:432c27–28).

22. *Lengqie jing* 4 (*T* 16:513b–514b) and *Ru lengqie jing* 8 (*T* 16:562b10).

23. *Yangju moluojing* 4 (*T* 2:540).

24. *WFL* 27, *T* 22:179a–b.

25. Ibid., 179c.

26. *WFL* 27 (*T* 22:179b19–23).

27. *sengba* 僧跋.

28. *SXC* 3C (*T* 40:137b18).

29. *NJNZ* 1 (*T* 54:209c14).

30. Yijing's transliteration: 三缽羅佉哆.

31. This same episode can be found in Yijing's translation of *GSP*(*N*) 8 (*T* 24: 445b8); see also *SSL* (*T* 23:464b–c).

32. *chuang* 床; fasc. 1, "Attendance at Meals," **[43]**.

33. *daifu* 大夫.

34. *shengchuang* 繩床.

35. *SXC* 1D (*T* 40:35b).

36. *SSL* 61 (*T* 23:466b25–26).

37. *changchuang* 長床, "long bed."

38. *SFL* 50 (*T* 22:938a16–18).

39. *NJNZ* 1 (*T* 54:206c–207a).

40. Fasc. 1, "Attendance at Meals," **[48]**.

41. *SFL* 13 (*T* 22:655c).

42. *SSL* 14 (*T* 23:100a24) and *SSL* 26 (*T* 23:188c14); see also *Binaiye* 8 (*T* 24: 886c).

43. *MSL* 29 (*T* 22:462c6–24).

44. *GSP(O)* 5 (*T* 24:121c28–122a3).

45. *MSL* 29 (*T* 22:462c22–23).

46. *Shishi huo wufubao jing* (T 2:854c–855a).

47. *JXXL* (*T* 45:872b3).

48. *SFL* 13 (*T* 22:655c25–26).

49. *SSL* 14 (*T* 23:100a29–b1 and *SSL* 26 (*T* 23:188c19–21).

50. Fasc. 1, "Attendance at Meals," **[50]**.

51. *SFL* 39 (*T* 22:848b27).

52. *WFL* 15 (*T* 22:103a23–27).

53. Fasc. 1, "Attendance at Meals," **[50]**.

54. See Rules 37, 38, and 49 pertaining to mealtime in Daoxuan's *JXXL* (*T* 45: 872a).

55. *Fu shukuhan hō* (*DZZ* 2:353–354).

56. Fasc. 1, "Attendance at Meals," **[50]**.

57. *SXC* 3C (*T* 40:137a11).

58. *T* 16:231c; cited in *SXCZ* (*T* 40:402c).

59. Rules 45–48 in *JXXL* (*T* 45:872a).

60. *SXCZ* 3C (*T* 40:403a11).

61. *DZDL* 32 (*T* 25:300c12–13).

62. *SXC* 3C (*T* 40:137a12).

63. *Niepan jing* 15 (*T* 12:703a6–26).

64. Fasc. 1, "Attendance at Meals," **[48]**.

65. Cited in *SXC* 3C (*T* 40:137c10).

66. *SFL* 49 (*T* 22:935c11–12).

67. *SSL* 10 (*T* 23:71a4).

68. *NJNZ* 1 (*T* 54:210a11).

69. For example, fasc. 1, "Taking Up Residence," **[30]**.

70. *SSL* 34 (*T* 23:242c); see also *WFL* 18 (*T* 22:121a), *SFL* 50 (*T* 22:940a18).

71. *xingzhe* 行者; fasc. 1, "Taking Up Residence," **[28]**.

72. *SJLP* 11 (*T* 24:753a23–25)

73. 畔頭波羅沙.

74. 何謂畔頭波羅沙、善男子欲求出家、未得衣缽、欲依寺中住者. *SJLP* 11 (*T* 24: 753a–25)

75. *ZSS*, 296b.

76. These are *gongguo xingzhe* 供過行者, *chuzhong juci xingzhe* 廚中局次行者, *zhu diantang xingzhe* 諸殿堂行者, *dazhong xingzhe* 打鐘行者, *menzi xingzhe* 門子行者, *huotou xingzhe* 火頭行者, *chatou xingzhe* 茶頭行者, *yuantou xingzhe* 園頭行者, *zhuzhuang xingzhe* 諸庄行者, and *chetou xingzhe* 車頭行者, respectively.

77. 童行.

78. *tongxing tang* 童行堂 or *xuanseng tang* 選僧堂. See also fasc. 2, n. 9.

79. Fasc. 1, "Attendance at Meals," **[52]**. Depending on their duties, purity-keepers are also referred to in the Vinaya texts as *shou sengyuan ren* 守僧園人 ("Sangha garden caretakers"); *shouyuan ren* 守園人, Skt. *ārāmika* ("gardeners";

GSP 5 [*T* 23:651c26], *GSP*[*N*] 5 [*T* 24:433c16]); *zhishi ren* 執事人, Skt. *vaiyyāvṛtya-kara* ("staff members"; *GSP* 20 [*T* 23:734c20, 741b16]); *zhi sishi ren* 知寺事人 ("People manage temple affairs," *SJLP* 13 [*T* 24:764c14–17]); and *sijia ren* 寺家人 ("people in the temple"; *GSP* 22 [*T* 23:741b18]). See also Jonathan Alan Silk, "The Origins and Early History of the *Mahāratnakūṭa* Tradition of Mahāyāna Buddhism with a Study of the *Ratnarāśisūtra* and Related Materials" (Ph.D. diss., Michigan University, 1994), 219.

However, these terms are only approximate in nature; the first three were often used interchangeably. For more information on the distinction among these Sanskrit terms, see Silk's dissertation, "The Origins and Early History of the *Mahāratnakūṭa*," 215–254.

80. *SSYL* 3 (*T* 54:303b26). 時苾芻眾告諸人日、清淨之業應可作之、不清淨事皆不應作、作淨業故日淨人

81. *GSP* 5 (*T* 23:651c24–25).

82. *SSL* 34 (*T* 23:250c17–251a14).

83. *WFL* 5 (*T* 22:30c25–31a11), *MSL* 30 (*T* 22:467b20–27), and *GSP* 5 (*T* 23:651a28–652b29).

84. *WFL* 5 (*T* 22:31a4) refers to them as the *shouyuan ren* 守園人 ("garden keepers"); *MSL* 30 (*T* 22:467b23) calls them *yuanmin* 園民 ("garden people"); and *GSP* 5 (*T* 23:651b24–25, 651c26) gives them the title "service givers" (*jishi-ren* 給侍人).

85. *SFL* 8 (*T* 22:619c1); *SSL* 7 (*T* 23:51b22); *SJLP* 13 (*T* 24:764c)

86. *SSL* 56 (*T* 23:415c11–12).

87. *WFL* 6 (*T* 22:37a22–23); *Sapoduo pini piposha* (*Sarvāstivādavinaya-vibhāṣā*) 4 (*T* 23:526c5–6).

88. *SFL* 43 (*T* 22:875b17–c, 876a17); *WFL* 22 (*T* 22:147b14–26, 152c1); *SJLP* 10 (*T* 24:740c).

89. *GSP* 36 (*T* 23:826b2); *GSP*(*Z*) 30 (*T* 24:356c22); *SJLP* 7 (*T* 24:721a).

90. *WFL* 69 (*T* 22:42a3); *SSL* 61 (*T* 23:467b26); *SJLP* 11 (*T* 24:753b1).

91. *WFL* 25 (*T* 22:168a9); *SSL* 57 (*T* 23:419b4).

92. *WFL* 9 (*T* 22:65c17–23); *SSL* 15 (*T* 23:108c3).

93. *SSL* 41 (*T* 23:299b15 and *SSL* 50 (*T* 23:363c19).

94. *GSP* (*Z*) 30 (*T* 24:356c20); *GSP* 33 (*T* 23:806c24).

95. *SJLP* 7 (*T* 24:721a4).

96. Cf. fasc. 2, n. 9. For more information on the purity-keeper, see Gregory Schopen, "The Monastic Ownership of Servants or Slaves: Local and Legal Factors in the Redactional History of Two *Vinayas*," *JIABS* 17, no. 2 (1994): 145–173; R. A. L. H. Gunawardana, *Robe and Plough: Monasticism and Economic Interest in Early Medieval Sri Lanka* (Tucson: University of Arizona Press, 1979), 99–100; and six articles written by Matsuda Shindō, "Indo Bukkyō kyōdan ni okeru zaizo-kusha *ārāmika* no kōsatsu (jo)," *SK* 54, no. 3 (1981): 264–265; "Indo Bukkyō kyōdan no yakushoku no kigen," *SKKK* 15 (1983): 114–131; "Indo Bukkyō kyōdan-shi ni okeru jōnin no kōsatsu," *SKKK* 14 (1982): 137–154; "*Daitō saiiki ki ni* miru Indo Bukkyō no jōnin," *BKN* 16 (1983): 53–61; "Shitsujinin *veyyāvaccakara* to shuonninārāmika," *IBK* 30, no. 1 (1981): 124–125; "Zenshū kyōdan no jōnin," *SGK* 25 (1983): 202–205.

97. *SFL* 35 (*T* 22:814c23); *WFL* 17 (*T* 22:119b20); *SSL* 21 (*T* 23:155b–c).

98. *SFL* 34 (*T* 22:811c14–21), see also in *WFL* 17 (*T* 22:119b18–20).

99. *SFL* 6 (*T* 22:855a–b); *MSL* 28 (*T* 22:454c–5a); *SSL* 27 (*T* 23:194c–5a).

100. *futian yi* 福田衣.

101. *Shimen guijing yi* 2 (*T* 45:862a25–27).

102. *Sanyi bianhuo pian* (*ZZK* 2-6-2:127d; cited in *ZSS*, 691a–b).

103. *SSYL* 1 (*T* 54:270c).

104. *GSP(B)* 10 (*T* 24:497b1–3).

105. Ibid.

106. For an illustration of the *guazi*, see Mochitsuki, 1257c.

107. *MSL* 32 (*T* 22:488a9–11); see also *GSP(Z)* 6 *T* 24:231c8).

108. 塔山.

109. Fasc. 1, "Preparation of Personal Effects," **[20]**.

110. Quoted in *ZTSY* (*ZZK* 2-18-1:120d).

111. *GSP* (*T* 23:786a, *T* 24:247b) also indicates that vessels for holding water must be divided into these two categories.

112. *NJNZ* 1 (*T* 54:207c11).

113. *JXXL* (*T* 45:870c).

114. *JXXL* (*T* 45:871b).

115. See Gregory Schopen, "On Avoiding Ghosts and Social Censure: Monastic Funerals in the *Mūlasarvāstivāda-vinaya*," *Journal of Indian Philosophy* 20 (1992): 18.

116. *CBQG* 5 (*T* 48:1139c).

117. *SXC* 1D (*T* 40:36c5).

118. *SXC* 3C (*T* 40:136b).

119. *NJNZ* 1 (*T* 54:209b3).

120. 國忌行香.

121. 觸禮三拜.

122. *NJNZ* 3 (*T* 54:221a8).

123. *JXXL* (*T* 45:871c).

124. *ZZK* 2-11-1:18d.

125. 儀禮沿革 (*T* 54:238c28).

126. 梵僧.

127. *T* 54:238c28.

128. *NJNZ* 3 (*T* 54:223a9).

129. 善來.

130. *ji shanlai* 極善來.

131. 寺制.

132. *ZTSY* 8 (*ZZK* 2-18-1:118c).

133. *Epidamo dapiposha lun* 26 (*Abhidharmamahāvibhāṣā* [*T* 27:135b29–c2]).

134. *ZSS*, 443a.

135. *jiushi canqing* 就室參請. *NJNZ* 4 (*T* 54:233a15).

136. *MSL* 5 (*T* 22:262b4–8).

137. *T* 16:803a1–2.

138. See Michihata Ryōshū, *Chūgoku Bukkyō to shakai fukushi jigyō, Chūgoku Bukkyōshi zenshū* (Tokyo: Shoen, 1975), 7:165–169.

139. *sengtang* 僧堂.

140. 寺院之最要佛殿法堂僧堂也. *DZZ* 2:400.

141. *Kutang* 庫堂.

142. One *zhang* 丈 equals approximately ten feet. See *Tiantongsi zhi* by Wen

Xingquan and Shi Dejie (Reprint, Taipei: Guangwen Shuju, 1976), 1:49–50; see also Yokoyama Shūsai, *Zen no kenchiku* (Tokyo: Shōkokusha, 1967), 176.

143. For more on the Holy Monk, see the section "Taking Up Residence" in Fascicle 1.

144. *yuntang* 雲堂.

145. *ZSS*, 33a.

146. *xuanfo chang* 選佛場.

147. For example, *SXC* and *JXXL*.

148. *sengfang* 僧坊.

149. *shichu* 食廚 or *shitang* 食堂.

150. *jiangtang* 講堂.

151. *ZZK* 2-6-2:155c5.

152. *LYSG* (*ZZK* 2-11-1:33a15–b5).

153. *T* 51:251a11; see also *SGSZ* (*T* 50:770c26).

154. *kanjing tang* 看經堂. Cf. **[129]**.

155. *shengseng* 聖僧.

156. *NJNZ* 3 (*T* 54:221b19).

157. *NJNZ* 1 (*T* 54:209b4); and *NJNZ* 4 (*T* 54:227a19).

158. *RRQG, Jiaoding qinggui, Beiyong qinggui,* or *CBQG.*

159. *T* 40:135c24.

160. *T* 32:784b–c.

161. For more on Daoan and Piṇḍola, see "Sangha Regulations before *Chanyuan qinggui*" in Chapter 1.

162. *T* 53:609c–611a.

163. *Fanwang jing pusa jieben shu* 1 (*T* 40:605b4–5).

164. See *Daizong chaozeng Sikong Dabianzheng Guangzhi Sanzang Heshang biaozhi ji* 2 (*T* 52:837b5–6), and Weinstein, *Buddhism under the T'ang,* 81.

165. *CBQG* 7 (*T* 48:1150b17).

166. *caodan* 草單.

167. *ZSS*, 1 19b, 115b.

168. *Keizan shingi* 2 (*T* 82:443b).

169. See Matsuura Shūkō, *Zenshū kojitsu sonzō no kenkyū* (Tokyo: Shankibō Busshorin, 1976), 233–244.

170. *Fo benxing jijing* (*T* 3:883c; cited in *ZSS*, 21a). The establishment of the Dharma hall and the imperial sponsorship of a lavish Dharma hall figure are discussed, respectively, in the following Vinaya texts: *SSL* 15 (*T* 23:105b12) and *GSP* (*Z*) 37 (T24:393b–c).

171. *Jingde chuandeng lu* 7 (*T* 51:251a9).

172. *Wujia zhengzong zan* (*ZKK* 2B-8-5:459c).

173. Deshan Xuanjian 德山宣鑑; Jianxing 見性.

174. *DZZ* 2:400.

175. *SFL* 43 (*T* 22:875a–b).

176. *WFL* 22 (*T* 22:152b11–13 and *T* 22:152b27–28).

177. See the biographies of Daoan (*GSZ* 5 [*T* 50:351c6]), Faxian (*GSZ* 3 [*T* 50:337b27]), and Tandi (*GSZ* 7 [*T* 50:371a4]), cited in Ikeda Rosan, *Maka shikan kenkyū josetsu* (Tokyo: Daitō Shuppansha, 1986), 271.

178. *LYSG* (*ZZK* 2-11-1:33b–34a).

179. *WFL* 25 (*T* 22:168b2–7).

180. *GSP(Z)* 14 (*T* 24:267c1–8).

181. *ZSS*, 350a.

182. For further information on the complex topic of the Song government's policies concerning monastic Buddhism, see Takao Giken, *Sōdai Bukkyōshi no kenkyū* (Kyoto: Hyakkaen, 1975); Moroto Tatsuo, *Chūgoku Bukkyō seidoshi no kenkyū* (Tokyo: Hirakawa Shuppansha, 1990); and Huang Minzhi, *Songdai Fojiao shehui jingjishi lunji* (Taipei: Xuesheng Shuju, 1989). For the material in this chapter, I am greatly indebted to all of the above.

183. Actually compiled in the later Jiatai 嘉泰 period (1201–1204), *QTS* bears the name of Qingyuan because it was thought to have been based on a set of statutes written in the era of Qingyuan (1195–1200). See Makino Tatsumi, "*Keigen jōhō jirui* no Dō Shaku mon-Sōdai shūkyō hōsei no ichi shiryō," part 1, *SK*, n. s. 9, no. 2 (1932): 68. There is one work in a Western language on the text of *QTS*; see W. Eichhorn, *Beitrag zur rechtlichen Stellung des Buddhismus und Taoismus im Sung-Staat* (Leiden: E. J. Brill, 1968).

184. *Da Tang liudian* 4 (Taipei: Wenhai Chubanshe, 1962), 101c; *FZTJ* 40 (*T* 49: 374b20).

185. *QTS* 51:481a, 483c–d. See Takao, *Sōdai Bukkyōshi*, 32.

186. *QTS* 51:480c.

187. For studies on the state tonsure system, see Michihata Ryōshū, *Tōdai Bukkyōshi no kenkyū*, in his *Chūgoku Bukkyōshi zenshū* (Tokyo: Shoen, 1975), 2:77–84. See also two articles by Ogawa Kan'ichi, "Hoku-Sō jidai no kōdosei to shibuchō," *Ryūkoku shidan* 58 (1967): 23–42, and "Sōdai no jukaisei to rokunen kaichō," *Ryūkoku daigaku ronshū* 385 (1968): 48–70.

188. *QTS* 51:480b.

189. The date of 747 c.e. cited in Buddhist historical documents as well as in the works of many scholars is based on information given in *DSL* 2 (*T* 54: 246b8–10), which in turn relies on *Tang huiyao* 49 (Shanghai: Zhonghua Shuju, 1955), 860.

190. Japan began issuing tonsure certificates in the fourth year of the Yōrō 養老 era (720 c.e.), twenty years before the supposed beginning of the custom in China. Since Japan adopted China's legal and political systems, its brand of Buddism, and important facets of its culture during the Sui-Tang period, it seems unlikely that the issuing of tonsure certificates would have originated in Japan and later be adopted in China. Yamazaki and Moroto hold that in China the system of government-authorized tonsure and clerical registration had been established as early as the Southern-Northern dynasties (fifth to sixth centuries). It seems reasonable to assume that the government would have issued some form of identification to the clergy at this time. See Yamazaki's *Shina chūsei Bukkyō no tenkai* (Kyoto: Hōzōkan, 1971), 571–572; and Moroto's *Chūgoku Bukkyō seidoshi*, 216–232.

191. *YZS* **[297]**.

192. The actual content of the examinations varied through the years.

193. See Weinstein, *Buddhism under the T'ang*, 60. Takao Gikan believes that the sale of tonsure certificates first began in the song period during the era of emperors Ren 仁宗 and Ying 英宗 (r. 1023–1067) and simply became more widespread during the reign of Emperor Shen 神宗 (r. 1068–1085), the period traditionally associated with the emergence of this practice. See Takao, *Sōdai Bukkyōshi*, 25.

194. See Huang, *Songdai Fojiao,* 385.

195. Both certificates were issued and sold by the Bureau of Sacrifices, but the printing took place at the Crafts Institute (*wensi yuan* 文思院), where it was overseen by the Directorate of Imperial Manufactories (*shaofu jian* 少府監).

196. See Takao, *Sōdai Bukkyōshi,* 26.

197. A sizeable body of research exists on the sale of tonsure ordination. See Tsukamoto Zenryū, *Chūgoku kinsei Bukkyōshi no shomondai* (Tokyo: Daitō Shuppansha, 1975), 1–92; Chikusa Masaaki, *Chūgoku Bukkyō shakaishi kenkyū* (Tokyo: Dōbōsha, 1982), 17–82; Takao Giken, "Dochō kō," *Rokujō gakuhō* 226 (1920): 6–26; Sogabe Shizuo, "Sō no dochō zakkō," *Shigaku zasshi* 41, no. 6 (1930): 99–114; Yuan Zhen, "Liang-Song dudie kao," part 1 and 2, *Zhongguo shehui jingji shi jikan* 7, no. 1 (1944): 41–104; 7, no. 2 (1946): 1–78; Lin Tianwei, "Songdai chushou dudie zhi yanjiu," In *Songshi yanjuiji* 4 (Taipei: Zhonghua congshu bianshen weiyuan hui, 1969), 309–359; and Huang, *Songdai Fojiao,* 384–398.

198. See Huang, *Songdai Fojiao,* 387–388; Moroto, *Chūgoku Bukkyō seidoshi,* 463.

199. *YZS* **[169]**.

200. According to the table provided by Huang, the cost of a tonsure certificate ranged from 50,000 coins to 1,500,000. The latter price is from 1212. See Huang, *Songdai Fojiao,* 389–393. Note that in Huang's table of contents *qian* 千, *guan* 貫, and *min* 緡 all refer to one thousand coins.

201. 壹貫; that is, one thousand coins.

202. 羡費錢; literally, "surplus money."

203. *QTS* 50:472d.

204. *YZS* **[113]**.

205. [*mianding*] *you* [免丁]由.

206. *T* 48:1113c.

207. *FZTJ* 54 (*T* 49:473a4–6). During the Tang, the fee paid for the tonsure certificate was referred to literally as "money for the purchase of scented water" (*xiang shui qian* 香水錢); the *mianding qian* certificate was called "money paid for leisure" (*qingxian qian* 清閑錢). *FZTJ* 40 (*T* 49:374b25); see also Weinstein, *Buddhism under the T'ang,* 60.

208. For a detailed discussion of "The Six Awarenesses," see fasc. 1, n. 128.

209. *YZS* **[39]**.

210. Ibid.

211. *QTS* 51:479a. The term *bensi* 本司 in the text should be *benshi* 本師. Cf. *QTS* 51:478c.

212. *QTS* 51:479a–b.

213. *QTS* 51:479a.

214. For the application format, see *YZS* **[41]**.

215. *QTS* 51:479a.

216. The edict also prohibits the traveling monk from entering the three border districts of Chuanxia 川峽 (the Huainan 淮南 East District, the Huainan West District, and the Jing West 京西 District). The edict erroneously refers to this area as Zhouxia 州峽. See Makino Tatsumi, "*Keigen jōhō jirui*," part 2, *SK,* n.s., 9, no. 4(1932): 55, 57. An exception was made for those monks who were studying permanently in these districts.

217. *QTS* 51:479a.

218. *YZS* **[113]**.

219. *QTS* 51:478c–d.

220. See Kosaka Kiyū, "Sōdai jiin sōni seido to shingi: toku ni sekichō no kyōshin to gyōyū no hanpyō wo chūshin ni," in *KBK* 26 (1968): 103–117; see also Makino, "*Keigen jōhō jirui*," part 2, 55.

221. *DSL* 3 (*T* 54:248c). An award of purple cords with a golden seal (*zishou jinzhang* 紫綬金章) was the highest mark of honor for government officials; thus the giving of the purple vestment (excluding the seal) to monastics was merely the adoption of a secular custom. See Weinstein, *Buddhism under the T'ang*, 192, n. 21.

222. *DSL* 3 (*T* 54:249b8–11).

223. *DSL* 3 (*T* 54:249b1).

224. *DSL* 3 (*T* 54:249b20).

225. See *Song huiyao jigao*, "Fangyu" 方域 14–34, p. 7557; noted in Huang, *Songdai Fojiao*, 453.

226. Huang, *Songdai Fojiao*, 453.

227. See *Shōbōgenzō* 39, "Shisho" 嗣書, *DZZ* 1:342.

228. A definition given by Dōchū in his *Zenrin shōkisen* (abbr. *ZSS*), 7b.

229. *ZSS*, 8a. For further discussion of these two categories see, Takao Giken, "Sōdai jiin seido no ichi kōsatsu," *SBS* 5, no. 2 (1941): 8–22; Huang, *Songdai Fojiao*, 305–313; Foulk, "The Ch'an School and Its Place," 62–72.

230. *QTS* 50:476c.

231. *YZS* **[263]**.

232. *QTS* 51:486b.

233. *YZS* **[264]**.

234. *QTS* 50:476d.

235. Ibid.

236. Ibid.

237. Ibid.

238. *QTS* 50:476c.

239. *QTS* 50:476a.

240. Ibid.

241. *YZS* **[264]**.

242. Takao, *Sōdai Bukkyōshi*, 67.

243. The Five Mountains referred to are Jingshan 徑山, Lingyinsi 靈隱寺, Jingcisi 淨慈寺, Tiantongsi 天童寺, and Eyuwangsi 阿育王寺. All were located in present-day Zhejian province. See Dōchū's *ZSS*, 3a. For the list of the Ten Monasteries, see *ZSS*, 5b–6a.

It is uncertain when this monastic system was established, but traditionally scholars follow the record written by Song Lian 宋濂 (1310–1381), who claims it was initiated in the Southern Song. In his inscription for monk Gufeng Mingde 孤峰明德 (1294–1372), *Zhuchi Jingci Chansi Gufeng De Gong taming*, Song Lian mentions that after the Song imperial court moved to south China (to avoid invasion by the Tartars at the beginning of the Southern Song period), Shi Miyuan 史彌遠 (1164–1233), who served as prime minister from 1208–1233 and was granted the posthumous title Weiwang 衛王, petitioned the emperor to establish this prestigious monastic system. See *Zhuchi Jingci Chansi Gufeng De Gong taming*, in *Song Xueshi wenji*, Sibu congkan edition (Shanghai: Shangwu Yinshuguan, 1929) 80:316a.

Chanyuan qinggui, compiled in the Northern Song, does not reveal any information on the Five Mountains and Ten Monasteries, hence it neither confirms nor contradicts the claim that this system was instituted later in the Southern Song.

This system operated much like the secular bureaucracy in that an official had to work his way up to the top positions, such as military general and civilian prime minister. When a monk attained the abbacy in the Five Mountains and Ten Monasteries category, his achievement carried no less honor in the religious realm than that afforded to secular official reaching the office of prime minister.

This type of monastic institution was not only found in the Chan school, but also later adopted in the Tiantai school. (A table listing these monasteries is given in Huang, *Songdai Fojiao,* 315–316). For a thorough study, see Ishii Shūdō, "Chūgoku no gozan jissatsu seido no kisoteki kenkyū," parts 1–4, *KBR* 13 (1982): 89–132; *KBR* 14 (1983): 82–122; *KBR* 15 (1984): 61–129; *KBR* 16 (1985): 30–82. Also Kusumoto Bunyū, "Gozan seidoshi kō," *ZBKK* 7 (1975): 137–153.

244. Merit cloisters were usually built beside the tomb of a noble family or converted from a private family shrine to gain the benefit of a tax exemption. The nobility maintained the right to appoint an abbot. For further discussion of the merit cloister, see Chikusa, *Chūgoku Bukkyō shakaishi,* 111–143; Takao, *Sōdai Bukkyōshi,* 71–73; Huang, *Songdai Fojiao,* 305–313.

245. *DSL* 2 (*T* 54:242c18) *GSZ* 6 (*T* 50:363b18).

246. See Xie Chongguang and Bai Wengu, *Zhongguo sengguan zhidushi* (Xining: Qinghai Renmin Chubanshe, 1990), 256–277; Tian Guanglie, "Woguo lidai sengguan zhidu lüeshu," *Neiming* 226 (1991): 41

Several studies in Japanese and Chinese examine in detail various aspects of the creation of a clerical hierarchy.

From the Southern-Northern dynasties to the Five Dynasties: He Guangzhong, "Lidai sengguan zhidu kao," in *Zhongguo Fojiao tongshi luncong,* Xiandai Fojiao xueshu congkan series. (Taipei: Dasheng Wenhua Chubanshe, 1978, 39:193–299.

From Southern-Northern dynasties to the Song dynasty: Hattori Shungai, "Shina sōkan no enkaku," part 1, *BS,* 2, no. 5 (1912): 65–81; part 2, *BS,* 2, no. 6 (1912): 55–63; part 3, *BS* 2, no. 8 (1912): 55–64.

Southern-Northern dynasties: Yamazaki Hiroshi, "Nanboku chō jidai ni okeru sōkan no kentō," *Bukkyō kenkyū* 4, no. 2 (1940): 63–92, and "HokuSei no sōkan shōgen jittō kō," *Shichō* 8, no. 1 (1938): 129–145.

Sui dynasty and Tang dynasty: Yamazaki Hiroshi, "Zuidai sōkan kō," *SBS* 6, no. 1 (1942): 1–15; "Tōdai no sōkan ni tsuite: sōtō, sōroku, sōjō," *Shichō* 9, no. 2 (1939): 18–68; and "Tō chūki irai no Chōan no kudokushi," *Tōhō gakuhō* 東方學報 4 (1933): 368–406. Also Weinstein, *Buddhism under the T'ang.*

Song dynasty and Yuan dynasty: Takao Giken, "Sōdai sōkan seido no kenkyū," *SKS* 4, no. 4 (1941): 1–17; Fujishima Takeki, "Genchō ni okeru kenshin to senseiin," *Ōtani gakuhō* 52, no. 4 (1973): 17–31; Nogami Shunjō, "Gen no kudokushishi ni tsuite," *SBS* 6, no. 2 (1942): 1–11 and "Gen no senseiin ni tsuite," *Haneda Hakase shōju kinen Tōyōshi ronsō* Kyoto: Haneda Hakase Shōju Kinenkai, 1950), 779–795.

Ming dynasty: Tatsuike Kiyoshi, "Mindai no sōkan," *SBS* 4, no. 3 (1940): 35–46; Mano Senryū, "Chūgoku Mindai no sōkan ni tsuite," *Ōtani gakuhō* 36, no. 3 (1956): 53–62; Hasebe Yūkei, *Min-Shin Bukkyō kyōdanshi kenkyū* (Kyoto: Dōbōsha, 1993), 77–92.

247. The areas included the prefectures Wenzhou 溫州, Hangzhou 杭州, Taizhou 台州, Huzhou 湖州, Chuzhou 處州, and Mingzhou 明州, which were all located in what is now Zhejian province. See Takao, *Sōdai Bukkyōshi*, 48.

248. The position of Sangha rectifier for the Ten Temples was attested to by Jōjin 成尋 (1011–1081), who visited Wutaishan in 1072. (See *STGK* 5, *NBZ* 115: 95b.) Nevertheless, this title had been in existence since the Tang, when Zhijun 智顒 (c. 791) was first granted this title (*SGSZ* 23 [*T* 50:855c21–22]). See Takao, *Sōdai Bukkyōshi*, 49.

249. See *STGK*, *NBZ* 115:17b; Takao, *Sōdai Bukkyōshi*, 49.

250. *QTS* 50:470a.

251. *QTS* 50:475c.

252. *QTS* 50:469b.

253. *QTS* 50:477b–d.

254. *QTS* 50:476c.

255. *QTS* 51:487d.

256. *QTS* 51:478d.

257. Takao, *Sōdai Bukkyōshi*, 36.

258. Takao, *Sōdai Bukkyōshi*, 42.

259. The authorship of these three texts is unclear. Both *Zhouli* and *Yili* were traditionally assigned to Duke Zhou (d. 1105 B.C.E.), but modern scholars have contended that the former was written at some point toward the end of the Warring States 戰國 period (403–221 B.C.E.), the latter during the so-called Spring-Autumn period 春秋 (770–403 B.C.E.). *Liji* is believed to have been written originally by the disciples of Confucius but, after being nearly destroyed, it was reedited by scholars Dai De 戴德 (hence the title "The Book of Rites by Senior Dai"; *Da Dai li* 大戴禮) and Dai Sheng 戴聖 ("The Book of Rites by Junior Dai"; *Xiao Dai li* 小戴禮). The text available to us today was reedited by Ma Rong 馬融 (79–166 C.E.), who added some chapters to the Dai Sheng edition.

Zheng Xuan 鄭玄 (127–100 B.C.E.) of the Han dynasty wrote commentaries on all three texts. Based on these commentaries (*zhu* 注), Jia Gonyan 賈公彦 (Tang dynasty) wrote treatises on both *Zhouli* and *Yili*. Kong Yingda 孔穎達 (574–648) annoted *Liji*. Jia's and Kong's treatises (*shu* 疏) are regarded as the authoritative commentaries (*zhushu* 注疏) on these texts.

I am indebted to James Legge's translation of the *Liji* (*Li Chi: Book of Rites*, 2 vols. [Oxford: Oxford University Press, 1885; reprint, New Hyde Park, N.Y.: University Books, 1967]) and John Steele's translation of the *Yili* (*The I-li: Book of Etiquette and Ceremonial* [London: Probsthain & Co., 1917; reprint, Taipei: Ch'eng-wen Publishing Co., 1966]).

260. *YZS* **[79]**.

261. *Liji*, "Yueling" 月令, in *SJZ* (Reprint, Taipei: Dahua Shuju, 1982), 1:1362a.

262. *Liji*, "Yueling," *SJZ* 1:1362a–b.

263. Legge, *Li Chi*, 2:3; *Liji*, "Yuzao" 玉藻, *SJZ* 2:1474b.

264. See the example given in the schematic diagram of Lingyin Temple in *GJZ*, *CHSS*, 1287, 1319.

265. Legge, *Li Chi*, 1:223; 天子七廟、三昭三穆、與大祖之廟而七 *Liji*, "Wangzhi" 王制, *SJZ* 1:1335b.

266. See also John Jorgensen, "The 'Imperial' Lineage of Ch'an Buddhism: The Role of Confucian Ritual and Ancestor Worship in the Ch'an Search for

Legitimation in the Mid-T'ang Dynasty," *Papers on Far Eastern History* 35 (1987): 110.

267. *ZZK* 2-17-1:32d–33d.

268. *T* 48:1111c–1112a.

269. *YZS* [79].

270. *Xin Tangshu* 48:1236, cited in *ZSS*, 417b. These English translations of the titulary terms are from Charles O. Hucker's *A Dictionary of Official Titles in Imperial China* (1985; reprint, Stanford: Stanford University Press, 1989).

271. Mizuno Masaaki, "Sōdai ni okeru kissa no fukyū ni tsuite," *Sōdai no shakai to shūkyō* (Tokyo: Kyūko Shoin, 1985), 193–224.

272. Ibid., 216.

273. In Yijing's record we find that offering sweetened drink was practiced previously in India. Yijing (*NJNZ* [*T* 54:223a]) noted that all visiting monks were offered a drink made with ghee, honey, sugar, or one of eight kinds of syrup.

274. Tanaka Misa, "Sōdai no kissa kittō," *Shisen* 66 (1987): 62–75 and "Sōdai no kissa to chayaku," *Shisō* 48 (1991): 279–285.

275. *YZS* [182].

276. *YZS* [187].

277. *YZS* [194].

278. For this English translation, I am indebted to Steele, *The I-li*, 1:145. The words in brackets are my own.

279. *YZS* [251].

280. The master of ceremonies is usually the host of the ceremony. When the abbot sponsors a tea ceremony for the assembly, however, his attendant usually presides as the master of ceremonies in his place.

281. *YZS* [184–185].

282. This translation is taken, with slight modifications, from Steele, *The I-li*, 1:125.

283. *YZS* [86].

284. That is, ninety days in total, or three months. As *Chanyuan qinggui* indicates, the summer retreat lasts from the fifteenth day of the fourth month to the fifteenth day of the seventh month.

285. *YZS* [91].

286. *Zhouli*, "Chunguan Xiaozongbo" 春官小宗伯, *SJZ* 1:766a.

287. Ibid. My translation follows: Legge does not translate the annotations.

288. 蒼日靈威仰, 太昊食焉; 赤日赤熛怒, 炎帝食焉; 黃日含樞紐, 黃帝食焉; 白日白招拒, 少昊食焉; 黑白汁光紀, 顓頊食焉焉.

289. *Zhouli*, "Tianguan Dazai" 天官大宰, *SJZ* 1:649b.

290. *Liji*, "Yueling," *SJZ* 1:1364c, 1369a, and 1370c. See Legge, *Li Chi*, 1:268, 272, and 276.

291. The attending spirit is Rushou 蓐收. See *Liji*, "Yueling," *SJZ* 1:1372c, 1373b, and 2:1379a. See Legge, *Li Chi*, 283, 286, and 291.

292. The attending spirit is Xuanming 玄冥. See *Liji*, "Yueling," *SJZ* 2:1380c, 1382b,. and 1383c. See Legge, *Li Chi*, 296, 302, and 206.

293. The attending spirit is Jumang 句芒. See *Liji*, "Yueling," *SJZ* 1:1353b, 1361a, and 1363a. See Legge, *Li Chi*, 250, 257, and 262.

294. According to the solar calendar, the lunar New Year usually falls in the month of February.

295. See *Dongjing menghua lu* 6 (Shanghai: Gudian Wenxue Chubanshe 1957), 33.

296. *Dongjing menghua lu* 10, 56.

297. *YZS* **[92]**.

298. Duanwu commemorates the deeply patriotic poet-official Qu Yuan 屈原 (of the Warring States period), who, after falling out of favor with King Chu 楚王, was so grieved that he threw himself into the River Miluo 汨羅 on the fifth day of the fifth month. Chinese peasants began the practice of casting bamboo canisters filled with rice into rivers as an offering. Later, during the Han dynasty, an officer named Ou Qu 區曲 was said to have been visited by a spirit who called himself the *Sanlü daifu* 三閭大夫 ("scholar officer of three regions," the same title given to Qu Yuan, who complained that the offerings placed in the river were being stolen by dragons. He suggested that the bamboo canisters be wrapped in bamboo leaves and bound with colored ribbons, which, he contends, would be sufficient to scare away the dragons. This story is said to be the provenance of the custom, still prevalent in China today, of eating rice dumpling wrapped in bamboo leaves (*Xu Qixie ji*, gushi wenfang xiashuo series, vol. 7 [Shanghai: Shangwu Shuju, 1934]

299. This Chinese folk holiday celebrates a romantic meeting, the annual reunion of the heavenly weaving woman Zhinü 織女 and the earthly cowherd Niulang 牛郎. The two had been separated by the emperor of heaven because, according to divine law, it is forbidden for an immortal to marry an earthling.

The origin of this legend is unclear. However, the earliest reference to it can be found in *Xu Qixie ji*. An immortal during the time of Wuding 武丁 (1324–1265 B.C.E.) was summoned to the Heavenly Palace. There he told his mortal younger brother the tale of Zhinü, who was permitted to cross a heavenly bridge once a year, on the seventh day of the seventh month, to meet her husband, the cowherd Chianniu [Niulang]. After its appearance in *Xu Qixie ji*, the legend of Zhinü and Niulang became immensely popular (*Xu Qixie ji*, 6b–7a).

300. This holiday is also called *Chongyang* 重陽 ("Dual Yang" or "Dual Nine") because the number nine, according to Chinese tradition, is considered a "Yang" number. On this day it is customary to carry *zhuyu* 茱萸 herb to a high place, such as a mountaintop, to stave off any unforseen disasters. The custom originates with the story of Huan Jing 桓景, who studied for several years under Fei Changfang 費長房. One day Fei told Huan that on the ninth day of the ninth month a calamity would take place within the Huan household. He advised Huan to go home, tie a sack filled with zhuyu herbs to his arm, and take the members of his family to a high place to drink chrysanthemum wine. Huan obeyed, and when the family returned to their house that night they found that all their domestic animals had died. (See *Xu Qixie ji*, 6a.)

301. *YZS* **[105]**.

302. *T* 48:1155a5, 19.

Chapter 3. The Author and His Work

1. The second character of Zongze's name, *"ze"* 賾, has often been miswritten as *"yi"* 頤. For example, see the spelling given in *Lushan lianzong baojian* 4,

in the edition of *ZZK* 2-13-1:26d12, and *Xu chuandeng lu* 12 (*ZZK* 2B-15-3: 202c16).

2. *Zhiyuan ji* (*ZZK* 2-10-4:302c4).

3. See *YZS*, *kaisetsu* 解説, p. 4.

4. Shiina Kōyū, "Sōdai no Shinshū Chōroji," *Chūgoku busseki kemmonki* (Tokyo: Komazawa Daigaku Chūgoku Shiseki Sankantan, 1989), 8:39–42.

5. *T* 16:335a.

6. *Xu chuandeng lu* 23 (*T* 51:625c10) and *Da Ming gaoseng zhuan* 7 (*T* 50: 926c29).

7. See Shiina, "Chōroji," 44.

8. A minor correction to Carl Bielefeldt's *Dōgen's Manuals of Zen Meditation*, 66: Luozhou Yongnian is located in what is how Hebei province, not Henan (Pinying) or Honan (Wade-Giles).

9. *Weixin jingtu zixing mituo* 唯心淨土自性彌陀. *Lianhua shenghui luwen* (*T* 47: 178a20–21).

10. *Nian er wunian sheng er wusheng* 念而無念生而無生. *Lianhua shenghui luwen* (*T* 47:177b23).

11. *Lianhua shenghui luwen* (*T* 47:177b27–28).

12. *YZS* **[151]**.

13. Both the *Wuliangshou jing* 1 (*T* 12:268a26–27) and the *Guan Wuliangshou Fo jing* (*T* 12:346a19–20) assert that a dying person should recite with sincerity the name of the Amitābha Buddha for ten *nian* 念 (instants), after which he or she will be reborn in the Pure Land. However, interpretations of the word *nian* have varied. Tanluan 曇鸞 (476–542?) and Daochuo 道綽 (562–645) asserted that one should recite the Amitābha's name for "a span of ten instants" (referring to the length of time one recites), while Shandao 善導 (613–681) held that one should recite the name with "ten utterances" (referring to the number of recitations). Zunshi advocated that *shinian* should be practiced in the morning. Each day, after getting dressed, the practitioner should face west, standing upright with both hands clasped, and continuously chant the name of Amitābha Buddha until he runs out of breath. This is counted as one *nian;* when repeated for ten breaths it is called "ten *nian*" (*shinian*). Thus the number ten refers to the number of breaths and not the number of times the name is repeated, as many have assumed. See *LBWL* 4 (*T* 47:210b7–13).

14. See *LBWL* 2 (*T* 47:178b11–12).

15. See *Lushan lianzong baojian* 4 (*T* 47:324c29–325a7); see also *FZTJ* 27 (*T* 49: 278c23–27) and *Guiyuan zhizhi ji* 1 (*ZZK* 2-13-2:123b).

16. See *Huayan jing*, "Li shijian pin" 離世間品 (*T* 9:631, *T* 10:279).

17. See *Wanshan tonggui ji* 1 (*T* 48:966b29–c4) quoted from *Da fangguang Rulai busiyi jingjie jing* (*T* 10:911c20–25).

18. *Wanshan tonggui ji* 1 (*T* 48:967a11–24). Yanshou cites from *Nuoxian biqiu jing* (*T* 32:701c25–28).

19. *LBWL* 4 (*T* 47:208a1).

20. *FZTJ* 27 (*T* 49:278c4–11).

21. *Wudeng huiyuan* 17 (*ZZK* 2B-11-4:334c); *Zhushang shanren yong* (*ZZK* 2B-8-1:53b).

22. *Zhushang shanren yong* (*ZZK* 2B-8-1:53d).

23. For illustrations of these and other monks' devotion to Pure Land practices, see the section "Wansheng gaoseng zhuan" 往生高僧傳 (Biographies of Eminent Monks Who Were Reborn in the Pure Land) in *FZTJ* 27 (*T* 49:271c–272b). It provides useful lists of Chinese monks from all traditions, from the fourth to the thirteenth centuries. For a discussion of possible connections in the thought of Zongze, Zunshi, and Yuanzhao, see Kondō Ryōichi's article "Zennen shingi ni okeru Jōdo shisō: sono shisōshiteki kigen," *HKDK* 1 (1967):25–43.

24. *LBWL* 3 (*T* 47:192c19–22).

25. It should be noted that there is an alternate ordering of the patriarchs of the Pure Land school. The Japanese monk Genkū 源空 (1133–1212), in his *Senchaku hongan nenbutsushū*, lists the six patriarchs as Bodhiruci 菩提流支 (?–527), Tanluan (476–542?), Daochuo (562–645), Shandao (613–618), Huaigan 懷感 (n.d.), and Shaokang 少康 (?–805).

26. I have reconstructed the details of this story by combining *Lushan lianzong baojian* 4 (*T* 47:324c20–23) and *FZTJ* 27 (*T* 49:279a).

27. See *Longshu zengguang jingtu wen* 6 (*T* 47:271a22–b4). This text is partially cited in *Lebang yigao* 2 (*T* 47:249a7–9) and *Jingtu jianyao lu* (*ZZK* 2-13-2:106d).

28. *Jingtu jianyao lu* (*ZZK* 2-13-2:106d).

29. See *Shishi tonglan* (*ZZK* 2-6-3:222a).

30. Zongze's discourse record, *Ciju Chanshi yulu*, was included in Korean scholar Ch'oe Nam-sŏn's 崔南善 collection entitled *Yuktang mungo* 六堂文庫. The text was said to have been later donated to Koryŏ University; however, when Japanese scholar Shiina Kōyū painstakingly searched the catalogue of donated books at the university, he could not find this work. Its whereabouts remain a mystery. See Shiina Kōyū, *Sō-Gen ban zenseki no kenkyū* (Tokyo: Daitō Shuppansha, 1993), 56, as well as this article "Chōroji," 38–39; and Ōya Tokujō, "Kōrai chō no kyūzan," in *Sekisui sensei kakōju kinen ronsan* (Tokyo: Sekisui Sensei Kakōju Kinen Ronsan Kinenkai Kankō, 1942), 87. According to Ōya, this three-volume discourse record was compiled by Zongze's attendants (Zuda 祖大, Pushi 普式, Faqiong 法瓊, Jingfu 景福, and Daojia 道浹) and includes a preface written by Lü Xizhe 呂希哲 in 1109.

31. *Fofa daming lu*, collected in Komazawa University Library. *Shishi zijian* 6 (*ZZK* 2B-5-1:56c–d); and *Jingtu jianyao lu* (*ZZK* 2-13-2:106d).

32. *YZS* **[77]**.

33. For a detailed discussion of the various editions of the *Chanyuan qinggui*, see *YZS*, *kaisetsu*, pp. 5–11.

34. See *YZS*, *kaisetsu*, p. 6.

35. For a table comparing the contents of the Kōrai edition with the circulating edition, see *YZS*, *kaisetsu*, p. 8. It seems that the Kōrai method of chapter division is more systematic and logical, grouping paragraphs together into fascicles by theme. For more information on the editions of *Chanyuan quinggui*, see Kosaka Kiyū, "Kanazawa bunko bon *Zennen shingi* to Kōrai ban *Zennen shingi* to no kanren ni tsuite," in *Kanazawa bunko kenkyū* 192 (1972): 1–8; Kagamishima Genryū, "Kanazawa bunko bon *Zennen shingi* ni tsuite," in *Kanazawa bunko kenkyū* 144 (1968): 1–6; and Carl Bielefeldt, "Ch'ang-lu Tsung-tse's *Tso-Ch'an I* and the 'Secret' of Zen Meditation," in *Traditions of Meditation in Chinese Buddhism*, ed. Peter N. Gregory (Honolulu: University of Hawai'i Press, 1986), 131.

36. Carl Bielefeldt has undertaken thorough studies of *Zuochan yi;* see his article "Ch'ang-lu Tsung-tse's *Tso-Ch'an I*" and his book *Dōgen's Manuals of Zen Meditation.*

37. See Kosaka, "Kanazawa bunko bon *Zennen shingi,*" 8.

38. See Yanagida Seizan, Kajitani Sōnin, and Tsujimura Kōichi, *Shinjinmei, Shōdōka, Jugyūzu, Zazengi,* Zen no goroku series, (1974; reprint, Tokyo: Chikuma Shobō, 1981), 16:228.

39. See *Shōwa hōbō sōmokuroku* 昭和法寶總目錄 3:1305a25–b19, and Yanagida Seizan et al., *Zazengi,* 229.

40. See *T* 80:12a14–16.

41. See *YZS* **[279–283]**.

42. See *Shōwa hōbō sōmokuroku* 3:1305a25–b.

43. *YZS, kaisetsu* p. 10.

Chapter 4. *Chanyuan qinggui* in translation

Preface

1. The Hongji Public Chan Monastery is in present-day Zhengding county, Hebei province.

2. *jiafeng* 家風.

3. *nazi* 衲子. The word *nazi* literally means "person who wears a patched cassock." Dōchū (*ZSS;* 702b) points out that the character *na* 衲 appears in earlier texts as 納, meaning "to receive." Monks relied entirely on the generosity of others, "receiving" their clothes from others. In the Vinaya texts the term consistently used is *nayi* 納衣 ("received clothes"), with one distinct exception (*T* 23:281a15), where it appears as 衲("to patch"). As its footnote indicates, however, this may be considered a scribal error. Monks' robes are indeed made by stitching (or patching) together pieces of any material available. (For the origin of cutting robes into strips in imitation of the rice paddy, see "Heritage from the Indian Vinaya" in Chapter 2.) Therefore, the erroneous *nayi* 納衣 was a natural mistake as the term "patched cloak" seemed equally suitable; in time 納 and 衲 eventually became interchangeable.

How the term "patched monk" came to refer exclusively to the Chan monk is explained by Dōchū. He simply notes: "Chan monks often wear [patched cassocks], therefore they are called 'patched monks'" (*ZSS;* 702b). This connection alone is perhaps not very convincing. As monks in the Lü school are said to follow the Vinaya more strictly than those in other schools, they, too, must have worn patched robes, for this is what the Vinaya demands. A more plausible explanation may be that during the Song dynasty the Chan school predominated throughout China. The Chan school occupied all the leading monasteries in the nation and the most prominent monks were Chan monks. Accordingly, what originally symbolized monks in general came to be associated wholly with the dominant Chan school.

4. That is, halting all spiritual progress. The phrase "facing a wall" (*menqiang* 面牆) is taken from *Lunyu* 論語 ([*The Analects of Confucius*], "Yanghuo" 陽貨, *SJZ* 2:2525b). Confucius says, "The man who has not studied the Châu-nan and the Shâo-nan [Zhounan 周南 and Zhaonan 召南, that is two chapters from the *Book*

of Odes 詩經] is like one who stands with his face against a wall. Is he not?" 人而
不為周南、召南，其猶正牆面而立也與, that is, "in such a situation, one can neither
advance a step nor see anything." See Legge's translation, *Confucius: Confucian
Analects, the Great Learning, and the Doctrine of the Man* (Oxford: Clarendon Press,
1893; reprint, New York: Dover Publications, Inc., 1971), 323.

   5. *kaishi* 開士. In the sutras "bodhisattva" is sometimes translated as *kaishi*.
Fanyi mingyi ji 1 (*T* 54:1060b24–25) indicates this translation seems to have originated with Daoan: "Master [Dao]an called [bodhisattva] *kaishi* or *shishi*[b] 始士 . . .
[that] means the mind begins to open or aspire." *SSYL* 1 (*T* 54:260c24) notes that
the ruler of Early Qin Fujian bestowed on virtuous and knowledgeable monks
the title of *kaishi*. The author of the present text has clearly adopted this custom
and here uses this term to refer to those with great virtue and wide knowledge.

   6. That is, our own monastic practices.

   7. It was said that Bodhidharma, an Indian monk who arrived in China
c. 480 C.E., practiced wall-facing meditation for nine years at the Shaolin Monastery (present-day Songshan 嵩山 in Henan province) after his confrontation
with Emperor Wu (r. 502–549) of the Liang. Modern scholars believe that the earliest existing text to establish a clear link between Bodhidharma and the Shaolin
Monastery is *Chuan fabao ji* (c. 713). In the earlier *XGSZ*, the biography of Bodhidharma records neither the encounter between Bodhidharma and Emperor Wu
nor any account of his taking refuge at Shaolin. See Sekiguchi Shindai, *Daruma
no kenkyū* (Tokyo: Iwanami Shoten, 1967), 133; see also T. Griffith Foulk and
Robert H. Sharf, "On the Ritual Use of Ch'an Portraiture in Medieval China,"
Cahiers d'Extrême-Asie 7 (1993–1994): 172. Bodhidharma is traditionally regarded
as the twenty-eight patriarch in India and the first patriarch in China within the
Chan school.

   8. Zongze here presents the rhetorical argument that Bodhidharma need not
have come from the West (that is, India) to develop Chan Buddhism in China because Buddhism was already fluorishing there in its earlier forms. The author
seems to suggest that it is superfluous to add another school to Buddhism in
China.

   9. That is, to protect the monastery and propagate the Dharma.

   10. *sanju* 三聚 *jingjie* 淨戒: Mahayana precepts observed by both clergy and
laity. The threefold pure precepts are: *she lüyi jie* 攝律儀戒, the precepts of avoiding all evil actions; *she shanfa jie* 攝善法戒, the precepts of doing all good deeds;
and *she zhongsheng jie* 攝眾生戒, the precepts of benefiting all sentient beings.

   11. *qipian* 七篇

   12. Here *śrāvaka* (*shengwen* 聲聞, "a hearer") refers to the Hinayana precepts
establishing the rules of monastic discipline. According to *SFL* 17 (*T* 22:678b9–11),
these precepts are arranged into seven categories: (1) *pārājika*, (2) *saṃghāvaśeṣa*,
(3) *sthūlātyaya*, (4) *pātayantika*, (5) *pratideśanīya*, (6) *duṣkṛta*, and (7) *durbhāṣita*.
(See Fascicle 1 and my Introduction for details and definitions.) However, another
kind of classification, outlined in *SFL* 59 (*T* 22:1004c8–9) divides the precepts
into five categories (*wupian* 五篇), namely, categories 1, 2, 4, 5, and 6 above.

   13. Yuba is most likely the eight son in the Yu family—probably Yuxiang 虞翔,
who appears as the publisher at the end of the text. *Chanyuan qinggui* gives only
his official position. The most striking information we have about Yuba is the account given in *Song huiyao jigao* 3890 (*Zhiguan* 職官, 71–12, 3977d), which indi-

cates that he was demoted in rank three full grades for failing to quell the rebellion instigated by Li Jin 李金 (?–1165) in the year 1162.

Fascicle One
1. Past, present, and future.
2. The Western Heaven is India, the Land of the Tang is China. *Baolin zhuan* 寶林傳, compiled by monk Zhiju 智炬 (also known as Huiju 慧炬) in 801 C.E., is considered the first text to proclaim the tradition of the twenty-eight patriarchs in India and the six patriarchs in China. Zhiju consulted the genealogical texts of the early Tang dynasty when he designed this Chan lineage of transmission. It was adopted by succeeding genealogical texts, such as *Shengzhou ji* 聖冑集 (898), *Zutang ji* (952), and *Jingde chuandeng lu* (1004). This schematic lineage was then firmly established by Qi Song 契嵩 (1007–1072), who wrote *Chuanfa zhengzong ji* 傳法正宗記 (1061) specifically to support the claims made by *Baolin zhuan*. For a detailed discussion, see Tokiwa Daijō, *"Hōrinden" no kenkyū* (Tokyo: Kokusho Kankōkai, 1973). Philip B. Yampolsky, *The Platform Sutra of the Sixth Patriarch* (New York: Columbia University Press, 1967) discusses the twenty-eight Indian patriarchs (pp. 8–9) and the biographies of the six patriarchs (pp. 3–23).
3. *shamen* 沙門: mendicants.
4. *yanjing pini hongfan sanjie* 嚴淨毘尼洪範三界. See *Lengyan jing* (*T* 19:106b13). The Three Realms within the cycle of birth and death are: the Sense-Desire Realm (*yujie* 慾界, Skt. *kāma-dhātu*); the Subtle-Matter Realm (*sejie* 色界, Skt. *rūpa-dhātu*); and the Immaterial Realm (*wuse jie* 無色界, Skt. *ārūpya-dhātu*).
5. *canchan wendao* 參禪問道.
6. The three robes are *saṅghāṭi* 僧伽梨, *uttarāsaṅgha* 鬱多羅僧, and *antarvāsaka* 安陀會. These robes must be made of cloth strips sewn together. The *saṅghāṭi* robe consists of nine strips of cloth, the *uttarāsaṅga* robe is made from seven, and the *antarvāsaka* robe from five. When a monk receives a piece of good cloth, he should cut the material into strips and then sew the strips together.
7. [*zuo*] *ju* 坐具, Skt. *niṣīdana*.
8. See "Heritage from the Vinaya Tradition" in Chapter 2.
9. *shouyong* 受用. This joy is obtained by a Buddha who has perfected all virtues and merits. His body, dwelling in a Pure Land and experiencing the permanent joy of Dharma, is regarded as the "enjoyment body," which is also referred to as the Reward Body (Skt. *saṃbhoga-kāya baoshen* 報身), one of the Three Buddha Bodies. The other two bodies are the Transformed Body (*nirmāṇa-kāya; yingshen* 應身), which has manifested in this world in response to the need of all sentient beings, and the Dharma Body (*Dharma-kāya; fashen* 法身), which signifies the essence of Buddhahood.
10. *kongmen* 空門; that is joins the monastery. Since the doctrine of *kong* (*śūnyatā*, "emptiness") is regarded as the ultimate truth in Buddhism, the Buddhist monastery is referred to as the Gate (or the House) of Emptiness.
11. For a detailed discussion of the sravaka and the bodhisattva precepts, see "Heritage from the Vinaya Tradition in Chapter 2." See also nn. 10 and 12 in the preface.
12. For the phrase 寧捨身命終不捨戒, see *Da baoji jing* 90 (*T* 11:516c11).
13. For an introduction to the *Four Part Vinaya* (*Sifen lü*), see "Introduction of the Buddhist Vinayas into China" in Chapter 1.

14. *pārājika* 波羅夷. The *pārājika* are those offenses that result in permanent expulsion from the order. These four gravest offenses are unchastity, stealing, taking life, and falsely claiming to have attained enlightenment. See *SFL* 1 (*T* 22: 568c–579a); *WFL* 1–2 (*T* 22:2b–10a); *SSL* 1–2 (*T* 23:1a–13c); *MSL* (*T* 22:229a–262a. For the Pāli Vinaya pertaining to *pārājika*, see the section "Defeat" in Horner, *Discipline*, 1:1–191.

15. *saṃghāvaśeṣa* 僧伽婆尸沙. The *saṃghāvaśeṣa* are serious offenses that do not require expulsion from the Sangha. These violations can be atoned for by immediate confession before the assembly. See *SFL* 2 (*T* 22:579a–600b); *WFL* 2–3 (*T* 22:10b–22c); *SSL* 3–4 (*T* 23:13c–28b); *MSL* (*T* 22:262a–289c); the section "Formal Meeting," in Horner, *Discipline*, 1:192–329.

16. *buding* 不定, Skt. *aniyata*. These are two transgressions for monks. (They do not apply to nuns.) The precise nature of these offenses and their consequent punishment are undetermined. They occur when a monk sits alone with a woman in an open space or in an enclosed space. The punishment depends on the given situation. See *SFL* 5 (*T* 22:600b–601b); *WFL* 4 (*T* 22:22c–23a); *SSL* 4 (*T* 23: 28c–29c); *MSL* (*T* 22:289c–291a); the section "Undetermined," in Horner, *Discipline*, 1:330–430.

17. *naiḥsargika* 尼薩耆. *Pātayantika* literally means "causing to fall into an evil existence, if not repented and expiated." (The two kinds of *pātayantika* are the *naiḥsargika pātayantika*, which consists of thirty offenses that require forfeiture of property, and the *pātayantika*, which consists of ninety offenses (see the following note). See *SFL* 6 (*T* 22:601c–633c); *WFL* 4–5 (*T* 22:23a–37b); *SSL* 5–7 (*T* 23: 29c–61c); *MSL* 8–11 (*T* 22:291a–324b); the section "Forfeiture," in Horner, *Discipline*, 2:1–163.

18. *pātayantika* 波逸提. Each of these ninety offenses requires simple expiation. See *SFL* 11 (*T* 22:634a–695c); *WFL* 6–9 (*T* 22:37b–71b); *SSL* 9–18 (*T* 23: 63b–130c); *MSL* 12–21 (*T* 22:324c–396b); the section "Expiation," in Horner, *Discipline*, 2:164–416 and 3:102.

19. *pratideśanīya* 波羅提提舍尼: "requiring confession." These offenses primarily concern food. See *SFL* 19 (*T* 22:695c–698a); *WFL* 10 (*T* 22:71c–73c); *SSL* (*T* 23:131a–133b); *MSL* 21 (*T* 22:396b–399b); the section "Confession," in Horner, *Discipline*, 3:103–119.

20. *zhongxue* 眾學. These are minor offenses. See *SFL* 19–21 (*T* 22:698a–713c); *WFL* 10 (*T* 22:73c–77b); *SSL* 19–20 (*T* 23:133b–141b); *MSL* 21–22 (*T* 22:399b–412b); the section "Training," in Horner, *Discipline*, 3:120–152. In Pāli Vinaya, there are only seventy-five rules for this category.

21. *miezheng* 滅諍, Skt. *adhikaraṇa-śamatha*: "the settling or appeasement of disputed questions." See *SFL* 47–48 (*T* 22:913c–922c); *WFL* 10 (*T* 22:77b); *SSL* 20 (*T* 23:141–147b); *MSL* 23 (*T* 22:412b); the section "Legal questions," in Horner, *Discipline*, 3:153–155.

22. The ten major offenses are killing, stealing, engaging in sexual conduct, lying, buying and selling intoxicants, finding fault with the four groups within Buddhism (that is, monastics and lay people who have taken the boddhisattva precepts as well as fully ordained monks and nuns), praising oneself while calumniating others, being avaricious while being uncharitable, being angry and refusing an apology from another, and slandering the Three Treasures. The minor transgressions include consuming any intoxicant, eating meat, eating any of

the five malodorous/alliaceous vegetables, and refusing to attend the sick (*Fanwang jing* [*T* 24:1004b–1009b]).

23. *chifan kaizhe* 持犯開遮.

24. These prohibited vegetables (*cong* 蔥, *jiu* 韭, *xie* 薤, *suan* 蒜, and *yuansui* 圓荽) are known as the five alliaceous vegetables (*wuxin* 五辛). However, the list varies from text to text. For example, *Fanwang jing* 2 (*T* 24:1005b14) lists *dasuan* 大蒜 (a large type of garlic), *gecong* 革蔥, *cicong* 慈蔥, *lancong* 蘭蔥 (three types of onions), and *xingqu* 興渠 (a vegetable found in Central Asia); while *SGSZ* 29 (*T* 50:890b) lists garlic, onions, *xingqu*, leeks, and scallions. *Honyaku myōgi taishū* (entries 5731–5734, 5815) lists garlic, onions, *xiaogen cai* 小根菜 (another type of onion), leeks, and *xingqu*. For the origin of the garlic prohibition, see "Heritage from the Vinaya Tradition" in chapter 2 for two accounts. The "economic version," applying to nuns, is found in *SFL* 25 (*T* 22:736c–737b); see also *SSL* 44 (*T* 23: 317a28–b24) and *GSP* 17 (*T* 23:997a). The account that mentions garlic's offensive odor appears in *SFL* 52 (*T* 22:956b14–19); see also *SSL* 38 (*T* 23:275b12–24) and *GSP* (*Z*) 6 (*T* 24:230a). As for the Pāli Vinaya, see Horner, *Discipline*, 3:243–245 (nuns) and 5:195–196 (monks). *WFL* 12 (*T* 22:86c) prohibits nuns from eating garlic for both reasons of odor and lay economy; however, it prohibits monks from eating garlic only on account of the odor (*WFL* 26 [*T* 22:176a]). *MSL* 31 (*T* 22:483b) prohibits monks from eating garlic for both reasons, but it prohibits nuns from doing so for purely economic reasons (*MSL* 38, *T* 22:530b). The same prohibition appears in commentarial literature: *PNMJ* 4 (*T* 24:826c–827a); *SJLP* 16 (*T* 24: 788a9) and *T* 18:800a15) and *SJLP* 18 (*T* 24:800a15).

25. See "Heritage from the Vinaya Tradition" in Chapter 2 for a discussion of the rules regarding meat eating in the Indian Vinayas.

26. *rubing* 乳餅.

27. *qicao luan* 蠐螬卵, used as an eye medicine. The biography of Sheng Yan 盛彥 in *Jinshu* 88 ("Liezhuan" 列傳 58, 2276–2277; cited in Morohashi 10:106a) tells the story of one of Sheng's servants, who having been whipped by her master, fed baked maggots to Sheng's blind mother out of spite. After unknowingly eating the maggots, the mother was miraculously cured of her blindness.

28. *yaoshi* 藥石; that is, supper. More precisely, this term means "herbal medicine and stone probe." Since meals after noon are prohibited by the Vinaya, the consumption of a meal at an "improper" time is justified by referring to it as "medicine"; accordingly one conceived of eating after noon purely as a way of sustaining oneself physically, and not to satisfy hunger. In *Chanyuan qinggui* any eating after noon, for whatever purpose, was not allowed. Permission to partake of a meal after noon appears only in *RRQG*, compiled in 1209. This practice was followed in a number of later monastic codes.

Although commonly associated with Buddhist ceremony, the term *yaoshi* was not originally monastic and can be found in the following citation from the earlier secular text *Zuozhuan* (*SJZ* 2:1977c): "Mengsun's severe treatment of me had a salutary effect like medicine (*yaoshi*)" 孟孫之惡我、藥石也. In the annotations to *Zuozhuang*, the word *yaoshi* is given a second interpretation as "mineral medicine," referring to the ingestion of alum shale and other minerals for health reasons. However, we must also consider a passage from an earlier text, *Zhanguo ce* ("Qin'er" 秦二 [Shanghai: Shanghai Guji Chuabanshe, 1985], 147), which records the strategies of statesmen during the Warring States period (475–221 B.C.E.):

"[The famous physician] Bianque was furious and threw away his stone probe" 扁鵲怒而投其石. This suggests that in ancient times the administering of herbal medicine may have been preceded by a stone probe, or the prodding of the body at various points with a sharp stone, somewhat akin to later acupuncture. Thus I prefer to translate *yaoshi* as "herbal medicine and stone probe."

29. *zhai* 齋 or *zhou* 粥.

30. In Buddhist literature, women are typically represented as poisonous snakes. For example, *Daaidao biqiuni jing* 1 (*T* 24:949b22). *DZDL* 14 (*T* 25:166a) insists that it is better for a man to catch a poisonous snake than to touch a woman.

31. *cinian zhongsheng youru chizi* 慈念眾生、猶如赤子. For this phrase, see *Fahua jing Saddharma-puṇḍarīka-sūtra* 4 (*T* 9:35b19); also *DZDL* 14 (*T* 25:167b5–6).

32. 皮之不存，毛將安傅. For the origin of this idiom, see *Zuozhuan* (*SJZ* 2:1803b), written in the fourteenth year of Xizong 僖宗.

33. 精進持淨戒、猶如護明珠. For this phrase, see *Fahua jing* 1 (*T* 9:4c19).

34. *daoju* 道具: "equipment of Dao." Many of the personal effects listed here are also indicated in the Vinaya texts. In *WFL* 20 (*T* 22:138a18–22), when Upāli asks the Buddha what personal items monks may possess, the Buddha answers they may own three robes, undergarments, an overcoat, bath clothes for rainy weather, cloth to protect wounds, mosquito nets, cloth for walking meditation, cloth used to block wall lice, a bed sheet, a sitting mat, a hip-protecting cloth, cloth to protect the lower legs, a head-protecting cloth, a cloth to clean the body, a cloth to clean the hands and face, a bag for needle and thread, a bowl sack, a shoe bag, and a filter bag.

According to *MSL* 3 (*T* 22:245a5–8), a monk's personal items include three robes, a sitting mat, cloth to bandage wounds, bath clothes for rainy weather, three bowls of varying sizes, a bowl bag, a bowl sack with a strap (to hang over the shoulder), a filter bag, two kinds of waist belts, a knife, a copper spoon, a bowl stand, a needle tube, a water vessel, a bath vase, an oil bottle, a tin walking stick, leather shoes, an umbrella, and a fan.

35. *shanli* 山笠.

36. *zhuzhang* 拄杖. The *Mūlasarvāstivāda Vinaya* includes an episode revealing the origin of the monastic walking stick (*GSP(Z)* 6 [*T* 24:229c8–12]). While the Buddha was sojourning atop Vulture's Peak, a number of aged monks fell when they were ascending the mountain to see him. This prompted the Buddha to instruct the monks to use walking sticks while in the mountains. Generally, walking sticks may also be used by those who are ill. A similar rule, holding that old and ailing monks are allowed to use walking sticks as well as a bag to hold their bowls during alms, is found in the *Five Part Vinaya* (*WFL* 26 [*T* 22:175b15]). An item similar to the walking stick and mentioned in the Vinaya is the "stick with a tin end" (*xizhang* 錫杖). According to the *Four Part Vinaya* (*SFL* 52 [*T* 22:956a7]), some unenlightened monks were frightened by centipedes and other insects. The Buddha told them to shake tin sticks to scare the insects away.

An elaborate description of the functions of the stick with the tin end is found in the *Mūlasarvāstivāda Vinaya* (*GSP(Z)* 34 [*T* 24:375a21–28]). To inform donors of the time of almsgiving, monks had taken to pounding on donors' doors, which soon brought complaints against the monks. In response, the Buddha told them to affix a ring as big as the mouth of a cup to the end of their sticks and to attach small rings to the big ring. The monks should then simply shake their sticks, and the sound would signal the donors inside their homes. On one occasion, when a dog barked at some mendicant monks, they used their sticks to hit the animal. The Buddha told them they should not have struck the dog but simply lifted their sticks to scare it away. In another instance, a dog appeared particularly malicious and the more the monks tried to scare it, the angrier it became. The Buddha then taught the monks to appease the dog by feeding it a lump of rice. In yet another related story, when monks shook their sticks in front of the houses of non-Buddhists, no one emerged, causing them to become exhausted by their futile solicitations. The Buddha told the monks that they need not shake their sticks continuously but only two or three times. If the signal was met with no reply, they should move on.

For a discussion of the various symbolic meanings of the stick, see *Dedao ticheng xizhang jing* (*T* 17:724a–5c).

37. *jiedao* 戒刀. The *Five Part Vinaya* (*WFL* 26 [*T* 22:174a1–5]) states that monks originally could not possess knives, so they used sharpened bamboo to cut their robes, ruining the material in the process. The Buddha then allowed the monks to keep knives specifically for the purpose of cutting robes. He further stipulated that the knives be the length of one finger and affixed to a wooden handle. A similar story appears in *GSP(Z)* 3 (*T* 24:217c–218a). After the Buddha witnessed monks tearing their robes by hand and thus ruining them, he gave them permission to use knives. He insisted, however, that the monks should not decorate the knives with any kind of jewel and that they be made between two and six fingers long. The knife must also be curved like a bird feather; it must not be straight.

PNMJ 3 (*T* 24:816a22–23) gives the six functions of a knife: to cut leather; to cut fingernails; to penetrate a wound; to cut robes; to cut off stray threads from robes; and to clean fruits or perform any other similar tasks during a meal. (See *SXZ* 3B [*T* 40:127a1–2].)

38. *cibu tong* 祠部牒. The use of *cibu* (Department of Sacrifices) for "tonsure certificate" identifies the document's place of issue. Unlike their counterparts in India, Monks in China were kept under governmental supervision through the issuing of tonsure certificates, the registration of all monastics, the required application for travel, and the bureaucratic system of cleric officials. Monks and nuns were also fully subject to secular law. ("Chinese Influences" in chapter 2 covers this topic in greater detail.)

39. *bonang* 缽囊. According to *SFL* 52 (*T* 22:953a28), when ailing and elderly monks returned from begging for alms, they needed to rest their hands after holding their bowls for so long. For this reason, the Buddha allowed monks to make a bag for holding their bowls and instructed them to hang the bags under their armpits. The Vinaya texts (ex., *WFL* 28 [*T* 22:180b3]) mention another type of bowl sack that has an affixed belt to hang the bag over the shoulder. This bag is called *luonang* 絡囊.

40. *zhenzi* 枕子. The pillow referred to here was probably a wooden one of the type still used in China and in some Japanese monasteries today. It was small and foldable. In his *NJNZ* 3 (*T* 54:221a28–b7), Yijing states that the wooden pillow was used only in China. In India and Southeast Asia, a pillow sack was stuffed with various kinds of soft materials: wool, linen, willow pollen, cotton, reeds,

soft leaves, dried moss, hemp, beans, etc. In short, these were somewhat like the modern pillow. Yijing commented further that the wooden pillow was hard and allowed wind to pass below the neck, which resulted in headaches.

41. *lingkou xie* 鈴口鞋. Here the term "bell-mouth" may refer to the outline seen when viewing the front of the shoe, which curved downward into points, resembling the shape of the bottom of monastic bells used during the Song dynasty. The illustration in *Butsuzō hyōshikigi zusetsu* (*NBZ* 73:132) seems to corroborate this, although, as no sources give the precise origin of this term, we can only speculate. Later these shoes were termed "nose-high" (*bigao* 鼻高) shoes, referring to the view of the pointed toe from the side.

42. *jiaobing* 腳絣.

43. *qianhou baojin* 前後包巾.

44. *baijuanfu* 白絹複. *YZS* punctuates this passage 白絹複包・絛包・枕袋, which is an error for 白絹複包・包絛・包枕袋. These terms are clearly indicated in the following section entitled "Packing." See *YZS* **[22]** and **[25]**.

45. *baotao* 包絛. According to the Vinayas (*WFL* 26 [*T* 22:174b28]; *SFL* 40 [*T* 22:855c5]), not only were monks allowed to possess "waist ropes," but they were prohibited from entering a village unless they had tied up their underskirt to prevent its falling down. They were also permitted to make knots and hooks to secure their robes.

46. *baozhen dai* 包枕袋. *ZD* (p. 1138b) indicates that the *baozhen* was used for holding the pillow. However, we are told explicitly in the section titled "Packing" that the pillow was inserted under the cloth belt. Although its main purpose was not to hold the pillow, this sack was called *baozhen* because after one packed a few items in it, such as the bath towel and skirt (see *YZS* **[22]**), it could be used to support the head like a pillow or could be placed on top of the pillow.

47. *gaibao* 蓋包, *xiao youdan* 小油單, and *shiyou dan* 柿油單.

48. *buwodan* 布臥單. To protect the body, the robe, and the bed, the Buddha allowed monks to use a bed sheet (*danfu* 單敷, "single sheet") to cover the mattress. Its size was the same as the mattress (*WFL* 20 [*T* 22:138a9–14]).

49. *mianbei* 綿被.

50. *xiao jingpin* 小淨瓶. This is referred to as *junchi* 君持 or *junchi*[b] 軍持 (Skt. *kuṇḍikā*) in Vinaya texts.

51. *yujin* 浴巾, *yuqun* 浴裙. *WFL* 26 (*T* 22:171b7) indicates that monks had been in the habit of bathing naked, scrubbing each other's backs and emerging from the bath naked. Such practices were censured by laypeople and reported to the Buddha. The Buddha then told monks to wear bathing clothes and prohibited them from washing each other.

52. *hangui xiaochao* 函櫃小巢. The compartments were usually part of the facilities in the Sangha hall. They were located in the wall at the end of each platform. For an illustration, see *ZD*, 175d.

53. *GSP(Z)* 15 (*T* 24:274b25–c3; quoted in *ZTSY*, 120b) states that monks used to travel with the three robes over their shoulders, soiling them with sweat and dust. The Buddha then taught them to make a sack to hold the robes. The size of the sack had to be three arms long (about six feet) and one and a half arms wide (about three feet), with an opening in the middle where the knot and hook are attached. In addition, the Buddha instructed that clothes used regularly be placed on the top and those rarely used be placed on the bottom.

54. *pianshan* 偏衫: literally, "side clothes." The short gown is the combination of *sengqi yi* 僧祇衣 (Skt. *saṃkakṣikā*) and *hujian yi* 護肩衣 (that is, "a piece of cloth to cover the left shoulder"). The *sengqi yi* is a piece of cloth covering the left shoulder and left armpit, tied under the right armpit and worn under the three robes by both monks and nuns. The *hujian yi* is a piece of cloth to cover the left shoulder and is worn only by nuns. *WFL* 29 (*T* 22:187c3) and *MSL* 40 (*T* 22:546b25) provide the following explanation: When women, some of them from noble families, became nuns, they wore the monastic robes, which usually did not cover the right shoulder. After a group of nuns was harassed by some laymen for their exposed shoulders, the Buddha allowed them to wear an extra piece of cloth to cover their right shoulders.

When Buddhism came to China, the Indian style of dress was not accepted by the Chinese. Given their deep-rooted, traditional sense of *li* 禮 (that is, propriety), the exposure of any part of the body was regarded as barbarian and improper. *Weilu* 魏錄, a missing text written by Zhu Daozu 竺道祖, reports that when imperial ladies saw monks with one arm exposed, they regarded it as an impropriety. Monks later made a cover for the right shoulder and sewed it to the *sengqi yi*. According to *CBQG* 5 (*T* 48:1139a), this is the origin of the short gown (*pianshan*). This account is also quoted in *ZSS*, 695a–700a; here Dōchū provides ample description of the origin and evolution of the short gown as the upper part of a monk's undergarments. (Below monks wore a skirt.) By the time *CBQG* was compiled in 1336, the upper and lower parts had been sewn together as one long garment and given the name *zhiduo* 直裰. The illustration of the short gown and the *zhiduo* can be seen in *Butsuzō hyōshikigi zusetsu* (*NBZ* 73:131). See also *ZD* (1114c) for *pianshan*.

55. *chuyi* 觸衣, i.e., items that have had contact with bare skin. Daoxuan's *JXXL* (*T* 45:873a24–25) indicates that "pure" clothes (*jingyi* 淨衣) must be placed on the "pure" pole, and "soiled" clothes on the "soiled" pole.

56. The hat was big enough to cover one's shoulders.

57. This is in direct contrast to Daoxuan's rule that when traveling one should carry bowls with the mouths facing away from the body. See *JXXL*, rule 11 in the section "Protecting the Bowls" (*T* 45:872c13–14).

58. That is, on his right side at the waist.

59. *chutou* 觸頭 and *jingtou* 淨頭. *ZD* (p. 506a) interprets these two "heads" as two distinct walking sticks rather than two parts of one stick. From this sentence, however, it is more logical to interpret the heads as two parts of the same stick. The walking stick handle was usually regarded as the "soiled" part, while the bottom end of the stick, that is, the "pure head," was kept in front while walking. Later in this text, the term *jingtou* refers to the latrine attendant.

60. *wenxun* 問訊. Here and throughout this text, I translate *wenxun*, the customary slight bow, as "bow." For the full bow and prostration, I use the Chinese terms. Both *wen* and *xun* literally mean "to inquire" (*ZTSY* 5:69b). *MSL* (cited in *SSYL* 2 [*T* 54:277b]) notes that while paying homage, monks should not be mute like goats but should "inquire" of, or greet, each other. *DSL* (*T* 54: 239a3–5) indicates that when monks encounter each other, they bend their bodies and press their palms together, saying, "*Bushen* 不審" (literally, "not knowing"; that is, "I do not know how you are and wish to inquire as to your well-

being"). However, Dōchū (ZSS, 383a), citing the descriptions given in monastic codes, argues that monks did not necessarily speak when performing *wenxun* (Jpn. *monjun*).

61. *sanmen* 三門; that is, the outer mountain gate. Referring to the outer mountain gate as the Triple Gate may have been adopted from *DZDL* 20 (*T* 25:207c10), which reads: "If the true form of all Dharmas [that is, all phenomena] can be represented as a castle, then this castle has three gates—Emptiness (*kong* 空), Formlessness (*wuxiang* 無相), and Non-Action (*wuzuo* 無作)." These gates are also referred to as the Triple Gate of Liberation, which leads to nirvana. The same idea can be seen in *Fodi jinglun* 1 (*T* 26:395c17), which lists Emptiness, Formlessness, and Non-Desire (*wuyuan* 無願) as components of the Triple Gate of Liberation.

62. *sengtang* 僧堂.

63. *chuangdang* 床䒓. The word *dang* should be pronounced in the fourth tone.

64. *Kāṣāya* literally means "yellowish red." However, this meaning was later lost in the Chinese translation *jiasha* 袈裟, which simply became a generic term for a Buddhist monk's robes.

65. *houjia* 後架. Translated literally as "rear stand," the *houjia* was used for refreshing oneself. The rear washstand was generally located behind the Sangha hall. *Shōbogenzō* (written by Dōgen, who based his observations on Tiantongshan) points out that the rear stand is a place for washing one's face, located close to the Sangha hall but west of the "illumination hall" (*zhaotang* 照堂). (In other words, the illumination hall was between the washstand and the Sangha hall. See the section "Washing the Face" in *DZZ* 2:428.) Generally, the toilet (*dongsi* 東司) was built next to the rear washstand. The rear exit of the Sangha hall led to the illumination hall, which in turn connected with the rear washstand, which was directly north of the toilet. Yokoyama Shūsai asserts that the standard Sangha hall was located to the right of the Buddha shrine, adjacent to the west corridor, and opening to the east. The rear washstand was usually located to the west of the illuminating hall, which was just outside the rear exit of the Sangha hall. This was the general format for monasteries during the Song dynasty (See Yokoyama, *Zen no kenchiku*, 212.) It is worth noting that a monastery may have had more than one rear washstand. In a diagram of Tiantongshan, a second washstand is located in the east wing of the complex, close to the assembly quarters and connected to the toilet. The term "illumination" hall does not appear in *Chanyuan qinggui;* it may be a building that was incorporated later.

This arrangement is illustrated in a diagram of Tiantongshan in *GJZ; ZD*, "Zuroku" 圖録, p. 12; see also *CHSS* 2:1286), a collection of diagrams illustrating monastic architectural layouts, the placement of liturgical vessels, and the locations of various rituals performed in the major monasteries of southern China during the Southern Song. It is believed that *GJZ* was first brought to Japan by Tettsū Gikai 徹通義介 (1219–1309) after his sojourn in Song China in 1259. (It is now preserved in the Eiheiji Monastery.) Later, circumstances led the monks of Eiheiji to trade the text of *GJZ* for a statue of Dōgen from Daijōji 大乗寺 Temple. Thus today scholars know this collection of diagrams as the Daijōji edition. Another version of this text, referred to as *Dai Sō shozan zu* 大宋諸山圖 was brought from China to Japan by Shōichi Enni 聖一圓爾 (1208–1280) in 1241 and has been preserved in Tōfukuji 東福寺 in Kyoto. Although the two versions are nearly identical in content, the Tōfukuji version contains three fewer diagrams and a number of other differences, leading Yokoyama Shūsai to conclude that the two collections were copied from different sources. (See his *Zen no kenchiku* [Tokyo: Shōkokusha, 1967], 49.) Basing his work on these two versions, Dōchū made a modified version entitled *Zenran zu kōka* 禪藍圖校訛, which was renamed *Dai Sō gozan zusetsu* 大宋五山圖式 and included in *CHSS* 2:1269–1334. For all future references to *GJZ*, I will provide page citations for both *ZD* and *CHSS*.

66. *tangsi* 堂司. This term is sometimes used interchangeably with *weinuo* 維那 (that is, Sangha hall rector), an can refer to either the person or his quarters.

67. *xiangkan* 相看.

68. *weinuo* 維那. For further details, see the section "Rector" in fasc. 3.

69. *guada* 掛搭.

70. [*zhong*] *liao* [眾]寮. The text does not specifically indicate to which quarters the word *liao* refers; however, judging from the context, it seems to refer to the assembly quarters. Monks did not sleep in the assembly quarters but in the Sangha hall.

71. *renshi* 人事. Literally translated as "people's affairs." Dōchū (*ZSS*, 399b) notes that this word has three meanings: to greet, to present gifts, and to present one's qualifications. The appropriate translation should be chosen by context.

72. *liaozhu* 寮主 and [*liao*] *shouzuo* [寮]首座. In *Chanyuan qinggui*, there are four positions referred to as "chief seat": the chief seat in the assembly quarters, called *liao shouzuo* 寮首座 (for details of his duties, see **[161]**); the chief seat in the Sangha hall, simply referred to as *shouzuo* (for details of his duties, see **[124–126]**); the chief seat in the sutra-reading hall, referred to as *kanjing shouzuo* 看經首座 (cf. *YZS* **[131]**); and the chief seat emeritus, or *liseng shouzuo* 立僧首座 (sometimes abbreviated as *liseng*), held by those who retired honorably from high administrative positions. For the appointment of the chief seat emeritus, see *YZS* **[248]** in fasc. 7.

73. *wenzi* 文字; that is, sutra literature.

74. *danguo* [*liao*] 旦過[寮]: literally "passing the dawn."

75. *ju weiyi* 具威儀. Dōgen (*DZZ* 1:420) indicates that when a student is going to visit the master, he should "get himself ready," that is, don his *kāsāya*, procure his sitting mat, properly arrange his shoes and socks, and bring a stick of incense. Although incense has brought when visiting the master, it was not a requirement for other social occasions. In general, the student prepared whatever the situation required. In Daoxuan's *JXXL* (*T* 45:873a; cited in *ZSS*, 402b), the first rule of entering the "warm room" (the bath house) was to prepare one's demeanor and to bring a sitting mat.

76. *kewei* 客位. The guest quarters was located within the overnight quarters. Its function was similar to that of a reception office, where tea or sweetened drinks were served to guests, whether monks or laypeople (see **[135]** and **[106]**). When the fundraiser returned to the monastery, the administrative staff received him at the guest quarters (see **[171]**). When a new abbot arrived at the monastery, he stayed at the guest quarters temporarily before taking up office. The *kewei* then was not only an office but also a place of lodging. It should be noted that in some passages of the present text, the term *kewei* appears to mean the guest seat (in contrast to the host seat).

77. *zhike* 知客. For a detailed discussion, see the section "Guest Master" in fasc. 4.

78. 觸禮三拜; i.e., each places a folded sitting mat on the floor in front of himself and bows down, touching his forehead to the sitting mat three times.

79. *huili* 迴禮.

80. *cantou* 參頭.

81. *xingzhe* 行者.

82. *daofeng* 道風.

83. *tang* 湯. In Yijing's record (*NJNZ* 3 [*T* 54:223a26]) we find that Indians observed the custom of offering sweetened drink. Yijing records that when a guest monk came, he would be offered a soup made with ghee, honey, sugar, or one of eight kinds of syrup while he took his rest.

84. *Shangzuo* 上座: literally, "upper seat." This term is used in the present text by monks addressing each other. A monk typically refers himself as *biqiu* 比丘 (bhikṣu).

85. *shengseng* 聖僧.

86. *shouzuo* 首座.

87. *bantou* 板頭. This word appears to have three separate but related meanings within the present text: the lead seat of each platform, the upright boards at the two ends of a platform, and the wall panel of a platform. The "second seat from the lead seat" is the third seat.

88. *chuangli* 床曆. The register gave each monk's name, date and place of birth, and years since ordination, using the information provided by his certificates. One copy was kept by the Sangha hall rector, another by the abbot (*CHSS* 1:557b).

89. *shangshou* 上手, i.e., stand in the higher position.

90. *choujie* 抽解.

91. I could not identify the enshrined statue mentioned here, and the text gives no further information as to its exact nature. However, *RRQG* (*ZZK* 2-16-5:478b) states that the holy statute in the assembly quarters is Avalokiteśvara (Guanyin 觀音). Similarly, the diagrams in *GJZ* (*ZD*, "Zuroku," p.10 and *CHSS* 2:1282–1283) clearly indicate that the image inside the assembly quarters is Avalokiteśvara. According to Menzan Zuihō 面山瑞方 (1683–1769), because the assembly quarters was often filled with the sound of voices reading aloud. Avalokiteśvara (*Guan shiyin* in Chinese, meaning "one who observes voices in the world") is the most logical deity for such a location. See *Tōjō garan shodō anzōki*, in *Sōtōshu zensho Shingi*, ed. Sōtōshū Zensho Kankōkai (1931; reprint, Tokyo: Sōtōshū Shūmuchō, 1972), 822.

92. *tangtou* 堂頭. This term may also refer to the abbot himself.

93. *shizhe* 侍者.

94. *rushi dizi* 入室弟子: "enter room" disciples; or *fajuan* 法眷, i.e., in the same Dharma lineage.

95. This may also apply to Dharma relatives. Those who enter the master's quarters as select disciples are chosen to inherit their teacher's Dharma lineage. The section entitled "Entering the Abbot's Quarters" (Fascicle 1) illustrates the ceremony of entering the abbot's quarters for instruction (see **[66]**). Although *Chanyuan qinggui* does not identify a special procedure for select disciples to follow when entering the abbot's quarters, William Bodiford cites a few traditions that seem to indicate a privileged status for select disciples within the monastic community in Japan. He writes:

Medieval *rinka* lineage, however, practiced an informal private instruction, conducted in secret only for selected individual students, who would visit the abbot's quarters alone. In purpose and content these secret sessions were completely different from the sessions conducted as part of the group ceremony. During the regular visits to the Abbot's Quarters, the teacher counseled and encouraged each member of the community of monks, one at a time. The secret instruction sessions, however, were limited to senior disciples who would inherit their teacher's dharma lineage. For these disciples alone the teacher conducted lengthy initiations into the entire kōan curriculum and into that lineage's own set of questions and answers used for each kōan.

See William M. Bodiford, *Sōtō Zen in Medieval Japan* (Honolulu: University of Hawaii Press, 1993), 148.

96. 兩展三禮, also *liangzhan sanbai* 三拜. To perform the formal *liangzhan sanli*, one fully unfolded the sitting mat, placed it on the floor, expressed congratulatory words or the purpose of the visit, bowed down three times, and collected and folded the sitting mat. Then one unfolded the sitting mat again, expressed a seasonal greeting, and bowed down three times. Finally, without unfolding the sitting mat, one bowed down three times. As *DSL* points out (*T* 54:238c29–239a2, see also n. 78 above), to prevent excessive formalities, the senior monk will stop the junior monk from performing repeated prostrations. Thus the *de facto* procedure is: unfold the sitting mat the first time without bowing down, express directly the purpose of visiting, unfold the sitting mat again without bowing down, deliver the seasonal greeting, then merely bow three times with the sitting mat touching the ground (*chuli sanbai*). The common courtesy of prostration, as indicated in the present text, can be divided into three degrees of veneration: nine bows with a fully unfolded sitting mat, *liangzhan sanli*, and *chuli sanbai*.

97. *gongjie zhi li* 公界之禮. The term *gongjie* in this text may refer to a practice carried out "in common," to an item that is considered "public" or "common" property, or to a fixed day of reception.

98. *dazhan jiuli* 大展九禮.

99. *zhishi* 知事. The administrators section included four offices: the prior, the rector, the cook, and the superintendent. For a detailed discussion of the appointment and termination of administrators, see *YZS* **[96–101]** in fasc. 2 and *YZS* [120–121] in fasc. 3.

100. *toushou* 頭首. The chief officers section included six positions: the chief seat in the Sangha hall, the scribe, the library director, the guestmaster, and the bathmaster. For a detailed discussion of the appointment and termination of chief officers, see *YZS* **[122–123]** in fasc. 3 and *YZS* **[176]** in fasc. 5.

101. *xiaoshi* 小師; that is, novices of fewer than ten years. Yijing observed that in India a monk who had been ordained for fewer than ten years was called *dahara* (*duoheluo* 鐸曷欏), translated into Chinese as *xiaoshi*. After ten years, he was called *sthavira* (*sitaxueluo* 悉他薛欏); in Chinese *zhuwei* 住位, meaning "remaining in the position." This referred to the fact that the monk was considered able to live without depending on his teacher (*NJNZ* 3 [*T* 54:220a21–22]).

102. *daojia* 道價.

103. *hanxuan* 寒暄.

104. *kusi* 庫司. This term can refer to either the person (the prior) or the

office (the priory). For further details, see the section of "Prior," *YZS* **[105–109]** in fasc. 3.

105. *shuji* 書記. See the section "Scribe" in fasc. 3.

106. *zangzhu* 藏主. See the section "Director of the Library" in fasc. 3.

107. *jiuzhu* 久住.

108. *yuzhu* 浴主. See the section "Bath Master" in fasc. 4.

109. *jiandian* 煎點. There are two types of tea ceremonies: *jiandian,* the tea and refreshment ceremony, and *chatang* 茶湯, the tea ceremony. In addition to these two terms, *Chanyuan qinggui* also uses *diancha* 點茶 and *diantang* 點湯. For a detailed discussion of these four terms, see *YZS* **[177]** in fasc. 5.

110. *tangyi banyue* 堂儀半月.

111. *dian ruliao cha* 點入寮茶.

112. *shengjie* 聖節, i.e., the emperor's birthday.

113. *mingde* 名德.

114. *duliao* 獨寮.

115. *jianyuan* 監院. A detailed discussion of the prior is given in fasc. 3.

116. *fangzhang* 方丈. *Chanmen guishi* (*Jingde chuandeng lu* 6 [*T* 51:251a8–9]) notes that "when a monk reaches the rank of abbot, he resides in the quarters called *fangzhang,* named after the room of Vimalakīrti." *Fangzhang* literally means "ten-foot square." *FYZL* 29 (*T* 53:501c8–13) records how this title came about. In the year of Xianqing 顯慶 (656–660), Wang Xuance 王玄策, under the emperor's edict, explored the Western Region, eventually reaching central India. There he visited the city of Vaiśālī, where he saw the ruins of Vimalakīrti's residence. In the *Vimalakīrti-nirdeśa-sūtra* it is written that the layman Vimalakīrti was a person of great achievement and high character. His tiny room was said to have supernaturally accommodated 32,000 visitors. During his visit to the ruins of Vimalakīrti's home, Wang measured this small room with his official tablet (*hu* 笏) and calculated the area to be the equivalent of ten tablets. Thus Vimalakīrti's room became known as "ten-foot square," and all masters' quarters came to be called by this name.

A *hu* was a tablet held in front of the chest during an audience with the emperor, The material used for this tablet was chosen according to one's official position. In *Liji* ("Yuzao," *SJZ* 2:1480b), a *hu* was about two feet six inches long and three inches wide. However, it can be inferred from *FYZL* that Wang's tablet was only one foot long. The unit of measure *chi* was the same throughout the centuries, but its actual length varied from dynasty to dynasty.

117. That is, they give official notice of their moving to the monastery.

118. *huazhu* 化主.

119. *qianzi liao* 前資寮.

120. *zhufang bianshi* 諸方辨事.

121. *mingfu shiming* 命服師名. *Mingfu,* taken from *Shijing* (Book of Odes, "Xiao Nancai" 小南采, *SJZ* 2:426a), originally referred to the garment a duke received from the emperor 服其命服. In ancient times, this piece of clothing represented his official status. The literal translation of *mingfu* in *ZD* (p. 1218b), "to follow an order," is erroneous.

122. *shangliao* 上寮.

123. *jiexia* 結夏. *SFL* 37 (*T* 22:830b–c) describes an episode in which six notorious monks were criticized for the unnecessary killing of insects and plants

during their continued travel in the summer months, when all non-Buddhist mendicants cease traveling. The Buddha then established the rule that monks should retreat for three months during the summer and should refrain from traveling throughout this period. See also *WFL* 19 (*T* 22:129a); *MSL* 27 (*T* 22:450c); *SSL* 24 (*T* 23:173b); *GSP(A)* (*T* 23:1041a–b). *Chanyuan qinggui* indicates that for Chan monasteries the beginning and ending dates of the retreat should be the fifteenth day of the fourth month and the fifteenth day of the seventh month, respectively.

124. That is, he must go through the Sangha hall orientation process again.

125. *panping shi* 判憑式. For further information regarding the traveling permit application, see "Influences of Chinese Culture" in Chapter 2.

126. Monks who wore brown robes were ordinary monks. Those who wore purple robes had received honoraria from the government. For a detailed discussion of the granting of the purple robe, see "Influences of Chinese Culture" in Chapter 2.

127. *wenzhang* 文帳.

128. *liunian* 六念. In Daoxuan's *SXC* 1C (*T* 40:30b–c), in the section entitled "Conditions for Ordination" 受戒緣集, it is stated that The Six Awarenesses were given to initiates after the bestowal of robes, bowls, and sitting mats. The Six Awarenesses are: one should know the present date; one should know whence one's meals will come each day; one should know the year of one's ordination; one should be mindful of one's robes, bowls, and righteously received alms; one should clearly know when one eats alone and when one eats with others; and one should know one's present state of health. Daoxuan's list itself was adopted from *Mohe sengqi lü da biqiu jieben* (*T* 22:549a). In contrast to the tonsure and ordination certificates, which first arose in China, the list is mentioned much earlier in the Vinaya texts as a document bestowed during ordination. During the Tang dynasty, monks and nuns carried tonsure and ordination certificates on their person while traveling. It was not until the third year of Xianping 咸平 (1000) in the Song dynasty that The Six Awarenesses became the third mandatory identifying document, serving as a passport for travel within China (cited in *YZS*, p. 40 n).

129. *shiya* 使衙.

130. *gongping* 公憑: "document attested to by the government."

131. *ditou* 地頭.

132. *piping shi* 批憑式.

133. *kaijing* 開靜: literally, "opening of the quiet." *Kaijing* may also refer to the break from meditation. In the early morning *kaijing* roused everyone from sleep, while in the evening it marked the break from evening meditation and reading.

There were two *kaijing* signals: big and small. According to *YZS* **[131]**, the peal of the small bell in front of the kitchen signified the "opening of small quietness," that is, when only some monks were awakened. The cloud-shaped metal sheet (*yunban* 雲板) was struck for the "opening of big quietness," when all the monks were awakened. Up to this moment, monks could only fold their comforters and roll up their mosquito nets. While the bell for small *kaijing* was struck for one sequence, the metal sheet was struck for three sequences. See also *ZSS*, 725b–28a.

134. *shiwei* 食位. In the Sangha hall, the monk's dining seat for meals and his

sleeping seat (*beiwei* 被位, "quilt seat") for meditation and sleep were not always the same. During mealtime, some monks were out performing other duties. For the sake of convenience when food was served, monks may have been required to change their seats to fill any empty places. Cf. *YZS* **[158]**.

135. *changban* 長板. See *ZSS*, 736b–737b.

136. Daoxuan's *SXC* 1A (*T* 40:6c11–12) clearly states that the three sequences (*santong* 三通) are also called *sanxia* 三下 (literally, "three times"). *WFL* 18 (*T* 22: 122c19: *ZSS*, 736b) indicate that the signal should be struck for three sequences.

137. *shangjuan* 上肩, i.e., the shoulder closest to the center of the room.

138. *muyu* 木魚. The wooden fish was a long piece of wood carved in the shape of a fish and used as one of the signaling instruments. For details on the source, see fasc. 6, n. 21.

139. *nanjia* 南頰.

140. In *JXXL* (*T* 45:872b), Daoxuan points out that when exiting the hall after a meal, one steps through the threshhold with the leg closest to the door. In *SXC* 1B (*T* 40:23b18–20) Daoxuan stipulates that if a monk is to sit on the west side of the hall, he enters through the west side, stepping through with the left leg. He also exits through the west side, but with his right leg, the leg closest to the door. If a monk sits on the east side, the procedure is just the opposite; he enters with the right leg and exits with the left.

As this is the universally accepted procedure, the wording in *Chanyuan qinggui* appears erroneous. It should be the left foot, the one closest to the left side of the door, that steps through first. In his *Fu shukuhan pō*, Dōgen adopts this section of *Chanyuan qinggui* but changes "right foot" to "left foot." See *DZZ* 2:349, line 3.

MSL 34 (*T* 22:502a8) specifies that an attendant disciple, having risen from bed before the others, "steps with his right foot first" into the master's door, bows to touch his head to the master's feet, then inquires whether the master has slept well. If we assume that the correct procedure is being followed, then the disciple steps through the right side of door. While *MSL* does not stipulate which side of the door must be used, it does indicate that monks followed a specific procedure when entering the hall or the teacher's room.

141. *beijia* 北頰.

142. *shangjian* 上間, i.e., the right section. The two divided sections and all doors are oriented (labeled right and left, etc.), according to the point of view of one looking in through the front door. If the Sangha hall was located in the western part of the compound and faced east, then the *shangjian* was on the north side and the *xiajian* on the south side.

143. *xiajian* 下間, i.e., the left section.

144. *chuang* 床.

145. It is not clear whether this is the right or left armpit.

146. *tachuang* 踏床. *GSP(Z)* 14 (*T* 24:270a; also quoted in *ZSS*, 811a) shows that the Buddha allowed monks to set up a stationary step at the foot of their platform or a portable stool below their chair.

147. This description is adopted from Dōgen. *Chanyuan qinggui* merely states that the monk sits "inside" the platform.

148. Cf. *SSL* (quoted in *SXC* 1B [*T* 40:23b14–15]): The proper way to descend

from the platform was to slowly lower one leg, then the other. One then stood up in a peaceful and composed manner. The method of ascending the platform was the same, in reverse.

149. Cf. *JXXL* (*T* 45:871c), rule 22 for mealtime: While in the seated position, the monk should be careful not to expose his undergarments.

150. Note: 垂衣"坐"床緣 should be 垂衣"於"床緣. See Dōgen's correction in *DZZ* 2:349, line 14. Cf. *JXXL* (*T* 45:871c) rule 23 for mealtime: While sitting on the platform, the monk should not let his robes drape over the edge.

151. *sanjing* 三淨.

152. *zhisui* 直歲. See the section "Superintendent" in fasc. 3.

153. *tantou* 炭頭.

154. *jiefang* 街坊. See the section "Prior" in fasc. 3.

155. [*yanshou* 延壽] *tangzhu* 堂主. See the section "Director of the Infirmary" in fasc. 4.

156. *shami* 沙彌 (Skt. *srāmaṇera*).

157. *zhenchui* 砧槌. The striking stand and hammer in the Sangha hall were not inventions of the Chan school. They were used at the time of Daoxuan and can most likely be traced back even earlier, to Daoan's time. Daoxuan's *SXC* 1D (*T* 40:35c26) describes the use of the stand and hammer. According to this text, the rector stood at the "place of striking the quietness" (*dajing chu* 打靜處) during the ceremony of precept instruction. It may be inferred that the stand itself represented the "quietness"; thus to hit the stand is to "strike the quietness." That this signal was struck to pacify or quiet (*jing*) the assembly is another possible interpretation. (See *ZSS*, 742b). This second interpretation is more plausible, since the rector stood with the roll-call stick on his left and the hammer on his right. For more information, see "Sangha Regulations before *Chanyuan qinggui*" in Chapter 1; for the proper way to employ the hammer, see *YZS* **[221]** in fasc. 6.

158. 洪濟, i.e., in Zongze's monastery.

159. *tudi zhou* 土地粥: the food offered to the earth guardians during the early meal.

160. *xingxiang* 行香. *DSW* 1 (*T* 24:914b4–7) stipulates that monks should sit down before receiving the incense offering. *GSP* 8 (*T* 23:666b3–12) describes the practice of holding the incense burner and circumambulating the pagoda (Skt. *caitya*): After the monks have received a drink, a senior householder bows down before the monks' feet, holding an incense burner. He then leads all the monks outside to circumambulate the pagoda. After they have all returned to their original positions, the senior householder kneels down in front of a senior monk. The senior monk preaches the Dharma to him. The next day after taking a bath, the householder again holds the incense burner before the senior monk and announces to the assembly that he would like to donate the use of his home for the monastery's summer retreat. *JXXL* (*T* 45:871c), rule 24 for mealtime reads: "At the time of *xingxiang*, monks should not cross their hands. Hands should be outside the sleeves with the palms pressed together. Monks should not laugh or joke."

When the Japanese pilgrim Ennin (794–864) went to China, he observed the practice of *xingxiang* performed in the Kaiyuan 開元 Temple (present-day Jiangsu province) and recorded the ceremony in detail in his diary (*Nittō guhō junrei kōki*, the third year of Kaicheng 開成 [838], *NBZ* 113:182). The following is taken from

Edwin Reischauer's translation (*Ennin's Diary: The Record of a Pilgrimage to China in Search of the Law* [New York: Ronald Press, 1955], 61–62):

> Early in the morning the monastic congregations gathered in this monastery and seated themselves in rows in the flanking building on the east, north, and west. At 8 A.M. the Minister of State and the General entered the monastery by the great gate. . . . In front of the hall were two bridges. The Minister of State mounted the eastern bridge and the General the western bridge, and thus the two of them circled around from the east and west and met at the center door of the hall. They took their seats and worshiped the Buddha.
>
> After that, several tens of monks lined up in rows at both the east and west doors of the hall. Each one held artificial lotus flowers and green banners. A monk struck a stone triangle and chanted, "All be worshipful and reverence the three eternal treasures. After that the Minister of State and the General arose and took censers, and the prefectural officials all followed after them, taking incense cups. They divided, going to the east and west, with the Minister of State going towards the east. The monks who were carrying flowered banners preceded him, chanting.

For two interesting articles on Buddhist cleric ceremonies, see Ōtani Kōshō, "Tōdai Bukkyō no girei: toku ni hōe ni tsuite," part 1, *Shigaku zasshi* 46, no. 10 (1935): 1183–1231; part 2, *Shigaku zasshi* 46, no. 11 (1935): 1377–1405; Ono Katsutoshi, "Ennin no mita Tō no Bukkyō girei," in *Jikaku Daishi kenkyū*, ed. Fukui Kōjun (Tokyo: Tendai Gakkai, 1964), 171–208.

161. "The one who has victoriously passed beyond" is one of the ten designations of the Buddha.

162. *shu* 疏.

163. Here reference is to the chanting of the ten epithets of the Buddhas and bodhisattvas. "The Pure Dharma Body" is the beginning of the first sentence, which, in full, reads, "The Pure Dharma Body Vairocana Buddha." Regarding the content of these epithets, see the discussion in the section "Daoan's Regulations" in Chapter 1. See also *DZZ* 2:351; Matsuura Shūkō, *Zenshū kojitsu gemon no kenkyū* (Tokyo: Sankibō Busshorin, 1981) 9–57.

164. Each strike of the hammer should correspond to one chanting of the Buddha's name. If the hammer is struck at the wrong word and during midsentence, it is considered akin to striking the Buddha's head or feet. Cf. *JXXL* (*T* 45:871c), rule 26 for mealtime: When one chants, one recitation of the name of the Buddha must be simultaneous with each bow. One must not chant too quickly or too slowly. One must chant with careful precision.

165. *shisheng fo* 十聲佛: the recitation of the ten epithets of the Buddhas. For the ten epithets of the Buddhas and bodhisattvas, see the section "Daoan's Regulations" in Chapter 1.

166. That is, the early meal.

167. See *MSL* 29 (*T* 22:462c22–23).

168. *sande liuwei* 三德六味. Food should be prepared with three "virtues" (it should be soft, clean, and correctly prepared) and six "tastes" (bitter, sour, sweet, spicy, salty and mild). The phrase "three virtues and six tastes" appears in the southern version of the *Dabo niepan jing* 1 (*Mahāparinirvāṇa-sūtra*; henceforth *Niepan jing* 涅槃經; *T* 12:606b1–3).

169. *wuchang* 五常. The Five Endurances given by Daoxuan in *JXXL* (*T* 45: 872b3) are the same as those listed above. Here it is worth noting that a footnote appearing on page 49 of *YZS* confuses these Five Endurances with the *wuchang* defined by the Confucian tradition.

170. *heshi* 喝食.

171. In *YZS* this term appears as *jieshi* 接食, meaning "receiving food." However, in the Korean version of *Chanyuan qinggui*, the term appears as *yishi* 揖食, meaning "in honor of the food." Here I have followed the Korean text. Cf. *YZS* **[52]**.

172. *kutou* 庫頭. For discussion of the position of supply master, see the section "Supply Master" in fasc. 4.

173. *xingchen* 行襯.

174. *hezhang* 合掌.

175. *fupa* 複帕.

176. *boshi* 缽拭. Dōgen describes the bowl wiper as a towel fourteen inches in length. See *DZZ* 2:350.

177. *jingjin* 淨巾.

178. *bodan* 缽單.

179. *fenzi* 鐼子.

180. *chijin* 匙筋.

181. *boshua* 缽刷.

182. *chusheng* 出生. See "Heritage from the Vinaya Tradition" in Chapter 1.

Another divinity who receives food offerings is Hārītī (Guizi mu 鬼子母). Yijing observed that in India and Southeast Asia, during the meal, food is offered to the Holy Monk before being distributed to the monks (*NJNZ* 1 [*T* 54:209b]). After all the food has been distributed, one dish of food is offered to Hārītī. Yijing explains the origin of this custom:

> The old lady [Hārītī] in a previous life swore to eat up all the children in the city of Rājagṛiha. Because of her evil vow, she was reborn as a *yakṣa* [yaocha 藥叉; evil spirit] and gave birth to five hundred children. As a *yakṣa*, she returned to the city and began eating other people's children and feeding them to her own. People reported this to the Buddha, who then hid her youngest child. She searched far and wide for this missing child and finally she came to the Buddha. The Buddha asked her: "Do you love your children? You have five hundred children and now that you have lost but one you feel pity. What about those people whose children you have eaten who had only one or two children?" The Buddha thereupon converted her and she received the five precepts to become a *upāsikā* [female lay follower]. She then inquired of the Buddha, "From now on how can I feed all my five hundred children?" The Buddha replied, "The temples and places where monks live will offer food every day to feed you." Accordingly, in all the temples of the West, in their doorways or on the side of their kitchens, there is an image of a mother embracing a child with several children at her knees. Here, every day, food is offered in abundance. The figure of this old woman is one of four divine guardians. This figure [of Hārītī] has a great deal of power. Those who are ailing or without offspring come to offer her food so that their wish will be fulfilled.

Hārītī is mentioned in the Vinaya: "In the Divine State [China] Hārītī appeared under the name Guizi mu ('the mother of demon children')." For the story of

Hārītī, see the sutra *Guizi mu jing* (*T* 21:290c–291c) and *Mohe moye jing* (*T* 12: 1006c18–1007a6). Guizi mu appears in the *Four Part Vinaya* as the goddess of fertility (*SFL* [*T* 22:782b, *T* 22:911a, and *T* 22:950b]).

Chanyuan qinggui apparently adopted the Kuangye 曠野 version of the story. *YZS* **[53]** includes the verse chanted during the food offering. The verse chanted by monks and nun in Chinese monasteries today during *chusheng* indicates that both Kuangye and Hārītī receive offerings. In addition, food is offered to the *Suparṇin* bird, who used to eat dragons but now lives on offerings. (*Da loutan jing* 大 3 [*T* 1:288b–c]). This verse is as follows: "May the *Suparṇin* bird, with its great wings, the spirit Kuangye, and Rākṣasī Hārītī be filled with sweet dews" 大鵬金 翅鳥、曠野鬼神眾、羅剎鬼子母、甘露悉充滿.

183. *jingren* 淨人: untonsured servers.

184. The same rule is found in *JXXL* (*T* 45:872a). See rule 37 regarding meal-time.

185. See *JXXL* (*T* 45:871c), rule 11 pertaining to mealtime: The bowl should be level with the chest, held neither too high nor too low.

186. *bianchui* 遍槌.

187. *wuguan* 五觀. The custom of contemplating the five virtues did not orig-inate with Chan practice. The same statement of five contemplations is given in Daoxuan's *SXC* 2C (*T* 40:84a9–12) and *SXC* 3C (*T* 40:128b3–c10). In the twenti-eth section, "Method of Offering Food" 對施興治篇, Daoxuan notes that the con-templations during mealtime can be divided into five categories as stated in [*Lü ershier*] *Mingliao lun*. I am unable, however, to locate the exact citation in the ver-sion of *Mingliao lun* in *Taisho shinshū daizōkyō* (*T* 24:665b–73a).

Matsuura Shūkō argues that the five contemplations given in *Mingliao lun* were compiled from fragments taken from other sutras or Vinaya texts. The dia-gram presented by Matsuura shows that the first contemplation was adopted from *Zengyi ehan jing* 12 (*T* 2:603c29) and *Sapoduo bu pini modelejia* 6 (*Sarvāstivā-davinaya-mātṛkā*, *T* 23:602b6); the second from *PNMJ;* the third from the Vinaya; the fourth from *Zengyi Ehan* 12 (*T* 2:604a6), *Bieyi za Ehan jing* 1 (*T* 2:375a28), and *SSL;* and the fifth from *Zengyi Ehan jing* 12 (*T* 2:604a2) and *Bieyi za Ehan jing* 1 (*T* 2:375a28). See Matsuura, *Gemon*, 5.

188. This verse may have been adopted from *Shishi fashi* (*ZZK* 2-6-3:215c), compiled by the Tiantai monk Zunshi 遵式 (964–1032), which, in turn, appears to have been taken from the Tantric monk Amoghavajra's *Shi zhu egui yinshi ji shui fa* (*T* 21:466c).

189. See *JXXL* (*T* 45:871c), rule 35 pertaining to mealtime: "One must lift the bowl up to one's mouth."

190. Similar concepts were adopted in both the Chan and Lü schools. In *JXXL* (*T* 45:871b26), rule 7 pertaining to mealtime, Daoxuan indicates, "The upper two-thirds of the outside of the bowl is considered 'pure,' the lower third is 'soiled.'"

191. The fourth and fifth fingers of both hands are considered the "soiled" fingers (*chuzhi* 觸指). They are used to wash away fecal waste.

192. The following are quoted from rules 26–47 in the "Hundred Myriad Rules to Be Learned" 百種學法 in *SFL* 20 (*T* 22:702b–709a). Corresponding sections may also be found in *MSL* 22 (*T* 22:403c–407b); *WFL* 10 (*T* 22:74c–75c); and *SXC* 2C (*T* 40:90b–c).

193. *T* 22:702c14.

194. *T* 22:703b9–10.
195. *T* 22:703c11.
196. *T* 22:704a9.
197. *T* 22:704b10.
198. *T* 22:704c14.
199. *T* 22:705a12.
200. *T* 22:705b15.
201. *T* 22:705c13–14.
202. *T* 22:706a10. Cf. *JXXL* (*T* 45:872a), rule 44 pertaining to mealtime.
203. *T* 22:706b6.
204. *T* 22:706c2.
205. *T* 22:706c22–23.
206. *T* 22:707a14–15. Cf. *JXXL* (*T* 45:872a), rule 52 pertaining to mealtime: If one spills the broth, juice, or rice onto one's napkin, one should not pick it up and eat it.
207. *T* 22:707b16–17. Cf. *JXXL* (*T* 45:871c), rule 35 pertaining to mealtime: One should not allow the cheeks to bulge with food like a monkey hiding its food.
208. *T* 22:707c11–12.
209. *T* 22:708a4.
210. *T* 22:708a25.
211. *T* 22:708b16. Cf. *JXXL* (*T* 45:872a), rule 44 pertaining to mealtime.
212. *T* 22:708c7.
213. *T* 22:708c29.
214. *MSL* 35 (*T* 22:513c6–10) presents some guidelines with regard to sneezing in the meditation hall. While in the meditation hall the monk should not sneeze with deliberate loudness. If he feels that he might sneeze, he should pinch his nose. If he still cannot avoid sneezing, he should do so only after covering his nose to prevent soiling his neighbors.

Concerning the proper response to another's sneezing, the Vinaya texts provide some interesting variations. According to *SFL* 53 (*T* 22:960b11–13) after the Buddha sneezed, a few monks responded with "[May the Honorable One have a] long life." Soon all the monks, nuns, and laypeople present began haphazardly to echo this phrase. The scene turned chaotic, prompting the Buddha's censure. *SSL* 39 (*T* 23:276b21–25) offers a slightly different version. After the monks response, the Buddha asked them whether he would indeed obtain longevity because of their words. The monks replied, "No." "Then from now on you should not say such things," replied the Buddha, thus forbidding the use of the phrase in this context. (The same episode is expanded in *GSP[Z]* 10 [*T* 24:248a18–249a2].) However, *SFL* 53 (*T* 22:960b13–19) continues the story. Sometime later a layperson sneezed and, because the monks were forbidden to respond, there was only silence. The layperson complained that the monks failed to bestow on him their blessing of longevity. The Buddha then relented, giving monks permission to extend the blessing to laypeople only. The same account is recorded in the Pāli Vinaya; see Horner, *Discipline*, 5:195.

MSL indicates that when a senior monk sneezes, a junior should say "Salute to you" *henan* 和南 skt. *Vandana;* When a junior sneezes, however, the senior remains silent. A different rule is given in *Genben sapoduobu lüshe* 13 (*T* 24:599b8–11).

The text states that when a senior monk sneezes, a junior one should say, "*Vandana* 畔睇"; when a junior one sneezes, the senior says "*Ārogya* 阿路祇" (literally "without sickness"). Indeed, one committed a misdemeanor if these remarks were not made after a sneeze. Regarding elderly women or *mahalla* 莫訶羅 (old and ailing laymen or monks), it was not considered a transgression to say aloud, "May you have a long life."

215. *zhenyan* 真言: literally, "true words."

216. That is, the Buddhas.

217. Another possible translation is: "Quaking with a power that rivals the heroes [that is, the Buddhas] in all ten directions, past, present, and future."

218. *huiyi zhuanguo* 回因轉果. According to Dōchū's annotation (*CHSS* 2: 818b–c), to "revert causes" means to move from *shijue* 始覺 (the enlightenment attained after cultivating religious practices) to *benjue* 本覺 (the original state of enlightenment). This is the wisdom that leads one to exit the cycle of birth and death. To "transform effects" is to exit *benjue* and move back to the state of *shijue*. This is the compassion that encourages one to leave nirvana. If one is able to "revert" or "transform" back and forth freely, it is because one has physical strength and energy after enjoying a meal.

219. *dazuo chatang* 大座茶湯. As the later text *CBQG* 7 (*T* 48:1152c) indicates, *dazuo chatang* is the tea ceremony held for the chief seat and the assembly. It is sponsored by the prior during the season of the four festivals, that is, the commencement and closing of summer retreat, winter solstice, and New Year.

220. *fangcan* 放參. The word *can* literally means "to inquire." A student inquires about the truth by consulting his teacher. *CBQG* 2 (*T* 48:1119b29) defines *can* as the time when the abbot gathers the assembly and preaches the Dharma. Here *fangcan* obviously refers to the occasions when monks were excused from the morning sermon.

221. That is, if the sermon is to be for the feast donor.

222. *zhantuo* 盞橐.

223. *tewei chatang* 特為茶湯.

224. That is, they should not forget the ceremony schedule.

225. *tangtou chatang* 堂頭茶湯.

226. *chayao* 茶藥: "tea medicine." This term refers to confections made from medicinal herbs. An excellent article on tea and confections is Tanaka Misa's "Sōdai no kissa to chayaku," *Shisō* 48 (1991): 279–285. Tanaka examines the term *chayao* (Jpn. *sayaku*) as it appears in historical records, the diary of the Japanese monk Jōjin (*San Tendai Godaisan ki*), and *Chanyuan qinggui*, to discern the word's meaning. She notes that the word *chayao* appears in the historical records as two separate terms: "tea" and "medicinal herbs" (p. 280). Jōjin's diary describes his visit to China, where the monks served tea, confections, and nuts (or fruit, *guo* 果), all of which were considered *chayao*. In *Chanyuan qinggui* the term appears as a single word, meaning "confection taken with tea."

Tanaka (p. 283) argues that during the Song-Yuan period *xiangyao* 香藥 ("fragrant medicine") and *shiyao* 食藥 ("food medicine") were actually confections made from medicinal herbs or fruits. She concludes that there is a long-standing Chinese belief that medicine and food derive from the same source. Although *chayao* may not be a monastic invention, it does reflect the idea prevalent in Buddhist temples that food is a primary source of medicine (p. 285). This is also evident in the monks' referring to supper as *yaoshi* ("medicine stone"): monks are said to partake of supper solely to sustain their health, not to please their palates.

227. *kuxia* 庫下.

228. That is, if he were to punish monks severely whenever they are absent.

229. *liaozhong laci* 寮中臘次.

230. *Qing yinyuan* 請因緣: the beginning of the period of time when the abbot's room will be open for students to enter and make their inquiries. The *qing ying-yuan* ceremony is referred to as *gaoxiang* 告香 ("an inquiry and offering of incense to the master") in the later texts *JDQG* (1274), *BYQG* (1311), and *CBQG* (1335). However, *RRQG* (1209) retains the term *qing yinyuan*. *JDQG* 2 (*ZZK* 2-17-1: 16b10) mentions that previous tradition forbade monks from engaging in the practice of entering the abbot's room to request instruction without first holding the *gaoxiang* ceremony.

231. That is, if there is a monk who has received the abbot's private instruction in the past.

232. *rushi* 入室. A diagram displaying the proper way of entering the abbot's room is provided by Dōchū in his *ZSS*, 647b. He also indicated that outside the abbot's quarters a statue of Bodhidharma was enshrined. Although this statue is not mentioned in *Chanyuan qinggui*, it is referred to in *CBQG* 2 (*T* 48:1120c21).

233. *Lang* 廊: literally, "corridor by corridor."

234. Originally, this kind of interview was not granted on a regular basis. As indicated in *Chanmen guishi* (*T* 51:251a14), the practice of entering the room to request instruction was subject to the learner's discretion. However, the later *JDQG* 2 (*ZZK* 2-17-1:16b13) states that interviews were arranged for days of the month ending in the number three or eight (e.g., the third, the thirteenth, etc.) with some exceptions. By the time *CBQG* 2 (*T* 48:1120c19) was compiled, the appointed meetings were firmly fixed on these "three" and "eight" days.

235. Here the right- and left-hand sides are determined by the orientation of the abbot sitting within. (See the diagram "Entering the Room" in *ZSS*, 647b.)

236. *toulou xiaoxi* 透漏消息.

237. *juhua* 舉話.

238. *tonghua* 通話.

239. *qingyi* 請益. For the term *qingyi*, see *Liji* ("Quli" 曲禮, *SJZ*1:1240a; Legge, *Li Chi*, 1:75): "When requesting (instruction) on the subject of his studies, (the learner) should rise; when requesting further information (*qingyi*), he should rise" 請業則起,請益則起.

Fascicle Two

1. *shangtang* 上堂. *YZS* **[79]** specifies that the ceremony in which the abbot ascends his seat to preach in the Dharma hall is held on the "fifth day." This "fifth day" can be interpreted in two ways: any day ending in a five (the fifth, the tenth, the fifteenth, and the twenty-fifth); or every five days (the first, the fifth, the tenth, etc.). However, according to the later *JDQG* (*ZKK* 2-17-1:15b), "four days—the fifth, the tenth, the twentieth, and the twenty-fifth—are known as *wucan shang-tang* 五參上堂 [the ascending of the hall on the 'fifth' day]." This supports the second interpretation. The number of "fifth days" was eventually reduced from six to four because the first and the fifteenth of each month coincided with the

new moon and full moon, respectively, when prayers were offered on the emperor's behalf. However, it is important to note that in *Chanyuan qinggui* this practice is carried out every five days, as was the custom among Chinese government officials. (See "Chinese Influences" in Chapter 2.).

2. *gongjie* 公界. This term has several possible meanings: a public or commonly owned item; a common practice; or a fixed date. Here the third meaning is used, and the fixed dates referred to are the fifth, the tenth, the twentieth, and the twenty-fifth of each month.

3. *zaocan* 早參.

4. *fatang* 法堂. See the section "Structure of the Monastery" in Chapter 2.

5. *yanxing* 鴈行. *SSL* 40 (*T* 23:289b14) relates how the Buddha, when he saw monks entering the hall in a haphazard fashion, instructed them to walk in "wild geese formation." *SFL* 49 (*T* 22:935a20–21) notes that if a donor arrived to extend an invitation, monks should present themselves in wild geese formation with senior monks in the front. Rule 8 of *JXXL* (*T* 45:872b12), which deals with exiting the hall after the meal, states, "After exiting the hall gate, monks walk on one side of the corridor, maintaining wild geese formation." A similar custom was observed in secular Chinese society. *Liji* ("Wangzhi" 王制, *SJZ* 1:1347b; Legge, *Li Chi* 2:244) notes that "A man kept behind another who had a father's years; he followed one who might be his elder brother more closely but still keeping behind, as geese fly after one another in a row. Friends did not pass by one another, when going the same way" 父之齒隨行、兄之齒鴈行、朋友不相踰.

6. *tuiyuan zhanglao* 退院長老. *ZTSY* 8 (*ZKK* 2-18-1:113c) notes that the abbot of the Chan monastery was called *zhanglao*, the senior one.

7. That is, the prior, the rector, the cook, and the superintendent.

8. *baixi* 拜蓆.

9. *tongxing* 童行. Historical usage of the term *tongxing* has been inconsistent and vague. Tang-era documents indicate that the word is a combination of *tongzi* 童子 ("boy [postulant]") and *xingzhe* 行者 ("[adult] server"). However, a Song legal document found in *QTS* 50 (p. 469) seems to assert that the word is derived from *Daotong* 道童 ("Daoist boy") and *xingzhe* 行者 ("Buddhist postulant"), sometimes interchanging *tongxing* with the title *xingtong* 行童, an inversion of the former. In any case, a *tongxing*, in either the Buddhist or Daoist hierarchy, was undoubtedly a person who had entered the order for a probationary period and not yet become a formal priest. In *Chanyuan qinggui, tongxing* is used to refer to Buddhist postulants only, including both the servers (*xingzhe*) and the purity-keepers (*jingren*). It was customary for a postulant to enter the monastery without shaving his head and to take the tonsure at a later date. A postulant was given a religious name and was registered with the government but, as *QTS* 51 (p. 480) stipulates, he was still obliged to pay a labor tax (*shending* 身丁) as long as his head remained unshaved.

A postulant (or anyone else) could take the tonsure by passing the sutra examinations or by imperial decree. Both of these were almost completely replaced by the trading of tonsure certificates on the open market when the Song government began selling large numbers of these certificates. For more discussion on the sale of tonsure certificates, see "Chinese Influences in Chapter 2." Once he had been tonsured and had taken the ten precepts, the postulant became a novice and was then required to undergo full ordination (two hundred and fifty precepts) to become a monk (*daseng* 大僧, bhikṣu). During the first ten years after full ordination, the monk was considered a junior monk (*xiaoshi*). *SJLP,* a commentary to the Pāli Vinaya, states that any man living in the monastery for a probationary period was called *paṇḍupalāsa* (*T* 24:753a23–25).

Moroto Tatsuo argues that the system of postulancy did not become prevalent until the end of the Tang and Five Dynasties (about the tenth century c.e.). Before this period, in the Southern-Northern dynasties, postulants did exist, but most monks simply entered the monastery and had their heads shaved immediately. The system of postulancy was first created solely by the central government in response to the fact that many citizens were taking the tonsure to avoid the state's compulsory labor law. (Tax exemption was not yet in effect for monastics. See Moroto, *Chūgoku Bukkyō seidoshi,* 439.) The government decided to assume control of the tonsure process rather than allow monasteries themselves to monitor the number of those admitted. Quotas were set for the monasteries, restricting the number of people who could be tonsured in a given time period. Furthermore, any individual who wished to become a monk first had to receive permission from the government and was later required to register after taking the tonsure to be eligible for labor exemption status. Private tonsure was strictly outlawed. The resulting backlog of tonsure candidates, and the delays caused by each step of the mandatory process, insured that at any given time a large group of monastic applicants could be found within the monastery waiting for official permission. Thus the status of postulant was born. See also Moroto's thorough discussion of the system of postulants, pp. 233–275. For a discussion of government regulation of the Buddhist postulancy in the Song period, see Tsukamoto Zenryū, "Sō jidai no zunnan shikyō tokudo no seido," in his *Chūgoku kinsei Bukkyōshi no shomondai* (Tokyo: Daitō Shuppansha, 1975). For a discussion of governmental regulation before the Song period, see Fujiyoshi Masumi, "Tō Godai no zunnan seido," *Tōyōshi kenkyū* 21, no. 1 (1962): 1–26.

10. *kutang* 庫堂. The storage hall functioned not only as storage space, but more importantly as a kitchen. Some scholars have preferred the translation "kitchen hall." In *Chanyuan qinggui,* terms such as *kuxia* 庫下 and *kusi* 庫司 tend to be used interchangeably with *kutang.* But these three terms also seem to have had subtle distinctions. Judging from context, one may conclude that *kusi* is the title of the position and the office, whereas *kuxia* refers to the department and *kutang* to the building itself. In later monastic texts, terms such as *kuli* 庫裡, *kuyuan* 庫院, and *chuku* 廚庫 also appear.

11. *[fa]zuo* [法]座.

12. *chanyi* 禪椅.

13. *shaoxiang shizhe* 燒香侍香.

14. 盧山圓通. The reference here is to the lineage of Fayuan Faxiu 法雲法秀 (1027–1090), who received the honorary title of Chan Master Yuantong from Emperor Shenzong 神宗. He is reported to have stayed at the Qixian Monastery 棲賢寺 in Lushan (present-day Jiangxi province). Faxiu is one of the Dharma heirs of Tianyi Yihuai 天衣義懷 and is of the same generation as Zongze's master, Changlu Yingfu. Before going to study with Yingfu, Zongze was tonsured under Faxiu.

15. *shizhu* 施主 (Skt. *dānapati*). Yijing (*NJNZ* 1 [*T* 54:211b10–12]) makes the following comments on the Chinese translations of this term: "The Sanskrit *dā-*

napati is best translated as *shizhu* 施主—*dāna* as *shi; pati* as *zhu. Tanyue* 檀越, another Chinese translation of *dānapati,* is incorrect from the start. This improper translation came about by omitting the syllable *na* from *dāna,* and then transliterating *dā* into Chinese as *tan.* Finally the word *yue* ('to transcend') was added, meaning that through donations, one may transcend one's own poverty. Although a wonderful translation, [*tanyue*] is still quite different from the original text."

16. "At the upper shoulder" of the administrators, that is, in a position closer to the Dharma seat and therefore higher in honor.

17. *zhushi* 主事. The meaning here is the same as *zhishi* 知事. See *SSYL* (*T* 54: 301c).

18. In this passage describing the ceremony as it moves from one hall to another, it is unclear precisely which action takes place in which hall. In this translation I offer what seems to me the most plausible interpretation.

19. *xiatang zhong* 下堂鐘. The bell is struck in a series of three sequences. Cf. *CBQG* 2 (*T* 48:1119b11) and fasc. 1, n. 136.

20. The Chinese text of this sentence is unclear; my translation is merely one possible interpretation.

21. *zhitang* 直堂. For a detailed discussion of the monitor's appointment and duties, see the section "Sangha Hall Monitor," *YZS* **[158]** in fasc. 4.

22. *touxiu* 頭袖: literally, "head sleeve." The use of the sleevelike cowl is generally said to have originated in an encounter between a master and an emperor, but the versions put forth by the Chan and the Tiantai traditions vary as to the time and place of the incident. The Chan account of the cowl's origination, according to Wuzhun Shifan 無準師範 (1177–1249), involves Emperor Dai 代宗 (r. 763–779) of the Tang dynasty and the first patriarch of the Jingshan lineage, Chan master Faqin Guoyi 法欽國一 (714–792), who was highly respected and patronized by the emperor. On one particularly cold day, the emperor is said to have cut the sleeve off his embroidered garment and wrapped it around the master's head. See *Wuzhun Fan Chanshi yulu* 無準範禪師語錄 6 (*ZZK* 2-26-5:483a).

The Tiantai school offers a similar story in connection with its founder Zhiyi 智顗 (538–597), who was favored by Emperor Yang 煬帝 (r. 605–616) of the Sui dynasty. *Shūhō zasshū* 宗鳳雜集 (cited in *ZSS,* 694a–b), a missing Japanese Tentai text, records an episode in which Emperor Yang, who at that time (591 C.E.) was still Prince Guang, invited Zhiyi to give him the bodhisattva precepts. Because of the cold weather, the emperor took the colorful sleeve from his imperial garment and wrapped it around the master's head during the ceremony. However, Dōchū comments that this incident is not found in any Chinese record.

SFL 41 (*T* 22:866a2–3) states that during the winter some monks caught a chill and reported this to the Buddha, who then allowed them to wear hats. The same text (*SFL* 40 [*T* 22:858a9–10]) indicates that when a monk caught a cold or had a headache and reported this to the Buddha, he allowed him to keep his head warm with a hat made of wool or cotton (*karpāsa* 劫貝). *DSW* 1 (*T* 24:916b17–18) states that one should not wear a hat while worshiping the Buddha.

23. *tangsi xingzhe* 堂司行者.

24. *dadian* 大殿. This may be an abbreviation for the Great Hero Treasure Shrine *daxiong baodian* 大雄寶殿, that is, the Buddha shrine. Master Baizhang neglected to build the Buddha shrine at his monastery, and Master Deshan Xuan-

jian 德山宣鑑 (782?–865) actively dismantled the shrine wherever he served as abbot. Both instances would seem to indicate not only the reduced importance of the Buddha shrine in the Chinese tradition, but also active opposition to its presence. However, as this shrine was symbolic of the Buddha's manifestation inside the monastery, it could not be cast aside so easily. Thus in Song texts and diagrams of Song monasteries, the Buddha shrine is still mentioned and is located at the very center of the monastic compound. See the diagrams of Tiantongshan, Lingyinshan, and Wannianshan 萬年山 in GJZ (ZD, zuroku, p. 12–13; CHSS 2:1286–1288).

GSP(Z) 26 (T 24:331b28–c1) relates a story in which the Buddha, in order to convert a non-Buddhist, used his supernatural powers to step on the floor of the fragrant shrine (xiangdian 香殿), causing the earth to shake. Yijing, in his translation, comments on the meaning of the term "fragrant shrine": "In the West, 'fragrant shrine' refers to the hall in which the Buddha dwells and is given the name gandhakuṭī, gandha meaning 'fragrance' and kuṭī meaning 'room.' Thus [gandhakuṭī] can be translated as 'fragrant room,' 'fragrant platform,' or 'fragrant shrine.' So as not to desecrate the honorable face [of the Buddha], one should refer to him only by the name of the place in which he dwells, just as here [in China] one refers to [the emperor only by honorific titles that indicate the emperor's location, such as] wangjie 王階 or bixia 陛下 ('Imperial Stairs'). To refer to [the place in which the Buddha dwells] simply as the Buddha hall or the Buddha shrine is to disregard [the great deference] intended [by the title as used] in the West."

25. tuditang 土地堂. The earth hall was the shrine of the guardian deities of the temple. Precisely what image was enshrined in this building is not known. Cf. n. 28 below.

26. lianzhong 斂鐘. It is said that the performance of lianzhong differed from school to school. In the Lü tradition, the bell was struck so that a tightly rolled trilling emerged, while in the Chan seven clear strokes were required. SXC 1A (T 40:6c14–5) describes the former: "Thus one strikes softly with the hammer. As the number of strikes increases, the strikes themselves should diminish in intensity until at last a quiet roll is achieved." SXCZ 1A (T 40:186c4), in its annotations to SXC, defines lian as "to finish [striking] with a quiet roll." In the Chan tradition, JDQG 1 ZKK 2-17-1:9d) indicates that "to lianzhong" is to strike seven times. Dochū (ZSS, 724a) remarks that seven strikes made in a tight roll could also be referred to as lianzhong. Daoxun's JXXL (T 45:871c), rule 10 pertaining to mealtime reads: "While waiting for the sound of lianzhong, the monk must fasten his towel [to his robe for use as a napkin] and hold his bowl, keeping the handle of his spoon turned toward his body." Rule 23 reads: "After entering the hall and before the striking of lianzhong, a monk should bow down and collect his sitting mat."

27. qielan [shen] 伽藍[神]. Qielan is an abbreviation of sengqie lanmo 僧伽藍摩 (Skt. saṃgha-ārāma), meaning "monastery." Here the word qielan refers to the guardians of the monastery. It is said that three shrines were erected within Chinese monasteries: the first was the "demon temple" (that is, the temple for Harītī, which in Chinese is rendered as Guizi mu); the second was the qielan temple (also referred to as the earth temple), in which the eighteen guardian deities were enshrined; the third was the Piṇḍola temple (SXC 3C [T 137a15–17]; SSYL 3 [T 54:303b]). Qi Fo ba pusa suoshuo datuoluoni shenzhou jing 4 (T 21:557c) lists

eighteen divine guardians who protect the monastery: sweet voice, divine voice, heavenly drum, ingenuity, praise of beauty, profundity, sound of thunder, lion's roar, wonder, divine echo, human voice, Buddha's slave, praise of virtue, wide eyes, wonderful eyes, profound hearing, profound sight, and penetrating vision.

28. *tudi [shen]* 土地[神]. *Chanyuan qinggui* does not specify which deities are considered guardians of the earth. Various names were used at different monasteries. For example, in the Jingshan 徑山 Monastery the earth guardian was referred to as *Lingze longwang* 靈澤龍王, "Dragon King in the Swamp of Miracles"; in the Lingyin Monastery he was called *Lingjiu shanwang* 靈鷲山王, "King of Vulture Mountain"; in the Xuefeng 雪峰 Monastery he was named *Songshan* 松山, "Pine Mountain"; and in the Xingshengsī 興聖寺 he was called *Qiansheng xiaowang* 千聖小王, "the Prince" (cited in *ZSS;* 143b–144a). Cf. Valerie Hansen, *Changing Gods in Medieval China, 1127–1276* (Princeton: Princeton University Press, 1990), 182.

29. This is the ritual chanting of the ten epithets of the Buddhas and bodisattvas, beginning with the first name: "The Pure Dharma Body Vairocana Buddha." See "Daoan's Regulations" in Chapter 1.

30. *Rulai dashi* 如來大師.

31. 元符, that is, 1099 C.E.

32. The verse 是日已過・命亦隨減・如少水魚・斯有何樂 can be found in *Faqu jing* 1 (*T* 4:559a). The story to which this line refers is first found in *Chuyao jing* 3 (*T* 4:621b–c). According to this text, the Buddha once lived in the Anāthapiṇḍika Garden inside Prince Jeta's forest in the region of Śrāvastī. Near this forest three fish were trapped in shallow water by a boat that obstructed their passage to deeper waters. The first fish gathered all its strength and leapt over the boat. The second fish managed to circumnavigate the vessel, passing through the grass. The third fish exhausted all its energy trying to escape and was caught by a fisherman. The Buddha witnessed this struggle through his divine eyes and, to preserve the right Dharma, he gathered the assembly and preached this gatha to illustrate the impermanence of all life.

33. *zhandao* 暫到.

34. *zhandan* 展單.

35. *ziazhang* 下帳. *Zhang* is an abbreviation of *huzhang* 戶帳 (the screen of the compartment).

36. *xiaocan* 小參. In contrast to the formal sermon that is given from the platform in the Dharma hall, the informal sermon is held in the abbot's private room. In *Chanyuan qinggui*, the informal sermon is described as an evening event and does not seem to be restricted to any particular day of the month. *ZTSY* 8 (*ZZK* 2-18-1:118d), a contemporary text, gives the following definition of *xiaocan*: "An informal sermon is any sermon given at a time not prearranged" (that is, not given according to the dictates of the regular monastic schedule). The later *CBQG* 2 (*T* 48:1119c11) indicates that the informal sermon was also held in the Dharma hall. In addition, *CBQG* 2 (*T* 48:1119c5–7) refers to evening sermons held on certain special occasions as informal sermons. These special occasions were: the arrival of a new abbot at the monastery; the visit of an official donor to the monastery; a special invitation for the abbot to give a sermon; a funeral service; and any of the four festivals.

37. *jiyang zongzhi* 激揚宗旨.

38. *faming jingu* 發明今古.

39. *jiaxung* 家訓.

40. *chuye* 初夜. According to Indian custom, day and night were each divided into three phases. The three day phases were morning (approximately 6:00–10:00 A.M.), midday (10:00 A.M.–2:00 P.M.), and sunset (2:00–6:00 P.M.): The three phases of the night were: early night (6:00–10:00 P.M.), middle night (10:00 P.M.–2:00 A.M.), and late night (2:00–6:00 A.M.).

41. *qintang* 寢堂: literally, "rear hall" (the room was located behind the Dharma hall). *Qin* originally referred to the rear part of an imperial ancestral temple. The *qintang* was located between the Dharma hall and the abbot's quarters. The abbot gave his sermon in the Dharma hall on formal occasions but withdrew to meet people and give sermons in the *qintang*. He slept in the abbot's quarters (*fangzhang*), a practice that was largely adopted from imperial custom. See also "Influences of Chinese Culture" in Chapter 2.

42. *binzhu wenchou* 賓主問酬. The first use of this term appears in *Zutang ji* 20 (Taipei: Xinwenfeng Chubanshe, 1987), 384; cited in *ZD*, 1057a.

43. 提唱: propagation of the doctrine of the school's tradition. This term is an abbreviation of *tigang changdao* 提綱唱道, meaning to focus on the major teachings and expound on them.

44. *zhengui* 箴規.

45. *shanmen zhushou* 山門主首.

46. Dōgen adapted this sentence in his *Shuryō shingi* 衆寮箴規 (*DZZ* 2:363). He interpreted the line quite differently and replaced the word "teacher" with "the Buddha and the patriarchs" (*fozu* 佛祖) to lend emphasis to his interpretation. He wroes, "Once [the assembly and the administrator have interacted] as guest and host for even one day, [the administrator] will be regarded [by the assembly members] for the rest of their lives as the Buddha [is regarded by] the Patriarchs [that is, their relationship will forever be that of master and disciple]." See Shinohara Hisao, "*Eihei daishingi*": *Dōgen no shūdō kihan* (Tokyo: Daitō Shuppansha, 1980), 359.

47. *youfang xingjiao* 遊方行脚. *GSP* (B) 7 (*T* 24:484b11–14) indicates that a monk was not permitted to travel the world until he had been ordained for five years and had gained knowledge in five dharmas (*wufa* 五法). These five dharmas were: knowledge of what constitutes an offense; knowledge of what does not constitute an offense; knowledge of all the minor offenses; knowledge of all the grave offenses; and memorization and understanding of the Vinaya texts.

48. The reason for this restriction is unknown; it may have been to prevent suspicion falling on a monk lodging in a private residence, or it may simply be an echo of the Vinaya's strict admonition that a monk remain in possession of his robes at all times while traveling overnight. Among those precepts pertaining to the use of robes, the prohibition of overnight travel without one's robes is the rule most often emphasized (*SFL* (*T* 22:603a–4b, 632b); *WFL T* 22:24a–b, 31c–2b); *MSL T*22:293c–4a); *SSL* (*T* 23:388c); *GSP* (*T* 23:712b–c).

49. *xun* 尋. *ZTSY* 3 (*ZKK* 2-18-1:36c) indicates that one *xun* is equivalent to six feet. However, Morohashi (4:37a) states that one *xun* may be as long as seven or eight feet.

50. *chuantang* 穿堂.

51. *xingdao* 行道.

52. *chencan muqing* 晨參暮請.

53. In *Shimen guijing yi* 2 (*T* 45:862a25–27), Daoxun contrasts the different ways of showing respect in China and India. In India, exposing one's shoulder and baring one's feet were considered a show of respect, while in China respect was shown by dressing as fully as possible, with a scarf covering one's head and shoes on one's feet.

54. The term used here is *jiaoban*, a gaiter-like cloth protecting the lower leg.

55. 袄衣. Dōchū (*ZSS*, 716a), citing *Zhenzi tong* (*shenji xia* 申集下, p. 11b) claimed that *chayi* were undergarments (*xiefu* 褻服). The precise meaning of *chayi*, Dōchū insisted, had been unclear in Japan until the arrival of the *Zhenzi tong* text, which gives a specific definition of the term. However, as we see in *Eihei shingi* (*DZZ* 2:317–319), Dōgen interpreted *chayi* (Jpn. *shae*) rather differently. *Shae* was used by Dōgen as a verb meaning "to fold the *kāṣāya* over the left arm," as opposed to placing it on the shoulder or simply as a noun referring to the *kāṣāya* itself (see Shinohara, *Eihei daishingi*, 103). Dōgen's *Bendōwa* (*DZZ* 2:317–318) gives the following description: "In the evening, the monks *shae* and enter the hall. They retrieve their cushions from their own units in preparation for meditation, but they do not display their bedding. There is also the time-honored method of half unfolding the mattresses, that is, the *kāṣāya* is taken from the arm and placed on the quilt before meditating."

Another example is given in the same text (*DZZ* 2:319): "Sometimes the director of the assembly quarters will *shae* before burning incense. Sometimes he will put his *kāṣāya* on his shoulder before burning incense." It would seem that the term *chayi* originally meant the undergarments themselves, but that its meaning evolved until it referred more to a practice than simply to a garment. After traveling to China, Dōgen adopted the practice of *chayi* in his own monastic code. At any rate, it seems to me most unlikely that *Chanyuan qinggui* would find it necessary to prohibit the wearing of undergarments alone while meditating or reading sutra; such an act would be unthinkable in this highly formalized and communal setting: I propose that this must be a caveat against wearing one's *kāṣāya* in an unseemly manner while engaged in sacred activity.

56. 掛子. This item of clothing was also referred to as *luozi* 络子 or *gualuo* 掛络. *CBQG* (*T* 48:1145b) identifies the *gualuo* as a five-strip robe See "Personal Possessions" in Chapter 2. For an illustration of the *guazi*, see Mochitsuki, 1257c.

57. *daidao youxie* 帶刀右脇. Lying on the right side has traditionally been regarded as the only legitimate sleeping position for the Buddhist. For example, see *Zhong Ehan jing* 8 (*T* 1:473c13) and *Zhong Ehan jing* 20 (*T* 1:560a3). The reference to sleeping as though carrying a knife stems from the practice of warriors of the time, who carried their knives on their left sides and therefore always slept on their right. Baizhang's biography (*GSZ* 10 [*T* 50:770c27]) mentions that one of Baizhang's regulations stipulated that a monk must lie sideways with his head on the pillow and with only his side touching the bed, as though he were carrying a knife.

58. *bantou* 板頭.

59. Holding the curtain as one passes and releasing it slowly is a practice intended to prevent noise. Rule 34 in Daoxuan's *JXXL* (*T* 45:869c) reads as follows:

"When releasing the curtain, one should not let it drop but should return it by hand."

60. *qingzhong* 清眾.

61. *zundian* 尊殿.

62. *shiluo* 尸羅 (Skt. *śīla*).

63. *shiseng* 師僧.

64. *bikong liaotian* 鼻孔撩天.

65. *youdi* 有底. See *Zengo jiten,* ed. Koga Hidehiko (Kyoto: Shibunkaku, 1991), 29a.

66. That is, if he shirks responsibility or is unwilling to face dangers.

67. *tisi* 提撕.

68. *weiqu* 委曲.

69. That is, if he fails to instruct, the teachings will die.

70. *fayao* 法藥, that is, when he hears the master's teaching.

71. *jiexia* 結夏.

72. *chatang renshi* 茶湯人事.

73. *niansong pai* 念誦牌.

74. *fashi*[b] 法事: "Dharma things" or "Dharma affairs." The term *fashi* in the present text has three meanings: the Dharma service; a monk who is appointed to preside over the Dharma service; and the items used in the Dharma service. The context suggests that the third definition is meant here.

75. *yandi* 炎帝. This is a reference to one of the Five Heavenly Emperors (*wu* [*tian*] *di* 五[天]帝, who were worshiped since ancient times. For further details, see "Influences of Chinese Culture" in Chapter 2.

76. That is, when the Buddha prohibits traveling—during the summer retreat.

77. That is, the monks.

78. *wande hongming* 萬德洪名.

79. *huixiang* 回向.

80. *hetang zhenzhu* 合堂真主.

81. *zunzhong* 尊眾.

82. Reference here is to the chant: "[Pay homage to] all the Buddhas in all ten directions and in all three ages, all the great boddhisattvas, and the great perfection of wisdom" 十方三世一切諸佛、諸尊菩薩、摩訶薩、摩訶般若波羅蜜. See *YZS* **[315].**

83. *fashi*[b] 法事.

84. *jiela pai* 戒蠟牌. This diagram indicates the year of ordination of each monk attending the summer retreat and their positions within the hierarchy of ordination seniority. One cannot discern the exact appearance of this document from *Chanyuan qinggui*; however, an illustration of this diagram first appeared in *Keizan shingi* (*T* 82:443b). In the upper center of the illustration there is a circle with the character *jing* 鏡 (mirror) written inside it. Below this circle, there is a rectangular shape with the words *qingjing dahuizhong* 清淨大海眾 ("Assembly of purity, in number vast as the ocean"). Below this line appears the character for the Holy Monk, written as Kauṇḍinya. There are four characters—*yuan* 元, *heng* 亨, *li* 利, and *zheng* 貞—written in each of the four corners indicating a counterclockwise direction. Surrounding the center the names of all the participants, beginning with the abbot, are arranged in counterclockwise order.

The four characters are cited as the fortune resulting from the first hexagram in *Zhouyi* The Book of Changes; *Qain zhuan* 乾傳, *SJZ* 1:13a): "Qian (represents) what is great and originating, penetrating, advantageous, correct, and firm" 乾、元亨利貞. In James Legge, *I Ching: Book of Changes* (Oxford: Clarendon Press, 1899; reprint, New Jersey: University Books, 1972), 57.

In the *Keizan shingi* diagram, which is in turn based on one from Tiantong shan, the Holy Monk is identified as Kauṇḍinya, the Buddha's first disciple. Seating in the hall begins with Kauṇḍinya and continues by ordination seniority. In Japanese diagrams of ordination seniority beginning with the 1718 text *Shō Eihei Shingi* 小永平清規 (*Sōtōshū zensho, Shingi*, p. 391), Kauṇḍinya was replaced by Mañjuśrī, who became a symbol of the Mahayana tradition as a whole.

The origin of using a mirror for meditation can be found in the following quotation from *SXC* 3B (*T* 40:127a3–4), which is in turn a citation (but with slight alterations) from *DZDL* 91 (*T* 25:705b): "[A bodhisattva will] provide the meditator with [his own] method of meditation: a Chan stick, a Chan ball, a Chan tablet (*chanzhen* 禪鎮), a skeleton, Chan sutras, a good teacher, 'good illumination' [*haozhao* 好照, mirror], clothes, etc." *SXCZ* 3B (*T* 40:387b) comments on the term *haozhao*, noting that some claim the illuminating mirror is suspended in the meditation halls to aid in exercising the mind 以助心行, some believe the mirror is meant to reflect a clear image, while still others hold that the mirror is intended to increase the amount of radiant light in the hall.

Going back still further, we find that placing a mirror in the temple or meditation hall is mentioned in the sutra *Lengyang jing* 7 (*T* 19:133b–c). When Ānanda asked for the Buddha's advice on proper decoration for the practice hall, the Buddha replied that the ground must be purified and leveled and a sixteen-foot-wide octagonal altar built. A lotus flower made of gold, silver, copper, and wood is placed in the center of the altar, and bowls containing water are then set inside the lotus. Eight round mirrors are arranged around the bowls and beyond these sixteen more lotus flowers are arranged. Sixteen incense burners are placed between the lotus flowers. Various cakes and excellent drinks such as milk, sugar water, and honey water are offered at the altar. Banners are hung, the images of Buddhas and bodhisattvas are suspended from the walls, and images of the guardian deities are placed on both sides of the gate. Moreover, eight mirrors are suspended in the air, facing the other eight mirrors at the center of the altar, so as to reflect the light and the images. In its explanation of the phrase "Assembly of purity, in number vast as the ocean," this same sutra states that if any one of the practitioners in the hall is impure, accomplishing the laws will be difficult (*Lengyan jing* 7 [*T* 19:133c10]).

For the above sources I am indebted to Matsuura Shūkō's excellent book, *Zenshū kojitsu sonzō no kenkyū* (Tokyo: Shankibō Busshorin, 1976), 500–507.

85. That is, the Sangha hall.

86. *jiezhi zhiyi* 結制之儀.

87. That is, prohibits leaving the monastery.

88. *huofeng jinping* 獲奉巾瓶, that is, to become closer to the abbot.

89. *sanye* 三業.

90. *liseng shouzuo* 立僧首座. The *liseng shouzuo* was a retired high-ranking monk serving as auxiliary chief seat. For a detailed discussion of this position, see the section "Appointment of Chief Seat Emeritus" in fasc. 7.

91. *jiexia*[b] 解夏.

92. *baidi* 白帝: one of the Five Emperors.

93. *juehuang* 覺皇: the Buddha.

94. *xun* 旬. The summer totals ninety days, or three months. As *Chanyuan qinggui* indicates, the summer retreat was held from the fifteenth day of the fourth month to the fifteenth day of the seventh month.

95. *diantang* 點湯.

96. *xunliao* 巡寮. This section refers specifically to the abbot's visit to the assembly hall. However, the term *xunliao* used in *Chanyuan qinggui* sometimes refers to visits to various other quarters. Also referred to in Eisai's *Kōzen gokoku ron* 3 (*T* 80:15a24).

MSL 5 (*T* 22:262b4–8) indicates that the Buddha visited the monks's quarters (*sengfang* 僧坊) every five days. See "Rituals of Indian Origin" in Chapter 2.

97. *xunliao pai* 巡寮牌.

98. *shuoshi* 説事: "explanation of matters."

99. *fajia* 法駕: exceptionally honorable.

100. *zunsu* 尊宿.

101. *kewei* 客位.

102. *menzhuang* 門狀. The *menzhuang* functioned much like a calling card. But unlike a card, the *menzhuang* varied in size. It indicated not only one's name but also the title and name of the person one was visiting. See *ZSS*, 622a.

103. *jiansi* 監司.

104. *shouling* 守令.

105. In *Chanyuan qinggui*, the high-ranking administrative members of the monastery (excluding the abbot) can be divided into two parallel categories: the administrators and the chief officers. The former comprised the positions of prior, rector, cook, and superintendent; the latter chief seat in the Sangha hall, scribe, director of the library, guest master, and bath master. The duties of these four administrators and five chief officers are elaborated in the fascicles that follow. In general the unifying characteristic of the four administrators was their supervision of financial matters; the chief officers dealt mostly with nonfinancial affairs.

The number of positions in each of these two categories was expanded in the descriptions given by the later text *CBQG*. Here the administrators are referred to as the east section (*dongxu* 東序) and their number was expanded to six. In addition to the aforementioned rector, cook, and superintendent, the role of prior was divided into two positions: first assistant prior (*dusi* 都寺) and second prior (*jiansi* 監寺). The supply master (referred to as the *kutou* 庫頭 in *Chanyuan qinggui*) was renamed and included in this section as the third assistant prior (*fusi* 副寺). The chief officers are referred to as the west section (*xixu* 西序). There were now thirteen positions in this section: chief seat of the front hall, chief of the rear hall, scribe, director of the library, guest master, bath master, director of the shrine, the abbot's five attendants (in charge of the burning of incense, secretarial matters, the entertaining of guests, robes and bowls, and medicine) and the Holy Monk's attendant. (For further details regarding the chief officers, see the section "Appointment of the Chief Officers," *YZS* **[122]** in fasc. 3.)

The term *zhishi* 知事, which is also an official imperial title, was without doubt adopted from the governmental system. Charles Hucker explains that the term *zhishi* (or *chīh-shih* in Wade-Giles) was used to refer to an administrative clerk in a governmental office. See Hucker, *A Dictionary of Official Titles in Imperial*

China, p. 162a, entry 1050. Hucker analyzes the word *zhi* 知 (Wade-Giles *chi*, literally, "to know, to take notice of"), which, beginning in the Han period (202 B.C.E.–220 C.E.), was commonly used as a prefix to an agent name. This added the meaning of manager or administrator, often in the form *chih . . . shih* [知 . . . 事] ("managing the affair" of) that is, "Administrator of" See ibid, p.155a, entry 934.

The administrative system of the monastery was obviously modeled on the governmental system. A further example of this is the east and west bifurcation that appears in *CBQG*, which closely resembles the division of the central government into two branches, civilian officials and military officers. See "Imperial System and the Monastic Practice" in Chapter 2.

106. *fuyuan* 副院.

107. *dianzuo* 典座. For the duties of the cook, see the section "Cook," *YZS* [116] in fasc. 3.

108. *qianzi* 前資.

109. *qinjiu* 勤舊. According to Dōchū's interpretation, the *qianzi* was a monk who had retired from the rank of third assistant prior (*fusi*) or lower and had served three terms. The *qinjiu* was one who had retired from a position ranking higher than *fusi*, such as the second assistant prior (*jiansi*) or first assistant prior (*dusi*), and had served three terms. After retirement, a *qianzi* moved into the quarters for retired staff (*qianzi liao* 前資寮), the former first assistant prior remained in individual lodgings (*danliao* 單寮), and the former second prior retired to the *mengtang* 蒙堂 (literally, "the hall of hiding one's illumination") (*ZSS*, 179b; *CBQG* 4 [*T* 48:1132a21–23]). Thus, we may conclude that both the *qianzi* and *qinjiu* were retirees, and that the latter was simply of a higher rank.

110. *qiju wanfu* 起居萬福.

111. *mou shangzuo* 某上座.

112. *jiaoge* 交割.

113. Throughout Chinese history silk was often used as currency.

114. *shangwen* 上聞.

115. 和尚: the abbot (Skt. *upādhyāya*).

116. *tewei jiaodai* 特為交代.

Fascicle Three

1. While the prior's (*jianyuan*) rank and authority was second only to the abbot's, the prior's tasks within the monastery were mainly financial in nature and, unlike the rector, he did not have the power to appoint candidates to staff positions. In general, it would seem that power and authority below the rank of abbot were not structured in a stratified, top-down pattern, but distributed laterally among several parallel positions. The models for the sharing of this power and the titles of the positions themselves undoubtedly varied from monastery to monastery. As is indicated by *Chanyuan qinggui*, some monasteries of the time had also established a position of assistant prior (*fuyuan*). As I have discussed, later, during the Yuan dynasty, the position of prior was expanded by adding a first assistant (*dusi*), a second assistant (*jiansi*), and a third assistant (*fusi*) (*CBQG* 4 [*T* 48:1132a10]). Thus the positions of the four administrators mentioned in *Chanyuan qinggui* (1103) were expanded at the time of *CBQG* into six new positions.

ZTSY 8 (*ZZK* 2-18-1:118d), a text contemporary with or perhaps preceding

Chanyuan qinggui, indicates that the title of *jiansi* had already appeared before the Southern Song dynasty. However, as *ZTSY,* citing *DSL* 2 (*T* 54:244c), points out, the Sanskrit term *vihārasvāmin* was first translated into Chinese as *sizhu* 寺主 ("temple master") rather than *jiansi,* and had already become known as an administrative position. The first appointment of an administrative position in a Chinese monastery was at the Baimasi 白馬寺 during the East Han dynasty (58–220), although at that time the position had not yet received the title of *sizhu.* It was not until the East Jin dynasty (317–419) that the term *sizhu* came into regular use. *ZTSY* adds that it was only in the present era that the title of *sizhu* was renamed *jiansi.*

2. *zhiqie hui* 炙茄會. The practice of roasting eggplant had been prevalent among Chinese monasteries since the Tang dynasty. *Youyang zazu* 19 (277:158), written during the Tang, depicts monks roasting eggplants frequently and testifies to the vegetable's delicious taste. One variety of eggplant, grown at the temple Ximingsi 西明寺, was brought especially from Korea and was lighter in color and shaped like an egg. The practice of roasting eggplant can also be found in Chan literature. Master Wuzu Fayan's 五祖法演 (d. 1104) discourse record, *Haihui lu* 海會錄 2 (*T* 47:657a9; cited in *ZSS;* 337b–8a), states that on the day of the eggplant-roasting feast, the abbot would ascend the platform in the Dharma hall.

3. I discuss the origins of these Chinese festivals in "Chinese Influences," Chapter 2.

4. *Chanyuan qinggui* does not give dates for these two ceremonies. However, *CBQG* 7 (*T* 48:1155a20, 1154c26) indicates that the use of the stove in the Sangha hall began on the first day of the tenth month, and ended on the first day of the second month.

5. 臘八, that is, the eighth day of the twelfth month. This festival marks the day when the Buddha attained enlightenment. Various sutras differ on the date: the eighth day of the second month, the eighth of the third month, the eighth of the fourth month, the eighth of the eighth month, or the fifteenth of the third month. Dōchū (*ZSS,* 506a) believed that Chinese monasticism adopted the tradition of *Yinguo jing* 因果經, which holds that the correct date is the eighth day of the second month. However, *Zhoushuyiji* 周書異記 (cited by Dōchū in *ZSS,* 506a) states, "On the eighth day of the second month, in the second year of the reign of Emperor Mu of the Zhou dynasty 周穆王 [1000 B.C.E.], the Buddha attained enlightenment at the age of thirty. [This second month] is equivalent to the La month 臘月 [the twelfth month] of the present calendar [Dōchū's note: the (late?) period of the Zhou dynasty]." Chinese tradition has for the most part adopted the eighth day of the twelfth month as the proper date of the Buddha's enlightenment. In modern times, on this day each temple prepares Laba porridge, a rice soup cooked with various kinds of beans, to share with visitors and distribute to donors.

6. This feast day is regarded as the day when the Buddha entered *parinirvāṇa.* Present-day Chinese monasteries celebrate the Buddha's birthday on the eighth day of the fourth month, the anniversary of his enlightenment on the eighth day of the twelfth month, and his entrance into *parinirvāṇa* on the fifteenth day of the second month. Some temples adhere to the lunar calendar, while others have adopted the solar calendar.

7. Another interpretation of this phrase 體面生拊 is given by Shinohara Hisao

(*Eihei daishingi,* 202): "matters without precedent." He translates the final character 柳 to mean "to create" or "to start." However, this word may also have the meaning "to wound" or "to injure" (Morohashi, 2:251c), and the first two characters are best translated as "reputation."

    8. *xingqian* 行遣.

    9. *faqian* 發遣.

    10. As the text here is rather vague, another interpretation is equally plausible: "However, even if [the prior should carry out punishment] in an inappropriate manner, [the monastery] should prevent this matter from attracting investigations by government officials."

    11. *jiefang huazhu* 街坊化主.

    12. *zhuangzhu* 庄主. See *YZS* **[146–147]** in fasc. 4.

    13. *jiangtou* 醬頭: person in charge of pickling and preserving.

    14. *zhoutou* 粥頭.

    15. *jiefang boretou* 街坊般若頭. See *YZS* **[141–142]** in fasc. 4.

    16. *huayantou* 華嚴頭. See *YZS* **[141–142]** in fasc. 4.

    17. *shuitou* 水頭.

    18. *yuantou* 園頭. See *YZS* **[145]** in fasc. 4.

    19. *motou* 磨頭. See *YZS* **[143]** in fasc. 4.

    20. *dengtou* 燈頭.

    21. *xingyi xingzhe* 行益行者. *Xingyi* is also referred to as *yishi* 益食 ("to serve food") by Faxian 法顯 (340–423?), who, in the diary recording his travels to India and South Asia (*Foguo ji* 佛國記, also *Gaoseng Faxian zhuan* [*T* 51:857b8–11]), reports that in Khotan 于闐 there was "a Mahayanist monastery called Gomati 瞿摩帝 that could accommodate three thousand monks. When this great mass of monks heard the signal for mealtime, they would enter the dining hall in a dignified and utterly silent manner. When the purity-keeper served the food (*yizhi*), the monks would not call to each other, but merely used hand signals."

    Incidentally, James Legge, in his translation of this text (*A Record of Buddhist Kingdoms* [Oxford: Clarendon Press, 1886; reprint, New York: Dover Publications, 1965], p. 18 and n. 1) incorrectly translates *yishi* as "to require food," a mistake that may be due to his initial mistranslation of the term *jingren*, which he identifies as "a denomination for the monks as *vimala*, 'undefiled' or 'pure.'" I find this definition inadequate, if not slightly misleading.

    22. *zhishi*[b] 職事.

    23. Yijing (*NJNZ* 4 [*T* 54:226b17–18]) pointed out that the common translation of *karma-dāna* as *weinuo* was erroneous because it combined a lexical translation of the first character *wei* and a phonetic transliteration in the second character *nuo*. He theorized that *wei* was taken from the Chinese word meaning "to enforce discipline," while the word *nuo* was transliterated from the Sanskrit *na*, which was the last syllable of *karma-dāna*. In his translation of the term *karma-dāna*, Yijing attempted to convey the precise meaning of the original word. *Karma* means "matters" or "affairs" and *dāna* means "to invest with authority" or "to grant"; therefore, Yijing reasoned, *karma-dāna* meant "to invest someone with authority over matters," which was best translated into Chinese as *shoushi* 授事. In India, Yijing observed, the *shoushi* was in charge of striking the signal instruments during ceremonies and supervising at mealtime. See Yijing's *DXQZ* (*T* 51:5c)

    In *SXC* (*T* 40:135b1–2), Daoxuan noted that *Chuyao lüyi* 出要律儀 (a lost text) put forth the notion that the Chinese title *weinuo* was actually based on a different Sanskrit term, [*vihāra-*] *pāla* (*poluo* 婆邏), which could also be translated into Chinese as *sihu* 寺護 ("temple protector") or *yuezhong* 悦眾 ("one who brings joy to the assembly"). However, in *DXQZ* 1 (*T* 51:5c25–26), Yijing considered the term *vihāra-pāla* as wholly separate from *karma-dāna* or *weinuo*, translating it as *husi* 護寺 and describing the position's duties as the supervision, carried out in shifts, of monastic affairs 作番直典掌寺門 and the making of announcements to the assembly 和僧白事. While most scholars agree that the term *weinuo* is derived from the Sanskrit *karma-dāna* rather than from *vihāra-pāla*, the definitions and duties of these original terms have become blurred over the years, resulting in a vague overlapping of categories that defies simple identification.

SSL 34 (*T* 23:250b) describes the establishment of the position of *weinuo:* "When the Buddha was living in the monks' hall within Prince Jeta's grove in the park of Anāthapiṇḍada, in the region of Śrāvastī, none of the monks knew the [correct monastic] schedule. No one struck the signal instruments to announce assemblies; no one cleaned the lecture hall or the dining hall; no one prepared the beds; no one taught [the purity-keeper] how to clean fruit or vegetables; no one guarded the bitter wine from insects 看苦酒中虫; no one served water during mealtimes; no one snapped his fingers [to silence the assembly] when all the monks spoke without order. This [chaotic] situation was reported to the Buddha, who announced that the position of the *weinuo* should be established." The Buddha further stipulated that there should be five qualifications for the *weinuo*. He should not exercise authority according to his personal biases, anger, fears, or ignorance. Finally, he should be able to distinguish the pure from the impure.

24. *yuezhong* 悦眾.

25. *zhufang banshi* 諸方辦事.

26. *zhuchi tie* 住持帖.

27. *kaitang shu* 開堂疏. See *YZS* **[256]** in fasc. 7.

28. *jiexia jiepai* 結夏戒牌.

29. *shengseng shizhe* 聖僧侍者. See *YZS* **[155–156]** in fasc. 4.

30. *gongtou xingzhe* 供頭行者. This position is also referred to as *gongguo xingzhe* 供過行者, which appears in *YZS* **[150]**.

31. *chuangzhang* 床帳.

32. *xiao toushou* 小頭首.

33. *tangtou shizhe* 堂頭侍者.

34. That is, the infirmary (*yanshoutang zhu* 延壽堂主).

35. *lutou* 爐頭. See *YZS* **[157]** in fasc. 4.

36. *gezhu* 閣主.

37. *dianzhu* 殿主.

38. *chuzhong* 出眾.

39. *yiliao* 移寮.

40. *xingqian* 行遣.

41. *beizhu* 被主: "the sufferer [of a loss]."

42. *gongju* 供具.

43. *daseng zhang* 大僧帳; "great monk register."

44. *jiaose* 腳色; "foot color." The word *jiaose* originally denoted a curriculum vitae that was presented to the government when an individual sought employ-

ment as an official. In addition to the basic biographical data such as place of birth, date of birth, age, etc., this document included the candidate's genealogical background extending back for at least three generations (Morohashi, 9:346b). The purpose of a monk's or a nun's curriculum vitae was to serve as a record of the monasteries he or she had visited.

45. *gongzhang qianwu* 供帳錢物. For the registration fee, see the discussion in "Influences of Chinese Culture" in Chapter 2.

46. *jinsong wangseng* 津送亡僧. For a detailed discussion, see the section "The Monk's Funeral," *YZS* **[237–240]** in fasc. 7.

47. *guchang* 估唱. For a detailed discussion of the auction, see *YZS* **[240–242]** in fasc. 7.

48. *baichui* 白槌.

49. *chatang* 茶湯.

50. *ruliao pai* 入寮牌.

51. *laci pai* 蠟次牌.

52. *puqing* 普請; "universal invitation." See "Communal Labor" in Chapter 2.

53. The word *dianzuo*, here translated as "cook," literally means "in charge of seating." It was applied to an administrative position described in the Vinaya. *MSL* 9 (*T* 22:280a20–24) states that when the Buddha was staying in Śrāvastī, a monk named Darva Mallaputra 陀驃摩羅子 received authority from all members of the Sangha to take charge of nine duties 僧拜典知九事. These nine duties, in order, were: assigning seating 典次付床座; designating which monks attend the feasts; assigning lodging; distributing clothing; allocating flowers and incense; distributing fruits and vegetables; appointing the water master (the person in charge of heating the water); distributing cakes and miscellaneous food; and assigning a person to preside over the ceremony of *pravāraṇa* at the end of the retreat. Thus the *dianzuo* is in charge of much more than seating (*DSL* 2 [*T* 54:245a8–9]). However, the term *dianzuo* itself does not appear in the Vinaya text *MSL*.

Among the Vinaya texts, Yijing's Chinese translation of the later *Mūlasarvāstivāda Vinaya* (*GSP* [*Z*] 19 [*T* 24:295b12]) is the only one in which the word *dianzuo* appears. This text records how the Buddha instructed the *dianzuo* to inform the donors of the number of monks who would attend any given feast. In Sasaki Shizuka's excellent article, "Tenzō ni kansuru ichi kōsatsu," *Zen Bunka kenkyūjō kiyō* 19 (1993): 59–76, he notes that *dianzuo* as used by Yijing corresponds to the Sanskrit *upadhivārika*, meaning "guardian of material objects" 物品管理人. He also points out that the term *upadhivārika* does not appear in any other Vinaya text; therefore, he posits, it represents a wholly new administrative position invented outright by the Mūlasarvāstivādain sect (ibid., 72–74).

Given that Yijing rendered *dianzuo* not as "cook" but as "manager," one is prompted to ask when the meaning of "cook" arose and when the original meaning was lost. In *Chanyuan qinggui* the word is used exclusively to designate the position of cook. As Sasaki points out, *dianzuo* had already come to be associated with the duties of the cook at the time of the writing of *Zutang ji* (952), but the question of precisely when this lexical transition took place still needs further study (Sasaki, "Tenzō," 75). In the diary of his journey to Tang China, Ennin frequently mentions the title *dianzuo* as an administrative position in the temple, not the kitchen. This meaning of the term is much like the one given in *DSL* (1019), which is itself adopted from *MSL*. It would seem then that the meaning of the term most likely underwent a change during the Northern Song. This serves as yet another example of how monastic administrative titles varied with time and place.

54. *kuzhu* 庫主.

55. *xingyi* 行益.

56. *gongguo* 供過.

57. *DSW* 2 (*T* 24:924b8–18) lists the ten virtues or duties of the *zhisui:* he must exert all his efforts for the sake of the three dharmas (that is, The Three Treasures); whenever a guest monk arrives at the monastery, he should greet the traveler and provide him with accommodation; he should provide guest monks with beds as well as lamps for as long as three or even seven days; if all the beds are full, he should be ready to yield his own bed to a guest; he should frequently inquire as to his guests' needs; he should explain the local customs and culture to the guests; he should be ever concerned about whenever provisions are low in supply; if there is a quarrel among the guests, he should not come to the aid of either party but try to resolve the conflict and reconcile the opposed parties; if guests should fall to quarreling, he should not publicly scold them or give them orders; and he should not compete with the *moboli* 摩波利 (the administrative staff, no Sanskrit equivalent). Jonathan Silk discusses the *moboli* in his dissertation "*Mahāratnakūṭa*," 245. In addition, the *zhisui* should neither frequently malign the *moboli* in the assembly nor take any possessions held in common to indulge others. From the above list of duties, the position of *zhisui* seems to have been closer to that of guest master than superintendent.

DSL 2 (*T* 54:245a9–10) indicates that the *zhisui*, as a monastic administrator, officially served a one-year term, although sometimes he served only a month, half a month, or even a day. No matter how long his term in office, it was the *zhisui*'s duty to bring comfort to the assembly. *DSL* does not seem to consider the *zhisui* a taskmaster. It seems that the term *zhisui*, like the word *dianzuo*, has lost its original meaning over time.

58. *zhuangke* 庄客.

59. The chief officers were the highest ranking administrative staff members in the monastery, equaled in rank only by the administrators (*zhishi*), who formed a separate but parallel group. As mentioned above, the number of chief officers was greatly increased by the time of the later text *CBQG* 4 (*T* 48:1131a7). In addition to the remaining positions of scribe, director of the library, guest master, and bath master, the chief seat was expanded (into the positions of chief seat of the front hall and chief seat of the rear hall) due to the increased number of members in the Sangha hall; other lower ranking staff members were also recruited, such as the director of the shrine, the abbot's five attendants (in charge of incense, secretarial matters, the entertainment of guests, robes and bowls, and medicine), and the Holy Monk's attendant. Cf. the section "Appointment of the Administrators" in fasc. 2.

Note that "chief officer" as it appears here is used not only to refer to the six major chief officers, but also at times to lesser chief officers who were appointed by the rector or the director of library.

60. *chabang* 茶牓.

61. *zhoushi* 呪食.

62. *zangxia dianzhu* 藏下殿主.

63. *jiefang biaobai* 街坊表白. In the present text, the precise duties of the *jiefang*

biaobai are unclear. *DSL* 2 (*T* 54:242a15) states, however, that the *biaobai* is also referred to as the *changdao* 唱導 ("chanting leader"). In the Western Regions, when senior monks were invited to a feast, they chanted and prayed for the well-being of the donors. This practice is said to have been started by Śāriputra, who was renowned for his eloquence.

Yijing (*NJNZ* 4 [*T* 54:227a–b]) described the practice of *changdao* carried out at the Nālandā Monastery in India. This monastery accommodated more than three thousand people, and gatherings were rather difficult to organize. The monks, lodged in some three hundred rooms divided among eight buildings, simply chanted within the confines of their own quarters. The monastery's custom was to send out a precentor, whose peripatetic chanting would then be heard at sunset by all the monks. The purity-keeper (*jingren*) and acolyte 童子 would lead the precentor on his rounds, carrying with them a variety of flowers. As they passed each building or shrine, the precentor would chant three or five verses loud enough to be heard throughout the monastery, completing the service only after sunset.

64. *yidan* 衣單.

65. Reference here is to the lineage of Huilin Zongben 慧林宗本 (1020–1099), who in 1082 was invited by the emperor to be the abbot of the Chan monastery Huilin, in the Da xiangguo Temple 大相國寺 in Luoyang 洛陽 (present-day Henan province). The designation "Chan Master Yuanzhao 圓照" was given by the emperor to Huilin, who was one of Tianyi Yihuai's Dharma heirs and the Dharma uncle of Zongze, the author of *Chanyuan qinggui*.

66. 放參.

67. 和尚放參.

68. 揖食.

69. *shuzhuang* 書狀. The scribe sometimes appears in *Chayuan qinggui* as *shuji* 書記. Both terms were used interchangeably; however, according to *Wuwen yinji longshou yanshu* 無文印寄隆瘦嚴書, the term *shuji* does not appear in the old monastic codes, which use the title *shuzhuang* exclusively. The word *shuji* only came about during the medieval period (cited in *ZSS*, 230b).

70. *zunbei* 尊卑.

71. *chujing* 觸淨.

72. *sengsu* 僧俗.

73. That is, while such behavior may seem innocuous, over time it builds up bad karma for the individual.

74. *qianli meimu yizhong guangcai* 千里眉目一眾光彩. The first four characters, 千里眉目, mean "a letter which carries its message a thousand miles away" (Morohashi 8:190d, 2:532b).

75. Chanyue 禪月 was the name given to the monk Guanxiu 貫休. The biography of Guanxiu (832–912) was collected in *SGSZ* 30 (*T* 50:897a–b; also *Sōden haiin* [*NBZ* 99: 300a]). Guanxiu joined the order at the age of seven and engaged in the propagation of the *Lotus Sutra* and *Dacheng qixin lun* 大乘起信論. However, he became renowned for his talents in poetry, painting, and calligraphy. His style of calligraphy came to be known as the "Jiang style" 姜體, after his family name. His poems rivaled those of the most famous poets of the Tang dynasty. He was treated with great honor by the prince of the Wuyue 吳越 region (Nanjing) and was later invited to visit the prince of the Shu 蜀 region (present-day Sichuan).

He was shown great favor by the Shu prince, who gave him the sobriquet *Dede lai heshang* 得得來和尚. When Guanxiu died, the prince ordered him buried in the manner of a government officer. Guanxiu was also renowned for his paintings of the arhats.

76. The biography of Qiji 齊己 also appears in *SGSZ* 30 (*T* 50:897c–8a; also *Sōden haiin* [*NBZ* 99:336a]). Qiji was tonsured at a very young age. He loved poetry and soon became famous as a talented poet. Because of a tumor on his neck, he was given the nickname "Poetry Growth" (*shinang* 詩囊). His collection of poems is entitled *Analects of the White Lotus* (*Bailian ji* 白蓮集). At the beginning of the Five Dynasties, he was invited by Gao Jichang 高季昌 to the Longxing Temple 龍興寺 (in present-day Nanjing) and was honored as the rectifier of clergy (*sengzheng*) in 921. The life of an officer did not interest Qiji, who preferred to live frugally, surrounded by nature. In *Chanyuan qinggui*, the single oblique mention of Qiji seems to imply that as a "poet-monk" he did not live as a true monk. In *SGSZ*, however, Qiji is depicted as a religious figure worthy of veneration, one who disregarded fame and fortune and refused to associate with government officers.

77. Jia Dao 賈島 was a contempory of Han Yu 韓愈, a famous Confucian scholar and officer. Jia was a monk in Fanyang 范陽 and later moved to Luoyang. He was saddened by the fact that the government prohibited monks from leaving the monastery after noon and composed a poem in which he complained of this restriction. Han Yu came to sympathize with Jia and took it upon himself to tutor the monk in secular literature. Jia later decided to return to secular life and was recommended to become a scholar (*jinshi* 進士), but he did not pass the civil service recruitment examination. It is said that when Jia was engaged in composing a poem, he concentrated to the point where he failed to notice the presence of the nobility, which often resulted in troublesome situations. Eventually Jia served in the local government as assistant magistrate 主簿 in the Changjiang 長江 region (*Xin Tangshu* 176, p. 5268). His poems were so revered that a statue was erected in his honor and he was given the name Jiao Dao Buddha 賈島佛 (*FZTJ* 41 [*T* 49:384a]).

78. 慧休. The reference here is unclear. *YZS*, in its annotations to the above text, identifies this monk as the same Huixiu mentioned in the *XGSZ*. However, this identification is erroneous. The monk Huixiu described in *XGSZ* 15 (*T* 50: 544b–5c) is said to be wholly devoted to the Vinaya practice and, more importantly, he is depicted as having shunned court life, repeatedly refusing (under the pretext of illness) to obey the emperor's summons to the capital.

79. *kanjingtang shouzuo* 看經堂首座.

80. The present text does not identify the holy statue in the sutra-reading hall.

81. *huijing* 會經: "meeting the sutra."

82. *bazhen* 把針.

83. *pianyun* 篇韻. Such reference works were arranged so that one could look up a character either by radical or sound.

84. *xiadeng ban* 下燈板.

Fascicle Four

1. *sengguan* 僧官. For a detailed discussion of the system of clerical officials in the Song, see "Chinese Influences" in Chapter 2.

2. The word given in the text is 師僧, translated literally as "teacher monks";

however, *ZD* (p. 442c) gives two definitions of the term: "teacher" and an "honorific title used to refer to monks in general." Here the latter interpretation seems more appropriate.

3. *CHSS* 1:461b–c.

4. Literally, to circumambulate the hall with burning incense.

5. *Chanyuan qinggui* gives no indication of how frequently monks were expected to bathe. A later text, *CBQG* 4 (*T* 48:1131b18–19), reports that in the winter monks bathed every five days and in the summer they bathed daily. According to the Japanese pilgrim Eisai, this was also the practice in Song monasteries (*Kōzen gokoku ron* [*T* 80:15a27]).

Taking a bath was considered essential for the monks' general hygiene. According to Vinaya texts, even at the time of the Buddha, the practice was recommended by the physician Jīvaka. According to *WFL* 26 (*T* 22:171b), when a group of monks ate an excessive amount of rich food and become ill, Jīvaka recommended that the monks bathe to alleviate their suffering, a proposal the Buddha accepts. In a separate but related story (*SFL* 39 [*T* 22:845c2–3]), the Buddha allowed monks of a particular area to bathe more frequently so as not to violate local customs.

6. *kaiyu* 開浴, *linhan* 淋汗, and *jingfa* 淨髮.

7. The bodhisattvas. The present text does not give a precise identification of the Holy Ones or any details of the ritual of inviting the Holy Ones to bathe. The biography of Daoan (*GSZ* 5 [*T* 50:353b27–c9]) informs us that the ritual bathing of the Holy Ones began during the time of Daoan. For this account, see "Heritage from the Vinaya Tradition" in Chapter 2.

A fuller account of the practice of inviting the Holy Ones to enter the bath is given by Daoshi 道世. In his *FYZL* (*T* 53:544c–5a) he indicates who the invitees are: first, the Buddhas of ten directions in all three ages; second, the bodhisattvas; third, the arhats (specifically Piṇḍola); fourth, the manifested spirits of the six realms; and fifth, the deities of the three realms 三界天眾, the dragon kings of the four oceans 四海龍王, the eight kinds of spirits 八部鬼神, all sentient beings 一切含識有形之類, and every crawling creature 蠕動之流. *Chanyuan qinggui* does not reveal whether its procedure is the same as the one depicted in the earlier *FYZL*, but at the very least scholars can safely rely on Daoshi's more detailed description for a general indication of the tradition.

The statue enshrined in the bathhouse seems to have changed during the Song and can be more precisely identified from this point on. The bathhouse of Tiantongshan, according to *GJZ* (*CHSS* 2:1316 or *ZD*, *zuroku*, p. 26), was called the "Illuminated One" (*xuanming* 宣明), after a common epithet of Bhadra-pāla, who attained enlightenment while in a bathhouse. At the entrance of the bathhouse stood a statue of Bhadra-pāla. This account is given in *Lengyan jing* 5 (*T* 19:126a10–16): Sixteen monks, led by Bhadra-pāla, entered a bath house. While bathing they suddenly realized the cause of water (*huwu shuiyin* 忽悟水因), thereby attaining enlightenment. Many present-day temples suspend portraits of the sixteen bodhisattvas led by Bhadra-pāla over bathhouse entrances. They include the temples Daitokuji 大德寺 and Myōshinji 妙心寺 in Japan (see Yokoyama, *Zen no kenchiku*, 223).

8. *fengyao* 風藥. *ZD* (p. 1060a) defines this item as cold medicine. However, after consulting Jōjin's diary *Santendai godaisan ki* 6 and 7 (*NBZ* 115:435a, 456b),

Tanaka Misa concludes that the word refers to a kind of confection taken with tea. See her article "Sōdai no kissa to chayaku," *Shisō* 48 (1991): 284–285. I find Tanaka's interpretation more convincing, for Jōjin (*NBZ* 115:456b) notes that *fengyao* was consumed with tea. *Chanyuan qinggui* mentions that tea sets were provided in the bathhouse, suggesting that bath day was considered a complete break from the usual routine and that after their ablutions, monks were allowed to relax and drink tea.

9. Cf. n. 7 above.

10. *dadie* 打疊. Die 疊 means "to strike the bell lightly." See *CHSS* 1:383c.

11. An alternative translation of this sentence is: "Monks should feel ashamed of their nakedness while bathing." However, the Vinayas indicate that monks should never bathe naked. *WFL* 26 (*T* 22:171b11) and *MSL* 35 (*T* 22:508c–509b) give elaborate descriptions of proper decorum when entering the bath.

12. In contrast to the fundraiser (*huazhu*), who traveled to distant regions and spent long periods of time soliciting donations, monks in these positions spent only short periods of time traveling, soliciting in regions close to the monastery and asking solely for food. Cf. the section "Fundraiser" in fasc. 5.

13. *zhou jiefang* 粥街坊, *mimai jiefang* 米麥街坊, *cai jiefang* 菜街坊, *jiang jiefang* 醬街坊, *shuitou* 水頭, and *tantou* 炭頭.

14. *tra. boretou* 般若頭.

15. *jingtou*[b] 經頭. Unlike the other preachers, the sutra preacher does not lecture on specific sutra.

16. *mitotou* 彌陀頭. *Chanyuan qinggui* does not give a detailed account of the activities of any of the preaching positions. The best description of these traveling preachers can be found in the diary of Ennin (*NBZ* 113:252a). During the Tang, Ennin observes, the sermons given by traveling monks were called *sujiang* 俗講 ("lectures for laypeople"). In the capital city of Chang'an, the imperial court had given orders that monks from various temples should lecture on the *Avataṃsaka Sutra, Lotus Sutra,* and *Nirvana Sutra.* Such monks were required to explain the profound teachings of the sutra in the plainest language so that the audience— the general public—could understand their meaning. Wandering preachers, Ennin records, would be invited by a monastery to speak, and their sermons could bring in large donations to the sponsoring temple. Throughout the Tang period, *sujiang* was performed during the three "observing months" (*zhaiyue* 齋月)—the first, fifth, and ninth months—and each time the preaching would last for one month. For the further reading on the *sujiang,* see Ōno Katsutoshi, *Nittō guhō junrei kōki,* 3:343, n. 4; Michihata, *Tōdai Bukkyōshi no kenkyū,* 281–296.

17. In the Tang and Song, the operation of a grinding mill became one of the major enterprises of large monasteries. Due to the great expense involved in running a mill, only the largest of institutions—such as those run by aristocratic families or those supported by big monasteries—could afford their upkeep. These mills, usually driven by waterpower or by animals, not only were for the use of the monastery, but were rented out to the public as well, thus ensuring a major source of income for the temple. *Chanyuan qinggui,* however, does not mention use of the mill by the public. For further information on the mill industry during the Song, see Huang, *Songdai Fojiao,* 209–211. For the industry before or during the Tang period, see Michihata Ryōshū, *Chūgoku Bukkyō shakai keizaishi,* 100–108; Jacques Gernet, *Buddhism in Chinese Society: An Economic History from*

the Fifth to the Tenth Century, trans. Franciscus Verellen (New York: Columbia University Press, 1994), 142–152; and D. C. Twitchett's review of the French edition of Gernet's book, "The Monasteries and China's Economy in Medieval Times," *SOAS* 19, no. 3 (1957): 533–535.

18. For an illustration of the fan mechanism, see *Nongshu* 16 Siku quanshu zhenben bieji edition (Taipei: Shangwu Yinshuguan, 1975), 174:9b. The descriptions of the various farming mechanisms given in *Nongshu*, fascs. 16 and 19, are useful for understanding the mill operations given here.

19. The term used here is *dou* 斗, a unit of measure roughly equivalent to one peck.

20. *luo* 羅.

21. See "Communal Labor" in Chapter 2.

22. *yuantou* 園頭.

23. *jiashi* 家事.

24. 寒食. This festival took place on the 105th (some say the 103rd or 106th) day after the winter solstice (December 22 or 23), placing it in the beginning of April, perhaps the third day of April. *Hanshi* literally means "cold-eating"; on this day Chinese were prohibited from using fire, thus food was eaten cold.

Tradition maintains that this custom arose from the tragic story of Jie Zitui 介子推 of the Spring-Autumn period (770–403 B.C.E.). Jie was living in exile with his king, Jin Wengong 晉文公, in poverty and hunger. When they began to starve, Jie, thinking only of his monarch's survival, cut off pieces of his own flesh to feed the king. Upon their return from exile, the king eventually regained the throne but forgot to show his gratitude to Jie. The latter expressed his disappointment in a poem and then sought solitude in the forest. Realizing his oversight, the king begged his former savior to return, but Jie refused. Finally, the king decided to force Jie to show himself by setting fire to the forest. Jie refused to emerge and chose instead to die among the flames. Deeply grieved by his own actions, the king decreed that thenceforth no fires were to be lit on that day each year.

The first occurrence of the story of Jie Zitui is found in *Hou Hanshu* 61 (p. 2024). No anecdote mentioning Jie or the king is recorded in any earlier dynastic histories, such as *Shiji* or *Zuozhuan*. However, the ban on the use of fire on this day had been a custom since the Zhou dynasty. Thus the linking of the fire ban to the story of Jie was most likely a later occurrence. According to *Jingchu suishi ji* Sibu beiyao edition (Shanghai: Zhonghua Shuju, 1936), 111: 5b–6a, Chinese observed this holiday by eating cold wheat porridge, holding cock fights, and playing on swings.

25. Farming villages were residential communities of tenants who cultivated temple land in return for money or grain. In the early period of Buddhism, the ideal monastic was a mendicant; in time, however, monks began to live together in communities and the need for regular housing arose. Vinaya texts reveal that as the numbers of a monastic community grew, lay followers donated increasing amounts of housing material, gardens, farming land, and even slaves to meet the Sangha's needs. (See *SFL* 43 [*T* 22:875a22–23]; *WFL* 26 [*T* 22:174a24–26]; *GSP(Y)* 15 [*T* 24:74b9, and 568a1–3]). When Yijing (*DXQZ* [*T* 51:6b20–22]) made his pilgrimage to the Nālandā Temple in India, he discovered that there were 200 villages belonging to one temple. The temple itself accommodated 3,500 monks.

The villages had been bestowed on the temple by successive emperors to support its needs.

In China, the earliest instance of a monastery receiving a land grant from an emperor occured during the North Wei dynasty, when Emperor Xiaowen 孝文帝 (r. 471–499) bestowed estates on Xuanzhongsi 玄中寺 Monastery (Mount Shibi 石壁山, present-day Shanxi 山西 province) in 495. See the inscription of pavillion Qianfoge 千佛閣 at Xuanzhongsi in Tokiwa Daijō and Sekino Tadashi, *Chūgoku bunka shiseki kaisetsu* (Kyoto: Hōzōkan, 1976), 2:57.

During the Tang and Song dynasties, the granting of lands to monasteries became a widespread practice, and the estates themselves became the major source of income for monasteries. In her book on monastic economy in Song China, Huang Minzhi lists six sources from which monasteries received or increased their estates: a grant from the imperial family; donations from monks and nuns or laypeople; purchases from landowners; development of an uncultivated forest or coast; acquisitions of official estates or unattended lands; and long-term rentals from the government or landowners. Huang also notes that some monasteries maintained estates located at great distances from the monastery. See Huang, *Songdai Fojiao*, 19–89.

26. *zhuangzhu* 庄主.

27. In the Song, there were two kinds of taxes imposed on tenants: one by the landholder, the other by the government. Both taxes were collected by the landholder. See Sudō Yoshiyuki, *Tō-Sō shakai keizaishi kenkyū* (Tokyo: Tōkyō Daigaku Shuppankai, 1965), 872. The monastery, in its capacity as landlord, paid taxes to the government twice a year, in summer (the sixth month) and in autumn (the eleventh month). See Kawakami Kōichi, *Sōdai no keizai seikatsu* (Tokyo: Yoshikawa Kōbunkan, 1966), 121; Huang, *Songdai Fojiao*, 102.

28. The tenant was also called *xiao zuoren* 小作人. Tenant farmers living in the villages were the main source of agricultural manpower; however, novices who had not yet received full ordination (such as the servers) and slaves also participated in farming. See Michihata, *Chūgoku Bukkyō shakai keizaishi*, 86 and 82.

29. That is, he should not seek extensive social contacts or excessive profits.

30. One function of the farming village was to provide lodging for both monastic and lay travelers.

31. Since horn and hide were used to make weapons, the Song government ordered them to be immediately transferred to the state as a kind of tax. This custom began in 952 during the Post-Zhou dynasty (Kawakami, *Sōdai no keizai seikatsu*, 125).

32. Sudō Yoshiyuki (*Tō-Sō shakai keizaishi*, 872) indicates that there were two methods of payment to the landlord: the first was the division of the harvest by a ratio (usually one-to-one), with a set percentage of the annual yield going to the landlord; the second was the payment of a fixed amount, regardless of the year's harvest. According to Huang Minzhi's study of gazetteers and stone inscriptions, there was no set rule governing how temples and their tenants shared the harvests; some monasteries demanded even more than 50 percent of the yield. The agreements varied not only from temple to temple, but between each landlord and tenant. Some tenants also had to rent their animals (usually cows) from their landlord. The payment could be in money, grain, hemp, or any other form previously agreed on (Huang, *Songdai Fojiao*, 108–109).

33. That is, he should be as yielding as possible with all his tenants.

34. *Xie* literally means "government office," indicating that this position was established to handle government matters. It is not mentioned in later texts, perhaps because its duties were thought to overlap with those of other positions, such as prior, fundraiser, and guestmaster.

35. In the original, this section is called "Director of the Infirmary and Latrine Attendant." For clarity, I have divided it into two separate sections.

36. See *Fanwang jing* 2 (*T* 24:1005c10).

37. *Fanwang jing* does not clearly define the Eight Merit Fields, and their meaning varies in the commentaries. Zhiyi (*Pusajie yishu* 2 [*T* 40:577c5–6]) lists the eight as the Buddhas, the sages, the preceptors (*upādhyāya*), the teachers (*ācārya*), the monks, the father, the mother, and sickness (based on the sentence 八福田諸佛聖人一一師僧父母病人 in *Fanwang jing* 2 [*T* 24:1007a15].

Fazang (*Fanwang jing pusa jieben shu* 5 [*T* 40:639a]) relied on *Xianyu jing*, which states that offerings to five kinds of people will accrue unlimited merit: people who know the Dharma; people who come from great distances; people who must leave for distant parts; starving people; and ailing people. To this Fazang added the obligatory triple gem: the Buddha, the Dharma, and the Sangha, bringing the total to eight. Fazang was critical of more "civic-minded" interpretations wholly unsupported by sutra, such as: the building of roads and wells; the building of bridges; the paving of dangerous roads; the feeding of parents; offerings to monks; offerings to the sick; the rescuing of those in danger; and the holding of unlimited feasts. Since Fazang deemed it necessary to criticize such a list, we may surmise that during the Tang period many believed the undertaking of public works was worthy of religious merit.

The Eight Merit Fields listed in *Chanyuan qinggui* does not correspond exactly to those given in *Fanwang jing*, but represents a later construction. See also Tokiwa Daijō, "Bukkyō no fukuden shisō," in *Shina Bukkyō no kenkyū* (Tokyo: Shūjunsha, 1943), 481.

38. For a detailed description of latrine decorum, see the section "Using the Toilet" in fasc. 7.

39. 更, that is, 4 o'clock A.M. In the ancient Chinese conception of time, one night (from 8 P.M. to 6 A.M.) was divided into five units (*geng*) of two hours each.

40. *maochou* 茆籌. These were used as toilet paper. *PNMJ* (*T* 24:808b3–6; see also *WFL* 27 [*T* 22:177b15–19; *MSL* 34 [*T* 22:504b5–8]) explains that monks were allowed to use *chou*, which could be made of wood, bamboo, or reed, to clean themselves. Rock, grass, soil, soft bark, leaves, or rare woods were not allowed. The length of the *chou* was between 4 *aṅgula* 指 (about 3 inches) and 1 *vitasti* 磔 (about 9 inches; 1 *vitasti* was equivalent to 12 *aṅgula*). Dōgen (*Shōbōgenzō* 54 [*DZZ* 1:471]) gave a similar description: bamboo spatulas could be painted or unpainted, were about 8 inches in length, about the width of a thumb, and formed in the shape of a triangle. Used bamboo spatulas were called *chuchou* 觸籌 ("soiled bamboo spatulas"); unused spatulas were called *jingchou* 淨籌 ("clean bamboo spatulas"). Soiled spatulas were thrown into a bucket (*choudou* 籌斗); clean spatulas were put on a rack in front of the latrine.

41. *shuixie* 水廁.

42. The text gives the compound *wanhou* 晚後 ("after night or evening"). I believe it should read *wanhou* 完後, that is, "after finishing."

43. *gezhu* 閘主 and *tazhu* 塔主.

44. *luohan tangzhu* 羅漢堂主. The arhat hall was said to enshrine sixteen or eighteen (or even as many as five hundred) arhats. The origin of the practice of offering to the arhats is given in Xuanzang's translation *Da Eluohan Nanri Miduoluo suoshuo fazhu ji* (*T* 49:12c–14c; henceforth *Fazhu ji*). We are told by Nandimitra, the narrator of the text, that when the Buddha was entering *parinirvāṇā*, he instructed sixteen arhats scattered throughout the cosmos to prolong their lives to maintain the Dharma. They were also told to receive offerings from lay patrons, so that the latter could receive merit. The text gives the locations (many of them legendary) of these sixteen arhats, each of whom was followed by his own retinue of arhats. Nandimitra lived in Sri Lanka after the Buddha's death: Xuanzang's text reflects the popular belief that the sixteen arhats also dwelled in Sri Lanka, or perhaps in India.

In China, belief in the sixteen arhats became popular after the Tang. Later the number of arhats was increased to eighteen, when Nandimitra and Piṇḍola were added to the list. This addition was based not on canonical texts but on Buddhist iconography. The most famous and earliest paintings of the eighteen arhats were those by the monk Guanxiu. Although eighteen figures are depicted in these paintings, the first of the original sixteen arhats and the seventeenth arhat (one of the two figures added later) are in fact the same person—Piṇḍola. He was mistakeningly identified as two separate individuals because his name was transliterated from Sanskrit to Chinese in two different ways (the first 賓度羅跋羅墮闍, the seventeenth 賓頭盧).

The later belief in five hundred arhats simply reflected the popularity among Buddhists of the number five hundred, which appears quite often in sutras and Vinayas and is sometimes given as the number of Buddha's retinue disciples and of those who gathered for the first council. In China, early descriptions of offerings to the five hundred arhats can be found in the collection of nuns' biographies, *Biqiuni zhuan* 4 (*T* 50: 945b21–2). The biography of the nun Jingxiu (418–506) describes how she invited each of the five hundred arhats from Anavatapta to Karashahr for a feast.

The arhat hall functioned not only as housing for the arhat statues, but also as the site of the routine offertory rituals. A detailed liturgical text of offerings to the arhats is found in Yirun's *Baizhang qinggui zhengyi ji* (*ZZK* 2-16-4:342a–345a). The names of the 16 arhats as well as a list of the 500 (a total of 501 names are given) are provided by Yirun.

For further information, see the excellent articles by Michihata Ryōshū, *Rakan shinkō shi*, in his *Chūgoku Bukkyōshi zenshū* (Tokyo: Shuen, 1975), 8:104–105; and Sylvain Lévi and Édouard Chavannes, "Les seize arhat protecteurs de la loi," parts 1 and 2a, *JA*, Juillet–Août (1916): 7–50; September–October (1916): 189–304.

45. *shuilu tangzhu* 水陸堂主. The ceremonies for feeding the hungry ghosts and spirits were held in the Water-land hall. The legendary origin of this ritual is given in the following anecdote from the *Jiu Mianran egui tuoluoni shenzhou jing* (*T* 21:465c–466b). One night a hungry ghost named Mianran 面然 (literally, "Burning Face") appeared before Ānanda and told him that he would die after three days and be reborn as a hungry ghost unless he offered food to the countless hungry ghosts and immortals (spirits). If such an offering was successfully made,

Ānanda himself would live longer and Mianran would be able to ascend to heaven. Ānanda appealed to the Buddha, who responded by preaching on the method of offering food to hungry ghosts and spirits—a practice that was to be carried out from that time forward.

The earliest ritual offering of food to hungry ghosts and spirits was not called "Water-land," a term that does not appear until the Song period. The first extant text to use the term is Zunshi's *Shishi zhengming* (*ZZK* 2-6-2:118c): "The temples in the Wuyue (the delta of Yangzi River) erect a separate hall with a tablet inscribed 'Water-land,' which signifies that all the immortals receive their food from the flow of water, while ghosts receive theirs from the pure ground." This indicates that "Water-land" was later misunderstood as a reference to all ghosts and spirits in the water and on the land.

The Water-land service is the most important ritual offering of food to the deceased or the spirits. This practice of feeding spirits began in China at the time of Emperor Wu of the Liang dynasty, who went so far as to order monks to compile a text based on the sutras that could accompany the ritual. The service was held for the first time in the temple of Jinshan 金山寺 in the year 505. The text of the ritual was lost soon thereafter and the service was not performed again until the Tang dynasty, when the text was recovered by Daoying 道英 and the service reinstituted (*Shimen zhengtong* [*ZZK* 2B-3-5:401c]; *Fozu tongji* 33 [*T* 49: 321b–c]).

During the Song dynasty this ritual was advocated by the famous scholar Su Shi, who compiled *Shuilu faxiang zan* (Eulogy of the Iconographs in the Water-land Ritual [*ZZK* 2-6-2:222a–223a]) in 1093. Zongze, the author of *Chanyuan qinggui*, consulted other versions of this ritual text and compiled his own four-fascicle text for the Water-land ritual in 1096, a compliation that unfortunately is no longer extant (see Zongze's *Shuilu yuanqi* [*ZZK* 2-6-2:222a]). The existing text *Fajie shengfan shuilu shenghui xiuzhai yigui* was originally compiled by the author of *Fozhu tongji*, the historian Zhipan (d. 1269), and later was reedited by Zhuhong (1532–1612). Based on Zhuhong's text, Yirun, an annotator of *CBQG* (c. 1823), reedited the text as *Fajie shenfan shuilu pudu dazhai shenghui yigui huiben* 法界聖凡水陸普度大齋聖會儀軌會本, creating a work of six fascicles that is still used today in Chinese temples.

For a study of the Water-land ritual, see the article by Makita Tairyō, "Suirikue shōkō," in his *Chūgoku kinsei bukkyōshi kenkyū* (Kyoto: Heirakuji Shoten, 1957), 169–193.

46. *zhen tangzhu* 真堂主. For a discussion regarding the hall of patriarchs, see "Influences of Chinese Culture." in chapter 2.

47. 付法藏因緣傳.

48. The present text is erroneous; the correct reference is to King Kaniṣka, or, more precisely, King Candana Kaniṣka of the Kuṣāṇa dynasty, a well-known historical figure. See *Fu fazang yinyuan zhuan* 5 (*T* 50:315b5–6).

49. *T* 50:317a. Also cited in *SXC* 1A (*T* 40:6c21–24).

50. In *XGSZ* (*T* 50:695b–c), the rector Zhixing is cited as the perfect example of someone who accrued merit through correct procedure and understanding. When the brother of one of Zhixing's fellow monks died while traveling, the deceased appeared to his wife in a dream, telling her that he had fallen into hell,

where he was tortured until Zhixing began striking the bell. The vibrations from this act had allowed him, along with other sufferers, to find relief and be reborn in a pleasant place. The dead man told his wife to donate ten bolts of silk to Zhixing, who humbly refused the gift and redonated the silk to the assembly in the temple. When people asked Zhixing how it was that he was able to accomplish such a great deed by striking the bell, he replied that he had read the story of King Kaniṣka in *Fu fazang yinyuan zhuan* and knew about the merit of striking the bell from *Zengyi Ehan jing* 24 (*T* 2:676c26–9).

It may be worth noting that both sources, *Fu fazang yinyuan zhuan* and *Zengyi Ehan jing*, appear in Daoxuan's *SXC* 1A (*T* 40:6c). Daoxuan also wrote the *Biography of Eminent Monks: Second Series*. Furthermore, both of these two sources were themselves collected in *FYZL* 99 (*T* 53:1017a) and in *Zhujing yaoji* 20 (*T* 54: 192a), both by Daoshi, who was Daoxuan's colleague at Xuanzang's translation institute. Thus these two figures, working side by side, made use of the same two sources in their separate works.

51. In the original, this section is called "Holy Monk's Attendant, Stove Master, and Sangha Hall Monitor." For clarity's sake, I have divided it into three separate sections.

52. *jieyuan* 結緣. The items listed here could not be considered especially valuable, and yet their number seems greater than would have been appropriate for any one monk to accumulate. It seems plausible that, once the attendant collected these articles, he redistributed them to all members of the assembly.

53. *WFL* 26 (*T* 22:171b27b–c1) indicates that in times of particularly cold weather, the Buddha allowed monks to light the stove outside the hall and bring it in once it had stopped giving off smoke; if the weather at a given locale was especially inclement, a stove might be installed directly inside the hall.

54. *tantou* 炭頭.

55. *MSL* 35 (*T* 22:512c16) indicates that the Buddha instructed all junior monks to take turns guarding the meditation hall.

56. *beiwei* 被位.

57. Here "senior" is an honorific title regardless of actual rank.

58. *shiwei* 食位. *Shiwei* was also called *bowei* 缽位 ("bowl seat"). The order of the eating seats was arranged according to ordination seniority, excluding the head seats of the platform sections (this number varied according to the size of the hall). For an illustration, see the diagrams in both *JDQG* 1 (ZZK 2-17-3:2d) and *CBQG* 7 (*T* 48:1151a).

59. The sleeping seats (lit., "comforter seats") were arranged according to seniority, but, unlike the eating seats, they included the head seat of each section. A diagram showing the difference between eating seats and sleeping seats may be found in *BYQG* 3 (ZZK 2-17-3:40c–d). This diagram clearly demonstrates that sleeping seats were arranged in a counterclockwise direction beginning with the side sections.

60. *Chanyuan qinggui* does not provide more information on this topic. However, *CBQG* 4 (*T* 48:1132a4 and *CHSS* 1:548d) indicates that one of the duties of the Holy Monk's attendant was to serve as the nighttime guard (*zhitang*).

61. In the original text, this section is called "Director and Chief Seat of the Assembly Quarters." For the sake of clarity, I have divided it into two separate sections. In *Chanyuan qinggui*, the director of the assembly quarters seems to oc-

cupy a position superior to the chief seat of the assembly quarters. In the later *CBQG* 4 (*T* 48:1133a), the chief seat of the assembly quarters is ranked higher than the director of assembly quarters, the title of the former having been changed to "chief of assembly quarters" (*liaoyuan* 寮元). In this text, the director simply assisted the chief and was therefore also given the title "assistant director of assembly quarters" (*fuliao* 副寮) or "*fuliao* candidate" (*wangliao* 望寮). This change can be seen as evidence of the later expansion of the administrative hierarchy of the monastery.

62. In his instructions for delousing or getting rid of fleas, as recorded in the Vinaya (*WFL* 26 [*T* 22:171b20–24]), the Buddha asked that these insects be carefully picked out and placed in the garbage or taken outside. Flea-infested mattresses were placed outdoors to sun.

63. The rest of the assembly sleeps in the Sangha hall.

64. In *Chanyuan qinggui*, the abbot's attendants are classified into two categories, outside and inside. The former tended to the abbot's personal needs, the latter dealt with the abbot's public relations. In the later *CBQG* 4 (*T* 48: 1131c9, 15, and 28), the "inside" attendants are medicine (nursing) attendants and robe-and-bowl (personal effects) attendants; the "outside" attendants are incense-burning (liturgical) attendants, secretarial attendants, and hospitality attendants.

65. *jiexia laci pai* 結夏蠟次牌.

Fascicle Five

1. *shizhe liao* 侍者寮.

2. It seems likely that monasteries often had special living quarters where fundraisers could gather and prepare their materials before departure.

3. During the Song dynasty, in addition to the semiannual agricultural tax, there were taxes on luxury items such as salt, tea, wine, and silk.

4. *guandie* 關牒: literally, certificates of travel. Cf. *YZS* **[39]**.

5. That is, collect "alms," raise funds.

6. *dinian mulu* 遞年目錄.

7. That is, wander idly, sightsee.

8. That is, the entire Sangha.

9. For a detailed discussion of the Song government's sale of tonsure certificates and conferral of the title of master, see "Influences of Chinese Culture" in Chapter 2.

10. 千佛出世不通懺悔. See *Qianshou qianyan Guanshiyin pusa dabeixin tuoluoni* (*T* 20:116a7).

11. *ruyao* 乳藥: literally, "milk medicine."

12. *renshi zhi wu* 人事之物.

13. *xiaoshu mulu* 小疏目錄.

14. *jiaotou bu* 腳頭簿.

15. *shili zhuang* 施利狀.

16. The various titles given to donors, such as *senggong* 僧供, *luohan* 羅漢, and *zhou* 粥, were used to indicate the donors' level of financial support. Thus the granting of a certain title meant a certain amount was expected for donation.

17. 錢: a monetary unit.

18. *fenwei* 分衛 (Skt. *piṇḍapāta*).

19. That is, those lesser chief officers appointed by the rector or the director of the library.

20. *qianzi liao* 前資寮.

21. *choujie* 抽解: literally, "disrobe."

22. *jiandian* 煎點. *Jiandian* literally means "to cook the food until dry and use it to dip into the empty stomach" (*ZSS*, 673a). *Dian* is an abbreviation of *dianxin* 點心, meaning "to dip into the empty stomach," that is, to serve a snack (ibid., 673b).

In the formal tea ceremony, not only was tea served, but also a snack, or, more precisely, a confection. In the lesser tea service called the *chatang* 茶湯, no confection was served. This minor difference can clearly be seen in the instructions of Chan master Furong Daokai 芙蓉道楷 (1043–1118) to his assistants. The master asked that the *chatang* prepared for the new trainees include tea and sweetened soup but not a confection (*Jiatai pudeng lu* 25 [*ZZK* 2B-10-2; quoted in *ZSS*, 673a]).

The term *diancha* 點茶 ("to dip into the tea"), which appears in this text also refers to the tea service. This term originates from the actual method of making the tea: powdered tea is placed in a container, boiling water is poured in, and then some cold water is "dipped" in before the mixture is stirred with a whisk. See *Qiugong jiali yijie* 1 (based on *Wengong jiali* 文公家禮), in *Qiu Wenzhuang gong congshu* (Taipei: Qiu Wenzhuang Gong Congshu Jiyin Weiyuanhui, 1972), 13a.

23. That is, confections.

24. *shacha* 煞茶. Cf. *YZS* **[183]**. The sentence "if higher-grade tea is served then sweetened drink should not be offered" would seem to indicate that average, lower-grade tea was probably served on most occasions.

25. That is, have these items brought in and offered.

26. That is, in the example of the present text.

27. *bang* 牓, *zhuang* 狀. The only difference between the two posters was size. For the form and content of the invitation posters, see *YZS* **[188]**.

28. *xing fashi ren* 行法事人: master of ceremonies or host.

29. Another possible interpretation: the entire assembly, including the host, first sat with legs dropped to the floor, then after a while the host asked everyone to sit in the lotus position.

30. That is, assume the lotus position.

31. The sitting mat was normally draped over the left arm under the robe (*kāṣāya*). In the above passage, the putting aside of sitting mats, as well as the use of fans and the covering of heads, indicates that this ceremony was considered less formal, and its participants were excused from certain stringent rules of monastic decorum.

The hanging of the sitting mat over the left arm under the *kāṣāya*, a practice still observed by Chinese monks and nuns today, is first recorded in Daoxuan's *Lüxiang gantong zhuan* (*T* 45:880c; *ZSS*, 708a). According to this account, monks first put their sitting mats on their left shoulders, *over* their robes, to prevent their *kāṣāya*s from being blown away by the wind. However, when a non-Buddhist asked why, given that the *kāṣāya* was considered nobler and worthier than the sitting mat (the former was worn underneath the latter), the monks changed their practice. From that moment on, monks were said to keep their sitting mats draped over their left arms but hidden beneath their *kāṣāya*s.

Fascicle Six

1. As this was not an event to which all monks were invited, the drum, which was used to summon the entire assembly, did not need to be struck.

2. Literally, "elephantine."

3. The host is only a guest because the abbot is the official host.

4. *zangxia* 藏下.

5. *fashi*[b] 法事. In *Chanyuan qinggui, fashi*[b] may refer either to the individual who presides over the ceremony or to the service itself, depending on the context.

6. *zuofan* 作梵.

7. *MSL* 34 (*T* 22:500a–501c) contains a section on monastic feasts that explains why lay patrons sponsored blessing ceremonies (*jixiang hui* 吉祥會): a birth in the family, a move to a new home, a long-distance journey, a wedding, etc. The "hungry ghost ceremony" (*egui hui* 餓鬼會) was for grave occasions, namely, to bring solace to the recently deceased.

8. *yugu* 魚鼓: "fish-shaped drum." Not a drum per se, but a piece of wood carved in the shape of a fish. Also referred to as *yuban* 魚板; see *ZSS*, 751a.

9. That is, from the position of the chief seat or a respectable senior monk, beside the abbot.

10. 恭敬頭.

11. The first line and title of a chant is a *lüefan* 略梵. Ono Katsutoshi (*Nittō guhō junrei kōki*, 2:155) maintains that the "three homages" may refer to the following verses of *Huayan jing* 6 (*T* 9:430c27–431a2):

> [I, with great respect,] take refuge in the Buddha and wish that all sentient beings may realize the great enlightenment and develop the ultimate mind. I take refuge in the Dharma and wish that all sentient beings may enter deeply into the sutras and gain wisdom as vast as the ocean. I take refuge in the Sangha and wish that all sentient beings may lead the assembly without hindrance.
> [一切恭敬]自歸依佛、當願眾生、體解大道、發無上意、自歸依法、當願眾生、深入經藏、智慧如海、自歸依僧、當願眾生、統理大眾、一切無礙

Another possible verse suggested by Ono appears in Zhiyi's *Fahua sanmei chanyi* (*T* 46:950b):

> We all, with great respect,/ Pay homage with one mind to the Buddhas who eternally dwell in all ten directions,/ [We] pay homage with one mind to the Dharma that eternally dwells in all ten directions,/ [And we] pay homage with one mind to the Sangha who eternally dwell in all ten directions."
> 一切恭敬、一心敬禮、十方常住佛。一心敬禮、十方常住法。一心敬禮、十方常住僧

12. 如來梵.

13. The entire verse of the *Rulai fan*, which is taken from *Shengman shizihou yisheng da fangbian fangguang jing* (*T* 12:217a21–24), reads:

> The magnificent body of the Tathāgata/ Is unrivalled in this world,/ Its ungraspability is beyond compare,/ Therefore [I] now pay homage to it./ The ex-

istence of the Tathāgata is without limits,/ As is his wisdom,/ [Which is] the permanently existing Dharma./ Therefore I take refuge [and faithfully bow down to the eternal Three Treasures].

如來妙色身、世間無與等、無比不思議、是故今敬禮。如來色無盡、智慧亦復然、一切法常住、是故我歸依

The above is my own translation. See also Reischauer, *Ennin's Diary*, 155.

By comparing this passage with earlier accounts of monastic chanting, we can see that this Chinese ritual remained largely unchanged for centuries. During the Tang period, Ennin (*Nittō guhō junrei kōki* [*NBZ* 113:208a]) recorded the following observations about a Korean temple that was located in Dengzhou 登州 (present-day Shandong 山東 province) and heavily influenced by Chinese methods of chanting: "After the bell was struck, the assembly was calm and silent. A monk in a low seat stood up and hit the hammer, chanting, 'We all respect and faithfully bow down to the eternal Three Treasures.' Then another monk began to chant the two verses beginning with 'The magnificent body of the Tathāgata.'"

14. The verse, taken from *Chao riming sanmei jing* (*T* 15:532a21–22), reads in its entirety:

Although located in this world, [one's mind] is in the emptiness, just as the lotus flower [though growing in muddy water] does not touch the water's surface. My mind is so pure and clean that it transcends [the material world]. Now I pay homage to the Ultimate Venerable One [the Buddha].

處世界如虛空、若蓮華不著水、心清淨超於彼、稽首禮無上尊

This verse was also chanted during the precept confession (*shuojie* 説戒) in the Lü school. See *XSC* 1D (*T* 40:37a9); see also *Nittō guhō junrei kōki* (*NBZ* 113:207b); Reischauer, *Ennin's Diary*, 152.

15. *baitang* 白堂.

16. 更. The fifth *geng* is 4 A.M.

17. That is, when only a number of monks are to be awakened.

18. *dengtou* 燈頭.

19. *yunban* 雲板. Although the radical for the character *ban* 板 means "wood," the *yunban* was not made of wood at all but of metal. Therefore this *ban* is sometimes written as 版, a character that does not signify wooden material (*ZSS*, 733b).

Sancai huitu ("Qiyong" 器用 12, 2:1339) informs us that the striking of the metal sheet was used to keep time at the monastery. According to *Tang liudian* 10 (117:16a), the Chinese government had long employed individuals known as *dianzhong* 典鐘 specifically for the task of striking a bell to keep time for townspeople. Thus we can conclude that the monastic use of the *yunban* to mark time was adopted from a preexisting secular practice.

20. That is, when all the monks are to be awakened.

21. Various extant sources provide us with interesting explanations for the fishlike shape of this instrument. *CBQG* 8 (*T* 48:1156a4–5) gives us the most straightforward explanation: As it was thought that a fish never closes its eyes, it was adopted as a symbol of unrelenting vigilance and rigor. An early source for this interpretation is *Liu Fu zhiyi* 劉斧摭遺 (cited in the later *Yunfu qunyu* 2, p. 47b),

which is generally considered the most reliable. This interpretation is the most popular among monastics today (*CHSS* 2:983c).

SSYL 3 (*T* 54:304a25–26) gives two different versions of the origin of the wooden fish instrument. In the biography of Zhang Hua 張華 (*Jinshu* 36 [p. 1075]), it is said that in the Wu region a stone drum emerged of itself from the ocean. When the drum was struck it failed to produce any sound, which prompted the emperor to ask Zhang Hua for an explanation. Zhang Hua suggested that a piece of paulowina wood be brought from Sichuan and carved into the shape of a fish. When this fish was used to strike the stone drum, the sound was heard for several miles around.

SSYL's second explanation is taken from *Gujin shiwen leiju* ("Xuji" 續集, fasc. 23, p. 20a). This text tells the story of a large beast named Pulao 蒲牢 who, when struck by a whale, screamed out in fright. After this impressive incident, bells were fashioned in the shape of Pulao and striking instruments carved in the shape of a whale. Dōchū (*CHSS* 2:983c), however, dismisses both stories, arguing that they refer to the origin of fish-shaped striking instruments rather than the fish-shaped drums in question.

The Tiantai monastic code *JYQG* 2 (*ZZK* 2-6-4:396a) cites an elaborate story allegedly adopted from *Abhidharmamahāvibhāṣā-śāstra*. A monk, who in his lifetime had betrayed his teacher by slandering the Dharma, was reborn as a fish with a tree growing from his back. Whenever the tree swayed in the wind, the fish bled and felt pain. Seeing his former teacher crossing the ocean in a ship, the fish spitefully attempted to hinder the boat's progress. But when the teacher realized that this fish was his student in a former life, he induced the creature to repent and performed the Water-land ceremony on the fish's behalf. That night the teacher dreamt that his former disciple had been reborn once again, and that the tree on his back had somehow been donated to the temple. When he arrived at his monastery the next day, the teacher saw the monks of his assembly marveling at a wooden fish that had mysteriously appeared inside the temple. After checking the two versions of this text available in Chinese translation (*T* 27:1545 and *T* 28:1546), Dōchū (*CHSS* 2:983d) was unable to find the source of this interpretation and declared the story too obscure to be relied on.

Perhaps the least accepted explanation of the origin of the wooden fish is the one relating to the life of Xuanzang 玄奘 (602–664) as recorded in *Zhigui qu* 指歸曲. It is said that while returning home from India, Xuanzang stopped at Sichuan, where he was invited to a funerary feast sponsored by a rich man whose three-year-old son had been drowned by his malicious stepmother. Much to the dismay of all those present, Xuanzang demanded that he be given a large fish to eat. The rich man complied, asking that such a fish be caught and brought before their honored guest. Presented with his meal, Xuanzang cut open the stomach of the fish, revealing the lost child still alive inside it. Xuanzang then instructed the rich man to have a piece of wood carved in the shape of a fish and hung in the temple. Again Dōchū (*ZSS;* 748b) found this story unacceptable, pointing out that it had no basis in Xuanzang's illustrious biography and therefore could not be considered truthful.

22. To be precise, the signal instruments mentioned here were located in the outer vestibule of the Sangha hall: the board was hung on the wall and was taken

down whenever it was to be struck; the wooden fish was suspended from the ceiling on the left-hand side; the drum sat on the right-hand side; and the small bell was suspended on the right-hand wall. Very similar arrangements can still be seen in the Sangha hall at Eiheiji.

23. *yuxia* 浴下.

24. That is, each day of the month ending in a three or an eight.

25. 三塗. The Three Paths refer to the three lowest states of existence: the path of heat, that is, hell; the path of knives, which is the realm of hungry ghosts; and the path of blood, the realm of animals. Those who are reborn in hell, due to the hatred they harbored in their former lives, are tortured in scalding pots, pans, ovens, etc. Those who are transformed into hungry ghosts, due to avarice in their former lives, are punished with knives and sticks. Those who become animals, due to the ignorant state in which they lived their lives are placed in a world of bloody and vicious struggle.

26. 八難. Those sentient beings who are born into the Eight Difficulties are unable to see the Buddha or hear the Dharma. These eight include the three realms mentioned above plus the heaven of longevity, which is the fourth level of the Subtle-Matter Realm; the remote region of Uttara-kuru; a state of blindness, deafness, or muteness; a disposition toward secular prejudice, the pursuit of secular knowledge, and lack of belief in the Dharma; and a period when there is no Buddha, that is, a time before or after that of a Buddha.

27. *Chanyuan qinggui* gives no indication of who should be assigned special envoy. *CBQG* 3 (*T* 48:1123c16–17), however, stipulates that only high-ranking administrators, senior retired staff, the chief seat in the west hall (that is, the chief seat emeritus), or second-rank chief officers can be appointed to this position.

28. *chengsishu* 承嗣書. A detailed discussion of the certificate of lineage inheritance is given by Dōgen in the section on "the certificate of transmission" (*shisho*) in his *Shōbōgenzō* 39 (*DZZ* 1:337–347). The certificate of transmission indicated that a direct transmission of the Dharma from master to disciple had occurred. The transmission of the Dharma refers to the passing on of true enlightenment, Dōgen explained, and just as all the Buddhas transmit the Dharma from one to the other, so it is with the patriarchs and within the temple, each transmission perpetuating the essence of enlightenment.

The certificate of transmission received by Dōgen from his Chinese master, Rujing, when he traveled to the Song has been preserved in the Eiheiji Temple. In the center of the certificate is written "Śākyamuni Buddha," surrounded by the names of all the patriarchs in clockwise order, from Mahākāśyapa, the foremost disciple of the Buddha, through the Chan patriarchs, to Rujing, and finally to the recipient himself. Under the names of the Buddha and all subsequent lineage holders (with the exception of the recipient) are the four characters *botuo bodi* 勃陀勃地 (*buddha bodhi*, "the enlightenment of the Buddha"), indicating that the Buddha and the patriarchs, who attained realization, are now transmitting the Dharma. A thin line is drawn through all the names to demonstrate the continuity of Dharma transmission. The attestation of Rujing is written at the bottom: "The life thread of the Buddha is connected when one attains enlightenment. With Dōgen, this connection has now been made complete" 佛祖命脈、証契即通、道元即通. The document is then signed, "Rujing, abbot of the Tiantongshan Monastery, in the third year of the Baoqing 寶慶 era [1227 C.E.] of the Song dynasty." The certificate is written on a silk brocaded scroll with the design of a raised plum blossom and measures about 5 feet, 7 inches in length and 15 inches in width. Some temples simply used ink to write these certificates while others used blood from a finger or the tongue.

To receive a transmission certificate, a disciple was obliged to study under and ultimately be selected by a master who had himself inherited a given Dharma lineage. In time, however, certificates were obtained by other means, such as influence, bribery, or coercion. The phenomenon was denounced by Dōgen (*DZZ* 1:341), who witnessed a number of these dishonorable practices. Some monks who studied under a renowned master commissioned personal portraits or scrolls inscribed with the master's words and presented these documents as certificates of transmission. There even arose the practice of visiting famous masters to obtain as many "celebrity" certificates of transmission as possible solely for the sake of personal fame. See Muramatsu Tetsuo, "Shisho no kōsatsu," in *Jissen shūjō kenkyū kai nempō* 6 (1937): 112–130; for an article in English on the Japanese Dharma transmission, see William M. Bodiford, "Dharma Transmission in Sōto Zen: Manzan Dōhaku's Reform Movement," *MN* 46, no. 4 (Winter 1991): 423–451.

29. *yishu* 遺書. When an abbot died, his will—or, more precisely, his farewell letters—was sent to his Dharma heirs at other monasteries, as well as to lay patrons and government officials. A detailed account of the procedure of issuing the abbot's will and the receiving of a will from a Dharma master is given in *CBQG* 3 (*T* 48:1129c16–1130b7 and *CBQG* 2, 1123b24–c4.

30. *ruyuan xianchi shu* 入院先馳書. For details, see the section "Appointment of the Honorable Senior—the Abbot" in fasc. 7.

31. *guowang xianchi* 過往先馳.

32. That is, for all private epistles.

33. *dangmian panping* 當面判憑; for example, a punishment or the sentencing of an individual.

34. That is, safeguard the monastery as a whole.

35. 省行堂. The name "hall of longevity" was criticized by the lay scholar Zhao Lingjin 趙令衿, who preferred that the infirmary be called *shengxing tang* 省行堂 (the hall of contemplating one's deeds). In his *Nanyue Falun si shengxing tang ji* 南嶽法輪寺省行堂記 (collected in *Zimen jingxun* 2 [*T* 48:1051c]), Zhao argues that the ailing monk should contemplate his past behavior and consider what changes should be made in his life, rather than automatically asking for or accepting medicine. Zhao considered the name "hall of longevity" vulgar and inadequate, insisting that the name *shengxing* would remind the patient to contemplate matters of life and death. This account may be considered indicative of the ferocity with which the secular community often criticized the clergy, sometimes even to the point of abandoning a basic sense of humanity.

Daoxuan (*SXC* 3D [*T* 40:144a13–20]) recorded that an infirmary was built in the northwest section of the Indian monastery in Jeta's grove in the park of Anāthapiṇḍika. Named "hall of impermanence" (*wuchang yuan* 無常院), the infirmary served as a place where ailing monks were brought to remove them from their rooms, where they were thought to be more prone to attachment to their belongings. A golden statue facing west was placed inside the infirmary (although the name is not given, we can assume it was a statute of the Amitābha

Buddha), its right hand lifted up and its left hand holding a colorful banner that draped to the floor. The sick were arranged behind the statue, where they could hold the end of the banner, signifying their willingness to follow the Amitābha Buddha and be reborn in the Pure Land.

Fascicle Seven

1. *dongsi* 東司. No one source explains the origin of the word *dongsi* (literally, "east office") for "toilet." As illustrated in the diagrams of Song temples in *DJZ*, *dongsi* was used no matter what the latrine's location in the monastic compound. An anecdote demonstrating this can be found in *Dahui Pujue Chanshi zongmen wuku* 大慧普覺禪師宗門武庫 (*T* 47, 949b22–26): After visiting with Master Zhenjing 真淨, Director (*langzhong* 郎中) Qian Yi 錢弋 asked to be shown to the toilet. Zhenjing had one of his servers lead Qian toward the westernmost part of the grounds, prompting the meticulous Qian to suddenly ask, "If it is called *dongsi*, why do we walk to the west?"

Dōchū (*ZSS*, 58a) hypothesized that *dongsi* may have been an erroneous transcription of *dengsi* 登司, the toilet deity. According to *Shiwu yiming lu* (cited by Dōchū), the deity's name from which *dengsi* is mistakenly derived is Guo Deng 郭登. However, Guo Deng is only one of several names for the toilet deity. Like the earth guardian, the toilet deity was known by several different names, depending on the text and varying local beliefs. Other designations for the toilet deity include: Zigu 紫姑, Qian Yi 錢義, Xu Tianzhu 項天竺, Bei 卑, and Houdi 後帝. See *Shiwu yiming lu* 28 (1788; reprint, Taipei: Xinxing Shuju, 1969), 14a; See also *Yiyuan*, Xuejin taoyan edition (Taipei: Yiwen Yinshuguan, 1965), 151:2b, 5a; *Gujin shiwen leiju*, Kanbun edition, 1661, 47:25a; Yale University Library; and the article by Minakata Kumagusu, "Shishin," *Minakata Kumagusu zenshū* (Tokyo: Kengensha, 1952), 3:136–144.

The Vinaya *MSL* 34 (*T* 22:504a17) stipulates that the toilet should be located in the southern or western sections of the monastery so as to be in the path of the prevailing winds. *GSP(Z)* 10 (*T* 24:247a19) states that the toilet should be erected in the northwest corner of the monastery; *Genben sapoduobu lüshe* 14 (*T* 24:606c25), a text from the same tradition as *GSP(Z)*, insists that the toilet be built in the northeast corner. No single direction seems to have been agreed upon. The most important factor for the placement of the latrine was simply good air circulation.

Although not given in *Chanyuan qinggui*, another word for "toilet" used in Chan monasteries was *xueyin* 雪隱. The second half of the word, *yin*, is said to have been taken from the second half of the name of Lingyin Temple 靈隱寺, while the first half, *xue*, is thought to have been derived from the name of either of two men who lived in this temple: Chan master Xuefeng Yicun 雪峰義存 (822–908), who attained enlightenment while he was cleaning the toilet, or Chan master Xuedou Chongxian 雪竇重顯 (980–1052), who secluded and cultivated himself while working as the latrine attendant. The term *xueyin* was written on a tablet and hung before the latrine in Lingyin Temple. See *Tōjō garan zakki*, collected in *Sōtōshū zensho Shingi*, ed. Sōtōshū Zensho Kankōkai (1931; reprint, Tokyo: Sōtōshū Shūmuchō, 1972), 852b; *ZD*, 665b.

2. See *SFL* 49 (*T* 22:932a15); *MSL* 34 (*T* 22:504a27, c25); *JXXL* (*T* 50:872c27).

3. See *SXC* 3D (*T* 40:148a17).

4. See "Personal Possessions" in Chapter 2.

5. *MSL* 35 (*T* 22:509a20) states that monks would tie their clothes together with their belts and hang them over a pole. A monk's belt identified his belongings. (As every monk was issued the same type of belt, one can only conjecture that a name or at least some kind of identifying mark was added to each belt.)

6. As the Vinayas indicate, a monk should snap his fingers before going to the toilet. See *SFL* 49 (*T* 22:932a18–19); *WFL* 27 (*T* 22:177a15); *MSL* 34 (*T* 22:504a28–29); *DSW* 2 (*T* 24:925b27); *SXC* 3D (*T* 40:148a7); *JXXL* (*T* 45:872c29). The custom of snapping the fingers was intended either to purify the place or to alarm the spirits. The latter is cited here (*CHSS* 2:825a; *SXC* 3D [*T* 40:148a7]).

According to *Zhengfa nianchu jing* 16 (*T* 17:92a28, 93b19–23), those who, as a result of their avaricious and spiteful nature, give unclean food to Buddhist monastics or Brahmans (non-Buddhist priests) will be reborn in the realm of the hungry ghosts who eat excrement.

An anecdote regarding the finger-snapping practice is given in *Za piyu jing* (cited in *Zhujing yaoji* 20 [*T* 54:190a23–25]; the original source has not been found). A monk once entered the toilet without snapping his fingers. Without the customary warning, the hungry ghost that dwelled inside the latrine had his face soiled. The ghost was furious but was prevented from killing the discourteous monk by his impervious virtue, for he was a monk who diligently upheld the precepts.

7. See *SFL* 49 (*T* 22:932a26–27); *DSW* 2 (*T* 24:925c2–3); *JXXL* (*T* 45:873a4).

8. See *DSW* 2 (*T* 24:925c5); see also *WFL* 27 (*T* 22:177b23–24).

9. Piles or intestinal ulcers.

10. For details regarding the bamboo spatula, see fasc. 4, n. 40.

11. See *SFL* 49 (*T* 22:932b20–21); *WFL* 27 (*T* 22:177b22); *JXXL* (T45:873a10–11).

12. In the Vinayas, the Buddha instructs monks to chew willow twigs and gives the following reasons for doing so: it reduces bad breath; it sharpens one's gustatory abilities; it balances the body's temperature; it aids digestion; and it improves eyesight. See *SFL* 53 (*T* 22:960c); also *WFL* 26 (*T* 22:176b); *MSL* 34 (*T* 22:505b1); *PNMJ* 6 (*T* 24:838b13–18); *DSW* 1 (*T* 24:914a16–17). It was not, however, appropriate to chew the willow twig while using the toilet. See *SFL* 49 (*T* 22:932a29); *WFL* 27 (*T* 22:177b9); *MSL* 34 (*T* 22:504b2).

13. See *DSW* 1 (*T* 24:914a17–18); see also *MSL* 34 (*T* 22:504b11).

14. See *Genben sapoduobu lüshe* 14 (*T* 24:607a27–29).

15. See *DSW* 2 (*T* 24:925b28); see also *WFL* 27 (*T* 22:177a15).

16. See *JXXL* (*T* 45:873a8–9).

17. See *JXXL* (*T* 45:873a19).

18. See *JXXL* (*T* 45:872c28–29).

19. For a wealth of information on the proper use of the toilet, see *SFL* 49 (*T* 22:932a14–b28) and 50 (*T* 22:942b25–c8); *WFL* 27 (*T* 22:177a5–b25); *MSL* 34 (*T* 22:504a14–505a22); *DSW* 2 (*T* 24:925b25–c11); *SXC* 3D (*T* 40:148a5–17); *JXXL* (*T* 45:872c27–873a16); *Shōbōgenzō*, 54 in *DZZ*.

20. See *YZS* **[114]**, fasc. 3.

21. *fosang hua* 佛喪花. *SSYL* 3 (*T* 54:307c17–18) notes that white paper was used to make these *śāla* flowers, which were meant to represent the eight trees that surrounded the Buddha's death bed (two at the roots in each corner) in

Kuśinagara. After the Buddha passed away, one of each pair of trees faded away while the other four flourished, thus symbolizing the polarities of "permanence and impermanence," "self and nonself," "happiness and unhappiness," "purity and impurity." See *Dabo niepan jing jijie* 2 (*T* 37:384a26–b10).

22. That is, the funeral.

23. *putong ta* 普同塔.

24. The practice of auctioning a deceased monk's possessions is recorded in the Vinaya texts. *SFL* 41 (*T* 22:862c) describes the auction's origins with the following anecdote: A monk died in debt, and the other monks of his monastery were at a loss as to how they might pay the debtors. The Buddha told them that the deceased monk's clothing (except for his three robes) could be sold to raise the necessary money. If, however, a monk had no possessions other than the three robes, then even these items could be sold. *SSL* 7 (*T* 23:53a) also indicates that the selling of clothing was permitted among members of the Sangha. During the auction, the buyer was allowed to change his mind until the third announcement of intended purchase.

Another Vinaya anecdote explains how the auction became a regular, systematized custom (cited in *SSYL* 3 [*T* 54:309b]). Once when a certain monk passed away, another monk was chosen to gather his belongings to distribute among the assembly. However, when the monk in charge seemed unable to do so equitably, the Buddha made some suggestions. Once the assembly has gathered and consented to the process, the Buddha advised, an auction should be held, and the monetary proceeds from it should then be distributed equally among the members of the Sangha.

25. Cf. *GSP(S)* 3 (*T* 24:652a13), which indicates that chanting was conducted before the distribution of the deceased's possessions.

26. *PNMJ* 3 (*T* 24:815b10–12) provides a detailed protocol for the distribution of the deceased monk's possessions. First, the deceased should be buried. After the mourners have returned to the monastery, the entire assembly should be summoned. Once everyone has gathered, the possessions of the deceased should be placed in public view.

An impressive defense of this particular procedure can be found in *SSL* 28 (*T* 23:202c29–203a4). The assembly began distributing a deceased monk's possessions before interring him. The spirit of the deceased, reluctant witness to these events, rose up in anger and berated the monks for dividing up his personal effects. The Buddha then instructed the monks to bury the deceased monk first, then distribute his possessions in a separate location. The deceased's possessions should never be divided in the presence of his body.

In *SXC* 3A (*T* 40:116a27–b2), Daoxuan offers several details that corroborate this order of events. When a member of Sangha passes away, Daoxuan insisted, the door to his room (where his possessions are kept) should not only be closed, but locked, and the key given only to the most trustworthy of disciples. If there is no such disciple, the key should be entrusted to the administrators. Only after the body has been interred may the disciple (or administrator) remove the deceased's belongings and distribute them.

27. *Chanyuan qinggui* does not give much detail on the auction itself. However, *CBQG* 6 (*T* 48:1149a5–12) describes the procedure in the following manner:

The rectory server selects and hands the items to the rector one at a time. The rector then lifts up each item, announces its identification number, then gives a description of the item, and its estimated value. If, [for example,] the [estimated value of] an item is set at one string of coins, the rector will start the bidding at one tenth of a string. The rectory server then repeats each of the rector's statements and waits for a response from [a bidder in] the assembly. [The bids are raised] incrementally until a full string of coins is reached, at which time the rector strikes the bell and announces, "[The bidding on] this item has now reached one string of coins." [Apparently this announcement indicates a ceiling beyond which bids cannot be raised.] This process is then repeated for each item until none remains. If there are two people who call out the same price [simultaneously], the rectory server will halt the proceedings by shouting, "Double break!" [signifying that neither bid can be accepted.] The bidding on that item must then start over. [Perhaps this may cause one of the bidders to rethink, negotiate, or simply yield to the other].

The striking of the bell shows that the bidding is over, [after which] the rectory server asks the [final] bidder to give his name. The guest master then records the name, and the attendant issues a document, in which is recorded the item, its price, and the name of bidder, to the delivery server, who then gives [the document] to the bidder. [Once the auction is over,] the delivery server collects all the items and places them in a trunk [for safekeeping until they are paid for. . . . If the bidder does not come to claim the item within three days, the item can be resold at the original price.

The text comments further that since the commotion generated by auctions was deemed unseemly, a less competitive, or at least less noisy, lottery system was introduced, with prices set in advance.

28. Within the Buddhist tradition there is a widespread belief in an intermediate existence (*zhongyou* 中有; Skt. *antarā-bhava*, also known as *gandharva*), which occurs after the moment of death and before the moment of rebirth. Theories about this period vary; some believe it lasts for seven days, others assert that it has no fixed duration, and still others completely disavow the possibility of any such period, claiming that rebirth is instantaneous. However, according to the Chinese tradition, the intermediate existence lasts for "seven sevens," that is, forty-nine days. In *Yuqie shidi lun* 1 (Skt. *Yogācārabhūmi*) (*T* 30:282a27–b4) it is written:

[After death], there is an intermediate existence. If it [that is, the being after death] does not find the proper conditions for rebirth, it remains [in this realm] for the full seven days. If it does find the proper conditions for rebirth, it stays for an unspecified number of days [that is, for as many days as it takes before the end of the cycle of seven days]. If, at the end of the seventh day, it has still not found the conditions for rebirth, it dies [that is, fades from all existence] and comes to be [that is, reappears in the intermediate existence] for another period of seven days. Thus the cycle of life and death repeats itself as long as the conditions for rebirth are not found and continues up to the full seven sevens [that is, seven periods of seven, or forty-nine days]. At the end of this period [of forty-nine days], it must decide where to be reborn. If this [being is unable to be reborn and] dies after [the first] seven days, it may still reappear [for the next cycle of seven days] in the same intermediate existence [where it has largely the same options for rebirth]. If, however, [the being's] karma has somehow been changed [for example, if friends and relatives from his former life transfer merit to the deceased], the seed of this [being] will change, allowing it to reappear in another cycle [where it will have different options for rebirth].

Accordingly, Chinese Buddhists performed meritorious acts for forty-nine days after the death of a loved one to transfer good karma to the deceased (now wandering between life and death) and to prevent their being reborn into an evil realm. Quoted from *SSYL* 3 (*T* 54:305b–c). The same theory of rebirth after forty-nine days is asserted in *Epidamo dapiposha lun* 70 (*T* 27:361b8–9).

29. That is, to illustrate to others the deceased's true detachment from material things.

30. Auctions were also used to distribute the possessions of a living monk who felt he had accumulated too many belongings. See *YZS* **[264]**.

31. The four great elements constituting the physical body are earth (solid), water (liquid), fire (heat), and wind (breath).

32. See the biography of Zongze in Chapter 3.

33. The Four Holy Names are: Amitābha Buddha, Avalokiteśvara Bodhisattva, Mahāsthāmaprāpta Bodhisattva 大勢至菩薩, and All the Bodhisattvas of the Pure Great Ocean 清淨大海眾菩薩 (that is, all the bodhisattvas in the Pure Land).

34. 恭敬歡喜去、還到安養國; that is, in the Pure Land. See *Wuliangshou jing* (*T* 12:273a27).

35. 生死交謝、寒暑迭遷. See *Wu buqian lun* 物不遷論 in *Zhao lun* (*T* 45:151a9).

36. 諸行無常、是生滅法、生滅滅已、寂滅為樂. See *Niepan jing* 14 (*T* 12:450a16, 451a1) and 13 (*T* 12:692a13, 693a1).

37. *Guan Wuliangshou Fo jing* (*T* 12:344c9–346a26) states that sentient beings are divided into three groups of three (upper, middle, and lower) in accordance with their deeds. Each of these groups in turn is divided into upper, middle, and lower. If any sentient being, no matter what its group, recites the name of Amitābha Buddha with sincerity and faith, it may be reborn in the Pure Land. Thus the various means of rebirth in the Pure Land can be classified into nine categories corresponding to a sentient being's deeds in a previous life.

38. 一生補處. See *Emituo jing* (*T* 12:347b5).

39. See fasc. 2, n. 82.

40. [十方薄伽梵]一路涅槃門. See *Lengyan jing* 5 (*T* 19:124c29).

41. That is, that the Buddha's wisdom will illuminate the spirit of the deceased.

42. That is, one hundred coins on a string.

43. This is more of a caveat than an admonition against intentionally fraudulent practices, warning monks that they may have "incomplete" strings of money in their possession.

44. That is, he should check to see that his coins do not include low-quality currency. During the Song, two types of coins were in circulation: copper and iron. The copper coin was intended to be more valuable than the iron, but when the value of copper began to surpass that of iron (most likely due to the high demand for copper in the forging of weapons), a nationwide shortage of copper

coins developed. In some areas, the local government went so far as to confiscate all copper coins in circulation and refrained from minting any more. Finally in 1102 Cai Jing 蔡京 ordered that coins be made of copper mixed with tin. Thenceforth a string of coins (one thousand) was made of copper, black tin, and white tin in the ratio of 8:4:2. This new admixture was referred to as "mixed-tin" (*jiaxi qian* 夾錫錢), or simply as "new tin." See Kawakami, *Sōdai no keizai*, 213–214.

45. According to *SFL* 21 (*T* 22:711b), some monks offended the guardian deities by carrying a dead body through the Buddha pagoda. A dead body was considered impure and to bring anything impure into the venerable Buddha pagoda was a sacrilege. There is an entire section in this Vinaya dealing specifically with proper decorum in the presence of the Buddha pagoda. For instance, while one is below, facing, or in any way proximate to the pagoda, one must not urinate, defecate, blow one's nose, spit, or chew willow twigs. One should not wear slippers, sleep near the pagoda, or hide one's personal belongings within the pagoda.

According to the Vinayas, the first Buddha pagoda was erected while the Buddha was still alive. *SSL* 56 (*T* 23:415b27–c3) gives an account of a layperson named Anāthapindada who asked the Buddha for permission to erect a pagoda to worship the Buddha's hair and nails. The Buddha himself was said to have erected a pagoda for Kaśyapa, a previous Buddha. In *MSL* 33 (*T* 22:497c24–26) King Prasenajit 波斯匿王, deciding to follow the example of the historical Buddha, also erected a pagoda in honor of Kaśyapa.

46. The chief seat emeritus is a retired high-ranking monk serving as auxiliary "chief seat." As the number of monks in a monastery increased, retired senior monks were called on to transmit their experience to the younger generation. This position was also called "chief seat of the rear hall" (*houtang shouzuo* 後堂首座) and later "chief seat of the west hall" (*xitang shouzuo* 西堂首座), referring to this person's seating in the Sangha hall. In Chinese tradition, the host sits in the eastern part of a hall, while a seat in the west is reserved for the guest. As most of the chief seat emeriti were chosen from other monasteries, they were considered guests of a sort. *CBQG* 4 (*T* 48:1133c) gives a detailed description of the ceremony of appointing the chief seat emeritus.

47. 法雲圓通. For the biography of Fayun, see fasc. 2, n. 14.

48. *juyang* 舉揚, that is, to give one final sermon.

49. *chushi* 出世, that is, if he has never served as the abbot of a monastery.

50. That is, if he often delivers sermons.

51. An "awl in the bag" is an idiom used to refer to a person whose potential virtue or talent is clearly discernable, just as an awl, though hidden in a bag, can still be recognized by its shape. The expression finds its origins in *Shiji* 76 p. 2366). During the period of Warring States (475–221 b.c.e.), the Lord of Pingyuan 平原君 attempted to gather a group of twenty honored statesmen (*menke* 門客) to send as negotiators to the neighboring state of Chu 楚國. When only nineteen suitable candidates could be found, one of the lord's subjects, Mao Sui 毛遂, promptly recommended himself for the mission. At first the lord was skeptical of the man's qualifications. "Just as when one places an awl into a bag the point of the instrument can be seen at the bottom," the lord observed, "so too would any of your talents have shown by now since you have already spent years at court."

"Place me in the bag," Mao Sui insisted, "and you will see not only the point of the awl below, but even the handle protruding from above." Persuaded by the man's determination, the lord acceded to his request, and later, during a crucial moment in the negotiations, Mao Sui stepped forward and won over the representatives of the Chu state with his arguments.

52. That is, virtue and talent cannot be hidden.

53. *xianshi* 顯示.

54. See *YZS* **[88–91]** in fasc. 2.

55. That is, most honorable.

56. *kaitang* 開堂; "the opening of the [Dharma] hall." The first ceremony performed by a newly appointed abbot was called the *kaitang*. However, according to *Chunming tuichao lu* 1, Jifu congshu edition [Taipei: Yiwen Yinshuguan, 1966, 72:9b–10a), the term *kaitang* originally referred to the ceremonies held in the imperially supported translation houses of the Song. These were "pre-readings" of newly translated sutras, which were held two months before their presentation in the court. A month later, that is, a month before the presentation, translators and editors would gather again to prepare the translation, an event called "the closing of the hall" (*bitang* 住持). (Note: *ZTSY* 8 [*ZZK* 2-18-1:118a] contains a transcription error in which *kaiting* is written instead of *bitang*.)

57. *zhuchi* 住持. The term *zhuchi* refers to the abbots' role as a holding vessel for the Dharma, where it may dwell safe from extinction. See *ZTSY* 8 (*ZZK* 2-18-1:118a).

58. *chuandeng* 傳燈. See *Da bore boluomiduo jing* 408 (referred to in *ZTSY* 8 [*ZZK* 2-18-1:113b]): "The Tathāgata preaches the essence of the Dharma to his disciples without contradicting the nature of Dharma. Based on the teaching of the Buddha, the disciples of the Buddha cultivate themselves vigorously and experience the reality of Dharma; therefore whatever they preach will not contradict the nature of Dharma. Accordingly, the teaching of the Buddha is like the *light which transmits and illuminates*" [italics mine].

59. Shanxian zunzhe zhanglao 善現尊者長老, that is, Śāriputra.

60. Jinsu Rulai 金粟如來, that is, Vimalakīrti's previous life. The author of *Shimen bianhuo lun* 1 (*T* 52:551b17–18), monk Fuli 復禮, noted that, according to Jizang 吉藏, the reference to Vimalakīrti's previous existence as the Golden Grain Tathāgata is based on *Siwei sanmei jing* 思維三昧經. However, since Jizang could not find this sutra in any of the canonical catalogues, he believed that, while the text may have existed in India, it was not translated into Chinese.

In both his *Jingming xuanlun* 2 (*T* 38:866b6) and *Weimo jing yishu* 1 (*T* 38: 915a15–16), Jizang refers to the Golden Grain Tathāgata as an epithet for Vimalakīrti's past incarnation. However, the two texts, which the above works cite as sources for this epithet, *Faji jing* 發跡經 and *Siwei sanmei jing*, cannot be found in the Chinese canon.

61. *sasao* 洒掃.

62. That is, he should rule by suggestion or intimation and not by overbearing interference.

63. That is, the teacher of human and heavenly beings. The biography of Chan master Lingshu Rumin 靈樹如敏 in *Jingde chuandeng lu* 11 (*T* 51:286c2–8) includes a story containing what may be the first use of this phrase. When Lingshu learned that a general in his region was planning a military takeover and was

coming to his temple to ask for advice, he decided to pass away (literally, "sit transformed"). The general arrived, learned of Lingshu's death, and became angry, demanding when Lingshu had become ill. The administrators replied that the Chan master had not been ill at all and had left a letter for the general to read. The general opened the letter, which simply read: "The eye of human and heavenly beings is the chief seat in the hall" (*rentian yanmu tangzhong shangzuo* 人天眼目,堂中上座). After contemplating the master's words, the general decided to abandon his plans and invited Chan master Yunmen Wenyan 雲門文偃 (864–949), who occupied the first seat in the Sangha hall, to serve as the next abbot.

64. *sangzhu* 喪主.

65. *kan* 龕.

66. *xiaozi* 孝子. According to Chinese custom, a son in mourning is called a *xiaozi*. The term "filial sons" is thus adopted from secular practice and is here meant to refer to the disciples of the deceased abbot.

67. That is, the day of the funeral.

68. That is, souvenir gifts.

69. For a detailed discussion of the selection of an abbot, see "Influences of Chinese Culture" in Chapter 2.

70. Goods such as tea, wine, or salt, the sale of which was monopolized by the government.

71. That is, his place of retirement. Song law (*QTS* 51 [486a]) stipulated that no retired cleric could build a cloister or hut on the grounds of a public monastery.

72. That is, while still an active abbot.

73. That is, he should not give private interviews or accept disciples.

Glossary

Characters for titles of books and their authors can be found in the bibliography.

Apan 阿潘
bafu lunzang 八輻輪藏
baichui 白槌
Baidi 白帝
baihei 白黑
baijuanfu 白絹複
baitang 白堂
Baiyun hall 白雲堂
Baizhang Huaihai 百丈懷海
BaiZhaoju 白招拒
bang 榜
bantou 板頭
baotao 包絛
Baoyou 寶祐
baozhen dai 包枕袋
bazhen 把針
beijia 北頬
beiwei 被位
beizhu 被主
benjue 本覺
bianchui 遍槌
biechang chanhui 別場懺悔
Bieli Chanju 別立禪居
Bieli zhongzhi 別立眾制
bigao 鼻高
bikong liaotian 鼻孔撩天
binzhu wenchou 賓主問酬
Biqiu 比丘
bixia 陛下
bodan 缽單
bonang 缽囊
bore hui 般若會

boretou 般若頭
boshi 缽拭
boshua 缽刷
bowei 缽位
buding 不定
busa 布薩
bushen 不審
bu shi 晡時
buwodan 布臥單
cai jiefang 菜街坊
canchan wendao 參禪問道
cantou 參頭
caodan 草單
ceshen 廁神
chabang 茶牓
changban 長板
changcan guan 常參官
Changlu Yingfu 長蘆應夫
Changlu Zongze 長蘆宗賾
Changlusi 長蘆寺
changpu cha 菖蒲茶
chanyi 禪椅
Chanyue 禪月
chanzhen 禪鎮
Chaodu 超度
chatang 茶湯
chatang renshi 茶湯人事
chatou xingzhe 茶頭行者
chayao 茶藥
chayi 衩衣
chencan muqing 晨參暮請
chengsi shu 承嗣書

309

Chen Shi 陳寶
chen shi 辰時
Chen Xu 陳詡
chetou xingzhe 車頭行者
Chi Biaonu 赤爆怒
chifan kaizhe 持犯開遮
chijin 匙筋
Chongfu Chansi 崇福禪寺
Chongjiu 重九
Chongning 崇寧
chou 籌
choujie 抽解
Chuanfa Cijue 傳法慈覺
Chuanfa zhengzong ji 傳法正宗記
chuangdang 床當
chuangli 床曆
chuangzhang 床帳
chuantang 穿堂
chuchou 觸籌
chujia 出家
chujia busa fa 出家布薩法
chujing 觸淨
chuli 觸禮
chuli sanbai 觸禮三拜
chushen 出生
chushi 出世
Chu shijie 處世界
chutou 觸頭
chuye 初夜
chuyi 觸衣
chuzhi 觸指
chuzhong 出眾
chuzhong juci xingzhe 廚中局次行者
cibu 祠部
cibu tong 祠部筒
Cijue Chanshi yulu 慈覺禪師語錄
Cijue Dashi 慈覺大師
cizhang 刺帳
cong 蔥
dachen 嗏嗅
dadian 大殿
dadie 打疊
dahui 大會
daidao youxie 帶刀右脇
dajing chu 打靜處
danfu 單敷
danguo liao 旦過寮
Danliao Jihong 澹寮繼洪

danliao 單寮
Daoan 道安
Daocheng 道誠
daofeng 道風
Daofu 道覆
daojia 道價
daoju 道具
Daoxin 道信
Daoxuan 道宣
daseng zhang 大僧帳
dashi 大師
Dawei 大魏
daxiong baodian 大雄寶殿
dazhan jiuli 大展九禮
dazhong xingzhe 打鐘行者
dazuo chatang 大座茶湯
dengtou 燈頭
Deshan Xuanjian 德山宣鑑
diancha 點茶
diandeng 點燈
diandu 點讀
dian ruliao cha 點入寮茶
diantang 點湯
dianxin 點心
dianzhu 殿主
dianzuo 典座
Dōchū 道忠
Dōgen 道元
Dong'an Temple 東安寺
dongjie 冬節
dongsi 東司
Dongta 東塔
dongxu 東序
Dongyang Dehui 東陽德輝
Duanwu 端午
dudi yuan 度弟院
dujiang 都講
duliao 獨寮
du sengzheng 都僧正
dusi 都寺
egui hui 餓鬼會
Eisai 榮西
Ennin 圓仁
Facong 法聰
Fadi jinglun 佛地經論
Fahua sanmei chanyi 法華三昧懺儀
fajia 法駕
fajuan 法卷

Falang 法朗
Fali 法礪
faming jingu 發明今古
fangcan 放參
Fangdeng sanmei xingfa 方等三昧行法
fangsheng ciji 放生慈濟
fangzhang 方丈
faqian 發遣
Fashe jiedu 法社節度
fashi 法師
fashi[b] 法事
Fatai 法汰
fatang 法堂
Faxian 法顯
Fayan 法眼
fayao 法藥
Fayu 法遇
Fayun 法雲
Fayun Faxiu 法雲法秀
Fazang 法藏
fazhu 法主
fazuo 法座
feishi jiang 非時漿
fengyao 風藥
fentong dasheng 分通大乘
fenwei 分衛
fenzi 鑷子
Foguo Weibai 佛國惟白
Foming dahui 佛名大會
Fosan hua 佛散花
fosheng hui 佛生會
Fotudeng 佛圖澄
Fu Jian 符堅
fuliao 副寮
fupa 複帕
fu senglu 副僧錄
fu sengzheng 副僧正
fusi 副寺
futian yi 福田衣
Fuxi shi 伏羲氏
fuyuan 副院
gaibao 蓋包
gangji tang 綱紀堂
Gao 高宗
gaoxiang 告香
geng 更
gezhu 閣主
gongde shi 功德使

gongde yuan 功德院
gongdu zhi 公度制
gongguo 供過
gongguo xingzhe 供過行者
gongjie 公界
gongjie zhi li 公界之禮
Gongjing tou 恭敬頭
gongju 供具
gongping 公憑
gongtou xingzhe 供頭行者
gongzhang qianwu 供帳錢物
guada 掛搭
gualuo 掛絡
guandie 關牒
Guanding 灌頂
guanglü 廣律
Guanxin shifa 觀心食法
Guanxiu 貫休
Guanzhong 關中
guazi 掛子
guchang 估唱
Guijing wen 龜鏡文
Guizi mu 鬼子母
guoji xingxiang 國忌行香
guotong 國統
hangui xiaochao 函櫃小巢
Hanshi 寒食
Han Shuniu 含樞紐
hanxuan 寒暄
haozhao 好照
Heluo 河洛
henan 和南
heshang 和尚
heshang fangcan 和尚放參
heshi 喝食
hezhang 合掌
Hongji Chanyuan 洪濟禪院
honglusi 鴻臚寺
Hongren 弘忍
houjia 後架
houtang shouzuo 後堂首座
Houzhu 後主
hu 笏
Huaisu 懷素
Huangdi 黃帝
Huan Wen 桓溫
Huan Xuan 桓玄
Huanzhu an 幻住庵

huayantou 華嚴頭

huazhu 化主

Huichang 惠常

Huiguang 慧光

Huiji Yuanxi 晦機元熙

Huijiao 慧皎

huijing 會經

Huiju 慧炬

Huike 慧可

Huikuang 慧曠

huili 迴禮

Huilin Zongben 慧林宗本

Huineng 慧能

huixiang 回向

Huixiu 慧休

huiyi zhuanguo 回因轉果

Huiyuan 慧遠

Huizhi 慧智

hujian yi 護肩衣

huofeng jinping 獲奉巾瓶

huotou xingzhe 火頭行者

huzhang 戶帳

Jia Dao 賈島

jiafeng 家風

Jia Gongyan 賈公彥

jiancha yushi 監察御史

jianci 鍵瓷

jiandian 煎點

jiang jiefang 醬街坊

jiangtang 講堂

jiangtou 醬頭

Jiankang 建康

jiansi 監寺

jiansi[b] 監司

Jianwen 簡文帝

Jianxing 見性

jianyi 鑒義

Jianyuan 建元

jianyuan 監院

jiaobing 腳絣

jiaoge 交割

jiaose 腳色

jiaotou bu 腳頭簿

Jiaping 嘉平

Jiatai 嘉泰

jiaxi qian 夾錫錢

jiaxung 家訓

jiayi yuan 甲乙院

Jibin 罽賓

jieben 戒本

jiedao 戒刀

jiedie 戒牒

Jiedu 節度

jiefang 街坊

jiefang biaobai 街坊表白

jiefang boretou 街坊般若頭

jiefang huazhu 街坊化主

jiejing 戒經

Jie jiurou cihui famen 誡酒肉慈慧法門

jiela pai 戒蠟牌

jielü 戒律

jiemo 羯磨

jiemo fa 羯磨法

jieshi 接食

Jie wuxin pian 誡五辛篇

jiexia 結夏

jiexia[b] 解夏

jiexia jiepai 結夏戒牌

Jiexiang 戒香

jieyuan 結緣

jiezhi zhiyi 結制之儀

Jile Jiedu 極樂戒度

jiming dudie 記名度牒

jingchou 淨籌

Jingcisi 淨慈寺

jingfa 淨髮

jingjie 淨戒

jingjin 淨巾

Jingli fa 敬禮法

jinglun shouzuo 經論首座

jingren 淨人

Jingshan 徑山

jingtou 淨頭

jingtou[b] 經頭

Jinguangming chanfa 金光明懺法

Jingxiu 淨秀

jingyi 淨衣

Jinhua Weimian 金華惟勉

jinsong wangseng 津送亡僧

Jinsu Rulai 金粟如來

jinzu 禁足

Jiqingsi 集慶寺

ji shanlai 極善來

jiu 韭

jiucan guan 九參官

jiushi canqing 就室參請

jiuzhu 久住

jixiang hui 吉祥會

jiyang zongzhi 激揚宗旨

juehuang 覺皇

juhua 舉話

junchi 君持

*junchi*ᵇ 軍持

ju weiyi 具威儀

juyang 舉揚

Kaifeng 開封

kaijing 開靜

kaishi 開士

kaitang 開堂

kaitang shu 開堂疏

kaiyu 開浴

Kaiyuansi 開元寺

kan 龕

kanjing shouzuo 看經首座

kanjingtang 看經堂

kewei 客位

Kie Bupposo bo 歸依佛法僧寶

kongmen 空門

kongming dudie 空名度牒

Kuangye 曠野

kusi 庫司

kutang 庫堂

kutou 庫頭

kuxia 庫下

kuzhu 庫主

Laba 臘八

laci pai 蠟次牌

lang 廊

Li 禮

liangsheng gongfeng guan 兩省供奉官

liangwang hou 兩王後

liangzhan sanbai 兩展三拜

liangzhan sanli 兩展三禮

Lianhua shenghui 蓮華聖會

lianzhong 斂鐘

Liao 遼

liaoshouzuo 寮首座

Liaowan 了萬

liaoyuan 寮元

liaozhong laci 寮中臘次

liaozhu 寮主

lingci 靈祠

lingkou xie 鈴口鞋

Ling Weiyang 靈威仰

Lingyinshan 靈隱山

linhan 淋汗

liseng shouzuo 立僧首座

liucan guan 六參官

Liu Jun 劉竣

liunian 六念

Liu Song 劉宋

Louyue 婁約

luefan 略梵

Lüjie 律解

Lüli 律例

luohan 羅漢

luohan hui 羅漢會

luohan tangzhu 羅漢堂主

luonang 絡囊

Luozhou Yongnian 洛州永年

luozi 絡子

luqin 路寢

Lushan Yuantong 廬山圓通

lutou 爐頭

maochou 茆籌

mao shi 卯時

Mao Sui 毛遂

mengtang 蒙堂

menzhuang 門狀

menzi xingzhe 門子行者

mianbei 綿被

mianding qian 免丁錢

miao 廟

miaoxi 妙喜

miezheng 滅諍

mifei qian 糜費錢

Mili 覓歷

mimai jiefang 米麥街坊

Ming 明帝

mingde 名德

mingfu shiming 命服師名

mitotou 彌陀頭

mokushō 默照

motou 磨頭

mou shangzuo 某上座

mu 穆

muyu 木魚

nanjia 南頰

Nanshan 南山

nazi 衲子

neng kandu zhe 能看讀者

niansong 念誦

niansong pai 念誦牌
panping shi 判憑式
pianshan 偏衫
pianyun 篇韻
piping shi 批憑式
piti qian 披剃錢
Puhui 普慧
Puli fa 普禮法
puqing 普請
Pusadichi jing 菩薩地持經
Pusa shanjie jing 菩薩善戒經
Putong ta 普同塔
Puxian 普賢
Puzhao 普照
qian 錢
Qianfeng Wan 千峰琬
qianhou baojin 前後包巾
Qiantang 錢唐
qianzi 前資
qianzi liao 前資寮
qicao luan 蠐螬卵
qielan shen 伽藍神
Qiji 齊已
qiju wanfu 起居萬福
qin 寢
Qing Guanshiyin chanfa 請觀世音
   懺法
qinggui 清規
qingtan 清談
qingxian qian 清閑錢
qingyi 請益
qing yinyuan 請因緣
Qingyuan Xingsi 青原行思
qing zhishi 請知事
qingzhong 清眾
qinjiu 勤舊
qintang 寢堂
qipian 七篇
Qi Song 契嵩
Qixi 七夕
quanzhang 全帳
Ran Min 冉閔
Ren 仁宗
rending 入定
renli 人力
renshi 人事
renshi zhi wu 人事之物
renxu 壬戌

rubing 乳餅
Rui 睿宗
Rujing 如淨
Rulai fan 如來梵
ruliao pai 入寮牌
rushi 入室
rushi dizi 入室弟子
ruyao 乳藥
ruyuan xianchi chu 入院先馳書
sanba 三八
sande liuwei 三德六味
sangzhu 喪主
sanjing 三淨
sanju jingjie 三聚淨戒
sanmen 三門
santong 三通
santu banan 三塗八難
sanye 三業
sengba 僧跋
Sengcan 僧璨
Sengchun 僧純
sengfang 僧坊
senggong 僧供
sengguan 僧官
senggui 僧規
senglu 僧錄
Senglüe 僧䂖
senglu si 僧錄司
Sengni guifan 僧尼規範
Sengni yaoshi 僧尼要事
sengpan 僧判
Sengqi jiexin 僧祇戒心
sengqi yi 僧祇衣
Sengqu 僧璩
Sengsheng 僧盛
sengsi 僧司
sengsu 僧俗
sengtang 僧堂
Sengxian 僧顯
Sengyou 僧佑
sengzheng 僧正
sengzheng si 僧正司
sengzhi 僧制
Senjō 洗淨
Senmen 洗面
shacha 煞茶
shamen 沙門
shamen tong 沙門統

shami 沙彌
shami shoujie wen 沙彌受戒文
shangjian 上間
shangjuan 上肩
shangliao 上寮
shangshou 上手
shangtang 上堂
shangwen 上聞
Shangzuo 上座
Shanjia 山家
shanlai 善來
shanli 山笠
shanmen zhushou 山門主首
Shanxi 陝西
shaofujian 少府監
Shaohao 少皞
Shaolin 少林
shaoxiang shizhe 燒香侍者
Shaoxing 紹興
sheli hui 舍利會
she lüyi jie 攝律儀戒
shengchuang 繩床
shengjie 聖節
shengseng 聖僧
shengseng shizhe 聖僧侍者
shengxing tang 省行堂
she shanfa jie 攝善法戒
she zhongsheng jie 攝眾生戒
Shi 釋
shichu 食處
Shi Dejie 釋德介
Shi Fajing 釋法鏡
shifang cha 十方剎
Shi Fayuan 釋法願
Shi Hu 石虎
Shijia 釋迦
shijue 始覺
shikan taza 只管打坐
Shilin Xinggong 石林行鞏
shili zhuang 施利狀
shiluo 尸羅
shinian 十念
shiseng 師僧
shisheng fo 十聲佛
shishi 施食
shishi[b] 始士
shisi sengzheng si 十寺僧正司
shitang 食堂

shiwei 食位
shiya 使衙
shiyao 食藥
shiyou dan 柿油單
shizhe 侍者
shizhe liao 侍者寮
Shi Zhixing 釋智興
shizhu 施主
shoubiao seng 手表僧
shouchi yi 守持衣
shouling 守令
shouyong 受用
shouyuan ren 守園人
shouzuo 首座
shu 疏
Shuilu fahui 水陸法會
shuilu tangzhu 水陸堂主
shuitou 水頭
shuji 書記
Shun 順帝
shuojie 説戒
shuoshi 説事
shuoyu 説慾
shuzhuang 書狀
sijia ren 寺家人
Siming Zhili 四明知禮
suan 蒜
suishun ren 隨順忍
sujian 俗講
Sun 孫
suoshi 鎖試
tachuang 踏床
tai 臺
taichang boshi 太常博士
Taihao 太昊
Taishi 泰始
Tai taiko goge jari hō 對大已五夏闍梨法
Tandi 曇諦
tang 湯
tangsi 堂司
tangsi xingzhe 堂司行者
tangtou 堂頭
tangtou chatang 堂頭茶湯
tangtou shizhe 堂頭侍者
tangyi banyue 堂儀半月
tangzhu 堂主
Tanmoshi 曇摩侍
tantou 炭頭

Tanwu jiemo 曇無羯磨
Tanwude lübu za jiemo 曇無德律部雜
　羯磨
tanyue 檀越
tazhu 塔主
tewei chatang 特為茶湯
tewei jiaodai 特為交代
Tianbao 天寶
Tiantai shan 天台山
Tiantongshan 天童山
Tiantongsi 天童寺
Tianzhu si 天竺寺
tichang 提唱
tisi 提撕
tonghua 通話
tongxing 童行
tongxing tang 童行堂
Tongzhao 通照
toulou xiaoxi 透漏消息
toushou 頭首
touxiu 頭袖
tudi shen 土地神
tuditang 土地堂
tudi zhou 土地粥
tuiyuan zhanglao 退院長老
Vimalākṣa 卑摩羅叉
Waisiseng jiedu 外寺僧節度
wande hongming 萬德洪名
wangjie 王階
wangliao 望寮
Wang Xuance 王玄策
Wannianshan 萬年山
Weilu 魏錄
weinuo 維那
weiqu 委曲
weiqu tisi 委曲提撕
wei shi 未時
weixin jingtu 唯心淨土
Wen Ruiquan 聞惢泉
wensi yuan 文思院
Wenxuan 文宣
wenxun 問訊
wenzhang 文帳
wenzi 文字
Wu 武后
wucan shangtang 五參上堂
wuchang 五常
wuchang yuan 無常院

wuda guanglü 五大廣律
wufa 五法
wufu 五福
wuguan 五觀
wujia 五家
Wuliang Zongshou 無量宗壽
wushan shicha 五山十剎
wushi 五事
Wutai shan 五台山
wu tiandi 五天帝
Wuxin 悟新
wuxin 五辛
xiadeng ban 下燈板
xiajian 下間
Xianchun 咸淳
Xianchun san zunsu 三尊宿
Xiangbu 相部
xiangdao 行道
xiangdian 香殿
xiangkan 相看
Xianglin Chengyuan 香林澄遠
xiangshui qian 香水錢
Xiangyang 襄陽
xiangyao 香藥
Xianqing 顯慶
Xiantong 咸通
Xiao 孝宗
xiaocan 小參
xiao jingpin 小淨瓶
xiaoqin 小寢
xiaoshi 小師
xiaoshu mulu 小疏目錄
xiao toushou 小頭首
Xiaoyin Daxin 笑隱大訢
xiao youdan 小油單
xiaozi 孝子
xiatang zhong 下堂鐘
xiazhang 下帳
xie 薤
xiefu 褻服
xieyuanzhu 廨院主
xingchen 行櫬
xingdao 行道
xing fashi ren 行法事人
xingqian 行遣
Xingshengsi 興聖寺
xingtong 行童
Xingwu Xinzong 省悟心宗

xingxiang 行香
xingyi 行益
xingyi xingzhe 行益行者
xingzhe 行者
xinliang 心量
xitang shouzuo 西堂首座
Xixi Guangze 溪西廣澤
xixu 西序
xizhang 錫杖
Xuan 玄宗
xuanfo chang 選佛場
xuanming 宣明
xuanseng tang 選僧堂
xuanxue 玄學
Xuechao Fayi 雪巢法一
Xuefeng shan 雪峰山
xunliao 巡寮
xunliao pai 巡寮牌
Xun zhishi ren 訓知事人
Yandi 炎帝
Yangqi 楊歧
Yang Wei 楊畏
Yang Yi 楊憶
yanshou tangzhu 延壽堂主
yanxing 鴈行
Yao Chang 姚萇
yaoshi 藥石
Yao Xing 姚興
Yedu 鄴都
Yi 懿宗
yidan 衣單
yiguan 壹貫
Yijing 義淨
yiliao 移寮
Yishan 一山
Yishan Chanshi shu 一山禪師書
yishi 揖食
yitang zuochan 依堂坐禪
Yitian 義天
Yongming Yanshou 永明延壽
youdi 有底
youfang xingjiao 遊方行腳
you shi 酉時
Yuanfeng 元豐
Yuanfu 元符
yuangui 遠規
yuansui 圍菱
Yuantong Faxiu 圓通法秀

yuantou 圍頭
yuantou xingzhe 圍頭行者
yuanwai lang 員外郎
Yuanzhao 元照
yuanzhu 院主
Yuba 虞八
yuban 魚板
yuezhong 悦眾
yugu 魚鼓
yujin 浴巾
yunban 雲板
Yunfeng Xiu 雲峰秀
yuntang 雲堂
Yunwai Ziqing 雲外自慶
Yunwu Zixian 雲屋自閒
yuqun 浴裙
yu shi 禺時
yuxia 浴下
Yu Xiang 虞翔
Yuxiang 虞翔
yuzhu 浴主
Zaijia busa yi 在家布薩儀
zangdian 藏殿
zangxia 藏下
zangxia dianzhu 藏下殿主
zangzhu 藏主
zan jibai 讚偈唄
Zanning 賛寧
zaocan 早參
Zeshan Yixian 澤山戈咸
zhai 齋
zhaiyue 齋月
zhandan 展單
zhandao 暫到
zhanglao 長老
zhantuo 盞橐
zhao 昭
zhaotang 照堂
Zhe 哲宗
zhechong dangfan 折衝當番
zhenchui 砧槌
Zhending 真定
Zhenghe 政和
zhengui 箴規
Zhengxi si 正喜寺
Zheng Xuan 鄭玄
zhentang 真堂
zhen tangzhu 真堂主

Zhenxie Qingliao 真歇清了

zhenyan 真言

zhenyan yuan 真言院

zhenzi 枕子

Zhi Daolin 支道林

Zhi Dun 支遁

zhiduo 直裰

zhi Guangji 汁光紀

zhiguan yuan 止觀院

Zhiju 智炬

zhike 知客

Zhimen Guangzuo 智門光祚

zhiqie hui 炙茄會

zhi sengshi 知僧事

zhishi 知事

zhishi[b] 職事

zhishi ren 執事人

zhisui 直歲

zhitang 直堂

Zhiyi 智顗

zhiyu 知浴

Zhong 中宗

Zhongfeng Mingben 中峰明本

zhongliao 眾寮

zhongtou 鐘頭

zhongxue 眾學

zhongyou 中有

zhou 粥

zhou jiefang 粥街坊

zhoushi 咒食

zhoutou 粥頭

zhuang 狀

zhuangke 庄客

zhuangzhu 庄主

Zhuanxu 顓頊

zhuchi ren 住持人

zhuchi tie 住持帖

Zhu Daozu 竺道祖

zhu diantang xingzhe 諸殿堂行者

zhufang banshi 諸方辦事

Zhu Fonian 竺佛念

Zhurong 祝融

zhushi 主事

zhuwei 住位

zhuyu cha 茱萸茶

zhuzhang 拄杖

zhuzhuang xingzhe 諸庄行者

Zongxiao 宗曉

Zongze 宗賾

zuisheng hui

zunbei 尊卑

zundian 尊殿

Zunshi 遵式

zunsu 尊宿

zunzhong 尊眾

zuofan 作梵

zuoju 坐具

Zuo shishi fa 作施食法

Bibliography

Lost Texts

An Fashi faji jiuzhi sanke 安法師法舊製三科. Daoan 道安 (312–385).

Beiyong yaoyu 備用要語. Xingwu Xinzong 省悟心宗 (n.d.).

Biqiu dajie xu 比丘大戒序. Daoan 道安 (312–385).

Biqiuni dajie 比丘尼大戒. Zhu Fonian 竺佛念 (c. 383).

Biqiuni jiedu 比丘尼節度. Huiyuan 慧遠 (334–416).

Boretai zhongseng jiyi jiedu 般若臺眾僧集議節度. Zhi Dun 支遁 (314–366).

Chujia busa fa 出家布薩法. Daoan 道安 (312–385).

Chujia busa fa 出家布薩法. Puzhao 普照.

Da jianzhi fa 打楗稚法. Daoan 道安 (312–385).

Daoshi yuanji 導師緣記. Daoan 道安 (312–385).

Famen qingshi ershisi tiao 法門清式二十四條. Daoan 道安 (312–385).

Fashe jiedu 法社節度. Huiyuan 慧遠 (334–416).

Jiaojie biqiuni fa 教誡比丘尼法. Sengsheng 僧盛 (c. 504).

Jiaoshou biqiuni ersui tanwen 教授比丘尼二歲壇文.

Jiedu 節度. Huiyuan 慧遠 (334–416).

Lüjie 律解. Daoan 道安 (312–385).

Lüli 律例. Chaodu 超度 (c. 489).

Qingxin shinu fazhi 清信士女法制. Prince Wenxuan 文宣王 (459–494).

Sengni guifan 僧尼規範. Daoan 道安 (312–385).

Sengni guifan fofa xianzhang 僧尼規範佛法憲章. Daoan 道安 (312–385).

Sengni yaoshi 僧尼要事. Sengqu 僧璩 (fl. 453–464).

Sengqi jiexin 僧祇戒心. Dharmakala (c. 249).

Sengzhi 僧制. Prince Wenxuan 文宣王 (459–494).

Sengzhi shiba tiao 僧制十八條. Huiguang 慧光 (c. 534–543).

Sengzhi sishiqi tiao 僧制四十七條. Sengxian 僧顯 (c. 493).

Shisong biqiu jieben 十誦比丘戒本. Tanmoshi 曇摩侍.

Sishi liwen 四時禮文. Daoan 道安 (312–385).

Waisiseng jiedu 外寺僧節度. Huiyuan 慧遠 (334–416).

Zaijia busa yi 在家布薩儀. Prince Wenxuan 文宣王 (495–494).

Primary Sources

Baizhang qinggui zhengyi ji 百丈清規證義記. 1823. Yirun Yuanhong 儀潤源洪. ZZK 2-16-4 and 5; *ZZKX* 111.

Baoyun jing 寶雲經. *T* 16, no. 656.

Beiyong qinggui 備用清規. See *Chanlin beiyong qinggui.*

Bencao gangmu 本草綱目. Li Shizhen 李時珍 (1518–1593). Shanghai: Hongbao zhai, 1888.

Bieyi za Ehan jing . *T* 2, no. 100.

Binaiye 鼻奈耶. *T* 24, no. 1464.

Biqiuni zhuan 比丘尼傳 517. Baochang 寶唱. *T* 50, no. 2063.

Butsuzō hyōshikigi zusetsu 佛像幖幟圖說. 1694. Gikai 義海. *NBZ* 73.

Chanlu Ze Chanshi wenji xu 長蘆賾禪師文集序. Yuanzhao 元照 (1048–1116). See *Zhiyuan ji.*

Chanlin beiyong qinggui 禪林備用清規. 1311. Zeshan Yixian 澤山戈咸. *ZZK* 2-17-1; *ZZKX* 112.

Chanlin leiju 禪林類聚. Ca. 1307. Daotai 道泰. *ZZK* 2-22-1; *ZZKX* 117.

Chanmen guishi 禪門規式. Yang Yi 楊億 (974–1020). See *Jingde chuandeng lu.*

Chanyuan qinggui 禪苑清規. 1103. Changlu Zongze 長蘆宗賾 (?–1107?). *ZZK* 2-16-5. *ZZKX* 111.

Chao riming sanmei jing 超日明三昧經. *T* 15, no. 638.

Chishō Daishi shōrai mokuroku 智證大師請來目錄. 859. Enchin 圓珍 (814–891). *T* 55, no. 2173.

Chixiu Baizhang qinggui 敕修百丈清規. 1335. Dongyang Dehui. *T* 48, no. 2025.

Chokki Tōgen shō 敕規桃源鈔. 1459–1462. Tōgen Zuisen 桃源瑞仙 (d. 1489). *Zoku Shōmono shiryō shūsei*. 續抄物資料集成 Vol. 8. Edited by Ōtsuka Kōshin 大塚光信. Osaka: Seibundō, 1980.

Chokushū Hyakujō shingi sakei, Yōshō yoroku 敕修百丈清規左觿 · 庸峭餘錄. 1700–1718. Mujaku Dōchū 無著道忠 (1653–1744). Zengaku sōsho 禪學叢書 edition. Vol. 8. Edited by Yanagida Seizan 柳田聖山. Kyoto: Chūbun Shuppansha, 1979.

Chuan fabao ji 傳法寶紀. Ca. 713. Du Fei 杜朏. *T* 85, no. 2838.

Chunming tuichao lu 春明退朝錄. Song Minqiu 宋敏求 (1019–1079). Jifu congshu 畿輔叢書 edition. Vol. 72. Taipei: Yiwen Yinshuguan, 1966.

Chunqiu Zuozhuan zhengyi 春秋左傳正義. See *Shisan jing zhushu.*

Chu sanzang jiji 出三藏記集. 510–518. Sengyou 僧祐 (445–518). *T* 55, no. 2145.

Chuyao jing 出曜經. *T* 4, no. 212.

Conglin jiaoding qinggui zongyao 叢林校定清規總要. 1274. Jinhua Weimian 金華惟勉. *ZZK* 2-17-1; *ZZKX* 112.

Conglin liangxu xuzhi 叢林兩序須知. 1639. Feiyin Tongrong 費隱通容 (1593–1661). *ZZK* 2-17-1; *ZZKX* 112.

Daaidao biqiuni jing 大愛道比丘尼經. *T* 24, no. 1478.

Da baoji jing 大寶積經. *T* 11, no. 310.

Da biqiu sanqian weiyi 大比丘三千威儀. *T* 24, no. 1470.

Dabo niepan jing 大般涅槃經. *T* 12, no. 375.

Dabo niepan jing jijie 大般涅槃經集解. 509. Baoliang 寶亮 (444–509). *T* 37, no. 1763.

Da bore boluomiduo jing 大般若波羅蜜多經. *T* 5–7, no. 220.

Da Eluohan Nanti Miduoluo suoshuo fazhu ji 大阿羅漢難提蜜多羅所說法住記. *T* 49, no. 2030.

Da fangguang Fo huayan jing 大方廣佛華嚴經. *T* 9, no. 278.

Da fangguang Rulai busiyi jingjie jing 大方廣如來不思義境界經. *T* 10, no. 301

Da Foding Rulai miyin xiuzheng liaoyi zhu pusa wanxing shou lengyan jing 大佛頂如來密因修證了義諸菩薩萬行首楞嚴經. *T* 19, no. 945.

Dai Sō gozan zusetsu 大宋五山圖説. See *Chokushū Hyakujō shingi sakei Yōshō yoroku* and *Zengaku daijiten* 禪學大辭典.

Daizong chaozeng Sikong Dabianzheng Guangzhi Sanzang Heshang biaozhi ji 代宗朝贈司空大辨正廣智三藏和上表制集. 778–800. Yuanzhao 圓照. *T* 52, no. 2120.

Da loutan jing 大樓炭經. *T* 1, no. 23.

Da Ming gaoseng zhuan 大明高僧傳. 1617. Ruxing 如惺. *T* 50, no. 2062.

Daoxuan Lüshi gantong lu 道宣律師感通錄. 664. Daoxuan 道宣 (596–667). *T* 52, no. 2107.

Da Song sengshi lüe 大宋僧史略. 978–999. Zanning 贊寧. *T* 54, no. 2126.

Da Tang liudian 大唐六典. Ca. 739. Taipei: Wenhai Chubanshe, 1962.

Da Tang neidian lu 大唐內典錄. 664. Daoxuan 道宣 (596–667). *T* 55, no. 2149.

Da Tang xiyu ji 大唐西域記. 646. Xuanzang 玄奘 (602–664). *T* 51, no. 2087.

Da Tang xiyu qiufa gaoseng zhuan 大唐西域求法高僧傳. 691. Yijing 義淨 (635–713). *T* 51, no. 2066.

Dazang yilan ji 大藏一覽集. Ca. 1157. Chen Shi 陳實. *Shōwa hōbō sōmokuroku* 昭和法寶總目錄 3, no. 75.

Da zhidu lun 大智度論. *T* 25, no. 1509.

Dedao ticheng xizhang jing 得道梯橙錫杖經. *T* 17, no. 785.

Dōgen Zenji zenshū 道元禪師全集. 2 vols. Edited by Ōkubo Dōshū 大久保道舟. Tokyo: Chikuma Shobō, 1969–1970.

Dongjing menghua lu 東京夢華錄. 1147. Meng Yuanlao 孟元老. Shanghai: Gudian Wenxue Chubanshe, 1957.

Epidamo dapiposha lun 阿毘達磨大毘婆沙論. *T* 27, no. 1545.

Emituo jing 阿彌陀經. *T* 12, no. 366.

Erya yi 爾雅翼. 1174; printed in 1270. Luo Yuan 羅願 (1136–1184). Xuejin taoyuan 學津討原 edition. Vols. 34–38. Taipei: Yiwen Yinshuguan, 1965.

Fahua jing 法華經. See *Miaofa lianhua jing*.

Fahua sanmei chanyi 法華三昧懺儀. Zhiyi 智顗 (538–597). *T* 46, no. 1941.

Fajie shengfan shuilu shenghui xiuzhai yigui 法界聖凡水陸勝會修齋儀軌. Ca. 1265–1274. Zhipan 志磐. Reedited by Zhuhong 株宏 (1532–1612). *ZZK* 2B-2-3 and 4, *ZZKX* 129.

Fanwang jing 梵網經. *T* 24, no. 1484.

Fanwang jing pusa jieben shu 梵網經菩薩戒本疏. Fazang 法藏 (643–712). *T* 40, no. 1813.

Fanwang jing pusa jieben shu 梵網經菩薩戒本疏. Zhizhou 知周 (678–733). *ZZK* 1-60-2; *ZZKX* 60.

Fanyi mingyi ji 翻譯名義集. Fayun 法雲 (1088–1158). *T* 54, no. 2131.

Faqu jing 法句經. *T* 4, no. 210.

Fayan Chanshi yulu 法演禪師語錄. Wuzu Fayan 五祖法演 (?–1104). *T* 47, no. 1995.

Fayuan zhulin 法苑珠林. Daoshi 道世 (?–668?). *T* 53, no. 2122.

Fo benxing jijing 佛本行集經. *T* 3, no. 190.

Fodi jinglun 佛地經論. *T* 26, no. 1530.

Fofa daming lu 佛法大明錄. 1229. Guitang 圭堂. Komazawa University Library.

Fo wubai dizi zishuo benqi jing 佛五百弟子自說本起經. *T* 4, no. 199.

Fozu lidai tongzai 佛祖歷代通載. 1341. Nianchang 念常. *T* 49, no. 2036.

Fozu tongji 佛祖統記. 1269. Zhipan 志磐. *T* 49, no. 2035.

Fu fazang yinyuan zhuan 付法藏因緣傳. *T* 50, no. 2058.

Gaoseng Faxian zhuan 高僧法顯傳. 399–414. Faxian 法顯. *T* 51, no. 2085.

Gaoseng zhuan 高僧傳. 519. Huijiao 慧皎. *T* 50, no. 2059.

Genben sapoduobu lüshe 根本薩婆多部律攝. *T* 24, no. 1458.

Genben Shuoyiqieyou bu baiyi jiemo 根本説一切有部百一羯磨. *T* 24, no. 1453.

Genben Shuoyiqieyou bu nituona mudejia 尼陀那目得迦. *T* 24, no. 1452.

Genben Shuoyiqieyou bu pinaiye 毘奈耶. *T* 23, no. 1442.

Genben Shuoyiqieyou bu pinaiye anjushi 安居事. *T* 23, no. 1445.

Genben Shuoyiqieyou bu pinaiye posengshi 破僧事. *T* 24, no. 1450.

Genben Shuoyiqieyou bu pinaiye song 頌. *T* 24, no. 1459.

Genben Shuoyiqieyou bu pinaiye zashi 雜事. *T* 24, no. 1451.

Gozan jissatsu zu 五山十剎圖. See *Dai Sō gozan zusetsu.*

Guan Wuliangshou Fo jing 觀無量壽佛經. *T* 12, no. 365.

Guang hongming ji 廣弘明集. 664. Daoxuan 道宣 (596–667). *T* 52, no. 2103.

Guiyuan zhizhi ji 歸元直指集. 1567–1572. Zongben 宗本. *ZZK* 2-13-2; *ZZKX* 108.

Guizi mu jing 鬼子母經. *T* 21, no. 1262.

Gujin shiwen leiju 古今事文類聚. 10 cases. –1604. Zhu Mu 祝穆, Fu Dayong 富大用,
    Zhu Yuan 祝淵, and Tang Fuchun 唐富春. Kanbun 寬文 edition, 1661. Yale Uni-
    versity Library.

Honyaku myōgi taishū 翻譯名義大集. Sakaki Ryōzaburō 榊亮三郎. 1916. Reprint
    Tokyo: Kokusho Kankōkai, 1981.

Hou Hanshu 後漢書. Fan Ye 范曄 (398–446). Beijing: Zhonghua Shuju, 1973.

Huayanjing 華嚴經. See *Da fangguang Fo huayan jing.*

Jianzhong Jingguo xudeng lu 建中靖國續燈錄. 1101. Foguo Weibai 佛國惟白. *ZZK*
    2B-9-2; *ZZKX* 136.

Jiaoding qinggui 校訂清規. See *Conglin jiaoding qinggui zongyao.*

Jiaojie xinxue biqiu xinghu lüyi 教誡新學比丘行護律儀. 634. Daoxuan 道宣 (596–
    667). *T* 45, no. 1897.

Jiaoyuan qinggui 教苑清規. Ca. 1347. Yunwai Ziqing 雲外自慶. *ZZK* 2-6-4; *ZZKX* 101.

Jiatai pudeng lu 嘉泰普燈錄. 1202. Leian Zhengshou 雷庵正受. *ZZK* 2B-10-1; *ZZKX*
    137.

Jingchu suishi ji 荊楚歲時記. Zong Lin 宗懍 (498?–565?). Sibu beiyao 四部備要
    edition. Vol. 111. Shanghai: Zhonghua Shuju, 1936.

Jingde chuandeng lu 景德傳燈錄. 1004. Daoyuan 道原. *T* 51, no. 2076.

Jingming xuanlun 淨名玄論. (Jizang 吉藏) (549–623). *T* 38, no. 1780.

Jingshan Wuzhun Fan chanshi lu 徑山無準範禪師錄. See *Zengji xu chuandeng lu*
    增集續傳燈錄.

Jingtu jianyao lu 淨土簡要錄. 1382. Daoyan 道衍. *ZZK* 2-13-2; *ZZKX* 108.

Jingtu shengxian lu 淨土聖賢錄. 1783. Peng Xisu 彭希涑. *ZZK* 2B-8-2; *ZZKX* 135.

Jinshu 晉書. Fang Xuanling 房玄齡 et al. Beijing: Zhonghua Shuju, 1971.

Jinyuan ji 金圍集. Zunshi 遵式 (964–1032). *ZZK* 2-6-2; *ZZKX* 101.

Ji Shenzhou sanbao gantong lu 集神州三寶感通錄. 664. Daoxuan 道宣 (596–667).
    T 52, no. 2106.

Jiu Mianran egui tuoluoni shenzhou jing 救面然餓鬼陀羅尼神咒經. *T* 21, no. 1314.

Kichijōzan Eiheiji shō shingi 吉祥山永平寺小清規. 1803. Gentō Sokuchū 玄透即中
    (1729–1807). *Sōtōshū zensho: Shingi* 曹洞宗全書清規, edited by Sōtōshū Zen-
    sho Kankōkai. 1931. Reprint. Tokyo: Sōtōshū Shūmuchō, 1972.

Kikyōmon gujakusan 龜鏡文求寂參. Printed in 1769. Honkō Katsudō 本光晿道.
    Komazawa University Library.

Kikyōmon monge 龜鏡文聞解. 1767. Menzan Zuihō 面山瑞方 (1683–1769). See *Sōtōshū zensho.*

Kōzen gokoku ron 興禪護國論. 1194. Eisai 榮西 (1141–1215). *T* 80, no. 2543.

Lebang wenlei 樂邦文類. 1200. Zongxiao 宗曉. *T* 47, no. 1969A.

Lebang yigao 樂邦遺稿. 1204. Zongxiao 宗曉. *T* 47, no. 1969B.

Lengyan jing 楞嚴經. See *Da Foding Rulai miyin xiuzheng liaoyi zhupusa wanxing shoulengyan jing.*

Lianhua shenghui luwen 蓮華勝會錄文. Changlu Zongze 長蘆宗賾 (?–1107?). See *Lebang wenlei.*

Lidai sanbao ji 歷代三寶紀. 597. Fei Changfang 費長房. *T* 49, no. 2034.

Lijing 禮記. See *Lijing zhengyi.*

Lijing zhengyi 禮記正義. Annotated by Zheng Xuan 鄭玄 (127–100 B.C.E.) and Kong Yingda 孔穎達 (574–648). See *Shisan jing zhushu.*

Linjian lu 林間錄. 1107. Juefan Huihong 覺範慧洪 (1071–1128). *ZZK* 2B-21-4; *ZZKX* 148.

Longshu zengguang jingtu wen 龍舒增廣淨土文. 1160. Wang Rixiu 王日休. *T* 47, no. 1970.

Longxing Fojiao biannian tonglun 隆興佛教編年通論. 1165. Zuxiu 祖琇. *ZZK* 2B-3-3; *ZZKX* 130.

Lü ershier mingliao lun 律二十二明了論. *T* 24, no. 1451.

Lunyu 論語. See *Lunyu zhushu.*

Lunyu zhushu 論語注疏. Annotated by He Yan 何晏 and Xing Bing 邢昺. See *Shisan jing zhushu.*

Lushan lianzong baojian 廬山蓮宗寶鑑. 1305. Pudu 普度. *T* 47, no. 1973.

Lüxiang gantong zhuan 律相感通傳. 667. Daoxuan 道宣 (596–667). T45, no. 1898.

Lüyuan shigui 律苑事規. 1325. Xingwu Xinzong 省悟心宗. *ZZK* 2-11-1; *ZZKX* 106.

Maoshi zhengyi 毛詩正義. Annotated by Zheng Xuan 鄭玄 (127–100 B.C.E.) and Kong Yingda 孔穎達 (574–648). See *Shisan jing zhushu.*

Miaofa lianhua jing 妙法蓮華經. *T* 9, no. 262.

Mohe Moye jing 摩訶摩耶經. *T* 12, no. 383.

Mohe sengqi lü 摩訶僧祇律. *T* 22, no. 1425.

Mohe sengqi lü da biqiu jieben 大比丘戒本. *T* 22, no. 1426.

Nanhai jigui neifa zhuan 南海寄歸內法傳. 691. Yijing 義淨 (635–713). *T* 54, no. 2125.

Niepan jing 涅槃經. See *Dabo niepan jing.*

Nihon Biku Enchin nittō guhō mokuroku 日本比丘圓珍入唐求法目錄. 857. Enchin 圓珍 (814–891). *T* 55, no. 2172.

Nisshū nichiyō shingi hisetsu 入眾日用清規秘説. 1696. Eken Mokugon 惠儉木. Komazawa University Library.

Nisshū nichiyō shingi shō 入眾日用清規鈔. Printed in 1655. Seisan Shōun 清三笑雲. Komazawa University Library.

Nittō guhō junrei kōki 入唐求法巡禮行記. Ennin 圓仁 (794–864). *NBZ* 113.

Nongshu 農書. 1313. Wang Zhen 王禎. *Siku quanshu zhenben bieji* 四庫全書珍本別輯 edition. Vols. 171–175. Reprint. Taipei: Shangwu Yinshuguan, 1975.

Nuoxian biqiu jing 那先比丘經. *T* 32, no. 1670.

Pini mu jing 毗尼母經. *T* 24, no. 1463.

Pusajie benshu 菩薩戒本疏. N.D. Yiji 義寂. *T* 40, no. 1814.

Pusajie yishu 菩薩戒義疏. Zhiyi 智顗 (538–597). *T* 40, no. 1811.

Qianshou qianyan Guanshiyin pusa dabeixin tuoluoni 千手千眼觀世音菩薩大悲心陀羅尼. *T* 20, no. 1064.

Qi Fo ba pusa suoshuo datuoluoni shenzhou jing 七佛八菩薩所説大陀羅尼神咒經. *T* 21, no. 1332.

Qing Bintoulu fa 請賓頭盧法. *T* 32, no. 1689.

Qingyuan fa 慶元法. See *Qingyuan tiaofa shilei.*

Qingyuan tiaofa shilei 慶元條法事類. 1201. Xie Shenfu 謝深甫. Taipei: Xinwenfeng Chubanshe, 1976.

Qiugong jiali yijie 丘公家禮儀節. Qiu Jun 丘濬 (1420–1495). *Qiu Wenzhuang gong congshu* 丘文莊公叢書. Vol. 2. Taipei: Qiu Wenzhuang Gong Congshu Jiyin Weiyuanhui, 1972.

Ruzhong riyong qinggui 入眾日用清規. 1209. Wuliang Zongshou 無量宗壽. *ZZK* 2-16-5; *ZZKX* 111.

Ruzhong xuzhi 入眾須知. Ca.1263. *ZZK* 2-16-5; *ZZKX* 111.

Sancai huitu 三才會圖. 3 vols. 1607. Wang Qi 王圻 and Wang Siyi 王思義. Shanghai: Shanghai Guji Chubanshe, 1988.

San Tendai Godaisan ki 參天台五台山記. 1072–1081. Jōjin 成尋 (1011–1081). *NBZ* 115.

Sanyi bianhuo pian 三衣辨惑篇. 1007. Zunshi 遵式 (964–1032). See *Jinyuan ji.*

Sapoduobu pini modelejia 薩婆多部毗尼摩得勒伽. *T* 23, no. 1441.

Sapoduo pini piposha 薩婆多毗尼毗婆沙. *T* 23, no. 1440.

Senchaku hongan nenbutsushū 選擇本願念佛集. 1198. Genkū 源空 (1133–1212). *T* 83, no. 2608.

Sengshi lüe 僧史略. See *Da Song sengshi lüe.*

Shanjian lü piposha 善見律毘婆沙. *T* 24, no. 1462.

Shelifu wen jing 舍利弗問經. *T* 24, no. 1465.

Shengman shizihou yisheng da fangbian fangguang jing 勝鬘獅子吼一乘大方便方廣經. *T* 12, no. 353.

Shiji 史記. Sima Qian 司馬遷 (135?–86? B.C.E.) Beijing: Zhonghua Shuju, 1972.

Shijing 詩經. See *Maoshi Zhengyi.*

Shimen bianhuo lun 十門辯惑論. 681. Fuli 復禮. *T* 52, no. 2111.

Shimen guijing yi 釋門歸敬儀. Daoxuan 道宣 (596–667). *T* 45, no. 1896.

Shimen jiseng guidu tu jing 釋門集僧軌度圖經. Daoxuan 道宣 (596–667). *Nihon daizōkyō* 22.

Shimen zhengtong 釋門正統. 1237. Zongjian 宗鑑. *ZZK* 2B-3-5; *ZZKX* 130.

Shisan jing zhushu 十三經注疏. Reprint of the Song edition. Taipei: Dahua Shuju, 1982.

Shishi fashi 施食法式. Zunshi 遵式 (964–1032). See *Shishi tonglan.*

Shishi huo wufubao jing 施食獲五福報經. *T* 2, no. 132.

Shishi jigu lüe 釋氏稽古略. 1354. Juean 覺岸. *T* 49, no. 2037.

Shishi tonglan 施食通覽. Ca. 1205. Zongxiao 宗曉. *ZZK* 2-6-3; *ZZKX* 101.

Shishi zhengming 施食正名. Zunshi 遵式 (964–1032). See *Jinyuan ji.*

Shishi zijian 釋氏資鑑. 1336. Xizhong 熙仲. *ZZK* 2B-5-1; *ZZKX* 132.

Shiwu jiyuan 事物紀原. 1447. Gao Cheng 高承. 1472. Li Guo 李果. Taipei: Shangwu Yinshuguan, 1971.

Shiwu yiming lu 事物異名錄. 1788. Reprint. Taipei: Xinxing Shuju, 1969.

Shi zhu egui yinshi ji shui fa 施諸餓鬼飲食及水法. *T* 21, no. 1315.

Shuilu faxiang zan 水陸法像贊. 1093. Su Shi 蘇軾. See *Shishi tonglan.*

Shuilu yuanqi 水陸緣起. Changlu Zhongze 長蘆宗賾 (?–1107?). See *Shishi tonglan.*

Shuowen xizhuan 説文繋傳. Xu Kai 徐錯 (920–974). Sibu beiyao 四部備要 edition. Vol. 42. Shanghai: Zhonghua Shuju, 1936.

Sifen biqiuni chao 四分比丘尼鈔. 645. Daoxuan 道宣 (596–667). *ZZK* 1-64-1; *ZZKX* 64.

Sifen lü biqiu hanzhu jieben 四分律比丘含注戒本. 630. Daoxuan 道宣 (596–667). *T* 40, no. 1806.

Sifen lü shanbu suiji jiemo 四分律刪補隨機羯磨. 635. Daoxuan 道宣 (596–667). *T* 40, no. 1808.

Sifen lü shanfan buque xingshi chao 四分律刪繁補缺行事鈔. 626. Daoxuan 道宣 (596–667). *T* 40, no. 1804.

Sifen lü shi pini yichao 四分律拾毘尼義鈔. 627. Daoxuan 道宣 (596–667). *ZZK* 1-71-1; *ZZKX* 71.

Sifen lü xingshi chao zichi ji 四分律行事鈔資持記. Yuanzhao 元照 (1048–1116). *T* 40, no. 1805.

Sōden haiin 僧傳排韻. Gyōjo 堯恕 (1640–1695). *NBZ* 99–100.

Songchao shishi 宋朝事實. Li You 李攸. Guoxue jiben congshu 國學基本叢書 edition. Shanghai: Shangwu Yinshuguan, 1935.

Song gaoseng zhuan 宋高僧傳. Zanning 贊寧. 982–988. *T* 50, no. 2061.

Song huiyao jigao 宋會要輯稿. Xu Song 徐松 (1781–1848). Taipei: Xinwenfeng Chubanshe, 1976.

Song Xueshi wenji 宋學士文集. Song Lian 宋濂 (1310–1381). Sibu congkan 四部叢刊 edition. Vol. 80. Shanghai: Shangwu Yinshuguan, 1929.

Sōtōshū zensho 曹洞宗全書. 18 vols. Edited by Sōtōshū Zensho Kankōkai. Tokyo: Sōtōshū Shūmuchō, 1970–1973.

Tang Hongzhou Baizhangshan gu Huaihai Chanshi taming 唐洪州百丈山故懷海禪師塔銘. 818. Chen Xu 陳詡. See *Chixiu Baizhang qinggui.*

Tang huiyao 唐會要. 961. Wang Pu 王溥 et al. Shanghai: Zhonghua Shuju, 1955.

Tang liudian 唐六典. Ca. 739. Siku quanshu zhenben bieji 四庫全書珍本別集 edition. Vols. 117–119. Reprint. Taipei: Shangwu Yinshuguan, 1975.

Tiantai pusa jieshu 天台菩薩戒疏. 777. Mingkuang 明曠. *T* 40, no. 1812.

Tiantongsi zhi 天童寺志. 2 vols. Wen Xingquan 聞性泉 and Shi Dejie 釋德介. Reprint. Taipei: Guangwen Shuju, 1976.

Tianzhu bieji 天竺別集. Zunshi 遵式 (964–1032). *ZZK* 2-6-2; *ZZKX* 101.

Tianzhusi shifang zhuchi yi 天竺寺十方住持儀. 1030. Zunshi (984–1032). See *Tianzhu bieji.*

Tōjō garan shodō anzō ki 洞上伽藍諸堂安像記. 1759. Menzan Zuihō 面山瑞方 (1683–1769). *Sōtōshu zensho.* Edited by Sōtōshū Zensho Kankōkai. 1931. Reprint. Tokyo: Sōtōshū Shūmuchō, 1972.

Tōjō garan zakki 洞上伽藍雜記. 1770, Futaku 不琢. printed in 1775. Edited by Keigan Eboku *Sōtōshū zensho.* Edited by Sōtōshū Zensho Kankōkai. 1931. Reprint. Tokyo: Sōtōshū Shūmuchō, 1972.

Wakan sansai zue 和漢三才圖會. 1712. Terajima Ryōan 寺島良安. Edited by Shimada Isao 島田勇雄, Takeshima Atsuo 竹島淳夫, and Higuchi Motomi 樋口元巳. Reprint. Tokyo: Heibonsha, 1991.

Wanshan Tonggui ji 萬善同歸集. Yongming Yanshou 永明延壽 (904–975). *T* 48, no. 2017.

Weimo jing yishu 維摩經義疏. Jizang 吉藏 (549–623). *T* 38, no. 1781.

Weishu 魏書. 554. Wei Shou 魏收. Beijing: Zhonghua Shuju, 1971–.

Wenshi jing yiji 溫室經義記. Huiyuan 慧遠 (523–592). *T* 39, no. 1793.

Wenshi xiyu zhongseng jing 溫室洗浴眾僧經. *T* 16, no. 701.

Wudeng huiyuan 五燈會元. 1252. Dachuan Puji 大川普濟. *ZZK* 2B-11-1,2,3,4; *ZZKX* 138.

Wudeng yantong 五燈嚴統. 1650. Feiyin Tongrong 費隱通容 (1593–1661). *ZZK* 2B-12-4; *ZZKX* 139.

Wujia zhengzong zan 五家正宗贊. 1254. Xisou Shaotan 希叟紹曇. *ZZK* 2B-8-5; *ZZKX* 135.

Wuliangshou jing 無量壽經. *T* 12, no. 360.

Wuzhun Shifan Chanshi yulu 無準師範禪師語錄. Wuzhun Shifan 無準師範 (1177–1249). *ZZK* 2-26-5; *ZZKX* 121.

Xianyu jing 賢愚經. *T* 4, no. 202.

Xinbian zhuzong jiaozang zonglu 新編諸宗教藏總錄. Yitian 義天 (1055–1101). *T* 55, no. 2184.

Xinghu lüyi 行護律儀. See *Jiaojie xinxue biqiu xinghu lüyi*.

Xingshi chao 行事鈔. See *Sifen lü shanfan buque xingshi chao*.

Xin Tangshu 新唐書. 1060. Ouyang Xiu 歐陽修 et al. Beijing: Zhonghua Shuju, 1975.

Xu chuandeng lu 續傳燈錄. 1368–1398. Yuanji Juding 圓極居頂 (?–1404). *T* 51, no. 2077.

Xuefeng Yicun Chanshi yulu 雪峰義存禪師語錄. Xuefeng Yicun 雪峰義存 (822–908). *ZZK* 2-24-5; *ZZKX* 119.

Xu gaoseng zhuan 續高僧傳. 645. Daoxuan 道宣 (596–667). *T* 50, no. 2060.

Xu Qixie ji 續齊諧記. Wu Jun 吳均 (469–520). Gushi wenfang xiaoshuo 顧氏文房小說 series, vol. 7. Shanghai: Shangwu Shuju, 1934.

Yakuchū Zennen shingi 訳註禪苑清規. Kagamishima Genryū 鏡島元隆, Satō Tatsugen 佐藤達玄, and Kosaka Kiyū 小坂機融. 1972. Reprint. Tokyo: Sōtōshū Shūmuchō, 1985.

Yangju moluo jing 央掘魔羅經. *T* 2, no. 120.

Yili 儀禮. See *Yili zhushu*.

Yili zhushu 儀禮注疏. Annotated by Zheng Xuan 鄭玄 (127–100 B.C.E.) and Jia Gongyan 賈公彥 (Tang dynasty). See *Shisan jing zhushu*.

Yiyuan 異苑. Liu Jingshu 劉敬叔 (?–465?). Xuejin taoyuan 學津討原 series, vol. 151. Taipei: Yiwen Yinshugnan, 1965.

Youyang zazu 酉陽雜俎. Duan Chengshi 段成式 (803–863). Congshu jicheng 叢書集成 series, vols. 276–278. Shanghai: Shangwu Shuju, 1937.

Yunfu qunyu 韻府群玉. Reprinted in 1590. Yin Jinxian 陰勁弦 and Yin Fuchun 陰復春 Yale University Library.

Yuqie shidi lun 瑜伽師地論. *T* 30, no. 1579.

Za piyu jing 雜譬喻經. *T* 4, no. 204–208.

Zengji xu chuandeng lu 增集續傳燈錄. 1417. Wenxiu 文琇 (1345–1418). *ZZK* 2B-15-4 and 5; *ZZKX* 142.

Zengyi Ehan jing 增一阿含經. *T* 2, no. 125.

Zenrin shōkisen 禪林象器箋. 1741. Mujaku Dōchū 無著道忠 (1653–1744). Kyoto: Baiyō Shoin, 1909. Reprint, Tokyo: Seishin Shobō, 1963.

Zhanguo ce 戰國策. Liu Xiang 劉向 (77–6 B.C.E.). Shanghai: Shanghai Guji Chubanshe, 1985.

Zhao lun 肇論. Sengzhao 僧肇 (384–414?). *T* 45, no. 1858.

Zhengfa nianchu jing 正法念處經. *T* 17, no. 721.

Zhengzi tong 正字通. 1635. Liao Wenying 廖文英. Yale University Library.

Zhiyuan ji 芝園集. Yuanzhao 元照 (1048–1116). *ZZK* 2-10-4; *ZZKX* 105.

Zhong Ehan jing 中阿含經. *T* 1, no. 26.

Zhouli 周禮. See *Zhouli zhushu*.

Zhouli zhushu 周禮注疏. Annotated by Zheng Xuan 鄭玄 (127–100 B.C.E.) and Jia Gongyan 賈公彦 (Tang dynasty). See *Shisan jing zhushu*.

Zhouyi 周易. See *Zhouyi zhengyi*.

Zhouyi zhengyi 周易正義. Annotated by Wang Bi 王弼 (226–249) and Kong Yingda 孔穎達 (574–648). See *Shisan jing zhushu*.

Zhujing yaoji 諸經要集. Daoshi 道世 (?–668?). *T* 54, no. 2123.

Zhushang shanren-yong 諸上善人詠. Daoyan 道衍. *ZZK* 2B-8-1; *ZZKX* 135.

Zimen jingxun 緇門警訓. 1469. Rujin 如巹. *T* 48, no. 2023.

Zuozhuan 左傳. See *Chunqiu Zuozhuan zhengyi*.

Zutang ji 祖堂集. Ca. 952. Monks Jing 靜 and Yun 筠. Reprint. Taipei: Xinwenfeng Chubanshe, 1987.

Zuting shiyuan 祖庭事苑. 1098–1100. Muan Shanqing 睦菴善卿. *ZZK* 2-18-1; *ZZKX* 113.

Secondary Sources in Chinese, Japanese, and Korean

Abe Chōichi 阿部肇一. *Chūgoku Zenshūshi no kenkyū* 中國禪宗史の研究. Tokyo: Kenbun Shuppan, 1986.

Chikusa Masaaki 竺沙雅章. *Chūgoku Bukkyō shakaishi kenkyū* 中國佛教社會史研究. Tokyo: Dōbōsha, 1982.

Ch'oe Pŏp-hye 崔法慧. *Koryŏp'an chungch'ŏm chokpon Sŏnwŏn ch'ŏnggyu* 高麗板重添足本禪苑清規. Seoul: Minjoksa, 1987.

Dai Jian 戴儉. *Chanzong siyuan jianzhu buju chutan* 禪宗寺院建築布局初探. Taipei: Mingwen Shuju, 1991.

Enomoto Fumio 榎本文雄. "Keihin: Indo Bukkyō no ichi chūshinchi no shozai" 罽賓ーインド仏教の一中心地の所在. In *Tsukamoto Keishō kyōju kanreki kinen ronbun shū: Chi no kaikō—Bukkyō to kagaku* 塚本啓祥教授還暦記念論文集「知の邂逅ー仏教と科學」. Tokyo: Kōsei Shuppansha, 1993.

Fan Wu 范午. "Songdai dudie shuo" 宋代度牒說. *Wenshi zazhi* 文史雜誌 2, no. 4 (1942): 45–52.

Fujishima Takeki 藤島建樹. "Genchō ni okeru kenshin to senseiin" 元朝における權臣と宣政院. *Ōtani gakuhō* 大谷學報 52, no. 4 (1973): 17–31.

Fujiyoshi Masumi 藤善真澄. "Tō Godai no zunnan seido" 唐五代の童行制度. *Tōyōshi kenkyū* 東洋史研究 21, no. 1 (1962): 1–26.

Furuta Shōkin 古田紹欽. "Nissō sō to cha" 入宋僧と茶. In *Cha no yu no seiritsu* 茶の湯の成立. Vol. 2. Sadō shūkin 茶道聚錦 series. Tokyo: Shōgakkan, 1984.

Hasebe Yūkei 長谷部幽蹊. *Min-Shin Bukkyō kyōdanshi kenkyū* 明清佛教團史研究. Kyoto: Dōbōsha, 1993.

Hattori Shungai 服部俊崖. "Shina sōkan no enkaku" 支那僧官の沿革. Parts 1–3. *BS* 2, no. 5 (1912): 65–81; *BS* 2, no. 6 (1912): 55–63; *BS* 2, no. 8 (1912): 55–64.

He Guangzhong 賀光中. "Lidai sengguan zhidu kao" 歷代僧官制度考. In *Zhongguo Fojiao tongshi luncong* 中國佛教通史論叢. Xiandai Fojiao xueshu congkan 現代佛教學術叢刊 series, vol. 39. Taipei: Dasheng Wenhua Chubanshe, 1978.

Hirakawa Akira 平川彰. "*Kyōkai shingaku biku gyōgo ritsugi* kaidai" 教誠新學比丘行護律儀解題. In *Kokuyaku issai kyō* 国訳一切経. Shoshū bu 諸宗部 14.

———. "Ritsuzō ni arawareta zen no jissen" 律藏に現われた禅の実践. In *Shikan no kenkyū* 止觀の研究, edited by Sekiguchi Shindai 關口真大. Tokyo: Iwanami Shoten, 1975.

———. *Ritsuzō no kenkyū* 律藏の研究. Tokyo: Sankibō Busshorin, 1970.

Huang Minzhi 黄敏枝. *Songdai Fojiao shehui jingjishi lunji* 宋代佛教社會經濟史論集 Taipei: Xuesheng Shuju, 1989.

Ikeda Rosan 池田魯參. *Maka shikan kenkyū josetsu* 摩訶止觀研究序説. Tokyo: Daitō Shuppansha, 1986.

Imaeda Aishin 今枝愛真. "Sarei to shingi" 茶礼と清規. In *Cha no yu no seiritsu* 茶の湯の成立 Vol. 2. Sadō shūkin 茶礼と清規 series. Tokyo: Shōgakkan, 1984.

Ishii Shūdō 石井修道. "Chūgoku no gozan jissatsu seido no kisoteki kenkyū" 中國五山十刹制度の基礎的研究. Parts 1–4. *KBR* 13 (1982): 89–132; *KBR* 14 (1983): 82–122; *KBR* 15 (1984): 61–129; *KBR* 16 (1985): 30–82.

———. "Hyakujō shingi no kenkyū: 'Zenmon kishiki' to Hyakujō ko shingi" 百丈清規の研究—「禪門規式」と「百丈古清規」—. *KZKN* 6 (1995): 15–53.

———. *Sōdai Zenshūshi no kenkyū* 宋代禪宗史の研究. Tokyo: Daitō Shuppansha, 1987.

Kagamishima Genryū 鏡島元隆. "Kanazawa bunko bon *Zennen shingi* ni tsuite" 金沢文庫本「禪苑清規」について. *Kanazawa bunko kenkyū*, 金沢文庫研究 144 (1968): 1–6.

Kawaguchi Kōfū 川口高鳳. "Chūgoku Bukkyō ni okeru kairitsu no tenkai" 中国仏教における戒律の展開. Parts 1 and 2. *BKN* 5 (1971): 132–154; *BKN* 6 (1972): 104–120.

———. "Shibunritsu gyōjishō ni arawareta in'yō tenseki no kenkyū" 四分律行事鈔にあらわれた引用典籍の研究. *BKN* 9 (1975): 25–59.

Kawakami Kōichi 河上光一. *Sōdai no keizai seikatsu* 宋代の經濟生活. Tokyo: Yoshikawa Kōbunkan, 1966.

Koga Hidehiko 古賀英彦. *Zengo jiten* 禪語辭典. Kyoto: Shibunkaku, 1991.

Kondō Ryōichi 近藤良一. "Chōro Sōsaku ni tsuite" 長蘆宗賾について. *IBK* 14, no. 2 (1966): 280–283.

———. "Hyakujō shingi no seiritsu to sono genkei" 百丈清規の成立とその原型. *HKDK* 3 (1968): 19–48.

———. "Zennen shingi ni okeru Jōdo shisō: sono shisōshiteki kigen" 禪苑清規に於ける淨土思想—その思想史的起源—. *HKDK* 1 (1967): 25–43.

Kosaka Kiyū 小坂機融. "Kanazawa bunko bon *Zennen shingi* to Kōrai ban *Zennen shingi* to no kanren ni tsuite" 金沢文庫本「禪苑清規」と高麗版「禪苑清規」との関連について. *Kanazawa bunko kenkyū* 金沢文庫研究 192 (1972): 1–8.

———. "Sōdai jiin sōni seido to shingi: toku ni sekichō no kyōshin to gyōyū no hanpyō wo chūshin ni" 宋代寺院僧尼制度と清規—特に籍帳の供申と行遊の判憑を中心に—. *KBK* 26 (1968): 103–117.

Kusumoto Bun'yū 久須本文雄. "Gozan seidoshi kō" 五山制度史攷. *ZBKK* 7 (1975): 137–153.

Lin Tianwei 林天蔚. "Songdai chushou dudie zhi yanjiu" 宋代出售度牒之研究. In *Songshi yanjiu ji* 宋史研究集 4. Taipei: Zhonghua congshu bianshen weiyuan hui, 1969.

Makino Tatsumi 牧野巽. "*Keigen jōhō jirui* no Dō Shaku mon: Sōdai shūkyō hōsei no ichi shiryō" 慶元條法事類の道釋門—宋代宗教法制の一資料—. Parts 1 and
2. *SK*, n.s. 9, no. 2 (1932): 64–84; *SK*, n.s. 9, no. 4 (1932): 44–58.

Makita Tairyō 牧田諦亮. "Suirikue shōkō" 水陸會小考. In Makita, *Chūgoku kinsei
bukkyōshi kenkyū* 中國近世佛教史研究. Kyoto: Heirakuji Shoten, 1957.

Mano Senryū 間野潛龍. "Chūgoku Mindai no sōkan ni tsuite" 中國明代の僧官に
ついて. *Ōtani gakuhō* 大谷學報 36, no. 3 (1956): 53–62.

Matsuda Shindō 松田真道. "*Daitō saiiki ki* ni miru Indo Bukkyō no jōnin" 大唐西
域記にみるインド仏教の淨人. *BKN* 16 (1983): 53–61.

———. "Indo Bukkyō kyōdan ni okeru zaizokusha *ārāmika* no kōsatsu jo" インド
仏教教団における在俗者 ārāmika の考察序. *SK* 54, no. 3 (1981): 264–265.

———. "Indo Bukkyō kyōdan no yakushoku no kigen" インド仏教教団の役職の
起源. *SKKK* 15 (1983): 114–131.

———. "Indo Bukkyō kyōdanshi ni okeru jōnin no kōsatsu" インド仏教教団史にお
ける淨人の考察. *SKKK* 14 (1982): 137–154.

———. "Shitsujinin *veyyāvaccakara* to shuonnin *ārāmika*" 執事人 veyyāvaccakara
と守園人 ārāmika. *IBK* 30, no. 1 (1981): 124–125.

———. "*Zenken ritsu bibasha* no jōnin" 「善見律毘婆沙」の淨人. *SK* 250 (1982):
142–144.

———. "Zenshū kyōdan no jōnin" 禪宗教団の淨人. *SGK* 25 (1983): 202–205.

Matsuura Shūkō 松浦秀光. *Zenshū kojitsu gemon no kenkyū* 禪宗古實偈文の研究.
Tokyo: Sankibō Busshorin, 1981.

———. *Zenshū kojitsu sonzō no kenkyū* 禪宗古實尊像の研究. Tokyo: Sankibō
Busshorin, 1976.

Michihata Ryōshū 道端良秀. *Chūgoku Bukkyō shakai keizaishi no kenkyū* 中國佛
教社會經濟史の研究. In Michihata, *Chūgoku Bukkyōshi zenshū* 中國佛教史全
集. Vol. 4. Tokyo: Shoen, 1975.

———. *Chūgoku Bukkyō to shakai fukushi jigyō* 中國佛教と社會福祉事業. Michihata, *Chūgoku Bukkyōshi zenshū* 中國佛教史全集. Vol. 11. Tokyo: Shoen, 1975.

———. *Rakan shinkō shi* 羅漢信仰史. In Michihata, *Chūgoku Bukkyōshi zenshū*
中國佛教史全集. Vol. 8. Tokyo: Shoen, 1975.

———. *Tōdai Bukkyōshi no kenkyū* 唐代佛教史の研究. In Michihata, *Chūgoku
Bukkyōshi zenshū* 中國佛教史全集. Vol. 2. Tokyo: Shoen, 1975.

Minakata Kumagusu 南方熊楠. "Shishin" 厠神. In *Minakata Kumagusu zenshū*
南方熊楠全集. Vol. 3. Tokyo: Kengensha, 1952.

Mizuno Masaaki 水野正明. "Sōdai ni okeru kissa no fukyū ni tsuite" 宋代における
喫茶の普及について. In *Sōdai no shakai to shūkyō* 宋代の社會と宗教. Tokyo:
Kyūko Shoin, 1985.

Mochizuki Shinkō 望月信亨. *Bukkyō daijiten* 佛教大辭典. 10 vols. Tokyo: Sekai
Seiten Kankō Kyōkai, 1958–1963.

Mogi Mumon 茂木無文. *Eihei Daishingi kōgi* 永平大清規講義. *Sōtōshū kōgi* 曹洞宗
講義 series, vol. 7. 1927. Reprint. Tokyo: Kokusho Kankōkai, 1975.

Morohashi Tetsuji 諸橋轍次. *Dai kanwa jiten* 大漢和辭典. 13 vols. Tokyo: Taishūkan
Shoten, 1957–1960.

Moroto Tatsuo 諸户立雄. *Chūgoku Bukkyō seidoshi no kenkyū* 中國佛教制度史の
研究. Tokyo: Hirakawa Shuppansha, 1990.

Muramatsu Tetsuo 村松哲雄. "Shisho no kōsatsu" 嗣書の考察. *Jissen shūjō kenkyū
kai nenpō* 實踐宗乘研究會年報 6 (1937): 112–130.

Nagai Masayuki 永井政之. "Chūgoku zen no minshū kyōka ni tsuite: Chōro Sō-saku no baai" 中國禅の民眾教化について―長蘆宗賾の場合―. *IBK* 34, no. 1 (1985): 291–298.

Nakamura Hajime 中村元. *Bukkyōgo daijiten* 佛教語大辭典. 1981. Reprint. Tokyo: Tōkyō Shoseki, 1985.

Narikawa Hōyū 成河峰雄. "*Hyakujō ko shingi* ni tsuite: *Chokki* hensanji ni mita" 百丈古清規について―「敕規」編纂時に見た―. *IBK* 31, no. 2 (1983): 337–340.

Nishio Kenryū 西尾賢隆. "Sōdai Nit-Chū Bukkyō kōryūshi: *Zemen shingi to Eihei shingi*" 宋代日中仏教交流史―禪苑清規と永平清規―. *Bukkyō shigaku kenkyū* 佛教史學研究 19, no. 1 (1977): 1–32.

Nogami Shunjō 野上俊靜. "Gen no kudokushi shi ni tsuite" 元の功德使司に就いて. *SBS* 6, no. 2 (1942): 1–11.

———. "Gen no senseiin ni tsuite" 元の宣政院に就いて. In *Haneda Hakase shōju kinen Tōyōshi ronsō* 羽田博士頌壽記念東洋史論叢. Kyoto: Haneda Hakase Shōju Kinenkai, 1950.

Nunome Chōfū 布目潮渢. "Tō-Sō jidai ni okeru kissa no fukyū" 唐宋時代における喫茶の普及. *Rekishi kyōiku* 歷史教育 14, no. 8 (1966): 27–34.

Ōchō Enichi 橫超慧日. *Chūgoku Bukkyō no kenkyū* 中國佛教の研究. Kyoto: Hōzōkan, 1958.

Ogawa Kan'ichi 小川貫弌. "Hoku-Sō jidai no kōdosei to shibuchō" 北宋時代の公度制と祠部牒. *Ryūkoku shidan* 龍谷史壇 58 (1967): 23–42.

———. "Sōdai no jukaisei to rokunen kaichō" 宋代の受戒制と六念・戒牒. *Ryūkoku daigaku ronshū* 龍谷大學論集 385 (1968): 48–70.

Ogisu Jundō 荻須純道. "Sōdai ni okeru nenbutsu zen no chōryū" 宋代における念佛禪の潮流. *Ryūkoku shidan* 龍谷史壇 44 (1958): 131–138.

Okimoto Katsumi 沖本克已. "*Hyakujō koki* ni tsuite" 「百丈古規」について. *ZBKK* 12 (1980): 51–61.

Ōno Hideto 大野栄人. "Tendai *Kanjin jikihō* no kenkyū" 天台「觀心食法」の研究. Parts 1 and 2. *IBK* 29, no. 1 (1980): 326–331; *Zen kenkyūjō kiyo* 禅研究所紀要 10 (1981): 219–230.

Ono Katsutoshi 小野勝年. "Ennin no mita Tō no Bukkyō girei" 圓仁の見た唐の佛教儀禮. In *Jikaku Daishi kenkyū* 慈覺大師研究, edited by Fukui Kōjun 福井康順. Tokyo: Tendai Gakkai, 1964.

———. *Nittō guhō junrei kōki no kenkyū* 入唐求法巡禮行記の研究. 4 vols. Tokyo: Suzuki Gakujutsu Zaidan, 1964–1969.

Ōtani Kōshō 大谷光照. "Tōdai Bukkyō no girei: toku ni hōe ni tsuite" 唐代佛教の儀禮―特に法會に就いて. Parts 1 and 2. *Shigaku zasshi* 史學雜誌 46, no. 10 (1935): 1183–1231; *Shigaku zasshi* 史學雜誌 46, no. 11 (1935): 1377–1405.

Ōya Tokujō 大屋德城. "Kōrai chō no kyūzan" 高麗朝の舊槧. In *Sekisui sensei kakōju kinen ronsan* 積翠先生華甲壽記念論纂. Tokyo: Sekisui Sensei Kakōju Kinen Ronsan Kinenkai Kankō, 1942.

Sakuma Ken'yū 佐久間賢祐. "*Nichiyō shingi* no kenkyū" 「日用清規」の研究. Part 1. *KDBKN* 24 (1991): 93–99.

Sasaki Shizuka 佐々木閑. "Tenzo ni kansuru ichi kōsatsu" 典座に関する一考察. *Zen Bunka kenkyūjō kiyo* 禅文化研究所紀要 19 (1993): 59–76.

Satō Shūkō 佐藤秀孝. "Gen no Chūhō Myōhon ni tsuite" 元の中峰明本について. *SGK* 23 (1981): 231–236.

Satō Tatsugen 佐藤達玄. *Chūgoku Bukkyō ni okeru kairitsu no kenkyū* 中國佛教における戒律の研究. Tokyo. Mokujisha, 1986.

Sekiguchi Shindai 關口真大. *Daruma no kenkyū* 達磨の研究. Tokyo: Iwanami Shoten, 1967.

Shiina Kōyū 椎名宏雄. "Sōdai no Shinshū Chōroji" 宋代の真州長蘆寺. In *Chūgoku busseki kenmonki* 中國仏蹟見聞記. Vol. 8 Tokyo: Komazawa Daigaku Chūgoku Shiseki Sankandan, 1989.

———. *Sō-Gen ban zenseki no kenkyū* 宋元版禪籍の研究. Tokyo: Daitō Shuppansha, 1993.

Shinohara Hisao 篠原壽雄. *"Eihei daishingi": Dōgen no shūdō kihan* 永平大清規：道元の修道規範. Tokyo: Daitō Shuppansha, 1980.

Shioiri Ryōdō 塩入良道. "Shoki Tendaizan no kyōdanteki seikaku" 初期天台山の教團的性格. In *Bukkyō kyōdan no shomondai* 佛教教團の諸問題, edited by Nippon Bukkyō Gakkai 日本佛教學會. Kyoto: Heirakuji Shoten, 1974.

Sogabe Shizuo 曽我部靜雄. "Sō no dochō zakkō" 宋の度牒雜考. *Shigaku zasshi* 史學雜誌 41, no. 6 (1930): 99–114.

Sudō Yoshiyuki 周藤吉之. *Tō-Sō shakai keizaishi kenkyū* 唐宋社會經濟史研究. Tokyo: Tōkyō Daigaku Shuppankai, 1965.

Suwa Gijun 諏訪義純. *Chūgoku chūsei Bukkyōshi kenkyū* 中國中世仏教史研究. Tokyo: Daitō Shuppansha, 1988.

Suzuki Tetsuo 鈴木哲雄. *Tō Godai Zenshūshi* 唐五代禪宗史. Tokyo: Sankibō Busshorin, 1985.

Tajima Tokuon 田島德音. "*Kyōkai ritsugi* senjutsusha in kansuru gimon" 教誡律儀撰述者に關する疑問. *Taishō Daigaku gakuhō* 大正大學學報 2 (1927): 97–110.

Takao Giken 高雄義堅. "Dochō kō" 度牒考. *Rokujō gakuhō* 六條學報 226 (1920): 6–26.

———. *Sōdai Bukkyōshi no kenkyū* 宋代佛教史の研究. Kyoto: Hyakkaen, 1975.

———. "Sōdai jiin seido no ichi kōsatsu" 宋代寺院制度の一考察. *SBS* 5, no. 2 (1941): 8–22.

———. "Sōdai sōkan seido no kenkyū" 宋代僧官制度の研究. *SBS* 4, no. 4 (1941): 1–17.

Tanaka Misa 田中美佐. "Sōdai no kissa kittō" 宋代喫茶・喫湯. *Shisen* 史泉 66 (1987): 62–75.

———. "Sōdai no kissa to chayaku" 宋代の喫茶と茶藥. *Shisō* 史窗 48 (1991): 279–285.

Tang Yongtong 湯用彤. *Han Wei Liangjin Nanbeichao Fojiaoshi* 漢魏兩晉南北朝佛教史. 2 vols. Reprint. Taipei: Luotuo Chubanshe 1987.

Tatsuike Kiyoshi 龍池清. "Mindai no sōkan" 明代の僧官. *SBS* 4, no. 3 (1940): 35–46.

Tian Guanglie 田光烈. "Woguo lidai sengguan zhidu lüeshu" 我國歷代僧官制度略述. *Neiming* 內明 226 (1991): 35–41.

Tokiwa Daijō 常盤大定. "Bukkyō no fukuden shisō" 佛教の福田思想. In *Shina Bukkyō no kenkyū* 支那佛教の研究. Tokyo: Shūjunsha, 1943.

———. "*Hōrinden*" no kenkyū 寶林傳の研究. 1934. Reprint. Tokyo: Kokusho Kankōkai, 1973.

Tokiwa Daijō, and Sekino Tadashi 關野貞. *Chūgoku bunka shiseki kaisetsu* 中國文化史蹟解説. 2 vols. Kyoto: Hōzōkan, 1976.

Tsuchihashi Shūkō 土橋秀高. "Chūgoku ni okeru kairitsu no kussetsu: sōsei shingi wo chūshin ni" 中國における戒律の屈折―僧制・清規を中心に―. In Tsuchihashi, *Kairitsu no kenkyū* 戒律の研究. Kyoto: Nagata Bunshōdō, 1980.

Tsukamoto Zenryū 塚本善隆. *Chūgoku kinsei Bukkyōshi no shomondai* 中國近世佛教史の諸問題. Tokyo: Daitō Shuppansha, 1975.

———. *Gisho Shaku-Rō shi no kenkyū* 魏書釋老志の研究. Tokyo: Daitō Shuppansha, 1974.

———. "Tō chūki irai no Chōan kudokushi" 唐中期以來の長安功德使. In *Tsukamoto Zenryū chosakushū* 塚本善隆選擇集 Vol. 3. Tokyo: Daitō Shuppansha, 1975. First published in *Tōhō gakuhō* 東方學報 4 (1933): 68–406.

Ui Hakuju 宇井伯壽. "*Hyakujō shingi* no rekishiteki igi" 百丈清規の歷史的意義. In *Dōgen Zenji kenkyū* 道元禪師研究. Tokyo: Dōgen Zenji Sangyōkai, 1941.

———. *Shaku Dōan kenkyū* 釋道安研究. 1956. Reprint. Tokyo: Iwanami Shoten, 1979.

———. *Zenshūshi kenkyū* 禪宗史研究. 3 vols. Tokyo: Iwanami Shoten, 1939–1943.

Xie Chongguang 謝重光, and Bai Wengu 白文固. *Zhongguo sengguan zhidushi* 中國僧官制度史. Xming: Qinghai Renming Chubanshe, 1990.

Yabuki Keiki 矢吹慶輝. *Meisha yoin kaisetsu* 鳴沙餘韻解說. Tokyo: Iwanami Shoten, 1933.

Yamada Kōdō 山田孝道. *Zenshū jiten* 禪宗辭典. Tokyo: Kokusho Kankōkai, 1975.

Yamazaki Hiroshi 山崎宏. "Hoku-Sei no sōkan shōgen jittō kō" 北齊の僧官昭玄十統考. *Shichō* 8, no. 1 (1938): 129–145.

———. "Nanbokuchō jidai ni okeru sōkan no kentō" 南北朝時代に於ける僧官の檢討. *Bukkyō kenkyū* 佛教研究 4, no. 2 (1940): 63–92.

———. *Shina chūsei Bukkyō no tenkai* 支那中世佛教の展開. Kyoto: Hōzōkan, 1971.

———. "Tō chūki irai no Chōan no kudokushi" 唐中期以來の長安功德使. *Tōhō gakuhō* 東方學報 4 (1933): 368–406.

———. "Tōdai no sōkan ni tsuite: sōtō, sōroku, sōjō" 唐代の僧官に就いて―僧統・僧錄・僧正―. *Shichō* 9, no. 2 (1939): 18–68.

———. "Zuidai sōkan kō" 隋代僧官考. *SBS* 6, no. 1 (1942): 1–15.

Yanagida Seizan 柳田聖山. *Chūgoku zenshū shi* 中國禪宗史. Kōza:Zen 講座-禪 series, ed. Nishitani Keiji 西谷啓治 et al., vol. 3. Tokyo: Chikuma Shobō, 1968.

Yanagida Seizan, Kajitani Sōnin 梶谷宗忍, and Tsujimura Kōichi 辻村公一. *Shinjinmei, Shōdōka, Jūgyūzu, Zazengi* 信心銘・證道歌・十牛圖・坐禪儀. Zen no gōroku 禪の語錄 series, vol. 16. 1974. Reprint. Tokyo: Chikuma Shobō, 1981.

Yokoyama Shūsai 橫山秀哉. *Zen no kenchiku* 禪の建築. Tokyo: Shōkokusha, 1967.

Yuan Zhen 袁震. "Liang-Song dudie kao" 兩宋度牒考. Parts 1 and 2. *Zhongguo shehui jingji shi jikan* 中國社會經濟史集刊 7, no. 1 (1994): 41–104; 7, no. 2 (1946): 1–78.

Zengaku Daijiten Hensanjo 禪學大辭典編纂所. *Zengaku daijiten* 禪學大辭典. 1978. Reprint. Tokyo: Taishūkan Shoten, 1991.

Zhu Chongsheng 朱重聖. "Woguo yincha chengfeng zhi yuanyin ji qi dui Tang Song shehui yu guanfu zhi yingxiang" 我國飲茶成風之原因及其對唐宋社會與官府之影響. *Songshi yanjiu ji* 宋史研究集 14 (1983): 315–411.

Secondary Studies in English, French, and German

Bielefeldt, Carl. "Ch'ang-lu Tsung-tse's *Tso-Ch'an I* and the 'Secret' of Zen Meditation." In *Traditions of Meditation in Chinese Buddhism*, edited by Peter N. Gregory. Honolulu: University of Hawai'i Press, 1986.

———. *Dōgen's Manuals of Zen Meditation.* Berkeley: University of California Press, 1988.

Bodiford, William M. *Sōtō Zen in Medieval Japan.* Honolulu: University of Hawai'i Press, 1993.

———. "Dharma Transmission in Sōtō Zen: Manzan Dōhaku's Reform Movement." *MN* 46, no. 4 (Winter 1991): 423–451.

Buswell, Robert. *The Zen Monastic Experience.* Princeton: Princeton University, 1992.

Collcut, Martin. "The Early Ch'an Monastic Rule: *Ch'ing-kuei* and the Shaping of Ch'an Community Life." In *Early Ch'an in China and Tibet,* edited by Whalen Lai and Lewis Lancaster. Berkeley: Institute of Buddhist Studies, 1983.

———. *Five Mountains: The Rinzai Zen Monastic Institution in Medieval Japan.* Cambridge: Harvard University Press, 1981.

Donner, Neal, and Daniel B. Stevenson. *The Great Calming and Contemplation.* Honolulu: University of Hawai'i Press, 1993.

Ebrey, Patricia Buckley. *Chu Hsi's Family Rituals.* Princeton: Princeton University Press, 1991.

———. *Confucianism and Family Rituals in Imperial China.* Princeton: Princeton University Press, 1991.

Edgerton, Franklin. *Buddhist Hybrid Sanskrit Grammar and Dictionary.* 2 vols. New Haven: Yale University Press, 1953. Reprint, Delhi: Motilal Banarsidass, 1985.

Eichhorn, W. *Beitrag zur rechtlichen Stellung des Buddhismus und Taoismus im Sung-Staat.* Leiden: E. J. Brill, 1968.

Foulk, T. Griffith. "The Ch'an School and Its Place in the Buddhist Monastic Tradition." Ph.D. diss., Michigan University, 1987.

———. "The *Daily Life in the Assembly* (*Ju-chung jih-yung*) and Its Place among Ch'an and Zen Monastic Rules." *The Ten Directions,* Spring/Summer 1991, 25–34.

———. "Myth, Ritual, and Monastic Practice in Sung Ch'an Buddhism." In *Religion and Society in T'ang and Sung China,* edited by Patricia B. Ebrey and Peter N. Gregory. Honolulu: University of Hawai'i Press, 1993.

Foulk, T. Griffith, and Robert H. Sharf. "On the Ritual Use of Ch'an Portraiture in Medieval China." In *Cahiers d'Extrême-Asie* 7 (1993–1994): 149–219.

Frauwallner, E. *The Earliest Vinaya and the Beginnings of Buddhist Literature.* Rome: Is. M.E.O., 1956.

Ganguly, Swati. "Buddhist Saṅgha and Monasteries in Medieval China: A Socio-Political Study." *Buddhist Studies* 11 (1987): 77–84.

Gernet, Jacques. *Buddhism in Chinese Society: An Economic History from the Fifth to the Tenth Century.* Translated by Franciscus Verellen. New York: Columbia University Press, 1994.

Gunawardana, R. A. L. H. *Robe and Plough: Monasticism and Economic Interest in Early Medieval Sri Lanka.* Tucson: University of Arizona Press, 1979.

Hansen, Valerie. *Changing Gods in Medieval China, 1127–1276.* Princeton: Princeton University Press, 1990.

Horner, I. B. *The Book of the Discipline: Vinayapiṭaka.* 6 vols. London: The Pāli Text Society, 1982–1986.

Hucker, Charles O. *A Dictionary of Official Titles in Imperial China.* 1985. Reprint. Stanford: Stanford University Press, 1989.

Ichimura Shohei. *Zen Master Eihei Dōgen's Monastic Regulations.* Woodville, Wash. North American Institute of Zen and Buddhist Studies, 1993.

Inagaki Hisao. *A Glossary of Zen Terms.* Kyoto: Nagata Bunshōdō, 1991.

Jackson, Roger. "Terms of Sanskrit and Pāli Origin Acceptable as English Words." *JIABS* 5, no. 2 (1982): 141–142.

Jorgensen, John. "The 'Imperial' Lineage of Ch'an Buddhism: The Role of Confucian Ritual and Ancestor Worship in the Ch'an Search for Legitimation in the Mid-T'ang Dynasty." *Papers on Far Eastern History* 35 (1987): 89–133.

Lamotte, Étienne. *History of Indian Buddhism.* Translated by Sara Webb-Boin. Louvain: Peeters Press, 1988.

Legge, James, trans. *Confucius: Confucian Analects, the Great Learning, and the Doctrine of the Mean.* Oxford: Clarendon Press, 1893. Reprint. New York: Dover Publications, 1971.

———. *I Ching: Book of Changes.* Oxford: Clarendon Press, 1899. Reprint, New Jersey: University Books, 1972.

———. *Li Chi: Book of Rites.* 2 vols. Oxford: Oxford University Press, 1885. Reprint, New Hyde Park, N. Y.: University Books, 1967.

———. *A Record of Buddhist Kingdoms.* Oxford: Clarendon Press, 1886. Reprint, New York: Dover Publications, 1965.

Leighton, Taigen Daniel, and Shohaku Okumura. *Dōgen's Pure Standards for the Zen Community.* Albany: SUNY Press, 1996.

Lévi, Sylvain, and Édouard Chavannes. "Les seize arhat protecteurs de la loi." Parts 1 and 2. *JA* (Juillet–Août 1916): 7–50; *JA* (Septembre–Octobre 1916: 189–304.

Mather, Richard B. "The Bonze's Begging Bowl: Eating Practices in Buddhist Monasteries of Medieval India and China." *AOS* 101, no. 4 (1981): 417–424.

Monier-Williams, M. *Sanskrit-English Dictionary.* 1899. Reprint. Oxford: Oxford University Press, 1988.

Reischauer, Edwin O. *Ennin's Diary: The Record of a Pilgrimage to China in Search of the Law.* New York: Ronald Press, 1955.

———. *Ennin's Travel in Tang China.* New York: Ronald Press, 1955.

Schlütter, Morten. "The Twelfth-Century Caodong Traditions as the Target of Dahui's Attacks on Silent Illumination." *KZKN* 6 (1995): 162–127 [*sic*].

Schmithausen, Lambert. *The Problem of the Sentience of Plants in Earliest Buddhism.* In Studia Philologica Buddhica Monograph Series, no. 6. Tokyo: The International Institute for Buddhist Studies, 1991.

Schopen, Gregory. *Bones, Stones, and Buddhist Monks: Collected Papers on the Archaeology, Epigraphy, and Texts of Monastic Buddhism in India.* Honolulu: University of Hawai'i Press, 1997.

———. "The Monastic Ownership of Servants or Slaves: Local and Legal Factors in the Redactional History of Two *Vinayas.*" *JIABS* 17, no. 2 (1994): 145–173.

———. "On Avoiding Ghosts and Social Censure: Monastic Funerals in the *Mūlasarvāstivāda-vinaya.*" *Journal of Indian Philosophy* 20 (1992): 1–39.

Silk, Jonathan Alan. "The Origins and Early History of the *Mahāratnakūṭa*: Tradition of Mahāyāna Buddhism with a Study of the *Ratarāśisūtra* and Related Materials." Ph.D. diss., Michigan University, 1994.

Steele, John, trans. *The I-li: Book of Etiquette and Ceremonial.* London: Probsthain & Co., 1917. Reprint, Taipei: Ch'eng-wen Publishing Co., 1966.

Strong, John S. "The Legend of the Lion-roarer: A Study of the Buddhist Arhat Piṇḍola Bhāradvāja." *Numen* 16, no. 1 (1979): 50–88.

Takakusu J. trans. *A Record of the Buddhist Religion as Practiced in India and the Malay Archipelago.* London: Clarendon Press, 1966. Reprint, New Delhi: Munshiram Manoharlal, 1982.

Tso Sze-bong. "The Transformation of Buddhist Vinaya in China." Ph.D. diss., Australian National University, 1982.

Twitchett, D. C. "The Monasteries and China's Economy in Medieval Times." *SOAS* 19, no. 3 (1957): 526–549.

Weinstein, Stanley. *Buddhism under the T'ang.* Cambridge: Cambridge University Press, 1987.

Yampolsky, Philip B. *The Platform Sutra of the Sixth Patriarch.* New York: Columbia University Press, 1967.

Yokoi Yūhō. *Japanese-English Zen Buddhist Dictionary.* Tokyo: Sankibō Busshorin, 1991.

Yu Chun-fang. "Chung-feng Ming-pen and Ch'an Buddhism in the Yüan." In *Yüan Thought: Chinese Thought and Religion Under the Mongols,* edited by Hok-lam Chan and Wm. Theodore de Bary. New York: Columbia University Press, 1982.

Index

abbot: attendant of (*tangtou shizhe*), 152, 173; Elder, 28; election of, 81; formal sermon, 11; front hall of (*qintang*), 87; funeral of, 217–219; Heshang, 149; hiatus from sermon of (*fangcan*), 129, 157–158, 265n. 220; *huazhu*, 28; inauguration ceremony of, 215; inauguration documents of (*kaitang shu*), 152; incense attendant of (*shaoxiang shizhe*), 135; "inside" attendants, 173, 293n. 64; office of (*tangtou*), 119; "outside" attendants, 173, 293n. 64; quarters of (*fangzhang*), 28, 87, 257n. 116; retirement of, 219–220; role of, 216–217; serving as abbot (*chushi*), 214; venerable senior (*zusu*), 145, 212; visit to the assembly quarters of, 145; *yuanzhu*, 58; *zhuchi*, 216
administrative system, 89–90
administrators (*zhushi* or *zhishi*); 89, 120, 136, 256n. 99; appointment of (*qing zhishi*), 146–149, 276n. 105; completion of their terms, 155; also referred to as "east section" (*dongxu*), 146, 276n. 105
ailing pavilion, director, 152, 169
alcohol in Vinaya, 16
announcement before meal (*sengba*), 57
announcing each course of meal (*heshi*), 125
annual list of donors (*dinian mulu*), 175

appointment: of abbot, 212; of administrator, 146–149; of chief officer, 156; of chief seat emeritus, 211
arhat hall, director, 169, 290n. 11
ascending the platform (*shangtang*), 11, 89, 135–136, 266n. 1
asking abbot for further instruction, 134
assembly of purity (*qingzhong*), 140
assembly quarters (*zhongliao*), 117, 254n. 72; assistant director of (*fuliao*), 293n. 61; candidate of assistant director of (*wangliao*), 293n. 61; chief of (*liaoyuan*), 293n. 61; chief seat of (*liao shouzuo*), 293n. 61; director of (*liaozhu*), 293n. 61
assistant director of assembly quarters, 293n. 61
assistant prior (*fuyuan*), 146, 277n. 1; first (*dusi*), 277n. 1; second (*jiansi*), 277n. 1; third (*fusi*), 277n. 1
assistant Sangha recorder (*fu senglu*), 85
assistant Sangha rectifier (*fu sengzheng*), 85
attendant (*shizhe*): of abbot (*tangtou shizhe*), 152, 173; of Holy Monk (*shengseng shizhe*), 152, 170; incense, 135; "inside," 173, 293n. 64; "outside," 173, 293n. 64
auction of deceased monks' property (*guchang*), 153, 302nn. 24, 27

Finding List

The following will help readers locate corresponding pages in *Yakuchū Zennen shingi* (YZS) and *Dai Nihon zokuzōkyō* (ZZK; series 2, case number 16, volume 5).

YZS	ZZK
Preface	
3	438a
Fascicle One	
13	439a3–13
16	439a14–b7
20	439b8–13
22	439b14–18
23	439b18–c5
23–24	439c5–12
25	439c12–d7
27	439d8–13
28	439d14–440a4
29–30	440a4–14
31	440a14–b2
32–33	440b2–440c1
35	440b2–c9
37	440c9–c15
38	440c15–d2
39	440d2–6
41	440d6–10
42	440d11–17
43	440d17–441a5
44	441a5–13

YZS	ZZK
46	441a13–b1
48	441b1–11
50	441b11–18
52	441b18–c3
52–53	441c3–8
54	441c8–18
55–56	441c18–d14
58	441d14–442a5
59	442a6–9
60	442a9–18
61–62	442a18–b8
63	442b8–11
64	442b12–442c1
65	442c1–9
66	442c10–18
67	442c18–d9
68	442d9–14

Fascicle Two

71	443a1–10
72–73	443a10–b3
74	443b3–6
75	443b6–11
76	443b12–17
77	443b17–c6
78	443c6–13
79	443c14–17
80	443c17–d6
81	443d6–444a2
83	444a2–9
84	444a9–16
85	444a17–b1
86	444b1–9
88	444b9–c4
89–90	444c4–13
91	444c14–d4
92	444d5–11
93	444d12–18
94	445a1–10

YZS	**ZZK**
96	445a11–b1
97–98	445b1–10
99	445b10–c3
101	445c3–18

Fascicle Three

105–106	445d11–446a13
109	446a13–b3
110–111	446b4–15
112	446b15–c6
113–114	446c6–12
114–115	446c12–18
116	446d1–17
119	447a1–6
120	447a7–14
121	447a14–18
122–123	447b1–16
124–125	447b17–c5
125–126	447c5–18
127	447d1–12
129	447d13–448a8
131	448a8–b4

Fascicle Four

135	448b10–18
136–137	448c1–12
138	448c12–17
139	448d1–6
140	448d6–12
141–142	448d13–16
143	448d17–449a13
145	449a13–18
146–147	449a18–b11
148	449b11–13
149–150	449b14–c8
151	449c8–15
152–153	449c15–d2
154	449d3–8
155–156	449d9–16

YZS	ZZK
157	449d16–450a3
158	450a3–16
160	450a17–b8
161	450b8–13
162–163	450b14–18
163–164	450b18–c4
164	450c4–8
165	450c8–15

Fascicle Five

167	450d3–11
168–169	45012–451a4
170	451a4–10
171	451a10–b1
172–173	451b1–b13
174	451b13–c3
176	451c4–12
177	451c13–d2
179	451d2–11
180	451d11–452a3
182	452a3–11
183	452a11–16
184	452a17–b4
184–185	452ab4–11
185	452b11–17
186	452b18–c4
187	452c4–13
188	452c13–d3
189–190	452d4–14
191	452d14–16
192	452d17–453a7
193	453a8–13
194	453a13–b8
196	453b8–c1

Fascicle Six

199	453c7–15
200	453c15–d13
202	453d13–454a8

YZS	**ZZK**
203	454a9–12
204	454a13–17
205	454a18–b6
206	454b7–12
207–208	454b12–c4
209	454c4–7
209	454c8–13
210	454c13–16
211	454c16–d2
211–212	454d2–8
213	454d8–14
214	454d15–18
215	454d18–455a8
216	455a8–14
217	455a14–17
217–218	455a18–b6
219	455b6–10
219	455b10–15
220	455b15–c5
221	455c5–d2
223	455d2–6
224	455d7–12
225	455d12–456a
226–227	456a2–10
228	456a11–17
229	456a18–b5
230	456b5–12

Fascicle Seven

233	456c3–11
235	456c11–d2
237	456d3–8
238	456d8–12
238–239	456d12–457a4
240	457a4–7
240–241	457a-15
242	457a15–b7
243	457b7–11
244	457b11–15

YZS	ZZK
245	457b15–16
245–246	457b16–c1
246	457c1–7
247	457c7–9
248	457c10–d1
250	457d2–10
251	457d10–16
252	457d17–458a4
253	458a4–12
254–255	458a12–b3
256	458b4–18
257–258	458c1–10
259	458c11–16
260	45816–d9
261–262	458d9–18
263	458a1–6
264	458a7–18
265–266	459a18–b9